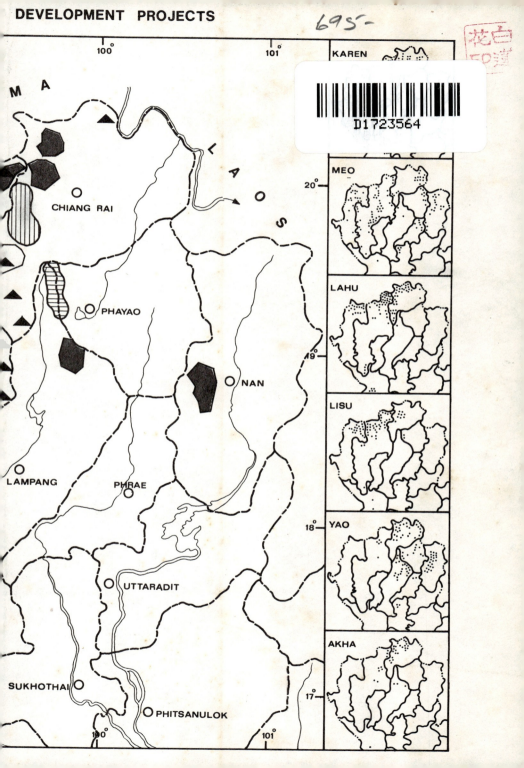

HILL TRIBES TODAY

HILL TRIBES TODAY

PROBLEMS IN CHANGE

by

John McKinnon

Bernard Vienne

White Lotus-Orstom (TRI-ORSTOM PROJECT)
1989

White Lotus Co.,Ltd.
G.P.O.Box 1141
Bangkok
Thailand

and

O.R.S.T.O.M. Institut Français de Recherche
Scientifique pour le Développement en Coopération,
213, Rue La Fayette
75480 Paris Cedex 10
France

© 1989 by O.R.S.T.O.M. All rights reserved
Distribution world wide by White Lotus Co.,Ltd.

Printed in Thailand
Produced by
Siripat Co.,Ltd.
ISBN 974-8495-25-6

Dedicated to the memory of
Bill Geddes and Lucien Hanks
in acknowledgement of their
contribution to the understanding
of *chao khao*

CONTENTS

                                      Page

List of Contributors ix
Acknowledgements xvii
Introduction: Critical Words for Critical Days xix
        John McKinnon & Bernard Vienne

INTERVENTION : POLICY & UNDERSTANDING 1

Government Policy : Highland Ethnic Minorities 5
        Wanat Bhruksasri

Facing Development in the Highlands : A Challenge
for Thai Society 33
        Bernard Vienne

The Poisoning Effect of a Lovers Triangle :
Highlanders, Opium and Extension Crops, a Policy
Overdue for Review 61
        Chupinit Kesmanee

PROBLEMS : POVERTY & IDENTITY 103

Highland Agriculture : From Better to Worse 107
        Chantaboon Sutthi

"Women and Children First?" A review of the
current nutritional status in the highlands 143
        Ralana Maneeprasert

Opiate of the People? A Case Study of Lahu Opium
Addicts 159
        Sanit Wongsprasert

Anarchists of the Highlands? A Critical Review
of a Stereotype Applied to the Lisu 173
        Prasert Chaipigusit

Lisu identity in Northern Thailand : A Problematique
for Anthropology 191
        Yves Conrad

RESETTLEMENT : OPINIONS & INTERPRETATIONS 223

Problem Solving Through Understanding : A Personal Opinion on How to Approach Development Problems in the Highlands 227
Wanat Bhruksasri

14 April 1986 : Eviction Orders to the Hmong of Huai Yew Yee Village, Huai Kha Khaeng Wildlife Sanctuary, Thailand 249
Ardith A. Eudey

Territorial Imperatives : Akha Ethnic Identity and Thailand's National Integration 259
Cornelia Ann Kammerer

Structural Assimilation and the Consensus : Clearing Grounds on which to Rearrange our Thoughts 303
John McKinnon

REFLECTIONS : FRAGMENTS & IMPRESSIONS 361

Hill Tribe People Blamed for Deforestation 363
Vithoon Pungprasert

Karen : When the Wind Blows 369
Pravit Phothiart

Highlanders as Portrayed in Thai Penny-horribles 393
Jean Baffie

Weddings, Wealth, Pigs and Coca Cola : *farang* Tourists in an Akha Village 409
Duangta Seewuthiwong

APPENDICES

I. Hill Tribe Population of Thailand 425
II. List of Swidden Plants 427
III. List of Non-swidden Plants 437
IV. List of Exotic Plants Introduced into the Highlands 451
V. Target Areas for Prevention of Forest Destruction by Hilltribes 471
VI. List of Plates 475

List of Contributors

Mr. Wanat Bhruksasri has been the Director of the Tribal Research Institute since it was established in 1964. He took his first academic diploma from Chulalongkorn University in Journalism, and his first degree in law, from Thammasat (1952). In 1953 he participated in the first course on social work to be offered in Thailand and subsequently took a graduate Diploma in Social Welfare from the University College of Swansea (1958). After attending the London School of Economics he returned to Thailand to be assigned a pioneer role in survey work in the highlands. Just before he was called back to establish the research centre he studied Research Methodology in Social Welfare at the University of California, Berkeley. Widely known in Thailand as a humanist and expert on the hill tribes he has consistently argued for their voluntary integration into the nation state. He has published numerous papers in both Thai and English and co-edited **Highlanders of Thailand** (OUP, 1983). In 1983 his outstanding contribution to social research in Thailand was acknowledged by a Pakorn Angsusingha Foundation Award.

Dr. Bernard Vienne is a French trained social anthropologist who holds a tenured position as senior researcher with ORSTOM. He has worked extensively in the Pacific Islands including Vanuatu, New Caledonia, Banks Islands and Motlav. He is well known in the French speaking world both as an advocated of equitable treatment and representation for indigenous people as well as his interdisciplinary work with archaeologists, geographers and a nutritionist. His recent book **Gens de Motlav; Ideologie et Pratique Sociale en Melanesie**

(Société des Océanistes, Paris: 1984) has been acknowledged with favourable comments from Louis Dumont and Claude Levi-Strauss. Since 1986, Vienne has been engaged in research in cooperation with personnel from the TRI studying the survival strategies of the Akha.

Mr. Chupinit Kesmanee is a senior researcher at the TRI who specialises in Hmong studies. He took his first degree in anthropology from Thammasat University, Bangkok and holds a graduate Diploma in Social Planning in Developing Countries from the London School of Economics and Political Science. Chupinit has worked in the highlands for over 12 years, undertaken joint studies with many foreign scholars of Hmong society and has published over 15 papers in Thai based on his own fieldwork. A review of his study of relocation activities in Kamphaeng Phet (1986) was recently published in ***Cultural Survival Quarterly*** (Vol. 12, No.3, 1988). He is currently undertaking graduate studies as Victoria University of Wellington, New Zealand.

Mr. Chantaboon Sutthi is a senior researcher with the TRI. Trained as an agricultural scientist at Kasetsat University, Bangkok, Mr. Chantaboon has spent most of his working life dealing with either practical and administrative issues affecting the welfare of hill tribe people or investigating their management of both indigenous and introduced genetic resources available in their rapidly changing ecological and economic environment. He commenced systematic survey work in this field by collecting over 1200 varieties of highland rice and lodged these in a genetic rice bank in both Thailand and the Philippines. He is particularly interested in the systemic, organisational and botanical changes taking place under increased commercialisation and intensification of highland agriculture. He has also written several scientific papers on the history, use and botanical nature of opium and special varieties of *canabis sativa*. In a forthcoming book he will list and index by scientific common English and Thai names, most of the plant materials used in the highlands.

Ms Ralana Maneeprasert, a TRI researcher, is a graduate of Chulalongkorn University and holds a masters degree in nutrition from the University of Queensland (1980). She is particularly interested in the role of women and the position of children in highland society. Most of her fieldwork has been conducted amongst the Hmong but she has also studied rice consumption in a Lisu community and is currently engaged in interdisciplinary cooperative research work on the Akha in which dietary information is being correlated with community access to, and management of, land resources and the annual round of customary rituals. She has presented papers at international gatherings in Australia, the Philippines and Thailand.

Mr. Sanit Wongsprasert has an ideal set of academic qualifications for an anthropologist. He first studied agriculture at Mae Jo College, subsequently took a degree in Social Administration from Thammasat University and then a masters degree in social anthropology from the University of Sydney. As a senior researcher at the TRI he has specialised in the Lahu but a list of his publications reveals the breadth of his interest in highland society. He has published work on population growth, agriculture, trade and commerce, leadership, food consumption, ritual and his most recently published article "Impact of the Dhammacarik Bhikkus' Programme on the Hill Tribes of Thailand" appeared in a book entitled ***Ethnic Conflict in Buddhist Societies: Sri Lanka, Thailand and Burma*** Mr. Sanit has been particularly active in NGO work associated with the King's Project and the University of Chiang Mai, Faculty of Agriculture.

Mr. Prasert Chaipigusit is the Lisu specialist and a senior researcher at the Tribal Research Institute. He took his first degree in social administration from Thammasat University and spent a year studying ethnology at the University of Vienna. He has published more than a dozen articles on various aspects of Lisu culture: altars, opium, traditional media, naming systems, folk songs, play, houses, leadership and evaluated the effectiveness of Buddhist missionary activities. This interest in research in nicely balanced by several years administrative and development work experience in the North-west and North-east of Thailand. Mr. Prasert has participated in project evaluation, studied people's participation in rural development and since 1968 has been engaged in a long term study of a Lisu village north of Chiang Mai.

Mr. Yves Conrad, a French social anthropologist prepared his masters dissertation in ethnology at the University of Paris IV (Sorbonne). Fieldwork took him to a Berber community in the Moroccan Atlas. He has been collecting information in Lisu communities for six years. Over the past four years he has worked in association with the French Centre National de la Recherche Scientifique, Paris (CNRS) and ORSTOM respectively on Lisu concepts of territoriality and scientific questions of identity. He is currently preparing his doctorate dissertation for the Ecole des Hautes Etudes en Sciences Sociales. He also holds an ORSTOM research fellowship and is engaged in the study of land use systems in the village of Doi Chang, Mae Suai in the province of Chiang Rai.

Dr. Ardith A. Eudey is a primitologist and visiting scholar in psychology at the University of California, Riverside, and regional coordinator for Asia of the IUCN/Species Survival Commission's Primate Study Group. In 1973 she began a longterm field study of primates in Thailand's Huai Kha Khaeng Wildlife Sanctuary in cooperation with the Wildlife Conservation Division of the Royal Forestry Department. The study was expanded into the region occupied by the Hmong in Huai Kha Khaeng and the contiguous Thung Yai Naresuan Wildlife Sanctuary in 1982. She has recently published an abbreviated account of events associated with the relocation of the Hmong of Huai Yew Yee and a commentary on the Nam Choan Dam in two consecutive issues of ***Cultural Survival Quarterly*** (Vol. 12, No's 1 & 2; 1988).

Dr. Cornelia Ann Kammerer is a graduate of the Department of Anthropology, University of Chicago, who has specialised in the Akha. Her doctoral dissertation *Gateway to the Akha World : Kinship, Ritual, and Community among Highlanders of Thailand* was completed in 1986 following nearly three years of field research. A revised version will be published under the same title in the Illinois Studies in Anthropology Series of the University of Illinois Press. Between 1986 she carried out a study of sociocultural change among Akha in Thailand, focusing on the impact of Christianity. She is currently a Research Associate in the Department of Anthropology, Brandeis University, Waltham, Massachusetts and a Fellow of the Cultural Survival Institute in Cambridge, Massachusetts. She most recently published "Shifting Gender Asymmetries among Akha of Northern Thailand" in *Gender, Power, and the Construction of the Moral Order: Studies from the Thai Periphery* edited by Nancy Eberhardt (University of Wisconsin-Madison, Center for Southeast Asian Studies, Monograph 4, 1988).

Dr. John McKinnon is a senior lecturer in geography at the Victoria University of Wellington. His first research was carried out on the island of Vella Lavella in the Solomon Islands. After a brief period at the University of the South Pacific, Suva, he worked as an advisor to what was then the Tribal Research Centre (1975 - 1978). During this assignment he assembled and co-edited the papers which appeared in *Highlanders of Thailand* (OUP: 1983). Between 1986 and 1988 as a researcher employed by ORSTOM and assigned to work with the TRI-ORSTOM Project he undertook a cooperative and comparative study of the dynamics of changing land use in Yao, Lisu and Akha villages in Mae Chan and Mae Suai districts of Chiang Rai. He is particularly interested in the position of minority people caught up in the process of national integration.

Mr. Vithoon Pungprasert. In 1986 Vithoon Pungprasert worked for **The Nation** as a reporter. At that time he wrote a series of articles on problems associated with the management of Thailand's forests. These short pieces were distinguished by their balanced and sensitive approach to what has always been a controversial issue. Foresters are seen either as the protectors of the national watershed and endangered wildlife or as secretly promoting cooperation with logging companies who sometimes illegally fell what remains of Thailand's forests. By firmly tying his reporting to people, concrete issues and places, Khun Vithoon dealt with the matter in a restrained and informative manner. He is currently in Paris furthering his career as a writer.

Mr.Pravit Phothiart is a TRI researcher with unusual qualifications. He enjoys a reputation as both a poet and a public speaker on hill tribe affairs, has been particularly active in the field of nonformal education and has special interests in Karen society which range from the performing arts to practical matters of nutrition, health and community development. His first academic interest was in physical science and he holds a Diploma in Analytical Chemistry from Chulalongkorn University. In the seven years before he joined the TRI he worked as both a researcher for the Chulalongkorn University Social research Institute (CUSRI) and as a Department of Public Welfare, Hill Tribe Welfare Division field worker resident in highlander villages. He is a TRI Karen specialist as well as the resident computer buff.

Dr. Jean Baffie holds a Doctorat de Troisieme Cycle from the University of Paris and completed his under-graduate work at Montpellier University. He specialises in the sociology, history and economy of Thailand and other ASEAN countries. He is particularly interested in urban minorities and since 1984 has carried out research in Ban Khrua, a former Cham village now lying in the very centre of Bangkok. During the course of ten years' stay in Thailand he has been employed as a representative and research worker for both the Centre de Documentation et de Recherche sur l'Asie du Sud-est et le Monde Insulindien (CeDRASEMI) and Asie du Sud-Est Continentale research centre (ASECO), Paris. He has contributed several articles on Thai society and culture to French academic journals and is co-author of a forthcoming book entitled **Ban Khrua, un Village Urbain de Bangkok.**

Ms Duangta Seewuthiwong is a research assistant employed by the TRI-ORSTOM Project. She took her undergraduate degree from Ramkhamhaeng University in Political Science and later studied philosophy at the University of Chiang Mai. After working with the Graduate Volunteer Programme run by Thammasat University she gained additional volunteer experience in the evaluation of a family planning project and a children's library project funded by the Komol Keemthong Foundation. Duangta has been a kindergarten teacher, a manager's assistant at a toy factory and a field fellow for the Mountain People's Cultural Development Project (MPCD) funded by the Dutch NGO, NOVIB. Her experience as a keen observer of human behaviour and capacity to participate in challenging situations resulted in her personal treatment of *farang* tourists in an Akha village witnessing weddings, bringing wealth, watching pigs being slaughtered and seeking cultural comfort in Coca Cola.

Acknowlegements

The editors would like to thank all the researchers of the Tribal Research Institute (TRI) who contributed manuscripts for consideration. Only a handful of those delivered appear in **Hill Tribes Today.** It is hoped that the many papers which were of a professional standard but did not fit into the theme of the present publication will subsequently be made available to a wider public.

We are especially grateful for: the professional and administrative assistance given by the TRI Director, Mr. Wanat Bhruksasri; financial support provided by the French Institute for Scientific Research for Development through Cooperation (ORSTOM) and the Royal Thai Government Department of Technical and Economic Cooperation; the many photographs provided by John Connell, Ardith Eudey, Bill Geddes, John Hobday, Ken Kampe, Ralana Maneeprasert and Supachai Sathirasilapin.

Editorial help was freely given by many people in Chiang Mai and special mention must be made of the contribution provided by Guy Dinmore, now the Reuters correspondent in Peking, Yves Conrad, a research anthropologist associated with both the Centre National de la Recherche Scientifique, Paris (CNRS) and ORSTOM, Philaivan Sindusopon of White Lotus and Geoffrey Walton of Chiang Mai.

Five of the Chapters (3, 4, 7, 9, 14) were written either partly or completely in Thai and translated by Duangta Seewuthiwong. Ms Duangta also assisted in general consultation with the contributors, provided valuable background research and critical comments.

Ms Luksanawan Sirisak typed most of the manuscript and without complaint entered a multitude of corrections and alterations.

We hope that publication of **Hill Tribes Today** is sufficient acknowledgement of the support and work these agencies and people provided.

Introduction

Critical Words for Critical Days

What is a proper perspective on the highlanders? One which argues a case that they should be entirely left on their own to follow some ancient cultural path in isolation from the rest of Thailand?

Such a position belongs to dreamers. It is not possible to keep apparently distinct minority cultures intact in imposed isolation. Absolute isolation was never a reality and such a policy has never been either an objective of Thai governments or of the highlanders. Before the first Tai states were formed in the thirteenth century highlanders maintained some commercial, political and social intercourse with lowlanders. Today, in modern Thailand, this link is stronger than ever before. A basic network on which the construction of a more permanent infrastructure of roads, administration and communications can be built is already in place. Highlanders are significantly dependant on trade to secure their food needs, increasingly look to modern scientific medicine for the treatment of illnesses, the more socially aware and better off want their children to receive a good Thai education and secure responsible, well paid jobs on the lowlands. A profound process of spontaneous, voluntary integration is taking place. For many of those who have not yet secured a firm place in the Thai polity, this remains one of their principal objectives.

If this process is so well advanced, why then should there be any need for critical words and talk of critical days? If, on one hand, highlanders identify their interests with lowlanders and are keen to more fully enter the Thai world, and if, on the other hand, state officials are willing to accept these people as full citizens, it would be reasonable to expect that this spontaneous process of integration would soon result in a harmonious accommodation: Thailand would provide an exemplar of a united, plural state.

The real situation is much more complex. Strong historical forces which are part of the structure of the changing mode of production may be carrying people together but it would be wrong to assume that this ground swell carries all before it. There are serious contradictions.

From a lowlanders point of view, until the twentieth century the highlands formed a no-man's-land, an obstacle between points of civilization occupied by "wild animals and primitive people". In the intervening years, given the minimum disruption to social confidence deeply challenged in neighbouring states by colonial take-overs and the facile ease with which modernisation has been managed, the strong hierarchical nature of the Thai social structure has largely survived. It remains divided horizontally by class divisions with ideas taken from *sakdina* and gravitating into intimate cellular groups organised around family, neighbours and entourage. Somehow highlanders, unless they are prepared to divest themselves entirely of their backward image, belong outside this society. Hence Thai officials, working from within a strong cultural tradition, in disregard of the firm highlander interest in becoming Thai, consider that projects must be mounted like that proposed by COHAN (Centre for the Coordination of Hill Tribe Affairs and Eradication of Narcotic Crops, 3rd Army) "To instill a strong sense of Thai citizenship, obligation, and faith in the institutions of Nation, Religion and Monarchy among the hill tribes". No-man's-land" has long since become a legal part of Thailand and there is a high level of anxiety to secure control over this estate to see that it becomes an integrated and well managed part of national territory: as to the people who traditionally occupy this land, that is another matter.

People count but are not always welcome: wishes count but are rarely fulfilled. The Royal Forestry Department, if not the state, would prefer the highlands to be unencumbered, to

Introduction

be unoccupied. This is difficult to achieve but the wish survives. The state has as yet been unable to extend citizenship to a large number of highlanders many of whom were born in Thailand. Then again, like most South-East Asian nations, it denies "tribals" land rights over what is considered to be public domain. Perhaps because of the gap between wish and fulfilment nearly everthing about highlanders is problematical. Any mention of "hill tribes" in official circles assumes that the following discussion will focus on problems. The problems are called "hill tribe problems" not because they are experienced directly by those after whom they are named but because highlanders are said to make problems for others. Nobody likes narcotics, land degradation or threats to security and so the wish is transformed from the positive ideal to the negative real; the danger then becomes the likelihood of a refusal to take the highlanders problems seriously and jump to the simple position "the problems are there because the people are there, therefore let us move the people out".

A proper perspective on the highlanders must address these widely accepted "problems", test their significance and make sure the context in which they occur has also been evaluated.

The most well known is the narcotics problem. Opium growing is a legacy of nineteenth century colonialism. Just thirty years ago perhaps as many as 45 out of every 100 highlander households grew the poppy *Popaver somniferum* L. and sold opium to help them make a living. It was an ideal crop, had a high weight/value ratio, kept well and the price was continually on the rise. Following international convention this crop was declared illegal and one of the principal "development" crusades over the past three decades has been to encourage farmers to grow something else and accept this restriction imposed on their livelihood. The international community has invested millions of dollars in the attempt to discourage farmers from growing opium and this in turn has become a cause in itself, the impact of which goes far beyond the original purpose.

xxi

INTRODUCTION

Land degradation said to follow solely from the felling of forests is believed to pose an urgent problem which threatens the national watershed, leads to rapid run-off, serious erosion, silting of major waterways and results in damaging floods. Even in the absence of reliable scientific evidence, some people still believe that following the felling of trees precipitation declines or at least that total water yield drops. Some prominent people even go so far as to speak of desertification. Nearly all of these notions can be questioned.

Security is a question that is a little more difficult to research. It raises questions of loyalty and allegiance. In 1967 Thailand believed it was facing a major insurrection in the highlands. The Communist Party of Thailand, in consultation with fraternal neighbours, had secured the support of a few highlanders. There was a moment of panic in which even vaguely suspect villages were attacked and the insurrection threatened to grow. When better advice prevailed and fewer attacks were mounted against highlanders, the problem subsided but this experience provided substance for suspicion. "All these people who are not Thai living in Thailand, can they be trusted?" And then the circle begins. "They are not citizens because we cannot be sure of their loyalty and because they are not citizens we cannot be sure of their loyalty."

A fundamental transformation is taking place that is not at all well understood. Should we then be asking different questions, "Do the interests behind current intervention block the development of a better understanding? What is a proper focus for research? How can research make a contribution to the development process and policy formation? What to do about opium production, the felling of the forest, matters of security, extending government services into the highlands and easing the burden of poverty?"

This book grew out of these questions in a truly cooperative undertaking in institutional development and scientific research conducted by personnel from the Tribal Research Institute (TRI) and the French Institute of Scientific Research

Introduction

for Development through Cooperation (ORSTOM). When these questions were first raised, the positions from which foreign and Thai researchers commenced the dialogue seemed far apart. As social scientists the participants found themselves considering matters in which they, *farangs* and Thai, became part of the subject of investigation as well as the highlanders whom both partners had a brief to study. Accepted ideas about what research really is had to be questioned. The commitment of all participants to the future of Thailand served as a basis from which to prepare critiques of specific aspects of policy and development and also made it necessary for the editors of this volume to reevaluate their position as both researchers and research advisors. The challenge was both personal and scientific and as part of this assessment, a decision was taken to look very carefully at research results prepared by the Tribal Research Institute.

This book commenced as a study of the considerable corpus of reports assembled by the TRI. Papers and reports written in Thai and circulated only in mimeograph form, little known outside the Institute and worthy of wider circulation were translated and discussed. Then, since so many offered a critical reflection on the contemporary situation, a decision was taken not only to share this work with a specialised academic research community but to publish it for a wider public. New pieces were written to cover specific issues such as opium addiction, nutrition and stereotyping. This material forms the core of the text and, taken as a whole, indicates a growing concern for the social, political, health and welfare of highlanders than cannot be ignored. To supplement Thai research, a few foreign researchers were invited to contribute chapters to broaden the scope of consideration on issues raised by the Tribal Research Institute. The combined effort presented here provides interesting comments on many of the questions posed above.

Is there a need for further research to make better information available to policy makers? Throughout the period 1986-1988 in the last years of the Prem administration, the

INTRODUCTION

growing impatience of the government with highlanders became clearer everyday. The idea took hold that since highlanders were cutting the forest, destroying the national watershed, endangering lowland property, were not citizens, constituted a security problem, grew narcotics and engaged in illegal trading activities then the quickest way to solve the problem was to simply move them out of the hills. This barrage of charges, advanced by leading national authorities provided a raison d'être for strong intervention, which was underscored by an increasing willingness to use the military and other paramilitary forces to move people from places like national parks, other forested areas and border zones where the government did not want highlanders to be, to places which the authorities considered more suitable.

Relocation became a highly sensitive issue. Events ran ahead of a humane understanding of the situation. Clearly better information was required on which to base national policy.

What sort of research is required? As an exercise in cooperative research, the TRI-ORSTOM Project held to the position that no science which explores the nature of the human species can be free of bias and value judgments. Good medical research is built on the assumption that any skills that can be brought to bear on the problems of maintaining a healthy body and mentally sound mind deserve attention. Social science is clearly subject to these contraints. Where researchers come from different cultures they may very well be unable to agree on what are important issues. Thai researchers working within a highly demanding socio-political milieu in which the voice of superiors must, at least publicly, be shown every respect do not come to specific research undertakings in the same way as their foreign colleagues. If work must be conducted in a conservative intellectual environment, especially when it comes to matters lying beyond the "hard" sciences and technology, what does not lie open to question? What questions will not in turn raise others concerning patriotism, loyalty, reliability and sincerity?

Introduction

One simple strategy is to avoid awkward questions altogether. It is something of a coward's way out but we all recognise the good sense in staying out of trouble. Issues can be avoided. But, regardless of their culture or nationality, good social scientists, as self-respecting practitioners of a broad spectrum of disciplines, cannot ignore matters which adversely affect those with whom they work. Such problems stare them in the face. Competent social scientists like good medical practitioners or engineers serve as vehicles to carry more effective ideas forward, promote skills, techniques and values that enhance understanding and by bringing a new perspective to bear on old problems, offer a way out.

Each of the contributors to this volume provides an interpretation of the situation in the highlands which offers another way of looking at issues; a result of this may well be to provide alternatives to current practices.

Expression of opinion is the first step out of cautious non-committal position characterized by the endless collection of basic socio-economic data. Serious questions signal a move to a positive position from which serious research can commence. In this book the opinion of Thai researchers from the Tribal Research Institute can be seen alongside those of a few foreigners. The bias of the treatment is clearly focused on problems which principally affect highlanders. It is the first collaborative book of its kind to move outside either a conventional scholarly treatment or a text commercially packaged for tourists who prefer to learn by looking rather than reading.

Once researchers begin to express opinions, they enter a territory in which the burden of proof becomes much more demanding. The shift marks a new beginning to research which can cross the boundary between different cultural values and move from old to new scientific methods. As the reader will discover, the differences between researchers are in several places well marked. What is evident throughout the book is a search for a proper voice to convey an understanding of the matters under discussion.

INTRODUCTION

In a society in which social conformity takes precedence by choice over assertive individualism, *farang* encouragement of more critical commentary was deemed to be presumptuous, demanding and politically risqué, if not naive. The position from which work was initiated challenged accepted ideologies of ethnicity, development, ecology and modernity. The democratic interpretation of cooperation as the sharing of work among equals rather than passing well defined tasks down the line caused frustration. The hope was present that research could be changed for the better solely by learning new techniques and refining old ones. The need for researchers to first examine their own preconceptions met with reluctance, and was only accepted by a few. For researchers already busy with demanding on-going research programmes it is not easy to respond to such a challenge.

Deliberate change is never easy. Analysis of situations in the light of new ideas and information may generate different results but if findings stand in contradiction to what important people think are the facts, it takes more than a scientific paper or two to change their minds. Too many interests are attached to established ideas for it to be possible to easily change people's way of thinking about opium, nutrition, security, land degradation and so forth which cluster around the very mention of "hill tribes". Projects are attempts to solve well-recongnised "problems" and the funds allocated to ameliorate these provide a living for many. All projects have answers which they consider the best and do not welcome criticism from outsiders engaged in different work who have the audacity to assume they know better.

A considerable potential for disagreement and conflict is built into the situation but any socially informed commentary worth its salt must address the contemporary situation in the highlands of Northern Thailand in such a manner that raises questions with which entrenched interests will take issue.

This book is not just a collection of articles about the highlands and their inhabitants, it is a challenge to established wisdom. These are critical days and this book has been prepared to answer this challenge with critical words.

Chiang Mai, December 1988

1. Akha Dzoema (Vienne)

2. Hmong (Hobday)

3. Mlabri (McKinnon)

4. Lua (Kampe)

5. Akha grandmother (Hobday)

6. Mien mother (Connell)

7. Lua boy (Hobday)

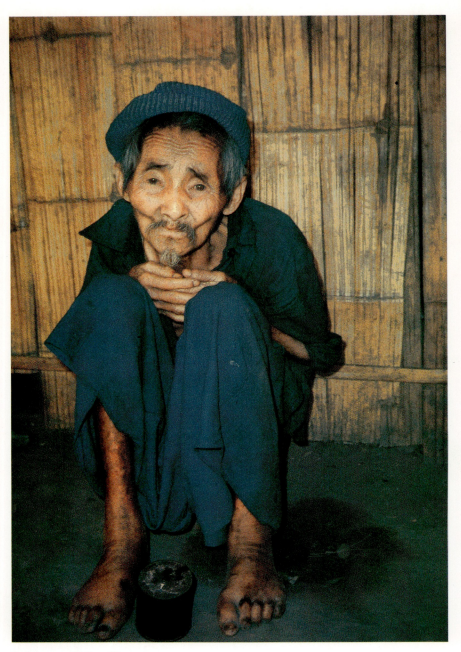

8. Lisu grandfather (Kampe)

INTERVENTION: POLICY & UNDERSTANDING

In this section each of the three contributors provides a commentary on current policy from the perspective of their professional experience.

Mr Wanat Bhruksasri, Director of the Tribal Research Institute, and with a long and distinguished career in the civil service behind him, provides an authoritative view of the pragmatic, humanitarian and liberal concerns which have contributed to the evolution of policy and changes in the administrative structure. This Chapter, originally written in 1985 as a lecture presented to visiting American academics, outlines the role that the Ministry of the Interior and its line agency (the Department of Public Welfare working through the Hill Tribe Development and Welfare Division) has played, and continues to play, in highland development work. The discussion provides essential background information.

Two powerful committees also deserve mention.

1) The Committee for Facilitating the Solution of National Security Problems Relating to Hill Tribes and Cultivation of Narcotic Crops working in consultation with the National Security Council which mounts its operations under the control of the Third Army's Centre for the Coordination of Hill Tribe Affairs and Eradication of Narcotic Crops (COHAN) (established 13 May, 1987).

2.) The Committee for the Prevention of Hill Tribe Intrusion into and Destruction of the Forest which has a close relationship with the Royal Forestry Department. This Department holds responsibility for management of both land and forest in the highlands (established, 1976).

Although the role of these agencies is not discussed in Chapter 1 some of the structural issues associated with their activities, plainly stated in their names, are raised by McKinnon in Chapter 12.

Bernard Vienne, an ORSTOM social anthropologist, provides a provocative anthropological analysis of the challenge posed by development policies in the highlands to Thai society as a whole. His observations provide a cautionary note for those engaged in development undertakings. Vienne argues that the state structure has uncritically incorporated so much of the ideological promise of technology and the techniques of industrial management that this forms a strong consensus which; because it accords poorly with reality, constitutes a potential hazard to both national interests and the well being of highlanders. His holistic approach identifies the contradictions between the spontaneous response made by highlanders to new economic opportunities and their restricted position within national life. This generates a tension which if not resolved may lead to a more problematic future.

Chupinit Kesmanee, a senior researcher at the TRI, discusses the complex interrelationships between the highlanders way of life and their survival strategies, the role of opium and the impact of new cash crops. He first reviews the history of opium in the region and how it became a part of highlander farming systems. He points out how highlanders, in servicing a market pioneered by the nineteenth century imperial powers, have in a sense, become the ultimate victims of the winners of the Opium Wars. Early acceptance of this commercial crop, well-suited to the relative isolation of hill tribe communities, provided the means to obtain lowland commodities which initially made their lives easier. But it has now become a risk to their survival. He argues that contemporary development policy brought to bear on opium crop replacement does not always serve long term highlander interests. He establishes this line of reasoning by demonstrating that the exclusive preoccupation with commercial agriculture too often endangers not only the ecological stability of indigenous farming systems but also undermines domestic food production. He sees this trend as leading to increased dependence on both costly agricultural inputs and unreliable markets for cash crop produce, on which farmers are then largely reliant for the income to purchase their food needs. This analysis is balanced by a set of development options which he believes would have a positive impact. He advocates more research to identify higher yielding varieties of rice, stronger promotion of self-sufficiency in food production and more investment in education. He closes with a plea for a more sociologically informed effort on the part of development agents.

Government Policy: Highland Ethnic Minorities.

Wanat Bhruksasri

This Chapter provides an interpretation and summary of Government policy towards the *chao khao* or hill tribes, the highland ethnic minorities, most of whom live in the north of Thailand. I will not include refugees from Laos and Burma who fall under a special policy package made up of measures passed by Orders in Council of Ministers to deal with refugees. Under these Orders, enacted in 1975 for Laos and 1976 for Burma, illegal immigrants were to be either arrested or repatriated. Many ethnic highlanders who became refugees are subject to this legislation. There are other minorities like the Yunnanese and Han Chinese who reside in government approved locations in the hill country of Mae Hong Son, Chiang Rai, and Chiang Mai close to the Thai-Burmese border. These people are the former Nationalist Kuomingtang Army units (KMT) and civilian refugees (see Hill, 1983: 123-134) who moved from Burma into Thailand in the early 1950's. They are called *chin haw* by the Northern Thai. Some of these people have been granted Thai citizenship. Most are registered aliens. These people fall under a different legal status and strictly speaking do not belong within a discussion addressed to ethnic minority groups well established in Thailand. Taking these qualifications into account I will now outline Royal Thai Government policy towards those people who are designated under the term "hill tribe".

INTERVENTION

First let me identify the ethnic hill tribes under discussion and provide an account of their historical background and some relevant socio-cultural aspects of their way of life. Finally, I shall review past policies and present a detailed report on present policy.

'Hill tribe': what's in a name?
The term *chao khao* or in English "hill tribe", is used throughout this paper as a collective name and has been in official use since 1959 when the Government set up the Central Hill Tribe Committee (CHTC), previously called the Hill Tribe Welfare Committee. Since then no one has attempted an official definition. Indeed, the term "hill tribe" is not accepted by some anthropologists, such as Peter Kunstadter, who prefer upland people, highlander or hill peasants to the term "hill tribe" (Kunstadter, 1969).

For all practical purposes the term provides a clear label for the Hill Tribe Development and Welfare Programme of the Department of Public Welfare. Since 1959 this agency has taken sole responsibility for hill tribe affairs, and the officially recognised ethnic groups which fall under this classification include the Lua (Lawa), Htin (H'tin, Mal, or Prai), Khamu, Meo (Miao, Hmong), Yao (Iu Mien, Mien), Akha (Ekaw), Lahu (Mussur), Lisu (Lisaw) and Karen (Kariang, Yang). Thus, among the 23 tribal ethnic groups found in Thailand, only nine tribal groups are currently included on the official list. The Hill Tribe Welfare Division and the Tribal Research Institute of the Department of Public Welfare are not empowered to handle the affairs of many of the highland ethnic minorities.

Seventy six percent of all hill tribes live in North Thailand. If viewed from the point of view of the indigenous Thai Northerners of *khon muang* as they call themselves, Northern Thailand is made up of eight provinces: Chiang Rai, Mae Hong Son, Chiang Mai, Lamphun, Lampang, Phayao, Phrae and Nan. The indigenous population of these eight provinces speak the same northern Thai dialect called *kham muang*. Some 24 percent of highlanders live in provinces to the south. Karen settlements are located as far south as Prachuab Khiri Khan in peninsular Thailand.

Ethno-linguistic groups.

According to Matisoff (1983: 65-66) the hill tribes of Thailand can be classified into what he calls three major linguistic superstocks. These are:

    1.0 **Sino-Tibetan.**

This superstock includes two linguistic branches relevant to our interests:

    1.1 **Karen.** The speakers of this language are called *kariang* in central Thai, or *yang* by northern Thai. The Karen call themselves according to their subgroups, Skaw, Pwo and so forth.

    1.2 **Tibeto-Burman.** The Loloish speakers of this branch of the Sino-Tibetan family comprise the Lahu the Lisu and the Akha.

    2.0 **Austro-Asiatic.**

Only one major branch of this family is found in Thailand, the **Mon-Khmer.** Speakers of this branch include: the Lawa or Lua as they are generally called; the Htin who call themselves either Mal of Prai according to their subgrouping; and The Khamu. A few Mlabri known in Thai as the *phi tong luang,* meaning "Spirits of the Yellow Leaves", live in Thailand but have no legal status as hill tribe people.

    3.0 **Austro-Thai.**

Following the linguist Benedict this superstock makes up a very diverse group which includes not only the languages of the indigenous people of the Pacific but also the **Tai-Kadai** and **Meo-Yao**. The ethnic minorites who concern us here belong to the last named group. The Meo (Miao) call themselves Hmong, and the Yao call themselves Iu Mien or Mien.

Population.
Up to the present, there has been no detailed comprehensive census survey of the hill tribe population. Five years ago, the most widely accepted estimate stated a figure of 350,000. In the absence of a proper survey, five government agencies, including the Department of Public Welfare acting as coordinator have agreed to cooperate in a two year population survey which commenced at the beginning of the 1985 fiscal year (October) and was supposed to be completed on the same date in 1987. At the moment the best figures available are those collected in the course of this survey and presented in Appendix I at the back of this book.

According to latest (September, 1988) Tribal Research Institute data, the nine officially listed tribal groups live in 21 provinces with a total population of 530,299 people. According to these figures, the hill tribe population makes up approximately one percent of the national population of Thailand (approximately 53 million in 1987).

Historical Background
There is general agreement among anthropologists that Austro-Asiatic language speakers belonging to the Mon-Khmer branch were resident in northern South-East Asia before the arrival, about a thousand years ago, of the first tribal Thai people (Manndorff, 1966: 5; Kunstadter, 1965: 2; Walker, 1979: 6). When the Thai established political control over the lowlands between 1200 and 1350 (Wyatt, 1985: 65-80) by extending the influence of their earlier city-states like Fang (860), they were following a pattern set down earlier by the Mon in Lamphun who founded the Haripunjaya kingdom in 769 (Penth, 1984: 5).

Many legends survive from the Mon period which indicate that the Lua had a close relationship with Haripunjaya. At this time the Lua appear to have been the largest ethnic group in the north. Some scattered settlements of these early inhabitants can still be found in the hills but if we follow Bradley (1983), we can assume that most Lua, following the rise of Thai influence, lost their separate ethnic identity and became Thai. This process of cultural-linguistic transformation has been much speeded up in modern times.

The other two principal Austro-Asiatic, Mon-Khmer speaking people are the Htin and Khamu. These people are found in both Thailand and Laos. The Htin are more numerous in Thailand than Laos, whereas the Khamu are found in greater numbers in Laos than Thailand (Walker 1979: 7). According to some evidence most Htin and Khamu, although they can be considered as ancient residents of the general region, are in fact recent immigrants from Laos. (LeBar, Hickey, Musgrav, 1967). However, David Fibecka Htin specialist argues that Htin have resided in Nan Province as long as the Lua (Lawa) have resided in the north of present day Thailand (Personal Communication, 9 August, 1985).

The Karen of the Sino-Tibetan linguistic superstock are recognized as having been resident in some parts of the country for a long time. A document written in Pali entitled **camthewiwong phongsawadan haripunchai** (or **Camadevi Dynasty Chronicle of Haripunjaya**) mentions that some Karen resided in the vicinity of the ancient city of Chiang Mai as early as the eighth century A.D. (Coedes, 1925: 12-13). However, according to other sources, these people began moving to Thailand in appreciable numbers from areas under Burmese domination in about the middle of the eighteenth century (Stern, 1968: 299; Hinton, 1975: 17; Marlowe, 1969: 1).

The remaining highlander groups such as the Lahu, Lisu and Akha who are part of the Sino-Tibetan linguistic family, and the Miao-Yao, classified under the Austro-Thai linguistic supergroup are, in general, relatively recent arrivals in Thai territory. The migrations of these peoples into Northern Thailand can be summarised as follows:

Meo - for the first time during 1840-1870 (Mottang, 1977: 52).
Yao - about 95 years ago or in the 1890's,
Lahu - about 1857 (DAP No. 550-107, 1970: 365),
Lisu - During 1919-1921 (Prasert Chaipiguist, personal communication)
Akha - about 1915 (Wanat Bhruksasri, 1985).

Agriculture is the hill tribes' most important activity. It can be said that in former days they were self-sufficient in food production. Rice, corn, vegetables, chillies and livestock were produced mostly for home consumption (Chantaboon, this volume). Today few villages are self-sufficient in food and the marketing of produce has become increasingly important. For some 30 percent, opium is the main cash crop. This is especially true for recently arrived migrants such as the Meo, Yao, Lahu, Lisu and Akha. For several reasons discussed by Chupinit in this volume these people brought opium cultivation with them into Thailand. Generally speaking the Austro-Asiatic people such as the Lua, Htin, Khamu as well as the Sino-Tibetan-Karennic speakers had no tradition of growing opium poppy before their recent association with poppy growing Loloish and Miao-Yao speakers.

Most highlanders employ slash-and-burn or shifting cultivation (swiddening). This involves the felling of forests either on a rotation or pioneer system. Following exhaustion of the soil and weed invasion the opium growers especially, prefer to move their settlements and pioneer new villages in forested land. However, the pattern of land use under shifting cultivation differs quite markedly depending on whether it is practised by opium growers or non-opium growers. The former generally practise primary or pioneer swiddening; the latter use a field-rotation system or, what is called by some anthropologists, a system of cyclical bush fallow which results in rather fixed village boundaries because the rotational system does not so rapidly exhaust the soil (Miles, 1969: 1).

Many of the cyclical swiddeners like the Lua and Karen, wherever possible, construct paddy or wet rice fields.

Animal husbandry is practised by every ethnic group mainly for the purpose of keeping pigs, cattle, buffalo and chickens for sacrifice and food consumption. Ponies are still used for transport in some locations, but pick-up trucks are seen everywhere.

Forest products are also gathered for household consumption and sale such as bamboo shoots, grass for thatching, mushrooms and so forth.

In traditional hill tribe cultures there are two corporate structures which constitute the institutional foundation of their society: the village and the household. Normally a village is formed of a main settlement with one or more small hamlets scattered around it. The village's most important resident is the headman who is selected by the adult male members of the community on the basis of a wide set of criteria: his popularity and skill, his leadership and knowledge and his wealth. The Akha and Karen headmen inherit the job.

The headman is in charge of administering village affairs, maintaining public peace, adjudicating disputes, accommodating visitors and so on. In carrying out his duties, especially those that affect community life, an informal council of elders and some local specialists in the community such as the religious leader or shaman are called in to assist. The headman also acts as a go-between in any village affairs which must be negotiated with Government agencies.

INTERVENTION

With this background in mind it is now possible to develop a better understanding of Government policy. Let me continue the assignment.

Government Policy Concerning the Hill Tribes.
As mentioned earlier the Government of Thailand first set up the Hill Tribe Welfare Committee (HTWC) in 1959. However, this does not mean that prior to 1959 Thailand did not have a policy towards these people. Although the historical literature on the subject is scanty, short accounts prepared by American anthopologists on the relationship of the Karen and Lawa to the Princes of Chiang Mai provide an indication of early policy. Marlowe says of the situation 200 years ago that, "As best as can be determined, the relationship between the newly settled Karen and the representatives of the Princes of Chiang Mai were essentially those of indirect rule...(and)..It would appear that the Karen were at first a semi-autonomous, tributary, dependent people under the protection of the Princes of Chiang Mai" (Marlowe, 1969: 2). A similar arrangement operated with the Lawa or Lua under which, "the Prince recognized the local authority of the hereditary Lua' leaders, known by the Thai title of Khun, and the Lua' title *samang*" (Kunstadter, 1969: 4).

This describes what can best be called a laissez faire policy. As long as the ethnic minority groups did not cause trouble or challenge the suzerainty of the Prince they were left alone. They enjoyed sufficient automomy to administer their own affairs and traditions.

This policy of non-interference remained in force up to the late 1950s. In 1951 the Government set up a Committee for the Welfare of People in Remote Areas (Ministry of Interior, Order No.653/2499, 7 August, 1951). This Committee's activities were directed at solving the urgent problems faced by all those living in isolated regions of Thailand. The term "hill tribe" was not yet in widespread use. This Committee however was successful in generating an increased interest and concern for highland people. The government's 1958 ban on the sale and consumption of opium also contributed to the growing interest (Proclamation of the Revolutionary Party, No. 37, 9 December, 1958).

The real reasons behind the Government's change of policy from that of non-interference to one of involvement were indicated at the time by General Prapas Charusathira, the former Minister of the Interior and the first chairman of HTW Committee, who said that,

> Because of their inefficient method of cultivation the tribes have been steadily despoiling the land of the region. Parts of it have been permanently ruined for agriculture. The removal of the forest cover has not only depleted timber resources but has interfered with the watershed of the rivers which irrigate the rice plains on which the economy of the national depends. Also, in the case of several of the largest tribes, their income has been derived from the cultivation of the opium poppy and the Government is determined to suppress opium growing for the sake of welfare of its own people and of others in the world.

> The third reason for the change from a relatively passive policy towards the hill tribes to one of active development brings us back to the security aspect. In their efforts to create disturbance in Thailand the foreign Communists are seeking to arouse dissatisfaction amongst the tribes. By radio propaganda and attempts to infiltrate agitators, they try to present our past tolerant policy as one of deliberate neglect, to create a sense of deprivation amongst the tribal peoples and to allure them with impractical promises.

(Gen. Prapas Charusathira 1967: 3-4).

INTERVENTION

On the same day the HTW Committee was established (3 June, 1959) the Council of Ministers also approved and empowered the Department of Public Welfare (DPW) to set up four Self-help Settlement Projects in Northern Thailand.

Soon after establishing the Doi Mussur (Tak Province) and Doi Chiang Dao (Chiang Mai Province) Settlement Projects, DPW felt a need for more reliable information on the hill tribes so that both planning and field operations under its responsibility could be made more effective. The first socio-economic survey of hill tribes in Northern Thailand was conducted between October 1961 and March 1962. The Department of Public Welfare in cooperation with the Ministry of Agriculture and the Border Patrol Police participated in the field survey. The services of an anthropologist, Dr. Hans Manndorff, were secured through the United Nations Narcotic Drugs Division to help in field work and write up the final report.

Several recommendations presented in this report were adopted by the Council of Ministers. Perhaps the most important recommendation was that which led to the establishment of Provincial Hill Tribe Development and Welfare Centres under the DPW. The first centre was set up in Tak province at what had been planned as a resettlement site. On the basis of another recommendation the Tribal Research Centre (now the Tribal Research Institute) was established (1964) as a joint project between DPW and Chiang Mai University (CMU). The Centre was built on the university campus.

The second socio-economic survey of the hill tribes was conducted by a United Nations team in 1967. The results of this survey led to the establishment of the Opium Crop Replacement and Community Development Programme under the assistance of a United Nations Fund for Drug Abuse Control (UNFDAC), launched in 1973.

Public Welfare Policy

Since 1959, many modifications have been made to the committee, its subcommittees and the policy itself. I shall outline only some of these modifications which will serve to show the direction of policy development and allow me to keep my paper within a reasonable length.

Late in 1967 Thailand witnessed its first outbreak of active insurgency at a Meo village in the district of Thoeng, Chiang Rai. Communist influence spread quickly in response to punitive raids by government forces and acts of terrorism increased. These incidents aroused the concern of both Bangkok and field agencies. Military, police and civilians were deeply disturbed by the aggressive response of some of the hill tribes. At this time (1969), His Majesty the King initiated what has become the most important of all voluntary services in the highlands, the Royal (Northern) Project. Just before the King took this initiative the government acting on advice of the planning committee of the National Economic Development Board, sanctioned by the National Security Council, agreed to change the name of the Hill Tribe Welfare Committee to the Hill Tribe Committee (1968) to acknowledge the wide range of problems and public agencies called into action in the highlands. This Committee is now called the Central Hill Tribe Committee. Policy modifications were made with the approval of the Council of Ministers on 15 December, 1969 (Letter from the Secretariate of the Council of Ministers, No. 0403/18577, 4). The policy which emerged is informally known as the Short-and Long-term policy.

The **Short-term Policy** was to arrange as soon as possible for government officials to work with hill tribes in vulnerable areas by providing civic action services to gain their confidence and encourage them to make a commitment of loyalty. The Government also mobilised their support in a defence effort to resist infiltration.

Where the armed forces undertook operations to suppress terrorism, all government units fell under the unified command of the military. In areas which were considered to be susceptible to infiltration, DPW was made responsible for quickly dispatching development and welfare teams to work with the people.

The **Long-term Policy** was to provide development and welfare services to highlanders to stabilize their residence and livelihood, discourage them from growing opium poppy and replace opium with other crops, cease deforestation and contribute to the nation in a manner expected of citizens. All this was to be implemented as part of the First Five Year Economic Plan prepared by the National Economic Development Board. In order to carry out his policy, four operational methods were laid down.

First, if communities were living in scattered hamlets rather than proper villages, or if these villages were difficult for government officials to reach, the hill tribes were to be persuaded to group together at suitable locations, as arranged by the authorities.

Second, communities already suitably located were to be given support to enable them to maintain their livelihood. DPW mobile teams were to provide various development and welfare services.

Third, those communities that did not wish to stay in the hills, or whose inhabitants had run away in fear of injury and who did not wish to live in the hills again, were to be grouped in evacuee centres. Welfare services would then be made available to enable them to integrate into lowland society.

Fourth, as an adjunct to the policy a general rider was made that all contact was to promote national security, encourage hill people to identify with Thai society and give their loyalty to the nation.

Public Welfare Policy

This Short-and Long-term policy was pursued until 1976 at which time the Government declared a general policy of integration.

Prior to this declaration, the composition of the CHT Committee was modified following submissions from the Ministry of the Interior. Under these modifications, designed to improve efficiency, the number of members was reduced and the Permanent Under-Secretary to the Minister of the Interior took the place of the Minister as the head of the Committee. All sub-committees in various fields such as education, health, vocation and etc., were dissolved.

Following this change, the Ministry of Agriculture and Cooperatives submitted and was granted (4 March, 1976) by the Council of Ministers, approval to form a Committee to Consider Ways and Means to Protect and Maintain the Forest and Watershed (Letter from the Secretariate of the Council of Ministers, No. 0202/3451, 4 March, 1976). This Committee is chaired by the Minister of Agriculture and Cooperatives and includes representatives of the Royal (Northern) Project. It is responsible for preparing projects to help:

1) broaden hill tribe employment opportunities, especially in agriculture and reafforestation schemes mounted to replace damaged forests; and,

2) train the highlanders in new occupations such as land conservation development and the maintenance of local watersheds.

Following on these changes, the year 1979 also saw the establishment of the Office of the Narcotics Control Board (ONCB) appointed under the Act for the Prevention and Suppression of Narcotic Drugs which had become law on November

16, 1976. This Board is chaired by the Deputy Prime Minister, and is charged with responsibility for minimising disruptions to work on the suppression of narcotics. Prior to this, work was often interrupted following changes of government.

Now, let's return once more to the policy of integration. This policy, originally prepared by DPW was submitted to the Ministry of the Interior and received the Cabinet's approval on 6 July, 1976 (Letter from the Secretariate of the Council of Ministers, No. 0202/11511, 13 July, 1976). This policy outlines the Government's intention to integrate the hill tribes into Thai society whilst respecting their rights to practise their own religions and maintain their cultures.

The objectives of this policy are stated quite clearly and precisely. They commit the Royal Thai Government to a policy under which assistance is given to the hill tribes for the express purpose of helping them to become first class, self-reliant Thai citizens. The policy is, especially in the last point, subject to the Ministry of the Interior's Regulations on Considerations for Granting Thai Nationality to the Hill Tribes involving Housing Registration Cards (1974). It also states the necessity to reduce the highlander population growth rate by promoting family planning. As for development approaches, the policy outlines three guidelines:

First, areas or zones for integrated development should be specified and the development task clearly entrusted to DPW, Ministry of Interior as the principal agency to carry out the work in cooperation and co-ordination with other line agencies.

Second, where hill tribe villages are not yet officially identified as belonging to development zones, mobile teams will be sent to work in these villages to build up a good relationship, gather baseline survey data for preparing plans, and assist with urgent problems.

Public Welfare Policy

Third, Thais who happen to live in highland areas will also receive services similar to those provided to hill people. It should be noted that this last guideline acknowledged for the first time the presence of Thai "lowlanders" living in the hills.

This **Integration Policy** as I have called it was modified again six year later in 1982. At that time, General Prem Tinsulanonda, who was Prime Minister until September 1988, appointed the Board of the Directorate for the Solution of Security Problems in Relation to the Hill-Tribes and Opium Cultivation. General Prachuab Suntarangkul was appointed the first Chairman and as Deputy Prime Minister was assigned the task of improving the administration of affairs dealing with highlanders and opium related problems by reviewing policies and measures undertaken in field operations, administration and development, including overall coordination between the project and agencies involved. It was expected that improvements would eventually enhance efficiency, and more quickly achieve objectives set down by the government. The Council of Ministers adopted resolutions which modified the policy on 7 December, 1982 and this revised policy remains in use up to the present time.

The present hill tribe policy of the Government in fact retains the accumulated intentions and wishes of all preceding policies, namely, to promote the welfare of the hill tribes as well as to solve problems relating to destruction of watershed and forests, opium poppy cultivation and security problems. The policy is quite precise and covers a wide set of objectives and measures to achieve these aims. It provides suggestions for improving administrative procedures and basic guidelines for the organization of committee planning, staffing, and evaluation. Criteria are given for the selection of development zones and sources of budgetary support. In recent months however there has been increasingly determined talk of resettlement on a large scale.

To present detailed information on all of these topics would take more space than I am allowed but it is worth while to summarize the principal policy objectives and measures, and the organization of the committees at different levels. Readers interested in the issue of resettlement should read my other chapter in this book "Problem Solving Through Understanding" (Chapter 9).

The policy objectives and measures can be divided into three categories: administration, eradication of opium production and consumption, and socio-economic development.

Administration. There are two objectives in this category.

The **first** aims to enable the hill tribes to live peacefully within Thai society and to enjoy a sense of belonging; to be good citizens, loyal to the nation; not to cause security problems and not place political or socio-economic burdens on the government.

The **second** aims at reorganizing the life-style of both hill tribes and Thai lowlanders resident in the highlands to secure a livelihood in a manner consistent with the law and local regulations.

The measures recommended as guidelines to administrative agencies responsible for achieving these objectives state that they must:

1. Create amongst the hill people a mutual understanding and a sense of belonging to the nation through the promotion of non-formal education, public relations and other related project activities provided specially for hill tribes.

Further, to ensure effectiveness implementing agencies should:

    1.1 See that the hill tribes be made fully aware of their place in Thai society, conscious of their right to maintain their way of life as Thai citizens.

Public Welfare Policy

1.2 Make sure that all rules and regulations are strictly followed particularly those relating to forest destruction, the depletion of watersheds and other natural resources. Also that every possible effort be made to promote self-reliance among the hill tribes and encourage them to participate actively in development activities.

2. Specify areas suitable for administrative and security control, natural conservation, and socio-economic development in order to settle people permanently ("settle" has come to increasingly mean "resettle").

3. Promote better ways of living and accelerate the carrying out of complete population and agricultural census surveys. Here again this includes Thai lowlanders resident in the highlands and making their living there.

4. Check immigration and push new migrants out of Thailand.

Policy papers also discuss the need to identify measures to discourage and if necessary punish new immigrants and those who assist them and that this be done in association with efforts to permanently settle those who qualify for citizenship. It is thought that such settlements will make it easier to distinguish between established residents and newcomers.

Eradication of Opium Production & Consumption. There are two principal objectives:

1. Reducing and eventually eliminating opium production and consumption among the hill tribes by encouraging them to engage in alternative activities which provide sufficient income.

2. Freeing the hill tribes from the influence of armed minority groups and disarming groups like the *chin haw* or Chinese Yunnanese (KMT).

The measures to be taken to achieve these two objectives are:

1. To decrease opium poppy cultivation and opium consumption by promoting the:
   1.1 Extension of substitute cash-crops;
   1.2 Elaboration of alternative occupations, which provide high, permanent incomes, supported by an established infrastructure for marketing, transport and processing of agricultural produce. Ethnic handicrafts are also to be promoted.
   1.3 Maintenance of public relations and educational programmes which identify the dangers of using narcotics and dissuade people from growing opium.

2. To minimize the influence of both ethnic minority pressure groups and the communists by means of staff efficiency, performance and morale should be improved to enable field workers to carry out their tasks competently.

3. To seek assistance from external sources to increase national effectiveness in solving problems related to hill tribe land use and opium production. This will be based on the support and control of key organizations whose responsibility is to monitor field work and make sure it is compatible with overall policy goals. Assistance should be given to Thai lowlanders as deemed appropriate.

Socio-Economic Development. There are two main goals:
1. To develop the productive capabilities of highlanders so that they are able to not only maintain their way of life, but also improve their standard of living.

2. To bring the hill tribe population growth rate down to 1.5% by the year 1986.

Other specific objectives laid down include the need to:
1. Improve the socio-economic status of hill tribe society by promoting a wide range of activities that will generate sufficient income, especially to promote economic development in the field of agriculture as well as other occupations. The emphasis should be on home industries. The promotion of, and training in, appropriate production technology should be in accord with the needs of the market and their culture. The private sector must also be allowed to participate in development efforts.

2. Make available primary health care services including advice on nutrition, health education, and also other useful public health information.

3. Intervene directly to slow the increasing rate of population growth in hill tribe and Thai communities located in the highlands.

4. Promote public relations and educational programmes as a way of creating a better understanding among the highlanders of the wide range of services provided by various government agencies.

Under this policy (1982) a three tiered organization of committees has been set up.

The **first tier** is the national level committee, called The Board of Directorate for the Solution of Security Problems Relating to Hill Tribes and Opium Cultivation. This Board is entrusted with considering and making policy recommendations to the Council of Ministers. It also has executive authority to promote and coordinate inter-ministerial cooperation and direct specific operations, as well as screen plans prepared at the provincial level. This Committee is chaired by the Deputy Prime Minister with the National Security Council acting in the capacity of the Committee's Secretariat.

The **second tier** committee is the earlier established Central Hill Tribe Committee. It is the inter-ministerial level committee headed by the Minister of the Interior. The Director-General of DPW acts as the secretary. This Committee is responsible for making policy and planning recommendations at the ministerial level consistent with national level policy. This Central Hill Tribe Committee coordinates the work of government implementing agencies that also carry out monitoring and evaluation tasks.

The **third tier** committee is the Provincial Hill Tribe Committee in each province headed by the provincial governor. This Committee is responsible for coordinating and preparing plans for solving practical problems relating to poppy cultivation and the like. Work includes directing, following-up and evaluating the results of all operations and projects. The head of the Provincial Office is the Committee's secretary assisted by the chief of each of the Provincial Hill Tribe Development and Welfare Centres.

To recapitulate, present government policy towards the hill tribes covers three matters, namely: administration; eradication of opium cultivation and consumption; and socio-economic development. For the sake of brevity I call this policy the **Policy of Three Aspects** to distinguish it from all preceding policies. It is implemented through a **three tiered** administrative hierarchy.

If the move towards resettlement is strengthen the policy may well have to be renamed. A change from current tolerance to forced resettlement would make it misleading to name a policy after the administrative arrangement under which it is implemented.

Concluding Remarks

Both the older **Integration Policy** and the current **Policy of Three Aspects** deserve fuller discussion but here I will offer only a few relevant remarks.

First, I am of the opinion that the **Policy of Three Aspects** is comprehensive, carefully thought out and its goals and objectives clearly identified. The long term or ultimate goal is clearly that of integration: the integration of hill people into the Thai state. This is an objective which presupposes that the path followed will "enable the hill tribes to become first class, self-reliant citizens".

In my experience, this policy has not always been popular with overseas anthropologists who tend to view its aim as incorporation by cultural assimilation. I have always argued strongly against this criticism on the grounds that Thai society is much more open than most and those who share this culture freely accept both miscegenation and cultural mixing. This mixing has occurred spontaneously without force and by the free will of those involved. Thus, if such mixing results in a diverse but unified population it seems more appropriate to call the process spontaneous or natural integration rather than assimilation with the overtone of force which that word conveys. It has always seemed unfair to me that anthropologists antagonistic to its use judge only the policy objectives without taking into account the nature of Thai society, culture and behaviour.

I myself believe that the objective of the 1976 Government policy implemented with tolerance and understanding truly reflects national ideology and the aspiration to form a united people linked in a common purpose for the national good as articulated in Article I of the Constitution of the Kingdom of Thailand. This Article states that the Kingdom is a unitary state and shall remain "undivided". This aspiration can be achieved only if the hill tribes are encouraged to become citizens.

The Department of Public Welfare in fact contributes a large part of its resources and manpower to integrate highlanders so that they can become full and equal citizens of the country. The number of hill people in contact with DPW mobile teams in 1986 amounted to 278,858; those whose names were recorded on official housing registration cards 166,759; as well as 67,663 with ID cards and 157,431 persons granted Thai citizenship. The DPW annual report (1984) indicates that the Department is administering 13 provincial Development and Welfare Centres in 18 provinces. In that year, 259 mobile teams were working in 1,155 villages with 40,832 households consisting of 48,548 families or 205,835 people.

Secondly, let me comment on programmes and projects based on the measures outlined in the **Policy of Three Aspects.** What activities are undertaken in pursuit of policy objectives? I have some suggestions for improvement. Some of these suggestions have been prepared in anticipation of a tougher government policy and are discussed in a separate paper (Chapter 9 this volume).

Then there is the matter of the administrative aspect of the policy. If we are to know how many people we are dealing with we need to carry out census and registration surveys. The census and registration surveys launched in 1985 will not tell us all we need to know. By the time this book is in print the survey of the highland population will nearly be complete (1988). This survey can not be called a census but the final figures will still provide valuable planning information for many agencies.

The **third** point I would like to make here concerns opium related problems and the ways and means by which a reduction of production and consumption by the hill tribes can be achieved. This issue remains a matter of central concern to which all government policies since 1959 have directed their attention. The opium problem is also of international interest and, as I said earlier, Thailand's request for UN assistance in the 1966/67 survey, and the manner in which it later welcomed the UN assisted

Public Welfare Policy

establishment of a crop replacement and community development programme in 1973, demonstrated the government's concern for this matter. These efforts, together with the results of socio-economic development in such fields as education, health, agricultural extension, promotion of other empolyment opportunities, public relations on the danger of opium as well as the continuing suppression of opium trafficking, etc., have brought about a great drop in opium production from approximately 150 tons in the 1965/66 season to 25 tons in 1986/87. This may lead to other problems.

In 1983 the TRI estimated the hill tribe consumption by calculating the ONCB rate of addiction (6.8 percent) for 400,000 people requiring a daily intake of 3.2 g. and came up with the total for annual demand as 31,956 kg. As the figures for supply and demand are so close further problems may be generated if suppression of production is too successful. As has been observed by Gammelgaard "A one-sided approach emphasizing only eradication of cultivation may have unwanted side-effects which are so common in the history of drug abuse control. One is to convert Thailand into an opium importing country. Another possible effect may be to pave the way for heroin dependence in the hill tribe villages" (Gammelgaard, 1985). To avoid this situation it is absolutely necessary to reduce the incidence of opium addiction among hill tribe populations.

The **fourth** and last point I would like to make here is given more thorough treatment in my Chapter, "Problem Solving Through Understanding": that is the question of how to solve the problem of destruction of the watersheds and forests brought about by shifting cultivation. At present there is a conflict of opinion between the advocates of human resource development and of natural resource conservation. This contradiction is likely to adversely influence the allocation of land to the hill tribes but the matter is such an important aspect of policy that it cannot be treated lightly. Support for administrative goals, security control as well as conserving natural resources appear to hinge on it. Through land grants, permanent settlements can be established in areas suited to sustainable cultivation practices. Ecologically informed and economically viable modes of production can only help achieve national goals. It would be a shame if the rhetoric on both sides precludes the possibility of a good outcome. I am confident that with the participation of the people, the hill tribes themselves, the goals of integration and the objectives of the **Policy of Three Aspects** are more likely to be achieved with a greater degree of success and with less pain than in other countries with a similar ethnic minority situation.

References

Bradley, David (1983) "Identity: The Persistence of Minority Groups" McKinnon & Wanat Bhruksasri (eds) **Highlanders of Thailand** Oxford University Press: Kuala Lumpur.

Coedes, G. (1925) "Document sur l'histoire politique et religieuse du Laos Occidental" **Bulletin de l'Ecole Francaise d'Extreme-Orient,** 25: pp. 12-13.

Department of the Army, (1970) **Ethnographic Study Series: Minority Groups in Thailand.**, Washington No. 550/107.

Gammelgaard, Joegen (1985) Keynote address "Workshop on the treatment of Hill Tribe Opium Addicts" Chiang Mai, 3-5 July, 1985.

Hinton, Peter (1967) "Introduction" **Tribesmen and Peasants in North Thailand** ed. Peter Hinton, Tribal Research Centre: Chiang Mai.

Hill, Ann Maxwell (1983) "The Yunnanese: Overland Chinese in Northern Thailand" **Highlanders of Thailand.** McKinnon and Wanat Bhruksasri (eds) Oxford University Press, Kuala Lumpur.

Kunstadter, Peter (1967) "Hill and Valley Populations in Northwestern Thailand" **Tribesmen and Peasants in North Thailand,** ed. Peter Hinton, Tribal Research Centre: Chiang Mai.

Le Bar, Frank et. al. ***Ethnic Groups of Mainland Southeast Asia*** Human Relations Area Files Press: New Haven.

McKinnon, John & Wanat Bhruksasri (eds). (1983) ***Highlanders of Thailand*** Oxford University Press: Kuala Lumpur.

Manndorff, Hans (1967) "The Hill Tribe Program of the Public Welfare Department, Ministry of Interior, Thailand: Research and Economic Development" ***Southeast Asian Tribal Minorities and Nations*** Peter Kundstadter (ed.) Princeton University Press: New Jersey.

Marlowe, David H. (1969) Upland Lowland Relationship: The case of the S'kaw Karen of Central Upland Western Chiang Mai ***Tribesmen and Peasants in North Thailand*** ed. Peter Hinton Chiang Mai: Tribal Research Institute.

Matisoff, J. (1983) "Linguistic Diversity and Language Contact" McKinnon & Wanat Bhruksasri (eds.) ***Highlanders of Thailand*** Oxford University Press: Kuala Lumpur.

Miles, D (1969) Shifting Cultivation, Threats and Prospects ***Tribesmen and Peasants in North Thailand*** Peter Hinton. (ed.) Tribal Research Institute: Chiang Mai.

Mottin Jean	(1977)	*History of the White Hmong (Meo),* Odean Store: Bangkok (in Thai).
Penth, Hans	(1984)	"The History of Lanna Thai" *Lanna Thai* Chiang Mai (in Thai).
Prapas Charusathira	(1967)	*Thailand's Hill Tribes* Department of Public Welfare, Ministry of Interior, Bangkok.
Stern, Theodore	(1970)	"A People Between: The Pwo Karen of Western Thailand" Paper presented to The Annual Meeting of the Association for Asian Studies: San Francisco
Suwan Ruengyote	(1969)	"The Hill Tribe Programme of the Thai Government" *Tribesmen and Peasants in North Thailand* Peter Hinton (ed.) Tribal Research Centre: Chiang Mai
UN Report	(1967)	*Report of the United Nations Survey Team on the Economic and Social Needs of the Opium-Producing Areas in Thailand* Government House Printing Office: Bangkok.
Walker, A	(1979/1980)	"Highlanders and Government in North Thailand" *Folk,* Vols. 21-22, Copenhagen.
Wanat Bhruksasri	(1985)	"Hill Tribes in Lanna Territory" Bangkok (in Thai).
Wyatt, David	(1985)	*A Short History of Thailand* Thai Watana Panich & Yale University Press: London.

Facing Development in the Highlands:
A Challenge for Thai Society

Bernard Vienne

> *"The king accused the gardener of putting poison in the mango. He ordered the gardener be executed...When everyone was quiet the chief minister threw a stone on the spot indicated. A cobra came out of a hole in the ground and bit the stone. The officials killed the snake...So he let the gardener look after the gardens as before."*
>
> The Laws of King Mangrai

Since the beginning when they spread out over the alluvial plains of what is now known as Northern Thailand the Tai have had something to do with highlanders if not the highlands[1]. Of course the interrelationship has changed from time to time and with this, reciprocal patterns of understanding. Unfortunately few historical documents are available from earlier periods to provide supporting evidence, but enough has been recorded to allowed us to identify a structural relationship[2]. Tracing the

---

1. See Wyatt 1984, Benchaphun Shinawatra 1985, Marlowe 1963.
2. The main sources are the recorded chronicles of the old principalities. This problem has been recently review by N. Tapp. (Tapp, 1986a, 1986b) and C.A. Kammerer, among others Cf. Sao Saimong Mangrai 1981, and the chronicles of Chiang Mai and Nan.

INTERVENTION

historical evolution of this pattern brings us to a deeper understanding of what has sometimes been described as the emergence of a drastic contemporary situation: a situation in which ideas of modernity mixed with geopolitical ambitions is bringing new populations and cultures into contact with each other followed by a cohort of profound problems. I am not the first to address myself to this situation but a review from a fresh perspective would make a contribution to our understanding of what is happening[3].

> From this point of view I would also argue against the common tendency to view the Hmong as an isolated, autonomous group who traditionally lacked relations with other groups. On the contrary, it is clear ... that they have had long and sustained·contacts with the members of other cultures throughout their history. The myth of self-sufficient tribe has been fostered by colonialists and early anthropologists as a useful administrative tool and a pretext for exploiting the people so categorized. But such a view does not do justice to the extensive interdependency which in the past ... characterised the relations between the uplands and lowlands (Tapp: 1986a: 3).

It is not my intention to present a comprehensive review of what has been said and done about what is presently undertaken in the mountains. Other papers in this book focus on these matters and emphasise the ideological and political aspects as well as the more pragmatic strategies one can observe at the empirical level[4]. I want to argue first the underlying objectives, aims and the choices made in research and development are

---

3. For the Karen see Renard 1980 and Keynes 1979. For the Hmong see Tapp 1985 and 1986a. For the Akha see Kammerer 1986 Chapter 11 this volume.
4. See Wanat, Chupinit, McKinnon, (this volume).

based on a stereotyped evaluation of the situation and that this has generated problems in the past which remain until today; and second, that these must be seriously confronted with contradictory statements founded on the results of a more scientific, critical and independent perspective. What I propose is not exactly an academic debate, as it concerns a serious issue which sooner or later will become a tremendous challenge. As an example, broad generalisations are used by policy-makers from time to time to reinforce arguments which often seem strangely dislocated from the logical content from which they are drawn and must be taken to mainly reflect political allegiance or loyalties, conflicts of interest, factionalism, business, ideology or whatever...more than comprehensive views centred on the regional specificity of Northern Thailand. The use of environmentalist ideology discussed in this volume by McKinnon is a case in point. This is not to say that the aims, the main objectives and priorities of the Royal Thai Government policy concerning either the highlands or the highlanders has to be criticised as such, from an external point of view, or for that matter reformulated, but rather to point out that the data required to provide an accurate analysis, if an efficient development policy is to be mounted, cannot rely on a collection of raw, unrelated facts and figures. Technology alone is no longer a keyword in this matter. New technologies that are not adopted by those for whom they are supposedly designed have generally failed everywhere.

Ethnic identity, minorities, and the historical process

During the past ten years, social scientists working with the so called hill tribes have been deeply concerned with the problem of ethnic identity as a manifestation of a culturally specific pattern of adaptation[5]. Since the pioneering work of E. Leach **The Political System of Highland Burma,** this problematique has been so well developed as to enter common use and to promote ethnicity as a quasi-official academic categorisation as well as an administrative label regardless of its

---

5. For a detailed and comprehensive summary see Conrad Chapter 8 this volume.

relevance. So the structural and critical perspective of Leach's masterpiece is unfortunately, in the case of Northern Thailand, often put aside. To be Karen, to be Hmong, to be Akha...is more or less to be credited with a predictable pattern of behaviour embedded in a stereotyped cultural pattern promoted as an idealised rationalisation which stands in contrast to the dominant society. As a result *chao khao*[6] are seen to oppose the supposed culturally homogeneous dominant society and provide a dissonant presence in the cultural harmony in such a way that emphasizes the modernity of one group against the primitiveness of the other. This comes to be a permanent performance which contains a strong sentiment in the exercise of self-identity founded on language, dress, daily behaviour as well as beliefs, ritual, and *savoir faire*. Even if this is not promoted by the people themselves it becomes part of "their" reluctance to make a choice between total assimilation and "their" ability to determining their own destiny: manifest "otherness" becomes from and outside point of view the prevailing reason advocated to account for problems. The implicit value judgements involved in terms such as "national integration", "land use management", "economic self-sufficiency", "demographic pressure", "social and political integration", to quote some of the problems to which administrators and development agents often refer, makes it necessary that these issues be cast in negative terms such as the "destruction of the environment", "increasing poverty", "dangerous population growth" and "state security" thus opening the door to interpretations which justify the implementation of

---

6. The term *chao khao* (ชาวเขา : chaaw khǎw) which literally means hill or mountain people has an official connotation. In this respect it is not use to refer to all people living in the mountains. Khon Muang, Hau, Shan and others....are excluded. The concept is restricted to the nine ethnic minorities, that is Karen, Hmong, Lisu, Akha, Lahu, Yao, Kamu, Htin, Lua, even though some of them are no longer mountain dwellers. It is also interesting to note that the Lua play the role of a residual category for the Thai, including people who use the term to distinguish themselves as long as they present characteristics such as customary differences in terms of language, dress, ritual etc...The concept of *chao khao* is a clear example of a normative concept founded on a dogmatic sociology of knowledge. If will be used in this paper accordingly. We have chosen to preserve the usual transliteration.

increasingly radical policies of assimilation.[7] Such a path poses major risks which I will later discuss.

Social scientists who take the risks for granted are as a consequence obliged to take a more defensive position than they might otherwise prefer and are forced, if they are rather conservative, to give priority to empirical and technical aspects of problems or if they are more radical, emphasize cultural aspects. In both cases the holistic and structural approach - the cornerstone of Leach's pioneer methodology-must be put to one side if not out of sight[8]. In a sense the attenuated sociological imagination and the knowledge which it has generated as a reflection on the problematique of cultural identity as the principal preoccupation (with all its contradictory statements) can be observed in the controversial implementation of state development policy if not in the political scene itself.

It is my opinion that until now problems in the highlands have been mainly approached empirically in terms of a technical problematique. "Uncontrolled migration", "increasing demographic density". "shifting cultivation" - if it still exists - "opium cultivation" and so on...are these in fact specific problems which one could expect to be solved by appropriate pragmatic measures or are they fragmented phenomena manifest in the face of a wider and more complex reality? Can we in fact consider problems without relating them to the more profound network of social relationships through which they emerge and in which

---

7. Cf. Prapas Charusathira 1967. Also the following.

"The government, therefore, is presented with a series of extremely thorny dilemmas. If it wants to protect the highland watersheds, it will be forced to institute widespread resettlement of hill farmers from such areas, protecting the watersheds thereafter with force, if necessary. In a democratic society, even if vitally necessary, such programs can be hard to push through" (Thailand Development Research Institute 1987).

8. This was already pointed out by Cooper ten years ago when he reviewed problems and prospects of the tribal minorities of Northern Thailand. Cf. Cooper 1979.

they are experienced in a quite specific way? Can we really handle the situation if we do not take into account the objective contradictions which so often appear between the idealistic views promoted and the inherent constraints of the real situation? A policy of cash crop replacement, the promotion of integrated farming systems as well as current policies of education or community development can be successful only if the "target people" really feel as though they are engaged as full participants in the challenges presented. This is exactly what can be observed when looking at the present situation in the highlands even through the shorthand methodology of rapid appraisal. People respond to development policies according to their own understanding rather than to the objective suitability of what is being implemented. Good will and an open mind are pre-requisites, if a reasonable chance for success is to be kept alive. Such participation cannot, of course, be created by force. Experience has already shown that force has a way of producing the very reverse of the desired outcome.

It is quite easy to advance such a provocative and even critical statement but it is not so easy to construct the matter in such a way as to ensure a better outcome. This is a crucial issue and research has something to do with it, not in terms of decision making but to better link it with the major problems faced by *chao khao*. In so far as the implementation of development has always been the result of a kind of political, social and economic compromise, research could help to adjust, if not reformat present policy in such a way as to solve or avoid making further problems. Weaving development as a social network of relationships into a greater potential for economic growth brings me to another observation. If economic change and even social welfare can be planned and implemented in such a way as to produce additional income, better education, efficient health services and so forth, the subsequent inevitable process of social transformation is, generally speaking, unpredictable. This is an extremely important point to keep in mind. How will people respond? How will they organize their own adaptation?

How will they adjust their strategies to the spontaneous pulses in the process of change which affect the environmental, economic and political contexts? Can we expect a homogeneous response secured solely through the processes involved in the transfer of technology? Unfortunately no, and there is still no easy way to do it.

Cultural adaptation and changes in behaviour go side by side with the emergence of latent conflicts, new patterns of self-organization, contradictory values. Praxis and underlying ideologies emerge through a quite complex process deeply embedded not only in cultural conciousness but also in the historical experience which moulds culture[9].

Success or failure of a development policy has always been dependant on the gap between incentive and response which cannot merely be fill up with empirical or pragmatic guess work. Developers are becoming more and more aware that problems are linked together and every operational project gets a chance to consider this fact. But, in most cases a proper understanding of the manner in which phenomenon are linked eludes us even if it is considered to be relevant. There are two ways of dealing with this methodological preoccupation and two contrasting modalities of intervention present themselves. One is to decide that problems are linked by the obvious fact of the priorities declared in state policy: the government serves its own interests and the subject people simply have to adapt themselves as best they can. The other alternative is to decide that the problems of the people come first and that the state has to adjust its policy to a de facto situation.

Although an argument for participation in development could be relatively easily documented for North Thailand by

---

9. Cf. N. Tapp for the case of the Hmong and A. Walker for the Lahu. The present study of N. Kammerer on Christian Akha will provide us with a deeper insight into those problems (personnal communication).

facts gleaned from official declarations and newspaper reports, it is my opinion that the social dynamic simply cannot allow such a radical alternative because of the disruption this would entail. In Thailand especially this would not be permitted even if there is some historical evidence to contradict me. Why? Because the structured opposition I pointed out above is such a widely accepted and coherent view that as an ideological reflection it has become, since the second world war, embedded as an objective *rapport de force* within such a powerful dialectic that it cannot easily be deflected let alone changed[10]. As can be seen in other East and South-East Asian nations this is a phenomenon not unknown to the region[11]. The negative examples of Burma and Sri Lanka are cases in point and help stress the serious nature of the subject matter: this is not an academic question but a real issue. Thailand must be careful the way ethnic minorities perceive the implemented policy if it is to avoid the fate of Burma, Sri Lanka or worse.

An argument on how to manage development problems in the highlands, centred on the dialectic of the relationship between the dominant rice growing lowland society undergoing a process of cultural homogenisation through state formation involving national integration and territorial consolidation in structural opposition to a mosaic of politically acephalous, minority settlements which must be recognized as a de facto reality, would still require a lot of explanation.

I don't want to fully argue the point, but let me attempt to develop the concept by discussing a few concrete examples already well documented in this book to see what happens.

---

10. I realise that this difficult point needs elaboration. To provide an adequate discussion will bring me into the domain of political science which is beyond my field of competence. However a futuristic analysis of how the political structure of Thailand would respond with contradictory statements to this challenge would provide a basis on which to arrive at a better understanding. This task exceeds the scope of this paper.

11. To limit myself to a Thai source, General Saiyud Kerdphol provides an insightful view of the role of colonialism consistent with the analysis of N.Tapp.

Even if the official policy has been slightly modified from time to time since its inception, as is well documented by Wanat (Chapter 1, this volume), the highland development problem and its correlative, the corrective welfare strategy advised remains the same.

The manner in which problems are classified at an empirical level still clearly reflects the basic understanding set down more than 30 years ago. What C.F. Keynes wrote in the 70's still enjoys wide acceptance because it repeats basic assumptions made about the hill tribe situation. The central place of this in peoples' understanding is a fixed reality quite apart from the dynamic process involved in development implementation.

> For the Thai government and its representatives, those who are hill tribes are distinguished by their practice of upland swidden cultivation, by their production of opium, by their low level of economic development relative to the rest of the Thai population, and by their "alien" status as recent, and illegal migrants into Thailand (Keyes, 1979: 13).

The stereotyped view found in early evaluations and subsequent publications persists as the dominant orientation to what can readily be described as a transformation scene. Researchers designing work appropriate to the current situation must assume that a reorientation is necessary and are the first to discover the innate conservatism of established "knowledge".

On the firm foundation of this dogmatic sociology of knowledge, development policy has been conducted on an empirical model according to the accepted classification of problems in terms of their hierarchical priority no matter how they are linked together in reality or how the structure of this linkage is at odds with what developers want to do. Controversial statements and obviously divergent interpretations put about by agencies who see themselves in competition with each other, emphasise this or that aspect of substantive issues which remind us, if such a reminder is necessary, that development work conducted outside market constraints, the dynamic of economic, political and social macro-structures and international political pressure is inconceivable. What R.C. Cooper wrote in 1979 remains true:

> In the past decade, the highlands of Northern Thailand have received an input of cash and development expertise per capita that may be the envy of any farming community anywhere in the world. However, this investment has been guided primarily by consideration of national and international interests and only secondly by consideration of the problems of the tribal and Northern Thai inhabitants (Cooper, 1979: 323).

Problem indentification

In many cases I have observed in the mountain area an artificial network of relationships has been progressively substituated for a more natural, outstandingly real one, in order to achieve successful implementation and good results. By this bias the technocratic structure of the state administration and its "bureaucratic, centralised model of development"[12] has been extented to the mountain situation regardless of its sociological specificity.

> Nevertheless, we should not blind ourselves to the side effects of its central premise, which is the penetration of a highly centralised bureaucracy to the remotest reaches of the national territory. It has led to high levels of domestic tension, to political disruption and protest, to regional revolts, and ultimately, in our own time, to the

---

12. Cf. Riggs, 1967.

weakening of the very state it was intend to support...But what I wish to emphasize here is that we need to be very clear about the need for serious domestic restructuring, and to carry this beyond ethnic Thai to the minority groups who share our national territory. I am talking of a new period of domestic reform and reorganization to meet the challenges of a new period in our history (Saiyud Kerdphol, 1986: 100).

In order to demonstrate the viability of the on-going process of development, management is more and more taking over by superimposing external structures in which action is more directed by their own interests than by proper consideration of the interests of the so called "target population". The centralised structure of decision making and the implicit resultant competition between participating agencies, more often committed to serve the best interests of their superiors - whoever they are rather than the highlanders themselves is clearly a distinguishing characteristic of what is undertaken. Intervention in the field is arbitrary, fragmented, uncoordinated, specified and evaluated according to technical, isolated goals. Those aspects are clearly documented by Chupinit (Chapter 3, this volume). Responsibilities are shared out between the agencies involved through careful negotiations reflecting social status and differing political strengths and alignments. As I mentioned previously this powerful reality "which encapsulates the imagination of planners, field agencies and personnel"[13] is largely determined by the historical confrontation of structures and values inherited from the past with the introduction of ideas about modernity borrowed from the West.

This heavy administrative structure has a natural propensity to develop bureaucratic patterns of interaction as a main paradigm modelled by the inherent patron-client hierarchical model of relationships and the dominant values of status confor-

---

13. Cf. Introduction (this volume).

mity, loyalty, *esprit de corps* as determined by the nature of Thai society and culture[14].

Hill tribe people become more and more excluded and isolated from the resultant process of decision making, even in their own sphere of activity, and they even have no proper way to express their allegiance, loyalty and confidence let alone their own point of view on current policy. In such a context, it could be a problem to bring national unity out of ethnic diversity, an area where "technique" doesn't seems to be so relevant.

> Our government, however, is pursuing the phantom of a **technical solution** (emphasis added) to the problems of the North in the belief that some yet-to-be-discovered agricultural innovation will end both the opium culture and the revolt in the hills...What is crucial is participation in the bureaucracy and real power to act as a coherent group in politics. Our failure thus far to recognize these dimensions of the problems is leading ineluctably to a crisis in the hills (Saiyud Kerdphol, 1986: 104).

The articulations of most development projects to the socio-economic reality is achieved by setting up a sophisticated and expensive management system which the people concerned could never handle for their own benefit in a post-project future[15].

Successful evaluation very often reflects good management rather than real and durable socio-economic results[16].

---

14. Cf.Han Ten Brummelhuis & Kemp, 1984; Klausner, 1981; Yoneo Ishii, 1986.
15. To get a more concrete idea the reader should consult the periodic reports and internal documents of the various development projects.
16. As a matter of fact evaluations are mostly conducted as an internal procedure, within the conceptual framework of the project itself.

Challenge of Development

The ability to convince people to play the game and support the project becomes the point. Irresistible technical innovations which sometimes have not even been carefully tested are extended in the field with no appropriate evaluation of their economic viability[17]. For what benefit? Each project is promoting its own ideas for its own renown and benefit in the knowledge that:

> Another problem involved is the lack of knowledge and skill on appropriate techniques which lowers production as well as destroys natural resources and environment (Department of Public Welfare, 1983: 10).

It is the *chao khao* who take the risk. Acceptance of the transfer of technology appears to be more or less mandatory, a kind of external constraint people have to take into account to please the host state and keep on good terms with the administrative structure. In a way they also hope to secure something for themselves, some advantage from the efficient tools introduced which they could use to improve the productivity of their own genuine agricultural practices[18].

This process of increasing dependency and precariousness, especially when it goes hand in hand with an objective impoverishment generates sentiments of disillusion, some kind of bitterness and a propensity to explore other channels, to set up alternative strategies of their own. Beside the formal allegiance to the official point of view, a strongly dynamic non-structured economic sector[19] is, as a result, developing its own momentum in an uncontrollable way, sometimes illegally, if not

---

17. The model of development goes hand in hand with technocratic management of the "mountain economy." What can be grown will be promoted and this sometimes becomes little more than just a tricky story.
18. That this is a critical problem is unfortunately well documented by the recent events reported in newspapers. Cf. **Bangkok Post, The Nation** (September, 1987).
19. Also referred to by economists as the informal sector.

INTERVENTION

always with negative effects[20].

As opium poppy cultivation has decreased[21], illegal traffic in narcotics with bordering countries has grown partly because of increasing demand from the national market. Groups which in the past had no connections in any way with the drug business have now become involved in response to factors which have disrupted the equilibrium of their economy of sufficiency[22]. This doesn't means that such trafficking is in the hands of *chao khao* Of course not. Once again they are caught in between as a matter of course rather than by choice. Some traditionnal opium poppy growers have moved themselves from the productive sector to the distributive one in order to preserve the basic structure of their bi-polar economy under the umbrella of new allegiances and the constraint of new dependencies. As has been said by Merleau Ponty :

> There is no absolute innocence nor for that matter, absolute culpability. Any action undertaken in response to a situation is not necessarily chosen freely and for that reason alone we cannot be held to be entirely and solely responsible (Merleau-Ponty, 1966: 68. My translation).

---

20. As it has often been observed in such a situation, precariousness and mistrust reinforce the process of cultural self-identification as a protection against the dominant culture.
21. In broad terms the production of opium has fallen from an estimated 133 tons/year in 1970 (UN Narcotics Commision) to 34.7 t/y (ONCB). Cf. TRI Internal Document.
22. One problem chosen at random out of many is population pressure on land which can not be solved at all solely by promotion of a cash crop oriented economy in preference to a more suitable, balanced economy which would take into account self sufficiency rice production. The underlying idea-even if not explicity expressed - is very often the need to recover land for other purposes. Of course - once again - the lack of legal access to land plays a key role. People are reluctant to invest financial profit or labour for permanent changes under such insecure conditions. This slows down the process of transformation and compromises economic success.

Challenge of Development

The effectiveness of both the policy of poppy growing eradication and cash crop replacement still need to be evaluated according to a more realistic point of view than that provided by current evaluations. In this respect *chao khao* can no longer be held to be the only ones involved with the problem, the only ones responsible. Do traditional cultures and ethnic identity still account for the problem? Is it not better to think that opium is still an objective and efficient "response to scarcity"? When farmers are able to secure suitable agricultural land with legal title I guess that the problem will disappear. The main problem, which has still to be properly evaluated by comparative case studies is the rate of objective dependency on opium production and how far it is affected by various policies of implementation.

Problems in the mountains have mainly been classified in such a way that precludes consultation with *chao khao*. This attitude is justified by the underlying paradigm. To change this point of view and set up some sort of consensus relies on first recognizing the fact that the current situation is the result of a change in the conduct of the relationship between lowlanders and highlanders which more or less acknowledges a kind of implicit "legitimacy" according to their own culture and history. The basic concepts used to understand the reality reflect more the political preoccupation of legitimacy from the point of view of the state rather than a scientific evaluation of what the problems are. One can use such an approach to try to answer the question but how then can the resultant problems be solved?

Problems have mostly been classified and documented in such a way that proper participation by the *chao khao* has been excluded, even thought to be dangerous, unrealistic as well as inefficient. So as a result all problems are subsequently identified according to their purely technical aspect, no matter what the context in which they appear.

A resume of various documents provides an indication

of the thinking involved[23]. *chao khao* by their territorial presence in the mountain area and their culturally oriented mode of existence brings problems to Thai society and the government. To be where they are is the original sin...maintaining a strong ethnic identity and not taking the necessary steps to conform to the dominant culture - that is to speak Thai, to be Buddhist, to secure a proper livelihood results in specific problems. Here the cultural differences must account for problems themselves.

The problems can be classified into two types:
- problems involved with the hill tribes themselves
- problems as an impact from the hill tribes' way of maintaining their unique life. (D.P.W., 1983: 9)[24]

This ethnocentric bias in the sociology of knowledge, because it assumes that cultural differences are the founding problem then generates conclusions which tautologically conform to their own premises: problems do not result from an historical process but emerge out of the inherent "nature" of the *chao khao*.

Nobody can contest that the problems so often pointed out in the mountains like deforestation, erosion, demographic pressure, uncontrolled migration...are a concrete reality and to implement an efficient policy according to the national interests is to act in a responsible as well as legitimate manner. But another point. The particular way in which they are enmeshed in the ecological and sociological reality of this specific context is the principal fact that must be taken into account and those who prepare such accounts must ensure that they keep as close as possible to the agreed understanding of empirical reality.

---

23. One can expect administrative documents, official declarations as well as political ones if not reports of various development projects to be neutral on this aspect.

24. Such a statement and the way it is developed later on in the report comes close to a socio-biological understanding of what culture is. Cf. Sahlins, 1984.

I believe that a more imaginative and critical perspective which will focus on interdependency and will question the categories currently used will be realy helpful to better ascertain the goals. It appears that macro-sociological structures and dynamics play a major role in such a context. It is a challenging field for further research. It is not easy to break away and use a more integrated approach using functional concepts in the place of formal categories which are unsuited to the task of accounting for processes. In a research milieu dominated by grass roots data collection, the results of which are not only used to fill up dogmatic, predetermined categories but also as pragmatic substitutes for proper research, what can investigation add to understanding? What is needed is to define problems clearly enough that investigation will reveal the extent to which they are embedded in a stereotyped, ideological context. This epistemological bias is also reflected in the way the policy itself has been implemented and is currently managed. The identification of problems through formal categories preserve and reinforce a hierarchical distance[25] between *chao khao* and the dominant culture which further validates a mixture of stereotyped judgements and naive evidence as a sort of meta-objectivity the main purpose of which is obviously to construct a good self image for those who devote themselves to the *chao khao*. This normative approach opens the door to an even more pervasive effect which is also well documented by Chupinit (Chapter 3, this volume). Again intervention appears fragmented and directed to serve the best interests of a client other than the highlanders themselves.

The time will come for a "reappraisal".

Clear objectives were formulated from the beginning and have since been firmly established as a pre-requisite for any kind of policy. It's a prerogative of the state whose legitimacy can't be contested at all from an outsiders point of view even if the challenge is mounted on scientific knowledge. But can a political rationality be substituted for a proper understanding of the

---

25. Very often expressed and sometimes formulated as an unquestionable feeling of superiority and hierarchical alterity.

reality without causing damage? Objectives are not generated by empirical facts, they are politically oriented. The way delineated objectives can help to solve problems depends on how implementation fits the reality.

A lot has been done to achieve those objectives in a proper way even in some cases with success. The question is not the objectives themselves but how to by-pass the inherent contradictions which emerge when the policy is implemented through a sociology of knowledge which provides an inadequate paradigm, how to stimulate peoples understanding and willingness to incorporate themselves as part of their way of life. To avoid possible misinterpretation of my argument I would now like better to clarify this issue.

As mentioned previously, the cultural diversity and cultural integration of modern Thailand are the result of continuing historical processes which still exercise an influence. As social facts they are dynamic phenomena. Cultural diversity can't be understood outside the referential process of the cultural integration of which it is a part, or against which it reacts. Such a statement emphasizes two relevant factors, adaptability and historical self-consciousness which are often encapsulated in oral traditions and ritual practices[26].

> This is that history that is not always to be read in books or written documents, or even archeological remains, and that the oral legends of the Hmong about their past have much to teach us about **real** history; that is a history which is being lived and felt **now**...Thus one is looking for a new kind of history, not one divided into "true" and

---

26. By adaptability I mean the genuine cultural potentiality to adjust strategies to the social economical and political context as was the case during the "Opium Wars" at the end of the last century. By historical self-consciousness I mean both the propensity to take into account and evaluate the present situation as well as what is supposed to have happen in the past based on some consciousness of the "historical" background of cultural identity.

Challenge of Development

"false", but one arising from a more phenomenological concern with historical consciousness as it affects current behaviour (Tapp, 1986: 7).

Any policy of national integration which "wishes to enable the Hill tribes to be first class, self-reliant Thai citizens" has to consider the historical basement of cultural identity and the way ethnic minorities entered a process under which they came to be incorporated in a Thai national history and sentiment rather than emphasize marginality as if it was the natural consequence of tradition and cultural diversity.

History reminds us, if necessary, that every nation was build up within a context of cultural diversity. This heterogeneity, when we come to see it as an integral part of our national heritage rather than as a receipe for conflict, can help us reformulate the paradigm and even reinforce national unity through political integration when assimilation is neither desired nor required. One acquires the sentiment of wanting to belong to a nation and one develops loyalty to the state through roles offered to responsible citizens more than by making a virtue of diminishing ethnic identity and promoting assimilation.

The history of this region (South East Asia) suggests that there is only one successful way to bring national unity out of ethnic heterogeneity. The way is not forced assimilation ,which only increases tensions. Nor is it isolation and exclusion from the body politic, which thus far has been our attitude towards the peoples on the periphery of our nation. The only method which has worked is a genuine sharing of power and responsibility (Saiyud Kerdphol, 1986: 102).

A national problem for security begins indeed when cultural identity, for one reason or another, becomes the rationale to place oneself outside the process of state integration and to construct a political power base and mount a movement against national and territorial integration. The modern state must integrate: nationalist ideology makes this imperative. Ethnicity, because it provides a clear basis on which to claim independent legitimacy is, as far as the state is concerned, grounds on which to reject the dominant culture. It is no comfort to know how easily this can emerge as a strong, political, integrative force even if founded on some kind of messianic dream. Then again the contrary is also equally valid or likely. True national unity has always emerged through some kind of cultural syncretism, even where the integrative trends are firmly established in the value system of an historically dominant culture.

The problem of dealing with questions of cultural identity and ethnic minorities are not, in such a perspective, only relevant to academic debate, but careful scientific investigation is not out of place if, to serve the purpose of national development, one wants to avoid serious difficulties in the future. One of the more important issues to be considered in this aspect is the participation of *chao khao* in national development and maintaining national security.

> If the tribal minorities are to find a permanent place in Thailand, they must come to terms with the Bangkok Government. Eventually, swidden and opium will have to go. In exchange, the tribes must be guaranteed adequate agricultural resources, given proper land tenure title and be made citizens of Thailand with all the rights and duties that this status implies...
> But there are now some sincere and competent people in those agencies most in contact with the tribes...Hopefully this could lead to participation by the tribal minorities in decision-making processes and a meaningful dialogue between interests (Cooper, 1979: 331).

Challenge of Development

This concluding opinion offered by Cooper ten years ago is clearly the point. After decades of development work it unfortunately seems to remain the essential problem: at least for the highlanders themselves. As a matter of fact, his view that better cooperation would result from a closer relationship is rather optimistic.

There are many reasons why the dynamic of social relationships is regulated - if not totally determined - more by objective structural factors and resultant contradictions than by the good will of competent technocrats. Among these factors centralized bureaucracy[27] is the prevalent structure which regulates the majority/minority interface in all of its aspects. By nature opacity is the rule, but obedience is required. No channels are provided to lodge appeals against policy decisions. Those who are affected by decisions which often appear rather arbitraty, even though they emerge from lengthy and complex procedures that are not always understood, have no recourse to acceptance. Corruption is sometimes better rewarded than loyalty[28]. Instead of increased identification with Thailand through responsible participation such a structure tends to exacerbate tensions rather that inspire the emergence of a balancing counterpoint.

> Generally however tribal villages have no channels of appeals against policy decisions made at national level. This lack of dialogue may be a key factor explaining the violence that sometimes erupts between tribesmen and forestry officials and Thai police stationed in tribal areas (Cooper, 1979: 325).

As I emphasised earlier this structural determination is somewhat difficult to correct or modify because it is anchored

---

27. Cf. Riggs, 1967.
28. The monetary transactions arranged "informally" from time to time between "new migrants" and "officials" provides an example.

on an historical tradition, justified by a specified sociology of knowledge which emphasises cultural values and full cognizance of this paradigm is a pre-requisite for scientific understanding of the social reality[29]. Although the statement of General Saiyud Kerdphol "The situation is clear: if we do not grant what is only reasonable and just, it will be taken by force of arms" sounds a little radical to someone acquainted with the current situation in Northern Thailand the way he refers to access to citizenship as a key problem is illuminating.

> ...We must bring a clear understanding of our present options when adressing the question of minority peoples who, for one reason or another, find themselves within our borders...For nomadic minorities, the modalities for a definitive determination of citizenship must be decided immediately. This matter has been in limbo for decades and needs to be resolved promptly. We can hardly ask the nomadic minorities to be loyal to Thailand if we ourselves are unable to make up our minds whether they are citizens or not. In practice, **present procedures are fraught with bureaucratic red tape calculated to alienate precisely those people we are trying to win over.** Whatever procedure is adopted must be simple, free and capable of rapid implementation
> (Saiyud Kerdphol, 1986: 108.) Emphasis added).

Every development policy so far implemented concerning *chao khao* is caught up in this reality. Technical solutions can't be secured outside the social and political context even if they are fully operative. In a later paper, Cooper, provided a comprehensive review of this point.

> One form of conservation farming system presently being seriously considered is agrosilviculture...

---

29. Cf. McKinnon, 1987.

> The problem with agrosilviculture is that tribesmen have no legal right to the land and therefore no right to the trees...Zonal development seems to make the best long term use of resources and to ensure that all interests are met. However, the scheme is not without problems. Development does not take place in a vacuum. Zones are full of people who have already worked out patterns of land tenure and structure of wealth and power. Classifying suitability of land is easy, reallocating land according to the classification could prove to be an impossibility...Unfortunately, many of the proposals for introducing crops are made on a base of inadequate or faulty research (Cooper, 1979: p.330).

This statement still stands. The models of intervention may be more sophisticated but not the way to construct a better understanding of the fundamental problems. What is interesting in fact is not to list again and again, the consequences of the main contradictions one can observe, but recognize that statements with some scientific credibility, those prepared ten years ago still provide an accurate analysis. But why are they ignored? Intervening agencies, development managers and even researchers don't seem to be concerned by the dependency created by technical solutions neither by the political problems this may generate nor the structural matrix so perpetuated. If *chao khao* interests are to be taken into some consideration this would make it necessary to adopt to more efficient approach to research design as well as agree to a more coordinated approach and the organization of a more realistic "tribal" administration. What needs to be done is to promote more studies of majority/minority relations instead of studying the so called "traditional behaviour" of *chao khao* in isolation. This would not be without political implications but it seems a more or less reasonable and necessary step to adjust modes of articulation to the reality. This in fact accounts for the reason why such a reorientation has not been taken into account.

In the final analysis the most important reason to call for a "reappraisal" is the imperative to maintain the predominantly positive attitude of the *chao khao* towards Thailand as a refuge of relative peace and order. Beyond any of the personnal reasons that brought them into Thailand, this stands above all: for most it was a choice, the end of long journey begun more than one thousand years ago. In their own view they chose Thailand in the hope that for better or worse it would be their mother country and homeland. The dominant attitude is one of respect and confidence which has been reinforced in a strong and positive way by the protection of His Majesty the King and the patronage of the Royal Family through what is well known as the King's Project. Evidence that most *chao khao* want to become Thai citizens is that they are well aware of what has already been done for them and don't question their allegiance to the Nation and to the Royal Thai Government even though they remain officially, for most of them, illegal immigrants. This is a real and positive factor, a success that Thailand can be proud of rather than appear to be insecure and afraid of the likelihood of a challenge being mounted by the *chao khao*. If the legitimacy of the state and current regulations are not really under challenge there is room for confidence in making sweeping changes but if these people are viewed and treated in an arbitrary and sometimes insensitive manner, their lives will become a perplexing if not a frustrating and sad experience.

> Is it really true that we are no longer allowed to establish fields? We are so sad. Now we have been living for years in this country which we have come to love as our home. We have never before had quarrels with the Thai and now we have to leave our villages and emigrate in order not to starve. (Statement from an Akha man).

If according to the usual analysis of the situation it seems that the nation is now confronted only with negative consequences stemming from their presence, who knows what kind of benefit *chao khao* will return to Thailand in the future?

References

Aroonrut Wichienkeeo & Wijeyewardene, G. (eds) (1986) — *The laws of King Mangrai*, A.N.U. Canberra.

Benchapun Shinawatra (1985) — *Highland-Lowland Interelationships in Northern Thailand: a Study of Production, Distribution and Consumption*, Ph. D. Michigan University.

Cooper, R.G. (1979) — "The Tribal Minorities of Northern Thailand : Problems and Prospects", *Southeast Asian Affairs*, ISEAS, Heineman pp.323-332.

Dessaint, W.Y. & A.Y. (1982) — "Economic Systems and Ethnic Relations in Northern Thailand." *Contribution to Southeast Asian Ethnography* No.1, pp.72-85.

D.P.W. (1983) — *A Directory of Development activities in the Opium Poppy Cultivation Area of Northern Thailand*, mimeo.

Durrenberger, E.P. (1983) — "The Economy of Sufficiency", McKinnon & Wanat Bhruksasri (eds) *Highlanders of Thailand*, Oxford University Press; Kuala Lumpur, pp. 215-226.

Han ten Brummelhuis & Kemp, J.H. (1984) — *Strategies and Structure in Thai Society*, Amsterdam.

Hinton, P. (1983) — "Do the Karen Really Exist?", McKinnon & Wanat Bhruksasri (eds) *Highlanders of Thailand*,

Oxford University Press: Kuala Lumpur, pp.155-168.

Kammerer, C.A. (1986) *Gateway to the Akha World: Kinship, Ritual, and Community among Highlanders of Thailand*, Ph. D. Chicago.

Keyes, C. (ed.) (1979) *Ethnic adaptation and Identity*, Institute for the Study of Human Issues : Philadelphia.

Keyes, C. (1979) "The Karen in Thai History and the History of the Karen in Thailand", Keyes (ed) *Ethnic Adaptation and Identity*, pp.26-61.

Klausner, W.J. (1981) *Reflection on Thai Culture*, The Siam Society, Bangkok.

Leach, E. (1954) *Political Systems of Highland Burma*, Cambridge Mass: Harvard University Press.

Lehman, F.K. (1979) "Who are the Karen, and if So, Why? Karen Ethno-History and a formal Theory of Ethnicity" Keyes (ed) *Ethnic Adaptation and Identity*, pp.215-267.

McKinnon, J. (1987) "Sociology of Knowledge, Ideology and Science: something to think about", TRI-ORSTOM Project, (Internal Paper) 14 p.

Marlowe, D.H. (1969) "Upland Lowland Relationship: the Case of S'kaw Karen of Central Upland Western Chiang Mai, in

Hinton, P.(ed), ***Tribesmen and Peasants in Northern Thailand.***

Marlowe, D.H. (1979) "In the Mosaic: The Cognitive and Structural Aspects of Karen-other Relationships", Keyes, C. (ed) ***Ethnic Adaptation and Identity,*** pp.165-213.

Merleau-Ponty, M. (1966) ***Sens et Non Sens,*** Nagel: Paris.

Prapas Charusathira (1967) ***Thailand's Hilltribes,*** D.P.W.: Bangkok.

Renard, D.R. (1980) ***Kariang: History of Karen-T'ai*** Relations from the Beginning to 1923, Ph.D. Hawaii.

Riggs, F.W. (1967) ***Thailand. The modernizations of a bureaucratic polity,*** East-West Center, Honolulu.

Saiyud Kerdphol (1986) ***The Struggle for Thailand,*** S. Research Center Co: Bangkok.

Sao Saimong Mangrai (1981) ***The Padaeng Chronicle and the Jengtung State Chronicle translated,*** University of Michigan.

Tapp, N. (1985) ***Categories of Change and Continuity among the White Hmong (Hmoob Dawb) of Northern Thailand,*** Ph.D. London.

Tapp N. (1986a) "Geomancy as an aspect of Upland-Lowland Relationship", Hendricks et.al. (eds), ***The Hmong in transition,*** University of Minnesota.

Tapp, N. (1986b) "Buddhism and the Hmong: A Case Study in Social Adjustment", *Journal of Developing Societies,* Vol.II, pp.68-88.

Task Force on Hill Tribes and minority Groups (1987) *Survey of Hill Tribes and Minority Groups in Northern Thailand,* (mimeo).

Walker, A.R. (1980) "Highlanders and Government in Northern Thailand", *Folk,* Vol. 21/22 pp.419-449.

Wyatt, D.K. (1984) *Thailand a Short History,* Yale University Press.

Yoneo Ishii (1986) *Sangha, State and Society,* University of Hawaii press, Honolulu.

The Poisoning Effect of a Lovers Triangle: Highlanders, Opium and Extension Crops, a Policy Overdue for Review.

Chupinit Kesmanee

It is generally believed that opium cultivation is an ancient highlander skill passed down from generation to generation. The fact is that highlanders and opium did not come into the world as a married couple.

Archaeologists are of the opinion that opium was first used in Neolithic times, in Anatolia in the eastern Mediterranean, and came to the Far East most probably after the death of Christ (McCoy, 1973: 3).

Early in the seventh century an Arab merchant took opium to China as a medicinal plant. There is some evidence that it was in use before this but this is difficult to confirm. Chinese literature makes reference to the use of opium in the historical saga of *The Three Kingdoms*. A Chinese surgeon, Hau-To, is said to have melted opium *Cannabis indica* in water and administered it to patients prior to surgery (Geddes, 1976: 201). Opium smoking did not become common in China until after a respectable European merchant introduced the habit in the 1500s.

By 1733 the principal portion of the opium trade was in the hands of the Portuguese. A few years later (1781), the British

East India Company jumped into the game when they started to export opium from India (McCoy, 1973: 59; Geddes, 1976: 202).

We could say that Great Britain found that the best way to dip its hungry hands into the riches of China was to first drug the people. The truth is that the imperial Chinese court never approved of this activity in much the same way that the Middle Kingdom of the contemporary world, the USA, now imperiously disapproves. In 1729 the Chinese Emperor prohibited the opening of opium dens, as well as the sale and smoking of opium for pleasure.

In 1839 the Governor of the Kwang-Tung Region destroyed 1,430 tons landed by the British who retaliated by indiscriminately bombarding the populated Chinese coast. Superior firepower ensured a British win. Under duress China opened designated ports to European merchants on the understanding that the landing of opium would not be opposed.

Seventeen years later the matter was reopened and the Opium War broke out again. Following the defeat of China, opium once again flowed in from British India as riches flowed out. China accommodated the problem by supporting opium growing and imposing an import tax from which they could draw revenue (McCoy, 1973: 63; Geddes, 1976: 202).

During this period I suppose we must conclude that the Chinese people smoked opium for pleasure. Let us not forget that this was also the situation in most of the colonised countries of Asia. It was Europeans who were the first to really promote, on any economy of scale, the smoking of opium for pleasure. When the noble merchants of civilized Europe sat in splendour on a wealth of gold and capital accumulated through opium trading, who asked about the morals of it all? The Chinese have reason to remember because the problem of opium addiction remained an issue until after liberation.

Grandstaff has said that the Hmong were growing opium before the middle of the nineteenth century and at this time they and other ethnic minorities from the South of China were marketing raw opium (Grandstaff, 1976: 171-173).

About one hundred years ago, hill people moving from China through Burma, Vietnam and Laos, brought their agricultural experience and skills to Thailand. They also brought opium seeds.

Since 1360, during the reign of King U-tong, and throughout history, up to the Fourth Chakri King, successive Thai rulers demonstrated their disapproval of the use of opium as anything other than a medical drug. However they experienced constant difficulties in implementing an effective policy of prohibition. Since the reign of King Rama III, the Ung Yi, a Chinese secret society, opposed Thai eradication policies. The British East India Company, by far the most successful international trader in opium, whose operations in China had proved to be so successful, was also making trouble for the Thai government. Chinese addicts and traders resident in Siam opposed restrictions on its use and special provision was made to keep them happy. The trade also promised to provide revenue. In 1807 the Thai government set up a state monopoly to manage opium imports and sales. In 1813 a secure opium store-house was built and between 1813 and 1840 opium trading was brought under a new system of management. This provided income for the government and helped reduce the amount of opium entering the black market (McCoy, 1973: 66-67; Geddes, 1976: 208; Chantaboon, 1983b: 14-15).

In 1955 the Thai government under a military regime declared opium illegal and in 1958 a bonfire of opium was lit at the Pramane Ground (Sanam Luang), a big ceremonial and recreation ground in the heart of Bangkok. In an attempt to deal with the problem of opium addicts an Opium Act was passed (1959). Unfortunately, even at this early stage, many addicts switched over to heroin. It was at this point that heroin started to be a problem (Geddes, 1976: 201.Chantaboon 1983b: 15).

INTERVENTION

During the early period when the government held a monopoly over the opium business it was cheaper for users to purchase their needs on the black market. Before 1830, although some Hmong and Yao had already moved into the North, supplies came in from China because there was not enough opium grown in Thailand.

After World War II, Lahu, Lisu and Akha from Burma had already begun, in greater numbers, to take up residence in Thailand. Some of those who arrived at this time clearly remember when and how much opium they sold to the government (Chantaboon, 1983b:-17). They brought with them not only a knowledge of how to cultivate opium poppies but they were also accompanied by Yunnanese entrepreneurs who managed the commercial relationship between highland producers and lowland markets (McCoy, 1973: 65-67; Geddes, 1976: 207).

In summing up we can say that the highlanders brought opium into Thailand from China where it had been forced on a reluctant government by European colonialism. Today the loudest contemporary voices raised against it are those whose grandfathers accumulated the original capital advantage in the trade which helped give them the economic predominance they enjoy today.

When Crop Extension Goes Marching In
Why this interest in eradication from overseas? Perhaps it is because when Europeans, especially the British, look in the mirror provided by history, they are ashamed of what they did in the past? Is it, as the Bible would have it, that the sin of the fathers is visited upon the children? Certainly the problem is now very much at home in the industrialized nations. The war against narcotics is a lesson learned rather late. We are all aware that heavily addictive drugs not only diminish human dignity (which is no doubt a cost the commercial establishment could profitably live on) but also that the cost in terms of the legal, medical and

social welfare services called on to combat the problem are very expensive.

In fact foreign awareness of the problem is not just a postwar phenomenon. Concern grew throughout the nineteenth century, especially in Britain where the British Royal Commission on Opium was set up (1893-94) to examine objections raised by missionaries and others. Perhaps not surprisingly, the Royal Commission examined the situation, noted the rising opinion against opium and declared that it was too profitable to give up.

A chronological list prepared by McCoy tells the story (McCoy, 1973: 137).

1906: The House of Commons unanimously declared trade in opium immoral (!).

1909: An international conference in Shanghai resolved to put pressure on colonial powers to stop the opium trade.

In 1946, at the first United Nations meeting on drugs Thailand was embarrassingly singled out as the only country in South-East Asia where the state maintained an opium monopoly.

1947: Thailand announced that is would only allow opium to be grown in the mountainous areas of the North. This provided a further incentive for highlanders faced with a civil war in China to migrate to Thailand and grow opium (McCoy, 1973: 137).

The declaration of the Opium Law (1959) which made the growing, smoking and trading of opium illegal coincided with the establishment of the Hill Tribe Welfare Committee. It was one legislative change in a policy package. The objective of this policy was not only to suppress the opium business but also to protect forests from the encroachment of shifting cultivators and remove what was and still is considered to be a threat to the national watershed system. This Committee subsequently became the Hill Tribe Committee (1968) (Public Welfare Department (Thai), 1978: 2-31).

In 1960 the Hill Tribe Division of the Department of Public Welfare commenced work. They were not the first. Several years before this the Border Patrol Police had worked with highlanders (with generous help from the U.S.A.) as part of a government effort to secure their loyalty.

Since 1960 many organizations have set up development work, especially agricultural development projects.

At the present time there are more than ten organizations carrying out experimental work in the highlands involving demonstrations and providing support for farmers. The policy of all agencies is to stabilise settlements by introducing permanent agricultural systems. This is done by providing extension advice and material support for farmers to grow cash crops in place of opium.

There are so many extension crops that a complete list would take a long time to read. Instead let me classify them into groups.

Temperate crops: This group includes field crops, fruit trees, perennial trees and also flowers. We could call this group of crops **superior** not only because of the social status of those who promote them but also because of their exotic (for Thai) names, growth habits, smell, and taste. There is a high expectation that plants from this group will replace opium because temperate crop growers enjoy a high market price for their produce.

Lovers Triangle

Sub-tropical crops have always been grown in Thailand such as corn, cotton, ginger, soya bean, red kidney bean, mung bean, cassava, mango, longan, etc. This group is not quite so difficult to grow but does not exhibit the promise of the first group. Moreover their harvests command lower prices. This group takes second place to temperate crops and extension personnel working with them also feel that this pegs their prestige at a lower level.

Varieties of indigenous crops bred overseas. Tropical plants such as the Wagashima soya bean, red kidney bean, giant sweet pea, garden pea, seedless pomegranate, coffee etc. This group appears to be more promising than the second group and, provided there are customers, growers enjoy a higher local price than that secured by the more common produce listed above.

This system of classification is my own. Some organizations support the first and third groups and try to avoid the second. Some support all, regardless.

Agricultural Extension: easier said than done
A list of long distance runners in highland development work includes the Department of Public Welfare which has been operating for more than 20 years; the Royal Project for more than ten years; the Thai-Australia highland Agricultural Project between 1972-1979 and the UN/Thai Programme for Drug Abuse Control (UNPDAC) which started work with extension crops and development in 1972. Much of the work pioneered by UNPDAC has been incorporated into the Office of the Narcotics Control Board (ONCB) set up under the Office of the Prime Minister (1977).

The Watershed Conservation Division of the Department of Forestry has supported agricultural extension activities for highlanders since 1976. In 1979 the Agricultural Extension Division started work. A little later a development project was set up in Mae Chaem managed by the Northern Agricultural Development Centre under the Ministry of Agriculture and Agricultural Cooperatives which received supporting funds from the U.S.A. (1981). The year before that a soft loan was provided by the World Bank for the Department of Public Welfare to set up a five year project which works in six northern sub-catchments.

There are many other projects but it is not the aim of this essay to record them all. The point is to offer the comment that until now none of these efforts has resulted in any of the agencies involved being able to say unequivocally that they have found the answer to development work in the highlands either in agriculture or conservation work. Opium is still being grown.

The highlanders standard of living is as low as ever.

As for the extension workers themselves, they face many problems that can be seen quite easily. The new crops pose a considerable challenge.

Growing them is a complex business. Land preparation, delivery of services, provision of inputs, plant care, weeding, application of fertilizer, handling both during and after harvest, storage and packaging are all new for both the highlanders and extension officers alike. Some types of plants need quite specific care; some need more labour than traditional crops; farmers require more money to purchase inputs and so on. The greater complexity ensures that many problems follow.

Pests and disease. Many of the new crops have very specific needs and a low resistance to infestation by insects and diseases. Where soils lack critical trace elements and minerals these need to be purchased along with fertilizers. There are always new types of pests and diseases making their presence felt in highland extension work.

Communication. Not only is there a language problem between extension workers and their clients, the sociology of knowledge of each side is mutually unintelligible. This creates a big obstacle to development work. Part of this problem concerns the fact the extension workers do not understand the customs, traditions and social behaviour of the highlanders just as the highlanders do not understand either the Thai or the foreigners who are also engaged in the work.

Market and Price. The price of agricultural produce is set in markets outside the highlands. Usually the farmer has no independent knowledge of the market and must accept what project officers tell him. This makes it extremely difficult for him to do any planning by himself.

The marketing side of hill crops is still relatively poor; government activities in this field are weak. This sometimes leads to a strange problem in which extension work precedes market planning. Highland framers are supposed to take extension advice in good faith even though it does not include such information as: likely returns from the harvest; who will buy their produce; where they will sell it; how they will get it to market; how it may have to compete with lowland produce that does not have to meet high transport costs. The good faith shown by highlanders is often amazing. They will go along with extension worker plans even though they are well aware that they face serious transport problems.

Another problem of introducing crops to the highland milieu is the adaptability of the new varieties to the physical situation and whether they will fit within both the framework of local cropping practices and the social system.

Bias in the "Balance"

In the past the government approach to problem solving has concentrated almost exclusively on the economic side of development. Many organizations provide rhetoric to the contrary but if we look carefully at their planning we can see that the balance between social and economic objectives definitely favours the latter. Economic plans are carefully prepared. The allocation of funds for research, experiments, demonstration workshops, training and extension work is always given on the promise of a fruitful outcome. In response to this optimism a lot of money is invested in infrastructural development for agricultural extension. When we look at the other side of the coin, at social considerations which make it necessary for us to consider issues of quality rather than quantity, the nature of the bias in development work becomes evident.

Education is one field in which society attempts to deliberately cultivate and nurture human qualities. Many agencies promote highlander education, open schools and provide extramural training. These are facts that can be quantified.

Assessing education policy, the Office of the Primary Education Commission has noted that "hill tribe education policy has never been clearly planned..." but remains part of a general educational policy rather than treated as a case in which special difficulties are involved in articulating theory and practice. The government has never paid any significant attention to hill tribe education and has never provided sufficient budget or other support. The state of highlander education is now no better than it was twenty years ago. Most courses are the same as used in general primary schools rather than specially designed for elementary school aged hill tribe pupils. Subject matter, teaching styles and learning conditions are not compatible with the highland milieu and as a consequence both pupils and parents are not convinced that either schooling or education is important (Office of the National Primary Education Commission, 1983: 76). The national, standard educational curriculum laid down in 1978 applies to most hill tribe schools. Courses defined then, remain in use.

This is not to say that the responsible government agencies have not attempted to face up to the education problem. In 1965 the General Education Department developed a curriculum for hill tribe schools but could not secure project support for lesson plans, textbooks and assessment methods. In the absence of an agreement between those responsible for professional tasks and administrators who had authority to allocate money, the project did not get off the ground (Ibid: 52). This collapse may be accounted for solely by a lack of funds. Another attempt was made (1977) by the Adult Education Project for the Hill Tribes. This project was a General Education Department project which arranged for instruction to be given to adults. The Department also prepared a texbook as well as a teachers' handbook (Department of General Education, 1978: 4). This undertaking was later transferred to the Department of Non-Formal Education which still runs it.

In fact the curriculum for Adult Education has not yet been adjusted to the needs of hill tribe people (Sunthorn, 1984: 7) but this does not imply absolute neglect. The work now associated with the Non-Formal Education Department commenced in 1978 as the Hill Areas Education Project (HAE) (Northern Regional Non-Formal Education Center, 1980).

This was a really serious effort because, for the first time, the government showed its mind and truely confronted in a comprehensive manner, the problem of highlander education. The HAE Project addressed itself especially to issues concerned with educational philosophy as it applies to the development process. In the 1981 curriculum these issues are identified as teaching aids (texts etc), organizing education services around clusters of villages focused on community education centres, setting up a monitoring system and making provision for self-supervision, indentifying new modes of administration, professional development of personnel and co-ordinating work between the different participating line agencies. These issues were all considered and define a huge task which remains to be done.

INTERVENTION

The curriculum is in fact the result of five years experimental planning (Ibid. 1985: 1-11). In 1983 the National Primary Education Commission Office hosted a seminar on the question of how best to provide primary education for highlanders. Matters considered included problems of administration, related services, supervision, budget, teaching and learning, equipment and instructional media, buildings, the role of teachers, pupils and parents, welfare and coordination. (Office of the National Primary Education Commission, Ibid, 1985).

The Office of the National Education Commission showed a great deal of interest in education for highlanders and in 1985 set up a project as part of a national level search to identify a primary education system which could be made available to all ethnic minorities. The object was to convince hill people that the Bangkok view of what it means to be Thai was not only politically correct but culturally acceptable. All of this was designed to unravel the endemic issues of alienation, isolation and poverty and enable the authorities to enhance their contribution to hill tribe advancement. The research provided an opportunity for preliminary discussions to be held on the social role of education.

Another matter undertaken as part of this exercise was the issue of public health. Not long ago public health services were not available in the highlands. Where they maintained any sort of presence the emphasis very definitely fell on curing sickness rather than preventing it. This curative approach has its limitations.

Suggestions as to how official methods of working could be changed were proposed by the Ministry of Public Health, Mahidol University and the National Research Council at a national seminar on the Psycho-Social Aspects of Public Health supported by the World Health Organization.

At that seminar a search was started to identify the social and cultural constraints operating in the national public health service. The gap between public health personnel and patients became a topic of investigation. The problem of poor communications attracted special interest and was seen to be the product of a situation in which medical officers trained in modern medical science are unsympathetically disposed towards patients who come from a small town or rural background. The researchers found that existing services emphasized curing in preference to preventative measures. Patients who were supposed to be the recipients of the service were not prepared to ask for help and were not willing to work together to improve the efficiency and effectiveness of local sanitary services (Ministry of Public Health, 1981a: 1). One of the speakers stated that for as long as he was aware, those in charge of sanitary services had chosen to give more attention to the acquisition of new curative medical technology rather than promoting public health and preventative medicine. (Perhaps all such ministries all over the world are misnamed and ought logically to be called Ministries of Illness!). No more progress has been made in preventive medicine which encourages people to maintain a healthy environment and help themselves but somehow new technology for dealing with illness and disease is much more attractive to the medical profession (Ministry of Public Health, Private Communication, 1981b: 1). These observations applied equally well to services available to both Thai and highland people.

The best way of tackling this problem is to use tools and communication techniques developed as a part of a health education curriculum (Ministry of Public Health, 1981c: 7).

Under the Fourth National Plan the Ministry of Public Health made provision for minority people but officers assigned to duties in the field met with many cultural obstacles and difficulties such as language, living conditions and transport. The hill tribes' low level of education in Thai and lack of knowledge concerning the manners and skills of modern society

INTERVENTION

as well as a lack of detailed data on hill tribe sanitary practices greatly impeded implementation of health care (Office of the Under-Secretary, Ministry of Public Health, 1984a: 1).

1981 was the year in which the first serious attempts were made to tackle hill tribe sanitary problems. The first area targeted for development was Mae Chaem district, Chiang Mai, where activities were mounted as part of a pilot project. The main objective of the work was to identify an appropriate approach to highlander problems consistent with public health service resources (Ibid: 2; Office of the Under-Secretary, Ministry of Public Health, 1984b: 2-3).

Starting from this project the Ministry of Public Health has made a serious effort to identify a package of public health provisions which would be most effective in the highlands. In 1984, with support from UNFPA, the Ministry of Public Health arranged a workshop where the ideas and experience of other concerned organizations could be brought together to set the parameters within which a new policy would be set up (Office of the Under-Secretary, Ministry of Public Health, 1984c: 1);

Although steps have been taken to formulate a public health policy we should keep uppermost in our minds the words of Dr. Charus Suwanwela and his team:

> Culture and the values of a community are the important factors in deciding on what are community problems, a process of decision making based on observations by third persons always misses the point. Health care for the people must be replaced by health care by the people. The problems people are working with now should be considered in the absence of prejudice and with careful judgement. The appropriate method and process should make for better practise as well as make use of development theory... (Charus et.al., 1980: 50).

We can summarize development efforts in the highlands back to 1960 relatively briefly. While much has been done in the economic field, this work lacks both continuity and coherence. Work in education started twenty years behind and public health behind that again. Nevertheless we have a proverb to comfort ourselves "Better late than never" (never mind who said it!). I myself feel that highlanders have developed a new appreciation of how education can help them and see it as a way to secure social promotion, command the respect of others and earn more money by securing better jobs. As in any period of rapid social change there are many inconsistencies. For example modern medicine is seen as a brand new spirit to cure sickness and gets rid of diseases quicker than old spirits. The material scientific understanding that should have accompanied this development is missing. There is a lack of balance here.

If we must always sit down and argue the case every time as to why the social side of development work should proceed as quickly as the economic aspect, we would spend all our time talking. Development literature reports on a lot of research and there are a lot of textbooks in which well documented casework is available. The preoccupation with economic development as the most important issue collapsed long ago.

Efforts We Ought to Review

If we set the question "What was the original idea behind promoting cash crops for highlanders?", the answer is most likely to be "to replace opium and bring their standard of living up to that of lowlanders". If this is true we should next consider that if the promotion of cash crops is to replace opium, a policy decision has been taken to extend this strategy throughout the highlands of Thailand. Certainly, among the many issues which stimulated government interest in the highlands, opium cultivation can be listed loosely alongside the matter of national security and deforestation.

In the beginning, policy was made on a very flimsy information base. Officials had to rely on their opinions and judgement in place of knowledge. As time passed we came to know better. We know there are four hill tribes struggling to grow opium as a part of their economic system, namely, the Hmong, Mien, Lahu and Lisu, and to complete the picture, a few Akha. Other ethnic groups such as the Karen, Htin, Khamu and Lua, at least 65 percent of all highland ethnic minorities do not traditionally grow opium. The significance of this is clearer when we realise that the number growing opium in the highlands make up at most only 35 percent of the total hill tribe population (statistics collected by the Tribal Research institute, 1983), and the figure today is likely to be as low as 15 percent.

The majority do not grow opium. Moreover, of those ethnic groups listed as growers neither every village nor every household in villages which grow opium are actually engaged in cultivating the crop. Today (1987) the proportion of growers is likely to be much lower than it was two decades ago.

Incidence (%) of Sample Villages Growing Opium (1983)
- Hmong   60.4%   of villages from a sample of   101
- Lahu   34.6%   222
- Mien   40.0%   45
- Lisu   66.6%   90
- Akha   14.2%   91

(Chantaboon, 1983d: 6-7)

We can see that projecting an opium crop replacement policy on all highlanders by extrapolating information from a minority of farmers is deeply faulted and quite unreasonable.

It is possible to argue that the extension of cash crops to strengthen highlander participation in the market is not just to replace the opium crop but also to improve their standard of living. This second objective needs to be explored but in the time being do not forget that the initial programme was begun for security reasons, to combat the opium problem and devise a strategy to tackle forest destruction. There is a surprising file

Lovers Triangle

of research results available (Binney, 1968; McKinnon, 1978; Lee, 1978, 1981; Durrenberger, 1983a: 87-98; 1983b: 221-223). Most of this information was collected in the course of anthropological research, and these professionals all confirm that opium is grown mainly because it is the only way in which highlanders can secure their rice needs.

Highlanders sell opium for money. They use the money to buy needed rice. If we look back twenty years a very clear picture emerges. Twenty years ago few anticipated that electricity would become available, that domestic water supply schemes would be set up. Transport was by mountain ponies and mules. The availablity of industrial goods which tempt people to earn more money so they can spend more was not very well developed. The neccessities of life were still rice, salt, gunpowder for muskets, iron for making knives and agricultural equipment, needles, thread and silver. Between 1936 and 1937 when the Dutch scholar Bernatzik travelled through hill tribe villages in Thailand he recorded that the Hmong traded with Chinese-Yunnamese for iron pots, metal pans, flint-stones and matches, sulphur for making gunpowder, salt, cowry shells, buttons, floral patterned cloth, silk, small mirrors, rope, needles and thread (Bernatzik, 1947: 424).

From this list we can sense the continuity of such trade but in more modern times the changes have been so great we should realise that we are scratching for information in the wrong place.

Because, in general, hill tribe communities have a strong preference for growing their own domestic foods it is not difficult to appreciate how important rice is as their staple. Not so long ago what opium was grown was for medicinal purposes (Grandstaff, 1976: 171). It was only in relatively recent times because of a variety of reasons (high price of opium, shortage of land and increased population) that highlanders started to grow more opium to make more money to buy rice.

Why do we direct nearly all of our attention, effort, intelligence and money to pushing people into the market? Do we want to encourage aggressive commercial farming in the highlands?.

Doesn't anybody wish to dissent? Does cultivation for domestic consumption have no value to either national planners or those responsible for carrying economic development forward? Is only one way to prosperity permitted? Does subsistence cultivation have no value because it is only for people rather than capital gains? Why don't we investigate in the right place instead of looking for cash crops to replace opium? Is this choice more difficult to pursue? Let us see.

Let me return to the point that the government is involved in the highlands to improve the people's standard of living. Let us accept this as a sincere manifestation of the development ideology of middle class, urban society.

By tradition, hill tribe communities invested their labour in a subsistence economy supplemented by trading but the main objective was to produce the bulk of their consumption needs. When, for various reasons, production fell short, they were forced to diversify their production strategies. If the resources available to them were inadequate, for example if there was no primary forest, they had to make use of secondary forest (Cooper, 1976: 298; Durrenberger, 1983, 2: 221).

> As all the primary forest is felled swiddeners are forced to clear gardens in secondary forest. If they can arrive at a symbiotic relationship with their new environment by devising by trial and error if necessary, an appropriate periodicity governing clearing and fallowing in a way that maintains soil fertility, then they have solved the basic problem of human survival: a stable relationship with a renewable and essential resource (McKinnon, 1978: 11-12).

Therefore to push highlanders into making money is not the only way to solve the problem. Having money doesn't mean they will be assured of good health, make optimum use of their environment or achieve greater social harmony.

Government offices and agriculture extension agents working in the highlands have found that it is really very difficult to persuade hill tribe people to stop growing opium and grow other crops. These officers have also found that it is even more difficult to persuade the non-opium-growing groups to cultivate cash crops. There are some villages in which such a policy has been successful but they are the exceptions rather than the rule. Their "success" is out of proportion with the effort put in by the extension agency.

Karen, whom the Thai call *yang* were renamed by a development worker *yang-ma-toi* (hot asphalt: sticky and slow moving). Clearly they demonstrate their reluctance by their behaviour (development workers want results fast!).

In this situation it is possible to see some important aspects of development policy, that is problems in **the economic system.** If we examine a survival based economy we focus on a system which lies deeply embedded in the reality of socio-cultural life whereas an **economy for trading** is a quite different system. If we try our best to replace the first system with the latter we challenge the total socio-economic system and its complex internal interrelationships.

We need not make the effort here to restate the sociological reality that economic and social systems of any society are closely interrelated with each other. Changing any single part of the system has a profound impact on every other part of the system.

When we can see this clearly we can begin to understand why the lot of hill tribe development workers like us is so very hard. We have extended a challenge to highlanders which our offspring will in turn extend. But even over two generations we will not get far at this creeping pace (or are we waiting for our great-grandchildren to help us out!).

To draw a clearer picture I would like to focus on something closer to home: food. For the hill people in general, rice and other domestic crops are the most important things to them, first for human consumption and next for animals (depending on the type of corn).

Highlanders have four farming systems (Chantaboon, 1983c: 2), the most unique of which is a mixed cropping system. Sanit Wongsprasert has surveyed crops planted in early maturing rice fields and found nine other crops. In slow maturing rice fields he found 17 crops and in opium plots 43 other useful plants scattered throughout the cultivated area (Sanit, 1979: 54-60, 77-88). In this respect corn fields are the same as rice and opium fields: many other crops are grown together.

Chantaboon Sutthi has collected data on the mixed cropping systems of six hill tribes: Hmong, Mien, Lahu, Lisu, Akha and Karen. Plants are intercropped for a variety of purposes but all are consumed in one way or another. Some are used as staple or supplementary food, others in the preparation of herbal medicines. Then there are fibre plants like cotton and hemp from which cloth is made. Some plant materials are used to make tools, and others as raw materials to produce whisky and other beverages; some feed those addicted to opium and tobacco; some provide cooking, seasoning and lighting oil (sesame, poppy, castor), and dyes, while others supply materials for ritual? purposes, ornaments, and talismans (Chantaboon, this volume). The Karen have a special plant to keep moisture levels down in rice stores (Chantaboon, 1983c: 1). Walker has prepared an inventory of crops planted in Lahu Nyi rice fields. His list includes rice and three other types of grain, three types of legume, two types of oil plants, four types (ten varieties) of tubers, two types of vegetable, seven types of squash and six spices (nine strains) (Walker, 1970: 382-384).

The use of these plants is closely integrated into the daily life cycle of highland communities. Another observation worth mentioning is that they do not think of diseases and insects as serious pests but they do have a big problem with foraging animals (Chantaboon, 1983c: 1). Fencing is important. Remember, these plants along with the farming systems into which they fit are deeply structured into highlander society.

Even the distinguished anthropologist Kunstadter shows amazement at "the ability of the Lua' and Karen, farmers (who) even as young children, (can) distinguish successfully between the 84 cultivated varieties (plants grown in swiddens) plus 16 useful uncultivated varieties that grow together with numerous weeds, even at the stage when plants are less than a centimeter in size" (Kunstadter, 1978a, 1: 90).

It is not unreasonable to ask "How can we presume to place extension crops within such a complex system let alone pretend we should replace it altogether?". Any simplification of the system in pursuit of cash rewards automatically implies that many valuable plants would be lost.

Some Karen and Lua have said that even though their harvests from irrigated fields are good they still grow hill rice in swiddens because they get the bonus of the 25 other plants they can grow there (Chantaboon, 1981: 79).

Even though they could grow extension crops there would be no great advantage in doing so. As an agricultural policy such a strategy has little to recommend it. This also applies to the opium poppy. When he looked carefully at the socio-cultural role of opium as distinct from its contemporary economic significance Chantaboon Sutthi found that is serves 11 economic functions, 14 social roles, and is used in 18 medicinal applications (Chantaboon, 1983b: 24-36). Opium belongs within highland society and cannot easily be eliminated solely on the strength of outside opinion.

The idea itself of changing the economic system of the highlands is best explored in the next case.

To my knowledge no extension cash crop has ever been offered that would fit inside the existing mixed cropping system. How realistic is it then to expect that the extension crops promoted in the highlands can replace the broad domestic purposes served by traditional crops when they do not fit into established farming systems and patterns of labour use, or use customary agricultural methods? If we think this problem can be avoided by indulging the optimistic hope that the new crops will fetch prices to enable the farmer to buy replacements to satisfy his subsistence needs are we not being more than a little crazy?

In the past all agricultural activities complemented social activities and cash crops faced considerable difficulty in penetrating this system.

The new cash crops come with their own technical superstructure: plants are first placed under investigation, then under trial as part of an extension experiment. Temporary and artificial marketing agreements are entered into in which the price is set by the co-operating parties. Information about the real market situation has always posed a big problem for Thai academic and civil service agriculturalists.

We must spend a lot of money to take care of cash crops promoted under development programmes. This includes special seed crops which require fertilizers and chemical pesticides to get rid of new pests, and new kinds of crops which make it necessary to buy new tools and equipment. It is not difficult

Lovers Triangle

to appreciate that given their lower standard of living, highlanders face many problems, not the least of which is a chronic shortage of funds. Poor transport is another and it is quite clear that the high cost of getting goods to market presents a considerable barrier to agricultural development. Many villages are perched on steep slopes where it is difficult to construct and maintain roads. Many new crops are very sensitive, fragile and quickly deteriorate: as observed by one humorist it would obviously be better if all villages were reached by asphalt or concrete roads, or best of all, by super highways! Seven years ago Peter Kunstadter observed "Under existing conditions, even the simplest modern technical devices are far too expensive for the average upland farmer, and the costs of modern technology, including fuel and agricultural chemicals, are bound to increase in the foreseeable future" (Kunstadter, 1978b: 302). He was right.

We cannot easily jump over every obstacle placed along the road of acceptance of all new cash crops. The technical problems are considerable. Let us imagine (again) that the hill tribes have accepted the **new economic system** and have already abandoned their old ways. What if for some reason the new crops fail? How would they retrieve something from the situation? With little or nothing growing in their fields, what can be eaten?

I would like to offer a research topic to anybody interested! Please review the policy of extending cash crops for hill tribe development. Is it suitable for them or not? Are we headed down the right path or not?

Is it a great leap forward or backwards? Are we able to appreciate that *yang* (Karen) are not *yang-ma-toi* (hot asphalt) but natural Yang who have their own modest and profound philosophy of life which runs much deeper than the development workers understanding or purpose?

I believe that it is **only by adjusting the traditional agricultural survival system** that we will be able to shore up the cracks that are appearing in highland society. Even attempting this task with the sincerity it deserves will make for a much more meaningful and close relationship with highlanders because the traditional system has strong roots in humanitarian ethics as much as reason. In the process of adapting themselves to their environment their forefathers accumulated experience and through trial and error built up a considerable wisdom concerning agro-eco systems. This knowledge has been passed down from generation to generation and must be acknowledged and understood: it is the means by which all the parties involved could come to a better appreciation of what must be done.

The highland mixed cropping system is adapted to high altitudes (Chantaboon, 1983c: 6-8) and for that reason highlanders choose locations in which they can replicate the traditional land use system. Many things must be considered: water sources (especially water for drinking while working in the field), distance from settlement, aspect of slope (orientation to solar radiation), altitude, soil moisture, wind direction, rock and soil type, nature of parent material and composition of established vegetation (Walker, 1970: 332-342, Chantaboon, 1981: 84-98). Such knowledge is only built up over many years experience.

It can be argued that once highlanders have become engaged in the cash economy it is no longer possible for them to turn back to a production system for domestic use only. Indeed the seductive power of the market is increasing. Farmers' needs increase in direct proportion to their knowledge of what is available and how it can be used. I agree with this argument (even though I can see some weaknesses).

Another good argument runs that to support the domestic economy implies support for swiddening (or "slash and burn" as it is sometimes dramatically described) but given current population densities and the amount of land claimed for other purposes (ie. forestry, national parks) there does not appear to be enough land available for everybody to continue with this system[1].

---

1. This observation originated with Dr. Nicholas Tapp out of one of our many informal discussions.

Lovers Triangle

I am caught in some doubt that I am able to choose the right gate to the patch of development. By this I don't mean to say that we must choose extreme change, abandon cash crops, turn our back on the market and return solely to a subsistence economy. Such thinking is too narrow. The decision making process should consider both systems. In other words we should target economic development strategies following a policy that asks us to first identify the most appropriate level of intervention between the two economic systems. In the past and up to the present the government has given heavyweight support to economic development by promoting cash crops almost exclusively and we dare to say that the state is remiss in this matter because the demise of subsistence cultivation will bring much trouble. To anticipate this end, to match the reality of the two systems, we must bolster the subsistence system so that it can continue to serve as the foundation of the highland socioeconomic system and keep entry into the market economy in second place. In this context cash crops would only have meaning as a necessary supplement when consumption needs can no longer be secured by domestic production. I do not think it is wise that they be promoted as part of a general policy of progress.

Such a new policy of balanced development would make it necessary to adjust project planning appropriately. The budget allocation formerly made and given over to research, experimentation, demonstration, training and the promotion of extension cash crops must be rearranged and readjusted. We should abandon the principle of a general allocation and provide special support for efficiency, effectiveness, and to accelerate efforts that can ameliorate the degenerating parts of specific systems.

By degenerating parts, I mean points of weakness, potential breakdown and crisis in the subsistence system. To ease crisis points in the system we still need more knowledge but there is a shortage of those knowledgeable enough to support such work. We do not have a strong research approach to mountain rice;

there is not much money available and few researchers are engaged in this field. It can be said that UNPDAC was a pioneer agency and consultant in this matter. One rice experiment station officer at San Pha Thong took up this work and expected to identify an appropriate hill rice strain (Chupinit, 1978: 18). He succeeded in breeding a rice strain suitable for some highland conditions (Ibid: 55-57, 60) but the matter was not taken up as part of a formal station work plan (Ibid: 42, 53-60, 64). The project is long since finished and no important development followed from it.

Between 1980-1983 the Faculty of Agriculture at Chiang Mai University also undertook research into highland rice production and produced a very interesting report (Faculty of Agriculture, CMU, 1983). The data from this report tells us that a collection was made of 300 highland rice varieties, about 200 of which are indigenous, and more than 100 exotic, brought into Thailand for cross-breeding (Ibid: 52). In the last year of the project the scientists were able to cross-breed six highly productive varieties (Ibid: 138) and these have subsequently been made available for wider distribution[2].

In 1980 the Rice Research Institute of the Department of Agriculture and the Department of Public Welfare agreed to start a rice field grain improvement project for the highlands. Between 1980-1981 the Public Welfare Department collected 300 varieties of highland rice grown by highlanders for the Department of Agriculture.

In 1982 the performance of these varieties was tested at different altitudes from a low of 330 metres to a high of 1,300 metres. The criteria for testing took into account taste as a priority issue as well as resistance to dry conditions, cold and disease. Production levels were recorded and the response to fertilizer measured.

---

2. Personal communication with Dr. Jakri Senthong.

Between 1983-1984 the Department of Agriculture arranged for numerous rice tasting sessions by hill people to help them select the most delicious variety. In 1984 the Department of Public Welfare again collected rice varieties and some 106 types were sent to the Rice Research Institute where they are still under investigation[3].

Observations on highland rice varieties are not readily available except to the few who have a special interest in the data. Distribution of information has always been limited and still remains at some remove from the eyes and ears of highland extension workers. When we switch our attention to corn, the second most important crop in the subsistence economy, we meet even fewer researchers. The remaining 40 crops so important in domestic consumption have failed to attract any interest at all.

Actually I wonder how much consideration has been given to the changes that occur when plant material is removed from its natural environment? Some edible plants brought down from the highlands and grown on the lowlands under completely different conditions did not grow well and tasted bitter. More research should be carried out on the relationship between grain crops and their nutritional status. Their food value is something that should be clearly established (this is an aspect which is invariably neglected).

Other important agricultural research which should be promoted is examination of the economic system as structured into highlander cultural traditions. Research on this issue would contribute much to our understanding of the adaptation process and direct the work of scientists and planners along more positive lines. Field research of this nature would also place us in a better position to understand the man-land relationship. If we could find a way to accelerate recovery of the biomass, then it is possible that cyclical swiddening itself could continue as a stable agricultural system which could support communities of sedentary farmers.

---

[3]. Personal communication with Mr. Chantaboon Sutthi of the Tribal Research Institute.

INTERVENTION

So far I have focused my attention on a critical review of a myopic development policy that deals solely with the commercial economic aspect of development. I have argued that much more attention should be given to social development. This aspect is no more or less important than the economic and it must be emphasized that development means improvements in the quality of life as much as an increase in the quantitative, material standard of living.

It is unlikely that we would hear of a university graduate educated to respect the law as well as his science driving a tractor into the forest to clear land for cash crops. Commercially succesful highland farmers with a capital surplus know only that they can extend their land holdings in this manner. In exploring the possibilities inherent in the capitalist mode of production what else can we expect of a rational, if less well educated farmer, with access to savings and a proven ability to mobilize labour? And do not think that I merely hypothesise. This has actually happened in Tak, Nan, Kamphaeng Phet and Phetchabun

If a well balanced development policy was being implemented we would not hear any more complaints from development workers that hill tribe people only ask for assistance and never help themselves. Perhaps we would also not hear how a highlander died after an injection given by a quack doctor because the people would be aware of such dangers and we would not allow such practitioners to administer "cures". Perhaps then we would not have to listen or face up to comments aired about the shortage of people of quality in the highlands (even if they are rich!): our sentiments would be formulated in a quite different way.

The wisdom of development priorities is overdue for critical examination. My case for putting the subsistence economy first and awarding second place to cash crop production should be considered as part of that reexamination.

If we are to adjust the contemporary cultivation system it would be easier if policy was based on the philosophy that people must first satisfy their own needs rather than have outsiders attempt to force change and convert them to a new system. This holds true because it would place the grounds for response on the profound level of basic human needs. The accumulated wisdom and skills of their historical experience and confidence developed in their own socio-cultural system would be called into play. It would be easier to intervene in small ways than to attempt to radically change the whole. Then again there are many plants grown by highlanders that have already passed the adaptation process. In such a case any adjustment in grain production should be carried out within the system rather than bringing all sorts of new varieties which face so many obstacles.

If we accept this point we must pay serious attention to the study of subsistence plants which naturally occur in the region (or in the culture), which could be engineered and reintroduced into the traditional mixed cropping system. Experiments should be mounted to identify a farming system close to highlander agricultural practices that will regain the ecological equilibrium maintained in the past.

My second point which needs to be explored is the assertion that the quality of social development is of equal importance to that of economic development.

The Problematical Future
If we insist on cash crop promotion for highlanders as a principle of policy we are heading for trouble. Not only the problems I've already indicated but others that we bring upon ourselves and may not know about until it is too late to do anything about them. Each case has its own characteristics.

The first point I would like to develop concerns highlander ecological systems. From the very first contact in modern times until today, the hill people have been punished by the accusation that they are destroyers of the forest and the watershed and that as a consequence of their method of cultivation upset the ecological balance of their environment. In these charges something is missing. Some research results conclude that swidden agriculture protects soil surface erosion even on high slopes under heavy rain (Nye and Greenland, 1960).

The argument that swiddening irrevocably destroys the forest, available organic matter and elements essential for plant growth is treated with scepticism by Nye and Greenland. They observe that a more dangerous situation is likely to develop from logging operations. As long as short periods of cultivation are followed by a long fallow, swiddening does not seriously diminish humus levels. The humus is renewed with regeneration of the forest and as a matter of fact most nutrients are locked in the biomass until released by fire (Ibid: 134; McKinnon, 1977: 13-16). The missing factor I mentioned is the increased population in the highlands. Lowlanders have moved to take up residence in the mountains. The number of highlanders has increased by natural causes and continuing immigration. All of this makes for the development of imbalances in the ecological system which do not justify blame. The stigma attached to the agricultural system known as shifting cultivation should be removed.

To come back to the cash crop economy, how does it help maintain the environment? How ecologically informed is this strategy?

We are able to see one point clearly. The advocates of the system appear to be willing to support monocropping even though many different crops have been introduced separately and with difficulty over a wide area in the face of rising costs. Irrigation systems have been extended and chemical fertilizers introduced. But an important feature of any monocultural agro-eco system is that over an extended period of intensive production pests and disease multiply considerably, especially in tropical regions (see Jazen, 1977). This problem was previously avoided by farmers because by planting in small scattered fields at some distance from each other and frequently moving their gardens, the hazard was avoided (Janzen, 1977: 52; Nye and Greenland, 1960: 75-76). Land rotation and burning fields reduced pests, diseases and weeds (Janzen, 1977: 52). The introduced cash cropping system made it necessary to use chemicals to combat pests and disease. This takes money and there is no guarantee that in the long run resistant strains will not develop (Janzen, 1977: 53-54).

It is unfortunate but true that the quantity of chemicals used must increase because there is no other way of combating the problem. Clumsy use of chemicals can quickly become a danger to both farmers and consumers. Highland farmers entirely new to their use and unaware of the dangers are especially vulnerable.

This could become a big problem in the future. What sort of residue is left behind? Chemicals that do not break down dissolve in moisture and flow into the headwaters of the river system. If this residue is absorbed by animals and plants, what impact does this have on human health? How badly is the water polluted for down-stream users? Then there is the recurring cost of replacing chemical fertilizers which break down quickly under tropical conditions. More fertilizers and chemicals means spending more money (Ibid: 52).

Single cropping systems inserted into mixed cropping systems have as yet unknown consequences. However, single cropping systems do increase the chances of pest and disease infestation. By definition other plants besides those grown for sale are weeded out and the nutrient up-take is confined to both a single root level as well as the same nutrients. For these reasons it is not surprising to see a post-harvest soil surface left wide open to erosion. In tropical regions where heavy rain is concentrated into relatively short periods it is little wonder that land under monocropping with generous use of chemicals is particularly vulnerable (Nye and Greenland, 1960: 136).

To document my case I must also point out that single cash crops other than opium do not make much money for small holder farmers. To optimise his resources the farmer needs access to more land, labour and capital. Where his access to these factors of production is strictly circumscribed the failure of a crop can mean disaster. How can he then survive?

On the other hand, swidden mixed cropping saves both labour and capital. Cutting and burning reduces the necessity to weed and provides materials for fencing. Cultivation is extended gradually and care of the garden always remains within the bounds of available labour. Swiddening, at the lowest cost, delivers the best results.

There are other advantages in such a system which inhibits the spread of pests and diseases. The shade from different plants helps retain soil moisture even through dry periods. The variable depth of the root systems and different food needs ensures a broader up-take of nutrients. If some crops fail there are others which remain (Chantaboon, 1983: 6-8, Webster and Wilson, 1971: 103).

One chronic problem constantly discussed is that of land tenure rights or land ownership. Any policy for hill tribe agricultural development that does not face this chronic problem must remain largely ineffectual (McKinnon, 1978: 14; Kunstadter, 1978b: 303-307). The promotion of cash crops, if such a policy is to be consistent, must also provide the means with which to raise money and as land has always been used as collateral to guarrantee repayment of loans, a firm and legal arrangement should be made (Kunstadter, 1978b: 305).

If the law cannot be changed to extend this right then it will remain very difficult for highlanders to secure credit on their own account. Will the government then provide loan money? It will be difficult to provide for all. If the government cannot do this, highlanders who stand at the expensive end of the credit business will soon find themselves in serious trouble.

Then again, if there are some successful cash crops in the mountains, surely they must attract traders from the lowlands anxious to invest money to secure healthy profits (Kunstadter, 1978b: 304). This has in fact happened at many places, even in the Doi Inthanon National Park (Tribal Research Institute and Northern Agricultural and Development Centre, 1984: 12). In such a site success can make trouble for all.

But by supporting subsistence cultivation as the main policy, the question of land ownership for highlanders remains an issue that cannot, if we are to solve these problems, be approached in a slapdash manner. Carelessness could well result in an unsatisfactory situation like that of the American Indians (U.S.A.) who quickly sold their allotted land cheaply, an act which led to their impoverishment and social breakdown (Kunstadter, 1978b: 307).

Kunstadter has written, "The issue is not that they should be unable to sell it, but that they should realize the benefits of keeping it" (Kunstadter, 1978: 307).

As we can see the promotion of cash crops has always been accompanied with terms of praise for adopter farmers who are next called "progressive farmers". Nearly all such "risk takers" enjoy an immunity from risk provided by a strong socio-economic position within their community. It is their socio-economic status which provides them with the courage to grow new crops and remain within the good graces of the authorities.

Along with the extension effort go the profound changes which accompany the development of capitalism and the rise of the attitude that the stronger we become the more we get. Commercial success in cash cropping brings profit and greatly increased capital. Those who understand how this more predatory system works are able to invest their wealth and with the use of machinery extend their fields well beyond the area worked by a household which relies on hand labour.

Good demonstrations of this bad example can be readily found at Ban Chedi Kho, Amphoe Mae-Sod, Changwat Tak. The growth of cash cropping has greatly extended the gap between the rich and the poor, the haves and those who have not. Communities wishing to achieve such development should know, extension crops provide a short cut to wealth. Take up cash cropping immediately: it is guaranteed to work for you even though it may destroy both the harmony of your community and the ecological balance of the environment.

An Inconclusive Conclusion

Six years ago Sanga Sabhasri wrote, "Some might state, suppose all hill people stopped growing opium in the next five years the UN would pull out their aid, and so would Thai agencies The hill people would be left with an unstable economy" (Sanga, 1978: 209). Fine! More than five years has passed and what some might have feared has still not happened. Highlanders are still growing opium. The United Nations is still helping. All the agencies engaged in work in the highlands five years ago are still there and have been joined by more. The number of foreign organizations has increased.

For how long should we develop the hill tribes? It seems to me that the more work we do, the more problems we create.

In this paper, I have made an effort to give reasons why the conduct of hill tribe development is unsatisfactory. For me there are two main reasons for this.

Lovers Triangle

First is the imbalance between economic and social development in the highlands. The second is that the cash crop policy as a central principle of economic development is inappropriate. I have suggested an alternative, a subsistence crops policy as a first priority to which cash crops should be given second place. Both government and non-government agencies must be involved. Plans could be adjusted to suit different needs. Research into the daily life of communities needs to be carried out to establish a real understanding of their farming systems and the nature of the plants they use and eat. Do not be discouraged by rumours spread by highland development workers that it is difficult to get money to mount such studies.

In writing this review I have not broached many new ideas. Many observations offered have been stated before. I am but a new wave to reach the shore, part of a well established school of scientific opinion which I have willingly joined. We must maintain an open mind so that we can accept that the success we have announced can be seen for what it is as an "unsuccessful success".

McKinnon has expressed this feeling, and he is one of few expatriate workers with the confidence to speak about experts who feel constrained to say quite misleadingly, "how rosy things are. (When in fact they should)...**admit to themselves as any competent scientist should that even in the best of circumstances it is in fact extremely difficult to achieve anything of real substance.** This is an ethical as much as a practical problem and this then becomes a call for a level of professional competence as a product not only of intelligence, qualifications, experience and that social mystique granted by age and status but something which is fundamentally dependent on personal honesty, integrity and receptivity" (McKinnon, 1977: 27-28).

As the Chinese proverb has it "change the mind, then find the shore", only then will the poisoning effect of the lovers triangle be no more.

References

Adams II, Leonard P. (1973) — "China: The Historical Setting of Asia's Profitable Plague" ***The Politics of Heroin in Southeast Asia*** Alfred W. McCoy et. al., Harper and Row: New York, pp. 357-375.

Bernatzik, H.A. (1947) — ***Akha and Meo: Problems of Applied Ethnology on the Indo-Chinese Peninsula*** Commission Press, Wagnerian University Printing Shop: Austria (English Translation, Vol. 2)

Binney, G.A. (1968) — ***The Social and Economic Organization in Northern Thailand*** Wildlife Management Institute: Washington D.C.

Cooper, R.G. (1976) — ***Resource Scarcity and the Hmong Response: a study of settlement and economy in Northern Thailand*** Ph.D. dissertation, University of Hull, subsequently published by the University of Singapore Press.

Chantaboon Sutthi (1981) — ***Highland Swidden Cultivation*** Tribal Research Centre, Department of Public Welfare, Ministry of Interior, (mimeo. in Thai).

Chantaboon Sutthi (1983a) — "Field Crops" ***Annotated Notes on Five Topics on the Hill Tribes of Thailand*** Tribal Research Centre, Chiang Mai, Department of Public Welfare, Ministry of Interior pp. 311-487 (in Thai).

Chantaboon Sutthi (1983b) "Hill Tribes and Opium Problems" Paper given at the seminar on Hill Tribes and the Addiction problem, Tribal Research Centre, 11 February (mimeo. in Thai).

Chantaboon Sutthi (1983c) "Slash and Burn Cultivation in the Highlands: Indigenous Technology-Cropping System" Tribal Research Centre, (mimeo. in Thai).

Chantaboon Sutthi (1983d) "Akha Slash and Burn Cultivation" Tribal Research Centre, (mimeo. in Thai).

Charas Suwanwela et al. (1980) "Public Health Service Research for Community Development: Case Study in Thai Hill Tribe Villages" *Journal of Environment Research for Rural Development* Vol.2, No.1, 1 December pp. 36-51 (in Thai).

Chupinit Kesmanee (1978) "Report on the Operations of Several Organizations in Hill Tribe Development and Welfare: Case Study of Ban Khun Wang 1977" Tribal Research Centre, Department of Public Welfare, Ministry of Interior, (in Thai).

Department of General Education *Report on the Evaluation of the Adult Functional Literacy for Hill Tribes Program,* Ministry of Education (in Thai.)

Department of Public Welfare (1978) *Public Welfare and the Hilltribe Development and Welfare* Ministry of Interior, (mimeo. in Thai).

Durrenberger, E.P. (1983a) "The Economy of Sufficiency", in *Highlanders of Thailand,* John McKinnon and Wanat Bhruksasri (eds.), Oxford University Press: Kuala Lumphur pp. 87-98.

Durrenberger, E.P. (1983b) "Lisu: Political Form, Ideology and Economic Action", *Highlanders of Thailand* John McKinnon and Wanat Bhruksasri (eds.), Oxford University Press: Kuala Lumphur pp. 215-226.

Geddes, W.R. (1976) *Migrants of the Mountains* Oxford University Press: Clarendon.

Grandstaff, T.B. (1976) *Swidden Society in North Thailand: a Diachronic Perspective Emphasizing Resource Relationships,* Unpublished Ph.D. dissertation, University of Hawaii.

Janzen, D.H. (1977) *Ecology of Plants in the Tropics,* Edward Arnold Ltd: London.

Kunstadter, P. (1978a) "Subsistence Agricultural Economies of Lua, and Karen Hill Farmers, Mae Sariang District, Northwestern Thailand", *Farmers in the Forest* Peter Kunstadter, E.C. Chapman and Sanga Sabhasri (eds.), East West Center Book, University of Hawaii pp. 74-133.

Kunstadter, P. (1978b) "Alternatives for the Development of Upland Areas", in *Farmers in the Forest* Peter Kunstadter, E.C. Chapman and Sanga Subhasri

Kunstadter, P. and E.C. Chapman (1978c) "Problems of Shifting Cultivation and Economic Development in Northern Thailand", in *Farmers in the Forest* Peter Kunstadter, E.C. Chapman and Sanga Sabhasri (eds.), East-West Center, University of Hawaii pp. 289-308.

Kunstadter, P. and E.C. Chapman (1978c) "Problems of Shifting Cultivation and Economic Development in Northern Thailand", in *Farmers in the Forest* Peter Kunstadter, E.C. Chapman and Sanga Sabhasri (eds.), East-West Center University of Hawaii pp. 3-33.

Lee, G.Y. (1978) **Development Assistance and Opium Production: a Case Study of the White Hmong of Thailand,** Department of Anthropology, University of Sydney (mimeo.).

Lee, G.Y. (1981) **The Effects of Development Measures on the Socio-Economy of the White Hmong.** Unpublished Ph.D. dissertation, Department of Anthropology, University of Sydney.

McCoy, A.W.,el.al. (1978) **The Politics of Heroin in Southeast Asia** Harper and Row: New York.

McKinnon, John (1977) "Shifting Cultivation Who's Afraid of the Big Bad Wolf?", Tribal Research Centre, (mimeo).

McKinnon, John (1978) "The Jeremiah Incorporation?", Tribal Research Centre, (mimeo).

Ministry of Public Health et.al. (1981a) "Summary and Suggestions from the National Seminar on the Psycho-Social Aspect of Public Health,", 15-17 December, (mimeo. in Thai).

Ministry of Public
Health et.al.
(1981b)
"The Principle of Health for All and the Psycho-Social Aspect" Group discussion at the national seminar on the Psycho-Social Aspect of Public Health, no. 24/1, 15 December (mimeo. in Thai).

Ministry of Public
Health et.al.
(1981c)
"Application of Research Results in the Psycho-Social Aspect of Public Health Planning and Implementation" Group discussion in the national seminar on the Psycho-Social Aspect of Public Health, no. 24/4 16 December (mimeo. in Thai).

Northern Region
Non-Formal
Education
Center (no date)
"Hill Areas Education Project" Department of Non-Formal Education, Ministry of Education (mimeo. in Thai).

Nye, P.H. and D.J.
Greenland (1960)
The Soil under Shifting Cultivation, Commonwealth Bureau of Soils Technical Communication No. 51: Harpenden, England.

Office of National
Primary Education
Commision (1984)
"Research Project Proposal on Education for the Minority Groups" Office of the Prime Minister (mimeo. in Thai).

Office of National
Primary Education
Commission (1983)
"Primary Education for the Hill Tribes" (draft) presented in seminar, Ministry of Education (mimeo. in Thai).

Office of National
Primary Education
Commision   (1984)

"Seminar Report on Primary Education for the Hill Tribe" Ministry of Education (mimeo. in Thai).

Office of Under
Secretary of Ministry
of Public Health
(1984a)

"Summary of Public Health Provision Project for Hill Tribes in Amphoe Mae Chaem Chiang Mai," Ministry of Public Health (mimeo. in Thai).

Office of Under
Secretary of Ministry
of Public Health
(1984b)

"The Result of the Mae Cham Project and a Proposal for Project Expansion" Discussion conclusion in the workshop on Modelling Public Health Services for the Hill Tribes Ministry of Public Health 24-27 October (in Thai).

Office of Under
Secretary of Ministry
of Public Health
(1984c)

Workshop Plan on Public Health Provision for Hill Tribes 1984 Ministry of Public Health (mimeo. in Thai).

Sanga Sabhasri
(1978)

"Opium Culture in Northern Thailand: Social and Ecological Dilemma", in **Farmers in the Forest** Peter Kunstadter, E.C. Chapman and Sanga Sabhasri (eds.), East-West Center, University of Hawaii: 206-209.

Sanit Wongsprasert
(1979)

The Socio-Economic Agriculture of the (black) Lahu Tribal Research Centre, Services for Hill Tribes. 24 October (mimeo. in Thai).

Sunthorn Sunantchai
(1984)

"The Ministry of Education Policy for Hill Tribe Development" Department of Non-Formal Education, Ministry of Education, presented in the workshop seminar on Modelling Public Health Services for Hill Tribes, 24 October (mimeo. in Thai).

Tribal Research Institute and Northern Agricultural Development Centre (1984)
Report on the Evaluation of Inthanon National Park Project 1983. No. 2 (mimeo. in Thai).

Walker, A.R. (1970)
"Lahu Nyi (Red Lahu) Village Society and Economy in North Thailand" Tribal Research Centre, Chiang Mai, Vol. 2 (mimeo.)

Wanat Bhruksasri (1978)
"Issues Hill Tribe: Measures necessary to solve problem" Tribal Research Centre, Chiang Mai, (mimeo. in Thai).

Webster, C.C. and P.N. Wilson (1971)
Agriculture in the Tropics, Longman Group Ltd: London.

9. Akha village (Hobday)

10. Akha village (Hobday)

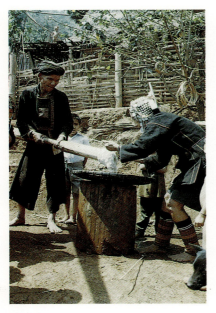
11. Akha pounding cooked rice (Vienne)

12. Lahu butchering a barking deer (Connell)

13. Lahu Sheleh cooking (Connell)

14. Akha bride (Ralana)

15. Pigs, Hmong village (Connell)

16. Pigs, Akha village (Vienne)

17. Mae Tho village 1964 (Geddes)

18. Mae Tho village 1987 (McKinnon)

19. Food demonstration (Connell)

20. Buddhist monks (Kampe)

21. Lisu students (Kampe)

22. Joys of school (Kampe)

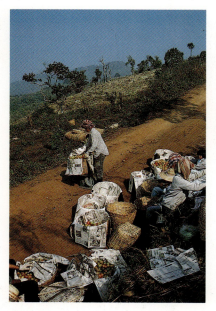
23. Lisu tomato harvest (Hobday)

24. Karen mat maker (Kampe)

25. Shan dentist: Akha patient (McKinnon)

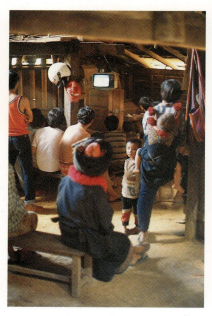
26. Mien house with TV (Connell)

27. School (Kampe)

28. School (Kampe)

29. Army consultants (McKinnon)

30. Villagers repairing road (Kampe)

PROBLEMS: POVERTY & IDENTITY

The grounds on which problems in the highlands can be identified are about as plentiful as the problems themselves. Mention of "problems" should immediately raise the critical question "Whose problems?"

The most common interpretation of "Hill Tribe Problems" refers not to problems faced by the highlanders themselves but problems seen to be made for the Royal Thai Government by their presence. The principal problems the government has with highlanders are usually listed as opium production, land degradation and security. These perceptions form a powerful raft of received knowledge on which is floated major policy decisions.

The "problems" discussed in this section fall into a quite different category. Rather than conforming to a politically accepted sociology of knowledge, the matters reported here are based on genuine scientific research into how highlanders have adjusted their lives to cope with a difficult situation. Each of the contributing professionals, committed to long term investigation in the field provides a quite distinct, individual range of reflections.

Chantaboon Sutthi, Deputy Director of the Tribal Research Institute reviews the condition of highland agriculture. In his Chapter he presents a case which makes initial reference to the established academic distinction between pioneer and cyclical swiddeners. He then goes on to discuss indigenous agricultural knowledge, land use, land tenure, crop assemblies and farming systems known to him from fieldwork, which provides the reader with a much better idea of the complex, concrete reality hidden by the sweeping description "shifting cultivation". His innovative classification and scientific identification of a broad range of native and introduced plant materials leads to a discussion in which he observes that commercialisation is leading to increased genetic impoverishment of highland farming.

Ralana Maneeprasert, trained in Thailand, the Philippines and Australia and with a great deal of experience in the field as a Hmong specialist at the Tribal Research Institute, provides a review of current scientific literature on the nutritional status of highlanders. Her discussion links nutrition to the dynamics of change and in her conclusion draws attention to the particularly difficult position of women and children. She warns that any further deterioration in the diet of highlanders is most likely to first weaken the position of those who have least authority.

Sanit Wongsprasert, a senior researcher and anthropologist at the TRI, on the basis of over 20 years field experience among the Lahu takes up the question of opium addiction. He asks "Who smokes and why?" The answer to who smokes reveals a high level of addiction including both young women and men. In his attempt to answer the more difficult question "Why?", he points out that endemic poverty and insecurity provide explanations for addiction and that cultural constraints which in the past limited abuse appear to have broken down. He identifies today's critical straw (the one that breaks the camel's back) as some kind of physical or psychological trauma. This raises further questions about whether or not the incidence of trauma is higher today than in the past. Aside from the material conditions which make drug addiction an attractive escape from the drudgery of an alienated existence, he observes, " 'drug addiction' must be seen for what it is: a culturally defined value judgement" and set alongside addiction to legal drugs such as tobacco and alchohol abuse, which also pose a danger to individual health and society at large.

Prasert Chaipigusit, a senior researcher at the TRI looks at an intellectual problem found in the manner in which the Lisu are said to be not only strongly individualistic but anarchistic.

Poverty & Identity

Drawing on his knowledge of the Lisu which dates from the early 1960's, he examines cultural characteristics which might account for the origins of such a stereotype and reviews the literature in which researchers and missionaries make reference to Lisu terms that have served to simplify their character. After reviewing the evidence he concludes that the appellation "anarchistic" is misleading and supports a largely negative assessment of highlanders by would-be developers. He argues that if these agents took more trouble to understand the people with whom they work, fewer misunderstandings would occur and that this would greatly increase project efficiency and effectiveness.

Yves Conrad, an anthropologist attached to the French, National Scientific Research Centre (CNRS) and ORSTOM explores a theme close to the heart of anthropology: the issue of identity. Popular demand for a stereotype as discussed by Prasert is matched in professional circles, by naive empiricists who see ethno-linguistic groups as genetic survivors of a more ancient past. Such an approach encourages scholars to invent an unbroken history which establishes a people's distinctness, provides them with a distant homeland and a stable identity that has most probably never been the case. In an attempt to get closer to the truth of the matter, Conrad focuses on the structural and material realities facing the Lisu today and explores their highly dynamic nature. He measures their adaptability by focusing on their response to the contradictions inherent in a situation which simultaneously promotes their integration into, and rejection by, Thai authorities Conrad argues not for an essential and stable identity maintained over millenia but for a series of periodic, pragmatic adjustments to external social, political and environmental conditions and a changing identity defined in terms of structural opposition to other groups. In challenging the idea of fixed identity, he also challenges the underlying validity of the Thai administrative classification system under which some groups are singled out for special treatment. Despite the apparent disadvantages faced by highlanders, many people such as Shan from Burma and Yunnanese from China choose to become Lisu in Thailand.

Highland Agriculture: From Better to Worse

Chantaboon Sutthi

This paper reviews agricultural practices and genetic resources used in the mountains and uplands of Thailand. It describes indigenous farming systems, presents an inventory of cultivated plants and indicates their wide range of uses.

It is the author's opinion that the contemporary impact of market forces and development projects combined with the diminishing availability of land, owing to administrative intervention and population increase, has led to a type of agricultural impoverishment. By "impoverishment" I mean that as some farmers have become unable to either find virgin forest to clear or maintain fallow periods exceeding ten years, they have had to rely less on nutrients released from the biomass and more on labour intensive methods. The range of plants cultivated has decreased. The move from subsistence to commercial farming has also been a move from complex multiple cropping systems to simple if highly demanding, monocropping regimes. This move from a highly diverse inventory of plants to specialisation is also evident in the loss of varietal diversity: fewer varieties of rice are grown today than in the past. Development in a commercial sense has brought more work for farmers, greater dependence on markets over which they have no control and a decline in the community bank of domesticated genetic resources.

PROBLEMS

Mountain Agriculture

High altitude agriculture is a type of slash-and-burn or swidden cultivation, an ancient form of farming widely practised by forest dwellers all over the world. There are many reasons why highlanders engage in this type of cultivation and experts affirm both its efficient use of labour and land and the fact that under low population pressure it is an ecologically informed system of management.

There are two quite distinct systems used in the highlands of Thailand.

1. Pioneer Swiddening (also known as slash-and-burn cultivation, primary forest swiddening, primary forest cultivation, shifting cultivation).

This pattern of cultivation is conducted by felling and burning the biomass and growing crops on the cleared land for as long as possible. The length of the cultivation period may vary from one to more than 20 years depending on fertility levels and composition of the soil. When the soil is exhausted, when there is a problem with weeds, disease, pests or the like, it is time to move to a new area, preferably of virgin forest. Highlanders using land in this manner periodically exhaust their resources and are forced to move again and again to find a better area in which to take up farming. We might say that this type of cultivation makes it necessary to move on forever.

This form of cultivation, known after Conklin as "pioneer swiddening", is followed by the Meo (Hmong), Yao (Mien), Akha, Lisu and Lahu. For this farmers require primary forest and in Thailand between 15 and 20 percent of all highlanders grow opium as their main cash crop. Opium is particularly suited to the cooler mountain climate of the north at about the 1,000 metre contour.

The area cultivated covers the main watershed catchments which give rise to the four most important tributaries of the Chao Phraya, the Ping, Wang, Yom and Nan which provide the principal source of irrigation for the central plains. We could say that highlanders who practise shifting cultivation are placing the national catchment at risk and threaten to cause a lot of damage. It was in fact this fear, as well as the growing of opium, which pushed the government to start development work in the 1960s.

2. **Cyclical Swiddening** (Secondary forest cultivation, secondary forest swiddening, bush fallowing, continuing cultivation, bush fallow rotation, recurrent cultivation, rotational bush fallow, cyclical bush fallow, land rotation). This form of cultivation is also a type of slash-and-burn which allows the vegetation to regenerate for subsequent clearing. This method provides the basis for permanent settlement by communities of Karen, Lua, Htin and Khamu. These people do not move with anywhere near the same frequency as pioneer swiddeners. Some Karen for instance have occupied their village sites for longer than 200 years.

The period for which land is used is largely set by the cultural preferences of the occupying group. The Htin and Lua prefer to use fields for one year after which they are abandoned to allow the vegetation to regenerate. One subgroup of the Htin are forbidden by custom to cultivate the same plot of land for more than one year. The length of the fallow depends not only on custom. Soil fertility, how much land the community has available and the intensity of cultivation are all taken into account. High population densities may make it necessary to return and clear the land before the natural vegetation has regenerated a biomass and nutrient bank of sufficient magnitude to ensure healthy plant growth.

There are three types of land tenure traditionally followed by cyclical swiddeners. These are distinguished as follows:

PROBLEMS

2.1 **Communal Estates.** All of the farm land belongs to the community. Nobody can either buy or sell it. At the beginning of each agricultural year all householders are consulted before a decision is taken about what farming activities will be undertaken and which areas will be cleared for cultivation. Sometimes one large area is cleared communally and subdivided into individual household lots. Sometimes two large areas are cleared. This pattern is followed by both the Lua and Karen. Land cleared under this system is preferably used for one year and left fallow for about ten.

2.2 **Private and Public Tenure.** Under this type of tenure some land belongs to individuals and some to the community. Both Lua and Karen use this dual system of tenure. The conditions under which individual ownership is allocated are decided upon by those holding rights of usufruct. How community land will be used is decided by the village. How private land will be used is decided by the owners. Householders who hold outright ownership are able to sell without refering the matter to the community.

Most of those who hold private land are descended from late-comers to the village who arrived after the best lands were already appropriated and worked on a communal basis. These people did not easily fit into existing reciprocal arrangements and were often constrained to work the remaining less fertile land.

As population has increased and people have become more aware of what lowland markets have to offer, land tenure arrangements have become increasingly complex. Generally villages that use this system have one or two areas which remain under traditional tenure as communal estates. Fields are used for one year followed by a three to six year fallow.

2.3 **Private ownership.** It is said that land has always been privately owned. As noted above, the conditions under which

Highland Agriculture

land in the vicinity of communal estates is claimed by individuals are arranged and agreed to by the people themselves.

The highland Lua do not generally recognise private ownership but this rule is either waived or ignored by more recently settled groups. Cultivation strategies are decided upon by the farm-owner who is not obliged to seek approval from fellow villagers. Owners may buy or sell at their discretion. Under this system Karen and Lua still use fields for one year and leave them fallow for three to six. Htin and Khamu cultivate for two to five years, and then abandon fields for three to ten.

Karen and Lua not only swidden hill sides they also construct irrigated terraces for growing rice. The labour invested in these is acknowledged as a qualification for private ownership and this can be transferred at the owner's discretion. The Htin and Khamu do not practise this form of rice cultivation.

Indigenous Technology
Even though swidden cultivation as practised by highlanders is often called backward or even destructive of the natural resource base, the system is, under normal conditions, ecologically viable, well adjusted to the environment and covers a wide range of activities starting with land selection, up to harvest and beyond including seed selection for the next season. Highlanders have practised agriculture for millennia and their accumulated wisdom is still pertinent to contemporary conditions. Traditional knowledge of the agricultural cycle can be summarised as follows.

Site Selection
Factors considered by farmers when selecting fields include location, aspect (orientation to the sun), wind, elevation, soil type, productive potential, and slope.

PROBLEMS

Farmers know where to grow early varieties of rice which are adapted to quite specific ecological niches, such as hill top sites where the soil is drier and less likely to become saturated. What may be called medium varieties must be grown on the middle slopes where soil moisture is higher. Annuals need much more moisture and must be grown on the gentle downhill slopes. Flat land on shoulders, beneath ridges and near large streams is generally more fertile but unsuitable for planting. Highlanders realise that if they sow in these places, plant maturation will be delayed, more weeds will grow and therefore more labour will be required to keep the garden clear. Opium latex grown on such sites is very viscous and easily lost because it does not congeal quickly, running irretrievably down the poppy stems.

Sunshine is also considered to be a matter of primary importance. Otherwise suitable areas with too much shade are avoided. This is particularly critical for opium poppy plantations, which require intensive care and much labour over a limited harvesting period (about 10 days, plus or minus three days). Highland opium growers know that sunlight stimulates the release of latex from the pod. Much attention is therefore given to the influence of site conditions on the speed of opium poppy maturation.

If there is enough land available, farrmers will choose several plots in different places. Most families maintain about one to three areas for opium growing but this also depends on their access to labour. Sites exposed to maximum sunlight are cultivated and planted first. This is called "hot land" where the poppies mature most quickly. The second plot is preferably chosen from land on which sunlight falls later in the day. There is usually one to two hours difference in the duration of radiation between the first and second fields. This "middle-hot land" is cultivated, planted and harvested after the first. The third area is called "cold land" and receives sunlight later in the day than the other two fields, about two to three hours less sunshine per day than

Highland Agriculture

the "hot land". The size of these fields is determined by available labour. Where only one site is developed a system of relay planting is practised. Ten to fourteen days after the first seeds are sown the exercise is repeated. The crop matures in the same sequence in which it was planted. The harvest can then be managed quite comfortably.

Differences in site selection and variations in planting times have led to some misunderstandings among those who study opium poppy growing in Thailand. The most widely accepted opinion is that there are three varieties of opium poppy where in fact there is only one.

Wind is also an important factor. On exposed sites where the wind is strong, turbulence is not only likely to damage young poppy plants but also makes it difficult to harvest the resin. If, after incisions have been made to bleed the latex, the pods are persistently knocked together, the harvest can be lost. What is not thrown to the ground is smeared on the pods in a thin layer which cannot be scraped off. Strong winds do not damage rice but fallen stalks make harvesting difficult.

Vegetation is also used as an indicator because it signals the presence of soil types specifically suited to various crops. The land on which *Gigantochloa albociliata* Munro grows is considered to be "lowland", hot and unsuitable for opium but good for rice. Here the clay content is always high. *Dendrocalamus hamiltonii* Nees grows at about 1,000 metres, thriving on loamy soils suitable for growing rice and fair to marginal for opium poppy. *Litsea cubeba* Pers. is an indicator of high altitude, good for poppy but unsuitable for rice. Where plants like the giant mountain fishtail palm, *Caryota obtusa* Griff. or *Dendrochide stimulans* Chew occur, they indicate a high productive potential for opium latex, much higher than obtained on the same soil in the absence of this vegetation.

PROBLEMS

Soil is another important factor. Many observers have reported that vegetation is more important but highlanders themselves say that it is possible for a wide range of plants to grow on land to which they are not well adapted and that the critical test in site selection is a careful examination of the soil itself.

Each ethnic group has its own method of soil classification, which involves physical tests. Soils are classified principally by examining the colour, texture, structure, weight, and composition. Parent material is assessed by examining rocky outcrops in the vicinity. If limestone is found, the soil is classified as having a satisfactory clay content and therefore suitable for growing opium. If there is sandstone, the soil is classified as sandy or loam suitable for growing rice. They not only carry out a visual check but also manipulate samples. If a soil has a high proportion of clay, it becames sticky and slippery when moisture is added. When this type of soil is dry, it crumbles into small pieces. Sometimes farmers dig 15 centimetre observation holes. If the soil sticks to the blade of the tool, it is classfied by its clay content. Some groups, particularly Lisu, inspect the soil by digging a hole about 15-20 centimetres deep, taking the fresh sample and squeezing it tightly in the palm then opening the hand. If the soil retains the shape of the palm, it is classified as clay. This test should be done during the winter season but not after recent rainfall. The Lahu also weigh soil. The Meo pull out a plant with a stem about one centimetre thick. If the soil sticks to the roots, it is classified as clay. After rain, the Lahu Sheleh check the underside of leaves to see if there is a deposit of soil particles thrown up by the explosive impact of raindrops. If there is a deposit the soil is classified as light. The absence of a deposit indicates that the soil is heavy and has a high clay content.

Frost is a hazard carefully avoided, especially for the opium poppy. Farmers always select steeper sloping land away from the valley floors on which frost is likely to form.

Highland Agriculture

Distance from the village is also a consideration. Bulky crops like rice are difficult to transport and because they attract the attention of scavenging birds and animals are best located near villages. This is not always possible and the condition of tracks and roads and the availability of transport is also considered.

Field Preparation

The cutting and felling of trees and other vegetation is the first operation. Generally speaking, pioneer swiddeners are more skilful at clearing primary forest than cyclical swiddeners. Trees are cut to fall in a position where they will not pose a danger when the rains come. If logs are felled incorrectly, they may slide or roll downhill and injure crops and people. Because clearing is a perilous activity, precise rules of conduct are followed. Trees are felled in sets rather than individually. To avoid accidents, cutting commences with axemen working uphill and abreast of each other on the same contour. The trees are cut so that they remain standing. When the axemen reach the top of the ridge, they wait until their group is entirely accounted for and out from under the canopy before the trees at the top of the ridge are felled. As these trees fall, their weight triggers a domino effect and with a loud series of cracks the forest comes crashing down.

Planting

From long experience hill people know how to space the plants out in a manner appropriate to different soils. If the soil is very fertile, farmers space plants well apart. The space between individual rice plants grown on the most fertile land is 50 centimetres, on soils with normal levels of fertility 45 centimetres, for lower than normal 25 centimetres, and for low fertility soil 20 centimetres. There is no exact standard measure; parts of the body are used in much the same manner as followed by lowland Thai farmers. The distance between the elbow and the end of the middle finger, about 45 centimetres, is suitable for planting rice on high fertility soils. When planting on low fertility soil, the placement of seeds is measured from the elbow to the wrist, about 25 centimetres.

It is a comment on the perversity of nature that the rice people prefer to eat is not as productive as less palatable varieties. To get around this problem, satisfy people's taste preferences and the need to produce a harvest of sufficient quantity, many types of rice are grown in the same field. A study of highland rice cultivation in the north and west of Thailand found that a typical field may have from one to five varieties of rice. Researchers have also discovered that single panicles often contained rice with a wide variety of characteristics.

Labour

It is often said that those who cultivate hill country use more energy than lowlanders because they walk up and down steep slopes and must constantly maintain their balance. It is assumed that this must put a heavier load on them than on lowland farmers. What truth there is in this I cannot say but it is clear to me that highlanders know how to conserve their energy.

When small family groups sow seed, they start at the bottom of the hill and work upward in a zigzag fashion walking back and forth along the contour. The harvest proceeds in the same fashion but from the top down. This is quite logical considering the nature of the work. If the work team is a large group organised under a system of reciprocal labour exchange, those planting move straight up the hill maintaining equidistance from each other. From the top they descend once more, moving in liens parallel to their ascent. This enables them to optimise their use of labour in the most efficient way.

When harvesting opium, a quite deliberate strategy is followed. The tappers keep incised poppies in their line of sight and sidestep backwards away from the pods as they cut. This is done so that the harvesters can avoid carrying away valuable latex stuck to their clothes and body.

Traditional knowledge of swidden agriculture as described above is an integral part of highland culture. It has been built up over the centuries on the basis of careful observation, trial and error and by exchanging information with neighbours. When Red Lahu (Lahu Nyi) select rice seed, they do not take it at random. They only take the rice which falls first in threshing. Other highlanders carefully collect the most perfect plants from their rice fields, tie these together in a bundle and thresh them before commencing the harvest in earnest.

Crop Species

Highlanders are principally rice-based farmers. Even though Meo, Yao, Lahu, Lisu and Akha started many years ago to grow opium as a cash crop, this does not mean that they have always grown opium. Each year some people, for reasons of their own, decide against growing opium. If they have suitable land, their first choice is to grow rice to eat.

Rice is their staple crop and by far the most important in their life. According to their way of looking at the world, reinforced to a large extent by their relative isolation, they favour the independence of self-sufficiency. The priority given to self-sufficiency makes it necessary for them to grow a range of crops wide enough to minimise their dependence on lowland markets. The plants grown in the cropping system are primarily for domestic consumption. If for some reason the rice crop fails, supplementary food crops provide a type of crop insurance which guarantees survival.

Opium is not only the most important economic plant but is also used as a medicine. Just as the opium derivative codeine is one of the world's most widely used drugs, so does opium itself hold a prominent place in indigenous herbal and esoteric medicine. Hill people still grow a wide range of medicinal herbs. There is another wide category of plants which they grow for use in traditional ceremonies. Most rituals require the use of some plant materials. The actual varieties used however, differ from group to group.

Another important group is the fibre plants used in weaving, dress making and making containers.

Pioneer swideners also grow maize. At the beginning of the rainy season, maize is planted in fields suitable for opium poppy. Towards the end of the rainy season (September and October), the maize is harvested and poppy sown. This double cropping of maize and opium is very well adapted to conditions. During this period it is impossible to fell, dry and burn vegetation and clearing the maize fields is a much easier task, especially if they have been well looked after. To plant opium poppy after maize not only minimises the task of soil preparation but also greatly reduces the need for weeding. When maize is grown, the field is weeded at least once (in fact usually twice). Maize not only keeps the land in good shape for the subsequent opium poppy crop but is also the principal source of fodder for pigs and chickens (used frequently as an offering to the spirits) and for making whisky.

Swidden Crops

Plant materials grown in swiddens can be classified by the uses to which they are put. A list of swidden crops is provided in Appendix II.

1. **Staple food crops.** Rice is clearly the most significant food. Meo, Yao, Akha, Lisu, Lahu, Karen and Lua all eat hill rice. The Htin and Khamu eat glutinous rice.

2. **Vegetables.** These plants are used frequently and the

Highland Agriculture

list includes, Chinese mustard, Chinese cabbage, Chinese radish, Chinese Kale, Chinese chives, Indian spinach, *Mesona* sp., peas, beans, garlic, shallot, cumin, Pe-tsai, lettuce, ginger, cucurbits, chilli, egg plant, cockroach berry, chives, okra, tomato, Australian arrowroot, yam bean and the very young opium-poppy. Altogether there are about 48 species of kitchen plants which are known to be used for cooking. There are many more not yet identified.

3. **Animal feed.** Plants used for animal feed include, maize (non glutinous type), the leaves of the grain amaranth, sweet potato, papaya, banana, rice, taro and pigeon pea.

4. **Supplementary food crops.** This group includes yams, yam bean, sweet potato, taro, cocoyam, cassava, arrowroot, Australian arrowroot, potato, sunflower, millets, sorghum, maize (glutinous type), popcorn, beans peas, opium-poppy seed, pumpkin seed, sesame and *Perilla frutescens* Britt. Of these, yams, taro, cocoyam, sweet potato, potato and maize are eaten if the rice crop fails.

5. **Fruits** eaten include papaya, pineapple, melon, water melon, bananas, peach and cucumber.

6. **Herbs, spices and condiments.** These are used to add taste to food. The list includes garlic, lemon grass, fennel, sweet basil, hoary basil, holy basil, chilli, coriander, cumin, parsley, kitchen mint, soya bean (fermented) and *Isodon ternifolius* Kudo, *Oenanthe stolonifera* Wall. and *Heracleum burmanicum* Kurz.

7. **Oil.** Opium-poppy oil and sesame oil are used as cooking oil as well as to keep the opium smoking lamp lit. Some Meo villagers know how to extract the oil from castor bean. This is used for lighting.

8. **Preserved and fermented** foods such as Chinese mustard (dry) and soya bean (fermented)

9. **Sugar:** sugar cane and kaoliang

10. **Fibre and utensils:** These include hemp, cotton, bird chilli, bottle gourd and smooth loofah. Hemp is used for making thread which is woven into cloth. Bottle gourds are used as water containers and receptacles for seeds and salt, as well as for spoons and ladles. The fibre of smooth loofah is used as a scrubber. Highland addicts use the stems of three year old bird chillies to make opium pipes. They believe that this prevents constipation.

11. **Religious and ceremonial crops.** These are planted as a matter of necessity for use in rituals and ceremonies according to the beliefs of each ethnic group. For instance the Akha grow shallot, taro and ginger in their swiddens before planting other crops. This is done to protect the field from the influence of bad spirits that might otherwise come and damage the plants and also bring bad luck to the farmer. Karen and Lua plant cockscomb, globe-amaranth, cosmos flower and marigold for a rice spirit calling ritual. Yao believe that safflower is an ancestor of opium poppy. They grow it in their opium gardens and hope that by looking after the whole family their opium will mature properly without untoward interruption from supernatural beings. Yao of the Tung sub-clan use fermented Chinese mustard as an offering to their ancestors. White Meo hold a pumpkin ritual. Akha still use the bottle gourd as a water ladle in a well ritual in which it is forbidden to use any other material. Almost every group uses rice (rice grains, cooked rice, pop rice) to make offerings to the spirits. The Meo use maize and finger millet powder in a ritual to exorcise bad spirits. Sorghum is used in the form of pop sorghum for spirit offerings. Opium is used in the highest form of spirit worship conducted by the Lahu Sheleh. Sesame oil is an essential item in the Yao ceremony of ordination. Lahu and Yao use many *Vigna unguiculata*(L.) Walp. (L.) in the new rice eating ritual and new year celebrations, which require spirit offerings.

Highland Agriculture

12. Decoration and cosmetics. Some ethnic minorities use plants from their swiddens for personal decoration. Akha woman and children use the small bottle gourd as an ornament by threading a string through a hole drilled in its neck and hanging it from the waist. Karen use Job's tears *(Coix lachryma-jobi)* Lin. of the *stenocarpa Stapf.* variety and *Coix puellarum* Bal. to sew on their jackets or thread into a necklace or bracelet. Lisu men weave wheat straw into their jackets. Meo grow a herb called "*foo*", which they bleed by scraping the underside of the leaf. The discharge is smeared on their cheeks as a rouge.

13. Cash crops. The most important economic crop of the Meo, Yao, Lahu, Lisu and Akha is opium. The Karen and Red Lahu are well known as chilli producers. Castor bean is grown even though it is not very profitable. The Pwo Karen grow sugar cane in small fields near their villages. The cane itself is not sold but crushed and boiled to make sweets for sale. Siam cardamom is grown by the Pwo Karen of Uthai Thani Province.

14. Alcohol and narcotics. Many plants in the gramineae family are grown for making alcohol. Rice, maize, sorghum, foxtail millet and finger millet are used for this purpose. Opium and tobacco are grown to supply habitual users but only opium is grown in any quantity.

15. Medicinal plants. Highlanders grow many medicinal plants. Unfortunately these have yet to be studied seriously, identified and chemically analysed. The scientific names of most of these plants are not yet known. The most effective of these medicinal plants are widely recognised and knowledge of their preparation and properties continually exchanged by the various groups. The medicinal usefulness of opium is known even to non-opium poppy growing people such as the Karen, Lua, Htin and Khamu. Other curative plants used widely include shallot, Indian spinach, lemon grass, ginger, cockscomb, pineapple, papaya, banana, peach, tobacco, para cress, sweet potato, castor bean, holy basil, cumin, fennel, *Kaempferia* sp., *Curcuma* *domestica* Valeton, *Cannabis sativa* Lin.. Some Karen use the "ivory" rice variety mixed with other herbs to treat some health complaints. They believe that "ivory" rice has the same curative properties as real ivory.

16. **Other Swidden Crops:** Maize stems are used as temporary wall fillers in field maize storage huts. Safflower is used to dye glutinous rice yellow, red or orange for special ceremonies. Maize, sorghum, kaoliang, foxtail millet, sunflower and castor bean are used as path and boundary markers. The Yao and Meo make soya bean curd (tofu).

Non-Swidden Plants

There are also many plant materials cultivated outside swidden areas. Under this heading, I will discuss the crops grown in household gardens and trees and shrubs established in small orchards and plantations. As in the previous section on swidden crops, this information will be classified by use. A list of scientific and common names is provided in Appendix III.

Kitchen plants are grown close to the village, around houses or in fenced-off gardens behind houses. Because of the nature of pioneer swiddening there is less need for the Meo, Yao, Akha, Lisu and Lahu to grow perennials. The only perennial grown in any quantity is the peach. This tree matures relatively quickly and is easy to look after. They are usually planted in swiddens that have become unprofitable to cultivate. Karen, Lua, Htin and Khamu, who practise cyclical swiddening centred on a permanent settlement, are more likely to grow perennials. They are more likely to find themselves in a position where they can secure some benefit from either exchange or sale of the fruit in lowland markets. Almost all orchard trees grown by highlanders are also grown by Thais. These annuals and perennials are identified below.

1. **Vegetable matter.** This classification covers both crops and perennials. Different parts of the plants are eaten such as the flower, fruit, trunks, shoots, leaves and young leaves. Any list should include, Welsh onion, *leucaena,* giant granadilla, citron, tea Asiatic penny-wort, hog plum, wild spider flower, sesban, horse-radish tree, yellow dock, *Cordyline fruticosa* Goppert, *Gymnema inodorum* Decne., *Oroxylum indicum* Vent., *Coccinia grandis* Voigt, *Sauropus androgynus* Merr.; bamboo *Zizania latifolia* Turcz., *Hibiscus sabdariffa* Lin., *Acacia pennata* Willd. subsp. insuavis Neilsen, *Talinum paniculatum* Gaertn., *Morinda citrifolia* Lin., *Solanum indicum* Lin., *Lasia spinosa* Thw., *Ipomoea aquatica* Forsk.

2. **Plants to Chew** (Masticatory). Highlanders such as the Lahu, Karen, Akha, and Lisu chew betel nut. Karen and Lua grow both the betel palm and betel pepper. Hill people who maintain close relations with northern Thai also make fermented tea or *miang*.

3. **Beverage.** The only plant in this group is tea. Coffee is raised commercially and promoted by many development projects but is not as a rule brewed by the highlanders.

4. **Fruit :** marian plum, mango, custard apple, sweet sop, carambola, durian, tamarind, star gooseberry, santol, jack fruit, mulberry, Malay apple, guava, pomegranate, coconut, giant granadilla, Indian jujube, Indian bael, pomelo, oranges, longan, Thai sapodilla plum, *Baccaurea ramiflora* Lour.

5. **Herbs, spices and condiments:** tamarind, garangal, citronella grass, Indian borage, roselle, lime, turmerics, *Piper sarnentosum* Roxb., *Polygonum odoratum* Lour., *citrus hystrix* DC., *solanum stramonifolium* Jacq., *Houttuynia cordata* Thunb., *Boesenbergia pandulata* Holtt.

PROBLEMS

6. **Other Non-Swidden Plants:**

6.1 **Construction.** Thirteen types of bamboo are used widely.

6.2 **Fibre.** Kapok is used for stuffing mattresses and pillows. *Stirculia guttata* Roxb. and three as yet unidentified species are used for making rope.

6.3 **Dye.** *Baphicacanthus cusia* Brem., indigo and turmerics.

6.4 **Utensils.** All bamboos are used as household and agricultural tools. Bamboo is one of the most frequently used plant materials in everyday life. *Sida acuta* Burm., and the substems of the coconut palm fronds are also used for making brooms.

6.5 **Fencing.** Physic nut is planted to serve as a living fence around houses.

6.6 **Soap and Shampoo.** As roads link villages with lowland markets, the use of *Sapindus rarak* A.DC., the soap nut tree grown in well-established villages of the Karen and Lua, is gradually being replaced by commercially manufactured soap and shampoo. Some remote Karen and other settlements still use this plant as soap and shampoo. During World War II when commercial soap was in short supply, the northern Thai also used the soap nut tree.

7. **Religious and Ceremonial.** Only a few non-swidden species are used for these purposes: *Acacia rugata* Merr., *Piper betel* Lin., *Zingiber ottensii* Valeton, *Zingiber cassumunar* Roxb., bamboo.

8. **Cash.** There are three types of cash crops: tea, betel pepper and Siam cardamom.

Highland Agriculture

9. **Ornamentals.** Thai people have long used ornamental plants. Most ornamental plants appear to have been adopted from the Thai by Karen, Lua, Htin and Khamu. There are many plants which can be listed including some medicinal plants such as blood flower, peacock's crest, Indian shot, chrysanthemum, cosmos flower, garden dahlia, zinnia, sponge tree, jasmine, gardenia, orange jasmine, queen of the night, cloth of gold, Indian rosebay, frangipani, trumpet flower, Cape lilly, cockscomb (var. cristata); *Hippeastrum* spp., *Chloranthus officinalis* Bl., *Kalanchoe pinnata* Pers., *Hibiscus schizopetalus* Hook.f., *Hibiscus rosasinensis* Lin., *Talauma candollei* Bl., *Pavetta* spp, *Celosia* sp., *Bougainvillea spectabilis* Willd.,d *Kalanchoe* sp., *Yucca gloriosa* Lin., *Rosa damascena* Mill., *Ixora* sp., *Zebrina pendula* Schnizl., *Strobilanthes* sp., *Cordyline* sp..

10. **Medicinal:** tea, Asiatic pennywort, cockscomb (var. cristata), sweet flag, bowstring hemp, Capelily lily, hog plum, trumpet flower, ringworm bush, coffee senna, tamarind, physic nut, star cactus, Spanish dagger, clove, nutmeg, betel palm, lime, tobacco, guava, betel pepper, pomegranate, Indian bael and cotton; *Baphicacanthus cusia* Brem., *Oroxylum indicum* Vent., *Kalanchoe pinnata* Pers., *Tinospora crispa* Miers ex. Hook., *Tinospora glabra* Merr., *Solanum indicum* Lin., *Boesenbergia pandulata* Holtt., *Curcuma* sp., *Zingiber cassumanar* Roxb., *Zingiber ottensii* Valeton, *Talinum paniculatum* Gaertn., *Strobilanthes* sp., *bougainvillea spectabilis* Willd., *Capparis* sp., *Garuga pinnata* Roxb., *Vibernum inopinatum* Craib, *Piper chaba* Hunt, *Ixora* sp., *Alpinia* sp.,

The plants listed above indicate the richness of genetic resources in both swidden and non-swidden fields. We can see, as expected, that food plants are more commonly grown than any others. There are 350 species which have been identified; of these 198 or 57 percent are staple food crops, vegetables, supplementary food crops, cereals, herbs, spices, condiments etc. Only 86 varieties of medicinal plants or 25 percent of the total have been identified. The role that these plants play in maintaining an economy of semi-subsistent self-reliance is clearly documented.

Cropping Systems

The traditional wisdom which regulates planting is an integral part of their economic system. Food is grown for both domestic consumption and livestock. Farmers know what is appropriate to a specific environment and they carefully determine the size of their fields according to available labour. Rice is clearly the most important crop and cultivation is managed in much the same way by all highlanders. However, what farmers call rice fields are planted with so many other crops that it would be more accurate to name them by the management systems used.

1. **Mixed cropping system.** In this system rice is the main crop usually found in association with maize and opium poppy. It is principally used by pioneer swiddeners such as the Meo, Yao, Akha, Lisu and Lahu but is also a feature of cyclical swiddeners such as the Karen and Lua. Minor crops such as those listed under "swidden crops" are scattered in appropriate microenvironments throughout a field where rice usually predominates.

These crops are not planted in rows. Green squash may be planted close to fallen timber, or next to the trunk of a burnt-out tree, or in the shelter of a field hut where it can climb onto the roof. Egg plant, chilli or lemon grass may be planted where it can be easily gathered on the way home. Millet, sorghum and kaoliang may be planted to indicate the perimeter of a field or to mark a footpath running through a garden.

Where this works well, farmers may harvest food from a single field for at least six months. Some crops can be left in either fields or field huts for a year; such as egg plant, cockroach berry, coco-yam, taro, cassava, chilli, pumpkin, wax-gourd and some types of cucumber, beans etc. Some plants grow all year round in swidden fields. Pioneer swiddeners grow crops to eat

Highland Agriculture

for ten to eleven months. Cyclical swiddeners appear to be less successful in this and can eat directly from their fields for only seven to eight months. Pioneer swiddeners have access not only to a wider variety of crops but also to greater quantities and are constantly harvesting from rice, maize and opium poppy fields. Cyclical swiddeners have only their hill rice fields to draw on. This practice of mixed cropping in swiddens is remarkably efficient in its use of labour committed to weeding. There is also a pleasing absence of the problems which plague kitchen gardens located closer to the village, which require both fencing and special weeding and are frequently invaded by hungry livestock.

2. **Sequential cropping system.** This is followed by pioneer swiddeners who grow opium, maize and rice. It is designed to enable the farmer to optimize household labour over a limited period, particularly between harvesting rice and planting opium poppy.

Glutinous maize is planted at the beginning of the rainy season, followed by rice. Both fields are intercropped with other food plants. Maize is harvested before rice. Soon after this, the opium poppy is sown as a second crop in the maize fields. Many other vegetables ands semi-annuals, such as chilli and egg plant, are grown among the poppies. After the opium is harvested, these are left to mature.

If conditions are right, this sophisticated system is very efficient. For how long it has been used is not clear but the words of one elder provide an indication, "We've used these systems for as long as I can remember". Perhaps they practised this form of management about a hundred years ago when they started to grow opium, long before cropping systems courses were introduced into the universities.

3. **Relay cropping system** This system is very much like sequential cropping only instead of glutinous maize, non-

glutinous maize is grown for animal feed. Opium poppy seed is sown under the maize before it is harvested.

Maize plays an important role in opium poppy cultivation because it not only reduces the amount of labour required by keeping down weed growth, it also protects seedlings from the explosive impact of late rain. Heavy rain can up-root the delicate seedlings and surface run-off wash them away. The maize canopy lets in enough sunlight for the seedlings to grow, keeps the ground temperature down, reduces the rate of soil moisture loss and maintains a better dew point ratio. Maize, then, serves the dual role of acting as a guard if precipitation is too generous, and enhancing both moisture retention and dew point condensation if there is no rain at all.

4. **Mono-cropping system.** Traditionally crops have rarely been grown in this system, under which a single type of plant is planted, but development project promotion of cash crops has now made it quite common. Hemp, cotton and sugar cane have been grown for sometime. Lettuce, cabbage, tomato and other temperate vegetables are more recent additions.

Research and Genetic Resources: current situation

In 1960 a major development programme was mounted with the stated objectives of stopping swidden agriculture, reducing opium growing, replacing opium with other cash crops and promoting permanent agriculture and settlement. Since then, many new crops have been introduced, mainly to replace opium. Most of the introduced plants are already well known to highlanders. They are improved varieties bred to provide a larger harvest. As most readers will appreciate, these plants place considerable demands on growers. They require careful management and expensive inputs (fertilizers, pesticides, herbicides etc.) and in this respect are quite different from the plants highlanders have habitually used. However, government extension workers report that they receive a good response from highlanders. Most of these new plant materials are grown in accessible areas that

Highland Agriculutre

extension workers can visit regularly without having to face too many difficulties. The range of introduced plants includes new varieties of rice, cabbage, lettuce, garlic, Jamaica sorrel, mung bean, black bean, longan, cassava, sugar cane, maize, Pe-tsai, dahlia, foxtail millet, sweet orange, sesame, ginger, egg plant, shallot, potato, peach, ground nut, mango, common bean, kapok, castor bean, pineapple, tomato, tobacco, tea, tarmarind. sweet sor, santol, jackfruit, Malay apple, guava, pomelo etc.

Many kinds of improved varieties have become highlander cash crops but of course the profitability of each depends on individual village market conditions. (A list of introduced crops is provided in Appendix IV).

Plants in this category include,
Vegetables: cabbage, Chinese cabbage, ginger, garlic, common bean, lettuce, shallot etc.
Field crops: soya bean, sesame, mung bean, black bean, foxtail millet, peanut, cotton, potato, cassava, sugar cane, maize etc.
Fruit and beverage: tea, peach, sweet orange, pineapple etc., and some improved varieties of tobacco (Virginia type).

Of these crops, maize is the most frequently planted. This is due to many factors but mainly because opium growing farmers such as the Meo and Yao at Nan, Chiang Rai, Tak, Petchaboon and Kampaeng Phet are well acquainted with it.

New cash crops have also been introduced:
Vegetables: celery, parsley, kohlrabi, Brussel sprout, turnip, cauliflower, Pe-tsai, aubergine, spinach, zucchini, bell pepper, fennel, head lettuce, Japanese cucumber, Japanese onion, leek, asparagus, tomato, sweet pea, etc.
Beverages: coffee, chrysanthemum tea, Jamaica sorrel etc.
Fruits: litchi, apple, Chinese pear, Japanese apricot, passion fruit, strawberry etc.

PROBLEMS

Field crops: red kidney bean, pinto bean, Lima bean, potato for processing into chips, etc.
Flowers: carnation, statice, gladiolus, strawflower, gypsophila, chrysanthemum etc.

However, even though there are now many improved crops varieties and cash crops in hill tribe communities, many villages have developed markets for their traditional crops. This depends on the environment and the market situation. Opium should also be included in this list because it is still grown in isolated spots.

This category of traditional crops includes a local variety of peach which is pickled, hemp grown for both its fibre and as a narcotic, coriander (seed), tea, rice, (plain rice sold in Chiang Mai as a vitamin rich rice), glutinuous rice (black grain type), lab lab bean, rice bean, Chinese mustard, Siam cardamon and betel pepper.

Research work also commenced about 1960. The Department of Agriculture, Ministry of Agriculture and Cooperatives, set up a research and experimental station in the highlands at Doi Mussur in Tak province on about the 950 metre contour. The extension crops subject to research and experiment included Arabica, robusta and liberica coffees, avocado, macadamia nut, cherri moya, litchi, longan, pomelo, sweet orange, mandarin orange, tea, mulberry, asparagus and strawberry. A considerable number of domesticated perennials have been added to the highlanders' inventory but lack of funds and personnel has limited the range of experimental work.

About 1963, the Department of Public Welfare (DPW) established four Hill-Tribes Self-Help Land Settlements (official translation). These were at Chiang Rai (Amphoe Mae Chan), Chiang Mai (Amphoe Chiang Dao), Tak (Doi Mussur in Amphoe

Highland Agriculture

Muang) and Petchabun. The settlements carried out basic work on crops such as carrot, kohlrabi, Pe-tsai, Kwang Tung, sweet pea, cabbage, beet, water melon, radish, turnip, lettuce, cauliflower, litchi, coffee, tea, apple, pear etc.

In Tak, at the DPW Doi Mussur "settlement", pasture experiments were set up as a component of a livestock extension project. This project received help from New Zealand and American Peace Corp volunteers. Pasture establishment experiments were carried out with clover and other legumes as well as the following grasses: Rhode, Guinea, Guatemala, Napier, paspalum, timothy, cocksfoot and sorghum. The adaptation trials also tested fodder crops such as rape, swede, velvet bean, kudzu, cow pea, centrosema, Lucernes (alfalfa) etc. This work ceased in 1967 when security became a problem.

The Rice Department (subsequently renamed The Rice Research Institute), in cooperation with the Department of Public Welfare, carried out experiments with more than 100 varieties of rainfed as well as irrigated rice, such as *nang mol* S4. The feasability of growing wheat was also explored. All this work was carried out at Doi Mussur, Tak between 1963 and 1966.

The Royal Project, which was set up in 1969 and commenced work in 1970, was the first agency to seriously analyse and experiment with various crops. Academic personnel from Kasetsart, the agricultural university in Bangkok, the Agricultural Faculty of Chiang Mai University and the Mae Jo Institute of Technology and Agriculture, also of Chiang Mai, and various offices of the Ministry of Agriculture and Cooperatives carried out work with support from the United States of America Department of Agriculture (USDA). Some 69 agricultural research projects involving both plants and animals were carried out between 1971 and 1985. Work concentrated on new and improved varieties of crops, only a few of which could be called traditional hill tribe plants.

PROBLEMS

Although USDA support was withdrawn in 1986 the Royal Project is determined to continue research and experimental work on highland agriculture with the support of private funds from his Majesty the King, other donors and the Narcotics Administration Unit located in the US Embassy, Bangkok.

The United Nations/Thai Programme for Drug Abuse Control (UNPDAC) also provided funding for research aimed principally at identifying opium replacement crops. This programme, started in 1973 introduced a considerable number of new and improved varieties, many of which have become important cash crops. The list includes:

Vegetables: Chinese radish, Chinese mustard, Chinese kale, Chinese cabbage, rhubarb, eggplant, heading mushlard, hot pepper, broad bean, tomato, musk melon, green pea, day lily, onion, cauliflower, head lettuce, broccoli, cabbage, carrot, Brussel sprouts, cucumber, sweet pepper, celery, parsley, sweet fennel.
Herbs and Spices, Condiments and Medicinal Plants: balm, summer savory, anise, rue, majoram, thyme, lavender, caraway, chicory hor, mint, cumin, tansy, coriander, sage, basil horehound, camomile, digitalis, clary, borage, dill, rosemary, dandelion, tarragon, elecampane, fenugreek, curcuma, wild majoram, sweet majoram, henbane, danggui, peppermint, cardamons, pyrethrum, hop, saffron, vanilla etc.
Field crops: sunflower, safflower, red kidney bean, Lima bean, pinto bean, sweet corn, sorghum, castor bean, potato etc.
Flowers: marigold, zinnia, alyssum, aster, carnation, dahlia, pansy, salvia, petunia, snapdragon, nasturtium etc.
Fruits: strawberry, apples, peaches, passion fruit etc.

UNPDAC also promoted perennial trees and shrubs, especially Arabica coffee. Arabica coffee varieties on which experimental work has been carried out include bourbon, catura, catuai, typica, catimor, Blue Mountain, Arusha, hybrido de Timor, coorge, coorge kent, geisha, kent, kaffa, Villalobos 954, K7, H - 17 - 1, DK 1 - 6, S-6, S - 12, S - 795, S - 947, S - 952,

S - 333, S - 645, S - 1934, S - 288 etc. The current extension favourites are varieties which also grow in the lowlands without shade, such as catimor, catuai and catura.

At about this time, the Thai-Australian Highland Agronomy project grew out of a cooperative arrangement between the Tribal Research Centre, Faculty of Agriculture, Chiang Mai University, and the Australian Development Assistance Bureau (ADAB). Its initial objective was to provide technical assistance to improve the nutritional quality of savannah grassland. Pasture agronomists introduced new germplasm from the legume and grass family such as *Desmodium* spp, *Panicum,* spp., *Stylosanthes* spp., *Macroptilium* spp, Macrotylona sp., *Glycine* wightii, *Trifolium* spp., *Lupinus* spp., *Setaria* spp., *Brachiaria* spp., *Paspalum* spp., Lucerne, Buffel and Kikuyu grass etc. This project also looked at livestock husbandry (especially cattle and pigs), perennials as fodder, plus also the impact of eucalyptus and pines. In the field, they looked at agricultural extension strategies and the provision of credit.

For nearly thirty years now, development work has been promoted by both government and private agencies. Their activities have brought about many changes in the way in which agriculture is practised in the highlands. The most important change has been the gradual realignment of highlander priorities from a subsistence orientation to one that places people in a much more dependent relationship on the world outside their villages. The emphasis on cash crops is aimed at enabling them to secure higher incomes. This often means that only one crop need be grown. Some farmers now expect to buy food crops for home consumption.

An example of such a community is the Meo village of Ban Khun Klang, Amphoe Chom Thong, Chiang Mai, who grow cabbage and strawberries as their cash crops and have to buy their rice and other food crops from either the Chom Thong district market or traders. The nearest market to the village clearly does not determine the price which is formed in the much wider context of the national economy. This makes for a high degree of vulnerability. In 1985, many of the Yao in Phayao who grow only cotton and maize for sale, suffered so severely when their crops were badly damaged that they had to ask for rice from the Phayao DPW, Hill-Tribes Development and Welfare Centre to get enough to eat.

Another detrimental impact which has accompanied the widespread adoption of monocropping systems is germplasm erosion. A recent survey in which I was involved found that many kinds of plants which used to be grown have disappeared. This is especially evident in communities favourably served by roads and transport services.

Specialisation also encourages farmers to change their scale of operation, fell more forest to increase the size of their holdings and bring marginal land under cultivation with machines, thus increasing the risk of serious soil erosion.

Rice is another crop which causes both academic researchers and development workers concern. The speed at which varieties possessing many good adaptive qualities are being replaced by higher yielding improved varieties that require careful management, especially the application of fertilizer, is a serious if incipient problem. In response to this, DPW along with the Rice Research Institute (RRI) undertook responsibility in 1980 to collect and conduct experiments with many varieties of hill rice. From 1983-1984 the International Board for Plant Genetic Resources gave support to this effort by passing through the International Rice Research Institute, the RRI and the Ministry of Agriculture and Cooperatives a request that the author, in cooperation with other field workers of the provincial Hill Tribe Welfare and Development Centres, collect samples of all available types of highland rice. Rice cultivars collected over the period 1980-1984 include more than 1100 varieties, all of which are kept at the National Rice Germplasm Centre, Pathum Thani Province.

Other traditional crops still grown are being collected. In 1986 the Tribal Research Institute, in a joint project with Chiang Mai University, began to gather legumes. Other plant materials are being collected to establish their scientific names, describe their structure, fertility, productivity, utility, chemical content and other characteristics. Legumes were singled out as a high priority because they are an important source of protein, alongside meat recovered from wild animals, fish and domestic livestock. At the time of writing more than ten distinct types had been identified.

Based on the experience of how subsistence and semi-subsistence traditional agricultural systems like those of the highlands of Thailand have changed in other parts of the world, profound underlying changes have yet to exhibit the full extent of their impact here. Aggressive "Top-Down" development projects which think for people and assume that as experts they know best can often come to decisions which in the long run endanger the wide variety of indigenous germplasm by replacing it with a few improved varieties. There are many examples of this having happened. *Pin kaew* rice used to be the best known rice grown in Thailand. It won many world rice competitions in the 1920s and 30s but already germplasm is difficult to find. The same thing has almost happened to the "400 variety" of rice grown by the Lahu Nyi and Meo. This variety grows very well on or about the 1,000 metre contour. The disappearance of this variety does not serve the government's policy to encourage highlanders to give up opium growing and to help them establish permanent villages. In the absence of the "400 variety" Meo and Lahu Nyi have been forced to abandon high altitude settlements and relocate in areas suitable for growing paddy rice and marketable cash crops. It is interesting to note that this variety first disappeared from communities served by extension workers who commenced work quite recently (1980). After searching for more than six years, we think that we have found a source of this seed with the Lisu. Good quality germplasm is required by plant breeders. In the sample found a single panicle sets from 300 to

400 seeds and under really favourable conditions spreads out to establish up to ten stems.

The Future

Clearly, rice is only one of many food crops traditionally grown by highlanders in a system of cultivation which includes a multitude of medicinal plants and others grown for use in rituals.

Many plants have recently been introduced into cropping systems by highlanders and extension workers to maintain favourable soil characteristics. Amongst these is found lablab bean *Lablab purpureus*(L.), sweet and rice bean *Vigna umbellata* (Thunb.) Ohwi & Ohashi. These plants will play an increasingly important role, particularly in the development of more intensive land use.

Since the 1970s, lowland Thai farmers in Kampaeng Phet province have developed a pattern of mixed cropping alternating between maize and rice bean which has proved to be quite successful in maintaining soil fertility. The rice bean can be sown by itself and also mixed with maize to inhibit weed growth until harvested in late December, early January. The germination of weeds in the following season will be greatly reduced, enabling farmers to single crop maize for a considerable period. Meo, Yao and Lisu have adopted this mixed cropping system. Since 1975 the rice bean has been introduced into their cropping systems on steep slopes and produced very encouraging results. Those who use it, especially the Yao, have found they can bring steep slopes classified as loamy soils under long term cultivation where previously they were restricted to two to three years before it became necessary to fallow. Some of the fields cultivated by this method have now been used continually for more than 10 years and produce good harvests, slightly reduced in more recent years, but still sufficient to justify farming. Good yields have been maintained even though clearing is restricted to burning instead

Highland Agriculture

of plowing. By planting maize and rice bean in a mixed cropping system farmers are able to extend the period of land use well beyond that which prevailed in the past.

As this system is extended to other highland villages we can expect, especially in communities which grow maize as animal feed (such as the Meo, Yao, Akha, Lisu and Lahu),that it will have a very positive impact on the development of land use intensification and enable more people to earn their livelihood than was possible under traditional extensive agriculture. Not only does the method reduce the need for weeding but it also produces a cash crop for sale. If it is to produce problems, one can expect them to be manifest in an increasing pest population. Highlanders have shown that they are willing to use pesticides on crops grown on fertile soils. However, if heavy use is made of pesticides,further problems are likely to be experienced.

During the period in which considerable attention has been given to highland development, both academics and agricultural extension workers have attempted to identify a cropping system focused on hill rice within a relay or sequential cropping system by selecting several plants, especially legumes, that would serve as a good second crop. Experiments have been carried out with several varieties of beans such as mung bean, soya bean and peanut, and also kitchen plants which could be grown before or after the harvest. An inter-cropping system has been tried unsuccessfully. Some of the plants used in the experiment need too much water. Some plants whose water requirements are low are intolerant of cold weather. Until about 1980, lowland farmers in Chiang Mai province planted lablab bean, which is tolerant of cold, dry conditions in their upland rice fields, under a sequential cropping system and achieved good results. Highlanders have adapted this system and also achieved good results as long as the rains do not stop completely in the critical period between October and November. Lablab bean has also been grown as a second crop after rice for as long as four years.

Even though rice and lablab bean are not grown in sequence as widely as possible, it may well prove to be important in the future. Intensive research needs to be carried out to see if this combination would enable farmers to reduce the fallow period of rice fields, particularly those of the Lua, Karen, Htin and Khamu, most of whom are subsistence farmers who grow rice for their own needs and very few cash crops. Lablab bean could provide a cash crop which contributes to soil conservation. The use of fertilizer may be necessary.

During this present period of rapid population growth any technique which would make it possible to intensify land use should be investigated.

Much more work should have been done earlier on traditional plant associations, cropping systems and the way in which these fit into the wider socio-economic system. Some of the traditional crops have proved to have greater commercial value than was anticipated. One example of this is: hemp *Cannabis sativa* Lin., which Meo use principally as a fibre to make clothing which is sold in considerable quantities on the Chiang Mai market. It has been estimated that the value of the hemp sold is worth about two million baht per year. Other examples include; peach (pickled), coriander (seed), betel pepper, Siam cardamon and even the trees which provide shade for coffee trees, *maa khaen (Zanthoxylum limonella Alston),* which can be used as a herb, spice or condiment. This is planted by Lampang highlanders as shade for their coffee and farmers have made so much money from them that they must be recognised as an important cash crop in their own right.

Conclusion

In this paper I have identified some of the salient characteristics of contemporary agriculture in the highlands and uplands. Most farmers have a long history of occupation and the agricultural systems developed over the centuries have only been subject to drastic change over the past few decades. These changes have involved a considerable loss of independence and self-sufficiency. If the genetic diversity of the indigenous systems is not to be lost, deliberate intervention on the part of researchers and other scientists is a matter of considerable urgency. Development projects themselves could gainfully pay more attention to the sophistication of traditional farming and help avoid a situation where exposure to soil erosion and vulnerability to both the lowland market economy and biological over-specialisation could place the welfare of highland communities at risk.

References

Anderson, E.F. (1986) "Ethnobotany of Hill Tribes of Northern Thailand. I. Medicinal Plants of the Akha" *Economic Botany* 40 (2): 38-53.

Anderson, E.F. (1986) "Ethnobotany of Hill Tribes of Northern Thailand II. Medicinal Plants of the Lahu" *Economic Botany* 40 (4): 442-50.

Black, Robert (1985) *Three language check lists of plant names* (Thai-English-Scientific), Klang Wiang Karnpim Co., Ltd: Chiang Mai.

Department of Agriculture (1979) *List of Plant Names* Germplasm Standard Subdivision, Field Crops Division: Bangkok (In Thai).

Isara Sooksathan et al (1983) "Research on Industrial Oil Crops for Opium Substitution on the Highlands of Northern Thailand" (Final report on research, July 1980 - June 1983) Highland Agriculture Project, Kasetsart University: Bangkok (mimeo).

Kunstadter, P., S. Sabhasri, and T. Smitinand (1978) "Flora of a Forest Fallow Farming Environment in Northwestern Thailand" *Journal of the National Research Council* Thailand Vol. 10 No. 1.

Kwanyeun Wichapan et al (1976) "Essential Oil Production in the Highlands of Northern Thailand"

Misc. Invest., No.85/Rep. No.4, Applied Scientific Research Corporation of Thailand: Bangkok (mimeo).

Lin, Chao-Hsiung (1975)
"Vegetable Herb and Flower Seed Production Trials", UN/Thai Programme for Drug Abuse Control, Bangkok: Thailand (mimeo).

Oradee Sahawatcharin (1985)
National Tree Planting Day 2529 P. Sampanpanit Ltd. partnership: Bangkok (In Thai).

Pavin Punsri et al (1984)
"Research on Small Fruit Production as Substitute Crops for Opium-Poppy" (Final report, October 1979 - September 1984) Highland Agriculture project, Kasetsart University: Bangkok (mimeo).

Pavin Punsri et al (1985)
"Exotic Fruit production as a Substitute for Opium Poppy in the Highlands of Thailand" (Final Report, August 1982 - July 1985) Highland Agriculture Project, Kasetsart University: Bangkok (mimeo).

Pisit Voraurai et al (1979)
"Ornamental Plants as Replacement Crops for Opium Poppy in Northern Thailand" (Final Report, May 1976 - May 1979) Faculty of Agriculture, Chiang Mai University: Chiang Mai (mimeo).

Purseglove, J.W. (1974)
Tropical Crops, Dicotyledons Longman: London.

Purseglove, J.W. (1975) — ***Tropical Crops, Monocotyledons*** Longman: London.

Reader's Digest Encyclopaedia (1972) — **Garden plants and flowers** Reader's Digest Association Limited: London.

Sanong Voraurai (1980) — Personal Communication, May - June.

Tang, Robert C., (1977) — "Report of the Vegetable and Flower Seed Production Consultant" UN/Thai Programme for Drug Abuse Control: Bangkok (mimeo).

Tang, Robert C., (1977) — "Report on the Vegetable and Flower Seed Production potential in Northern Thailand" UN/Thai Programme for Drug Abuse Control, Bangkok, Thailand (mimeo).

Tem Smitinand (1980) — **Thai Plant Names** Funny Publications Ltd., Bangkok.

"Thai-Australia Highland Agronomy Project First Report" (1972-1975) — Report to the Department of Public Welfare and Chiang Mai University on Pasture Agronomy Research (mimeo).

Zeven, A.C. and P.M. Zhukovsky (1975) — **Dictionary of Cultivated Plants and their Centers of Diversity, Excluding Ornamentals, Forest Trees and Lower Plants** Centre for Agriculture, Publishing and Documentation: Wageningen.

"Women and Children First"? A Review of the Current Nutritional Status in the Highlands.

Ralana Maneeprasert

When a ship is sinking it is a long standing maritime tradition for women and children to be among the first assigned to the life boats. It is often remarked upon in feminist literature, that within disadvantaged societies women and children make up a further disadvantaged minority which makes rescue necessary in the first place. Is there a nutritional crisis developing in the highlands which requires that a rescue be mounted? What is the position of women and children?

Although a comprehensive survey of nutrition in the highlands has yet to be carried out, research by various anthropologists, medical doctors and development teams has so far pointed to endemic malnutrition among highlanders. Women and children appear to be the worst affected.

Highlanders are heavily dependent on rice as a source of nutrition but this is in critical short supply in some areas. Protein Energy Malnutrition (PEM) and Vitamin Deficiency are the most serious problems observed. More research is urgently needed.

At a workshop held recently in Chiang Mai, Dr Sorenson a Danish medical doctor and paediatrician, stated that the consequences of a poor diet, if not corrected, could result in a population already disadvantaged politically becoming totally demoralised and eventually physically and mentally handicapped (Vryhied & Sorenson, 1986: 225-269).

A recent formal talk given by Dr Vichai Poshyachinda of the Drug Dependence Research Center, Institute of Health Research, Chulalongkorn University at the Tribal Research Institute emphasize that tribal people have for some time been facing nutritional problems, traceable in part to the impact of development programmes (see also Chupinit, Chapter 3). The establishment of rice mills alone has resulted in riboflavin deficiencies manifest in angular stomatitis.

These are serious charges made by professional people who have carried out fieldwork in the highlands. Their opinions must be acknowledged and examined carefully. Such observations cannot be ignored.

Even relatively brief and simple studies can highlight the seriousness of malnutrition and disease in the highlands. A pilot anthropometric assessment I conducted among Akha children in August, 1986, showed that only nine out of 53 children in the village of Mae Salaep were of normal weight for their age. All children between the ages of 1-60 months were measured, 53 altogether, 23 were found to be under weight while 19 exhibited acute levels of malnutrition and two fell into the chronic malnutrition bracket. Both were in a critical state.

Infants in their first year were the healthiest, 80 percent of these children showed no sign of malnutrition. The most disadvantaged group were children between one and five years of age. The majority of these suffered from first and second degree malnutrition. The most dangerous period for children occurs immediately after they are weaned.

The month after the survey, I learned that two of the children had died, a boy and a girl, both five years old. The boy had been suffering from chronic malnutrition. When I had interviewed the boy's father, the child was suffering from a high fever, looked pale and was occasionally shaken with muscular spasms. The spasms could well have been a manifestation of infection, bronchiolitis, as well as vitamin B deficiency. His paleness indicated anemia which could also have been caused by vitamin B deficiency and parasites.

There is a close relationship between nutritional shortfalls and infection. An inadequate diet greatly increases the risk of acquiring infection which in turn is more likely to intensify in those who have a poor diet. When children contract an infection during a critical phase of malnutrition, the effect is always very serious.

Protein deficiency
This is one of the most serious aspects of malnutrition in the highlands. One of the first studies of highlander diets was carried out by a team led by Dr Thatsanai Parsingha in 1976 among Akha and Yao communities in Chiang Rai for the Department of Public Welfare. In his final unpublished report he stated that the main nutritional problems faced by these people was that of protein deficiency. The hardest hit group were children between two and five years of age. He also found a high incidence of parasitosis.

In 1986, the Thai-Norwegian Church Aid Highland Development Project found evidence of PEM and vitamin A and B deficiencies in project villages but on the basis of superficial observations, a consultant, Miriam Krantz, concluded that the problems had not yet reached a severe stage.

Vitamin Deficiencies
The most commonly reported vitamin deficiencies are of A and B. Some of these shortfalls can be traced to overmilling

of rice and inappropriate cooking methods. as well as general lack of food.

A survey of Hmong and Mien in a refugee camp in Nan province carried out by a team led by Dr Atireg Na Thalang in 1977 showed that while the weight and height of tribal refugee children were better than that of Thai rural children, clinical examinations found a high prevalence of vitamin A and B deficiency.

A more recent study of Lahu children in Chiang Rai province in March, 1985, by Vibon and Nithiya Rattanapanone showed vitamin A and B_2 deficiencies, as well as a high incidence of anemia and dental caries. It is well known that fat facilitates the absorption of certain vitamins, such as A, D, E and K, but the amount of fat eaten in hill tribe diets is low (Ralana Maneeprasert, 1978; CATAD, 1986). In the highlands vitamin A is readily available from green-leaf vegetables and many kinds of fresh fruit, such as papaya, grown in backyard gardens. One possible explanation of vitamin A deficiency is not the supply of the vitamin itself but the lack of fat.

Malnutrition Disorders
  Goitre. There is no need for this to appear as an endemic disorder because it is easily avoided. Goitre, caused mainly by lack of iodine, is closely associated with PEM, vitamin A and B_1 deficiency, urinary bladder stone disease and malaria. People take this disorder for granted because the clinical signs develop slowly and the host becomes accustomed to the discomfort. People do not realise that it is an impediment to health.

  Nutritional Anemia. This is a condition where hemoglobin levels are lower than normal. The normal hemoglobin level (HBAA) for adult Thais recommended by the World Health Organisation should not drop below 12 or 13 per

Nutritional Status

100 ml. (Aree Valyasevi, 1977:-186). As with many other disorders, nutritional anemia is prevalent in the highlands. Characteristic paleness is a common clinical sign easily identified and usually occurs in association with other disorders. The most common are parasitosis, PEM and vitamin deficiencies. Dietary factors are clearly the principal causes of nutritional anemia.

Beri-beri. This is a disease associated with polished rice. Generally, infantile beri-beri is found in babies of 2-6 months who are breast-fed while their mothers are suffering from a thiamin (B_1) deficiency. Viseshakul (et. al., 1978: 29) estimated that infantile beri-beri may account for up to 33 percent of hill tribe infant deaths in Mae Chan. But because tribal infants are usually breast fed and milled rice is used widely, it is highly likely that this problem is common. In some villages there is more than one mill. I found three rice mills in the Lua village of Pa Pae in the course of a survey carried out in 1981. By reducing the workload of women, mills can make a positive contribution to their standard of living but the overmilling of rice so that thiamin (B_1) and riboflavin (B_2) are polished off actually adds to their difficulties.

The Role of Rice

Rice is the staple food in the highlands, providing the main source of energy and protein, but is often in short supply for a variety of reasons, including lack of land and population growth. The situation in some villages is critical.

Rice is mainly cultivated for family consumption; corn is grown for feeding domestic animals and opium can provide a source of cash to meet shortfalls in the household production system. In the extended family, the rice and corn harvest is shared between all members but cash earnings from the sale of opium belong to those who managed the fields. Today opium is no longer a secure source of income even though many households still rely on it.

Where suitable land is available, rice is by far the most important crop. Surplus rice and corn may also be sold. Where rice cannot be grown then corn, potato, soya bean, sesame, cotton, garlic, chilli and tea may become the main source of income. Rice means security. The greater the harvest the greater the security. The principal objective of highland farmers is to satisfy their domestic needs in anyway possible rather than simply grow everything they need to eat.

Rice not only plays a significant role in nutrition but also provides the raw material for many other significant functions in daily life. Glutinous rice is used for making both liquor and a cake *(khaw pook)* served at ceremonies. Most ceremonies within the ritual cycle of all ethnic groups involve the use of rice. The Lahu Sheleh for example have nine rites for rice and four rites for opium poppy (Chantaboon Sutthi, 1982).

Duangmanee Viseshakul led a survey of an Akha village in Chiang Rai in 1982 and found that so long as rice was sufficient to cover calory needs then enough protein with respect to nitrogen and essential amino acids was also provided. When supplies of rice fell short, it was young children, pregnant women and lactating mothers who were most likely to suffer from deficiencies.

A nutritionist, Petra Windisch, working with a team from the Technical University of Berlin in a study of Wawi village, Chiang Rai, found that symptoms of malnutrition were more evident among women and children than in men. She noted that the situation could well deteriorate in the near future because of short supplies of upland rice, low consumption and associated nutritional problems (Schubert et. al. 1986: 102-121).

A paper prepared by Peter Hoare (1985) on Lahu communities in Chiang Mai and Chiang Rai provinces observed that rice provided between 59 and 95 percent of household energy

Nutritional Status

intake. Higher income households purchased both more rice and also other sources of protein from the market. Villagers did not buy any source of carbohydrate other than rice. His weight for height survey revealed that infants aged 0-5 years suffered from chronic malnutrition.

In a 1978 survey of Meo (Hmong) which I co-directed, it was found that highlanders ate 833 grams of rice per day per head as against 525 grams eaten by lowlanders although both highlanders and lowlanders ate much the same amount of meat (Ralana Maneeprasert, 1978). Hinton's figure for the Karen indicates a similarly high consumption of rice, 770 grams per day per man unit. Rice provides the additional calories required when hard work is undertaken. If highlanders have enough rice, it provides their protein and energy needs but exclusive consumption is not recommended for women and children who need a more adequately balanced diet of nutrients if they are to perform both field and domestic tasks (Duangmanee Viseshakul, 1976). Women breast feeding their children must be well fed themselves to ensure healthy growth rates for their offspring. PEM is much too high in tribal women and children to guarantee good health.

Although their home pounded rice contains a higher quantity of protein nutrients, 8.5 grams of protein per 100 grams compared to 7.4 grams in lowland milled rice (Ralana Maneeprasert, 1978), much of this advantage is lost in washing, rinsing and in the method of cooking.

The average yield of highland rice is about 20-40 *tang* per rai and for paddy field 50 *tang* (1 *tang* = 15 kilos). Typically, farmers at best produce enough to feed themselves for ten months (TRI, 1985). For at least two months they must cope with a shortfall. Food shortages are widespread and highland populations are growing at a faster rate than food production. Farmers expect to face, sometime during the year, a "hungry season".

Raised under healthy conditions where communities established in virgin forest have access to a wide range of food, children may, however, achieve better growth rates than lowlanders. A survey of hill tribe refugees in Nan who had recently arrived from Laos exhibited a better growth status than Thai rural children (Atireg Na Thalang, 1977).

Food and Sexism

Highland women and children are regarded as second class citizens in their own communities. As a consequence they are sometimes ignored, perhaps inadvertently, when assistance. is offered by outside agencies. In a very real structural sense they belong to a disadvantaged group within a disadvantaged population. In most highland societies the men eat first and women and children have what is left over. Where householders eat from a common bowl, young children often face fierce competition to get a fair share of the food. The household head and male members of the family are favoured with larger portions of available food especially meat. Such eating practices have a marked detrimental impact on the nutritional status of woman and children.

The status of girls or daughters is generally beneath that of male offspring; consequently fewer resources are invested in them including food, health care and education, because it is expected that on marriage they will leave the family. Sons are expected to look after their parents in their old age and by enhancing their economic position parents are ensuring their own future.

The study of nutrition in the highlands cannot ignore the structural matters which determine distribution of food among household members. In my experience the head of the family shows little awareness of the need to see that the nutrient intake of women and children is adequate, although it should be noted that women generally prepare meals. Extensive animal studies

Nutritional Status

have shown that malnutrition retards the development of the brain. If the socio-political position of women and children is lower than that of men, and if this group is denied enough food to ensure healthy maturation, then this deprivation may actually be structured into their physiology and adversely affect their ability to secure a good living. As their position deteriorates so does their ability to deal with it.

More research is needed into the structural position of women and children within highland societies with respect to the highlanders' overall nutritional condition.

Cultural Influences

Food is more than just a source of nutrients and there can be close associations between cultural practices and malnutrition.

In the course of a recent field trip to an Akha village I carefully observed the eating behaviour of three different families. Women and children did not share meals with us but ate on their own in a separate room or in the kitchen after the men. On the first day I ate with the men green mustard prepared in two different ways, as a boiled vegetable available at the season and as a home-made pickle.

The second day was the monthly holiday, rabbit day. Most people stayed at home. One pig was killed and butchered with pieces sold to neighbours. Two special side dishes of spiced pork were served. One was raw (c.f. Bernatzik, 1947: 88) and the other cooked in oil served with various fresh green vegetables.

Usually, the whole family eats together. An exception is made to this custom on holidays or if guests appear. On special days members of the family prefer to eat separately. Only men eat with outsiders. Children eat with their mothers.

Rice is the main component of every meal. It is soaked overnight in water and steamed in a wooden steamer. The family with whom I ate had 11 members: nine adults and only two children. Every day 10 kilograms of rice are cooked, enough for three meals. This was done by the mother on the morning of the day I first visited her. She steamed the rice twice. The first time took an hour, the second about 40 minutes. The method of cooking rice differs from that described by the anthropologist Bernatzik some 40 years ago:

> The Akha soak it overnight in water and boil it in the same water for about ten minutes. The excess liquid is then squeezed out with the hands and finally the rice is steamed in a wooden steamer until it is done (Bernatzik, 1947:88).

These methods are quite different from those used by the Hmong and are scrupulously clean. Wherever possible they pipe water into their kitchens. It is only when community workers attempt to change things that cultural barriers become evident. Hill tribe people are attached to traditional ways of preparing food. Food habits and methods of cooking are known to belong to their ancestors. Socialization is so effective people do not question the old ways.

The many different cultures in the highlands each have different ideas about how food should be cultivated, harvested, prepared, served and eaten. Culture determines dietary beliefs and practices at a very deep level. Cultural knowledge systems classify food into groups such as hot and cold, sacred or profane, medicinal or social, the last category being food that may only be consumed in the presence of guests.

Dog meat is eaten by the Akha. It is also used as a medicine as well as a social food. Mothers are known to recover their strength quickly after giving birth if they have enough dog meat.

Such meat is also served as a special dish to welcome visitors. Buffalo are very important in the funeral ceremonies of both the Hmong and Akha.

From a clinical perspective cultural influences may affect nutrition in two ways. First, people may exclude much needed nutrients from their diet by imposing a negative classification such as non-food or lower-class food or hot-food. Second, they may encourage the taking of certain food or drinks injurious to health by defining them as sacred or medicinal to reinforce social, religious or ethnic identity. These food categories can become confused or disposed of altogether. For example, when liquor traditionally used for religious purposes becomes a popular social beverage then problems can occur. It can be difficult for people to adjust to a new diet when forced to in times of change and environmental degradation.

Where Next?
The need for better data on nutritional problems in the highlands is evident. Surveys should firmly identify the importance of the main staple crops in their diet, their origin, their distribution and when the "hungry season" occurs. A wide variety of methods needs to be used such as anthropometic assessment, clinical examination and biochemical tests.

From this review of nutritional problems in the highlands it is clear that life is much more difficult for hill people than for the majority of lowlanders. This is not to say that lowlanders are immune to this problem so closely associated with poverty. The many Thais who have yet to enjoy the benefits of development should not be ignored for they also have their "hungry season". Highlanders, both Thai and those belonging to discrete ethnic minorities, demand our professional attention not only to establish the parameters of their deprivation but also to find out what can be done about it.

PROBLEMS

There can be little doubt that the hill tribes are a disadvantaged population. Although women remain in charge of cooking, for reasons that are not clear, women and children are most likely to be the victims of malnutrition. This needs to be more firmly established. The itinerant eating habits of children and the unavailability in an impoverished environment of foods on which to snack may provide one explanation.

One possible way to reduce malnutrition among infants and children is to set up day care centres. Experiments in their use have already been mounted at Phra Bat Huai Tom, a Karen village in Lamphun. Dr Ousa Thanungkul has reported (1983) the direct benefits of providing supplementary foods which greatly reduced anemia and PEM among children there. However, as a solution on a wider scale, this strategy leaves much to be desired. Making welfare recipients of highlanders is no substitute for enhancing their overall ability to secure a living from the land by their own labour.

As to the future, all that can be said is that it looks grim. Lao Tsu has advised us in a moral, political strategy. "The wise ...rule by emptying hearts and stuffing bellies, by weakening ambitions and strengthening bones." Although we have much to learn before we can answer the question, "Is nutritional crisis developing in the highlands?" it is clear that our professional strategy must be to look first at the position of women and children.

References

Aree Valyasevi et al. (1977) — *Nutritional Diseases* Bangkok: Faculty of Medicine, Mahidol University, Vol. 1 (in Thai).

Atireg Na Thalang, Surin Chaithachawong, Yingsak Jiemchaisri (1977) — "The Health Survey in Anthropometic Assessement and Nutritional Status of the Hill Tribe Populations in the Refugee Camp at Ban Nam Yao, Poe, Nan Province" *Chulalongkorn Medical Journal* Vol. 21, No. 4: 304-09 (in Thai).

Bernatzik, H.A. (1947) — *Akha and Meo: Problem of Applied Ethnology in the Indo-Chinese Penninsula (Southeast-Asia)* Vol 2 Army Translation Service Washington D.C., Translation No. J-0643.

Chantaboon Sutthi (1982) — *Rice in Swidden Agriculture* Chiang Mai: Tribal Research Institute (in Thai).

Charas Suwanwela, et al. (1987) — *Primary Health Care in the Hill Tribe Village* Bangkok: Institute of Health Research, Chulalongkorn University.

Duangmanee Viseshakul et al. (1978) — "The Nutritional Status of the Hill Tribe Children and Their Lactating Mothers" *Journal of the Medical Association of Thailand* Vol.61, No. 1, January: 26-32.

Duangmanee
Viseshakul et al.
(1979)

"A Field Trial of Supplementary Feeding in Hill Tribe of Supplementary Feeding in Hill Tribe Children (1-4 years old): One Year Follow-up Study" *Journal of the Medical Association of Thailand* Vol. 62, No. 4, April: 190-199.

Duangmanee
Viseshakul
Vasanti Na Songla,
Sin Punsa
(1982)

"Rice Consumption of Hill Tribe People of Northern Thailand" *Journal of the Medical Association of Thailand* Vol. 65, No. 3, March: 133-138.

Hinton, Peter
(1975)

Karen Subsistence: The limits of a swidden economy in north Thailand Unpublish Ph.D. dissertation, The University of Sydney.

Hoare, Peter, W.C.
(1985)

"The Movement of Lahu Hill People Towards a Lowland Life stlye in Northern Thailand: A Study of Three Villages". In Walker, Anthony, R. ed., *Contributions to Southeast Asian Ethnography* No. 4, August 1985: 75-77.

Krantz, Miriam
(1986)

Nutrition Report Chiang Mai: Thai Norwegian Church Aid, Highland Development Project.

McKinnon, John
(1983)

"Introductory Essay; a Highlander's Geography of the Highlands: Mythology, Process and Fact" *Journal of Mountain Research and Development,* Vol. 3, No. 4: 313-317.

Mead, Margaret (1943) "The Factor of Food Habits" *The Annuals of the American Academy of Political and Social Science Nutrition and Food Supply: the War and After* John D. Black (ed.) Volume 225, Philadelphia: The American Academy of Political and Social Science.

Ousa Thanangkul (1983) *Infant and Child care Centers Project.* Chiang Mai: Research Institute for Health Sciences, Chiang Mai University, Final (unpublished) report to the Asia Foundation.

Panja Kulapongs (1985) *Nutritional Anemias in Recent Advances in Hematology 1985* Chiang Mai: Department of Clinical Microscopy, Chiang Mai University (in Thai).

Ralana Maneeprasert (1979) *A study of Human Food Consumption in Selected Meo Villages at Doi Pa Kia, Chiang Dao, Chiang Mai* Tribal Research Institute: Chiang Mai (mimeo, in Thai).

Scrimshaw, N.S., C.E. Taylor and J.E. Gordon (1968) *Interactions of Nutrition and Infection* Geneva: World Health Organization (WHO Monograph Series No. 57).

Tribal Research Institute and Department of Political Science, Chiang Mai University (1985)
A Socio-Cultural Study of the Impact of Social Development Programs on Tribal Woman and Children Tribal Research Institute: Chiang Mai.

Viboon Rattanapanone, Nithiya Rattanapanone. (1985)
"Nutritional Status of Musur (Hill Tribe) Children at Huay Pong Village in Chiang Rai" *Nutrition Conference'85. Programme and Abstracts* Bangkok: Institute of Nutrition, Mahidol University.

Vryheid, Robert E. and Birte Sorensen (1986)
" 'Too Many People Are Selling All Their Beans without Eating Any'. Nutritional Problems and Agricultural Practices Among Thai Hill Tribes" *Data Requirements For Highland Farming System Development* Proceedings of a Workshop sponsored by FAO & Payap Research Center. Payap University: Chiang Mai.

Weteki, Catherine E. (1986)
"Dietary Survey Data: Sources and of Limits to Interpretation" *Journal Nutrition Reviews, Supplement* Vol. 44, May: 204-212.

World Health Organization (1974)
Handbook on Human Nutritional Requirements Geneva: World Health Organization (WHO Monograph Series No. 61).

31. Akha swing (Vienne)

32. Akha consulting liver (Vienne)

33. Akha ceremony (Vienne)

34. Lahu Sheleh ceremony (Supachai)

35. Preparing Akha cakes (Vienne)

36. Akha sacrifice (Vienne)

37. Burning forest (McKinnon) 38. Burnt-over garden (Hobday)

39. Cut swidden ready to burn (Connell)

40. Wheat field (Connell)

41. Fields of Red Kidney bean (Connell)

42. Irrigated rice terraces (Connell)

43. Akha ploughing, Doi Chang (McKinnon)

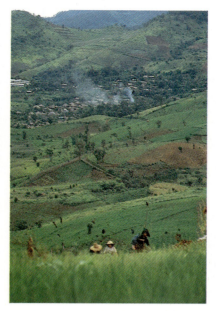 

44. Highland town, Doi Chang (McKinnon)   45. Doi Chang fields (McKinnon)

46. Akha land use, Mae Salaep (Vienne)

47. Grass strips, Doi Chang (McKinnon)

48. Tomato field; Doi Chang (McKinnon)

Opiate of the People? A Case Study of Lahu Opium Addicts

Sanit Wongsprasert

In the **Communist Manifesto** Karl Marx refered to religion as the "opiate of the people". What did he mean? In his lifetime educated people's opinion of opium changed drastically from one of amused tolerance to real concern: the smoking of opium for pleasure was seen to have a strongly demoralising influence on society. Surely religion provides a strong moral influence on society? We can expect an atheist to show his mistrust of religion but how exactly was Marx using the term?

The image is a weapon of criticism used against religion. Marx sees religion as if it were opium used as a sedative to reduce pain, soothe feelings and dull critical judgement. Is this what opium does for highlanders living on the margins of a modern state which is very much involved in the realities of the twentieth century? What is it that makes people become addicts? Who are those most likely to become victims? How successful are the rehabilitation treatments? Do the highlanders themselves see addiction as a problem?

In this Chapter I shall discuss these questions with reference to three Lahu villages in which I worked as the social science advisor to a project set up principally to identify a better agricultural extension strategy for use in hill tribe villages. I speak Lahu and have worked in other Lahu communities since 1965.

PROBLEMS

The information presented here focuses on the villages Huai Pong, Huai Nam Rin and Doi Mod located in Wiang Pa Pao district, Chiang Rai but also draws on my field work experience in many other villages. The specific research in this report was carried out by the Tribal Research Institute, the Hill Tribe Development and Welfare Centre, Chiang Rai and the Faculty of Agriculture of Chiang Mai University. Field work was supported by the Royal (Northern) Project and the United States Department of Agriculture and was carried out between 1982-86.

When field work commenced nearly all households in these villages were growing opium (1982/83). By 1985 Huai Pong, which in 1982 had produced a small crop of only 2 kilograms per household, had stopped growing opium altogether. Huai Nam Rin, which also relied on opium production (average production of 1.9 kilograms per household (1982/3)), had stepped back production to approximately 0.5 kilogram per household. Despite this fall in production, addiction rates remained high. None of the villages were self-sufficient in rice and many of the poorer households had to struggle for a living. Although the average gross income per houshold per annum had increased from baht 3,227 to 13,313 in Huai Pong and from baht 9,421 to 12,893 in Huai Nam Rin, small farmers cultivating only 2 rai were, materially speaking, not much better off.

Who are the addicts?
Out of a total population of 480 living in 87 households I counted 79 addicts: 16.5 percent of the total population. Addiction was determined on the criterion of habitual and compulsive smoking of at least one pipe daily (3.3 grams). Sixty three percent of addicts were men (50 individuals) and 37 percent women (29 individuals). In Doi Mod all of the men between the ages of 20-24, some three individuals, were addicted and all save one individual in the 25-29 cohort (again three individuals). By far the most vulnerable were not the older people who could claim to have earned the right to be self-indulgent and to have chosen to spend the last years of their life in a drugged state (as might

Lahu Opium Addiction

be true of the Hmong) but those who had just entered into their majority and were in the prime of their lives. In my sample villages, males between the ages of 20 and 39 made up nearly 30 percent of all addicts (24 individuals) and females in this same age group made up over 21 percent of the total (17 individuals). The impact on both the reproductive and the productive capacity of the community is considerable.

A better idea of the distribution of addicts can be gained from an examination of the population pyramids on the opposite page. If addiction rates are any indication of the morale of a community, then Doi Mod was the most demoralised village. Out of a total population of 40 above the age of twenty years nearly 50 percent or 19 people smoked opium everyday. In this village two men under the age of 20 smoked, surely a clear indication of the pessimism with which this community faces the future.

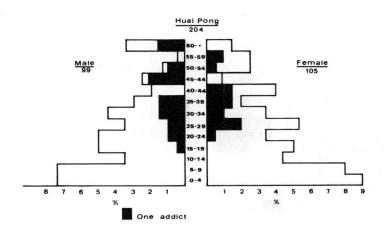

PROBLEMS

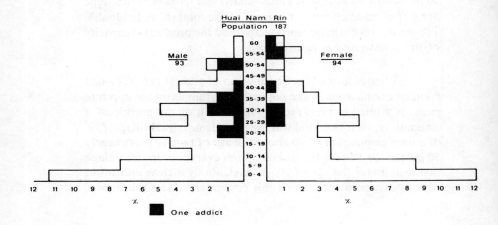

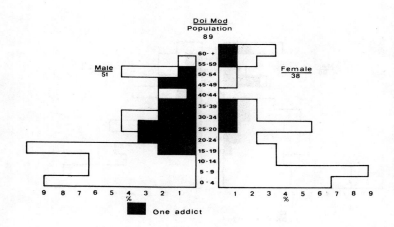

On average most smokers were married (over 60 percent) and had been addicted for 9-10 years. I did not find any unmarried females who smoked but 14 percent of all male addicts had not been married. Those who had suffered marital trauma by death of a spouse, been abandoned or divorced were more highly represented in the addicted group than the general population. Table 1 below summarises the data from which I have drawn these observations.

Table 1 Addicts by Sex, Average, Age and Duration of Addiction; Marital Status

Village	Number	Sex		Average		Marital Status (%)				
		M: F:	male female	Age	Years Addicted	Married	Widowed	Divorced	Separated	Single
1. Huai Pong	36	M	20	36	9	83	4	4	–	9
		F	16	35	4	92	–	4	4	–
2. Huai Nam Rin	22	M	14	42	8	76	5	–	–	19
		F	8	42	11	37.5	37.5	12.5	12.5	–
3. Doi Mod	21	M	16	38	14	40	13.3	20	20	13.3
		F	5	41	8	50	33	–	–	–

Source: Field survey 1983/84

Why do people smoke?

There can be no doubt that the principal reason why people smoke is not only that opium is available but that a general sense of malaise and hopelessness pervades much of the highland world. Broad structural issues that define their precarious position in wider society exert an overall negative influence on their daily existence, making it more likely that in a crisis, they will choose this self-destructive alternative, even where their own cultural values caution them against making this choice. Endemic poverty, high infant mortality (40 percent of children die in their first year), low life expectancy (36-39 years) all contribute to this malaise. It is not surprising that so many turn to opium as a way to forget troubles.

Is it specifically because they are poor? This is a much more difficult question to answer. The short answer must be that it definitely helps. If your hold on land is precarious, if you do not have citizenship, if you do not feel strong and do not have access to health services when you are unwell, it must be a comfort to give up, forget your troubles and become a smoker.

When I ask the poverty question and review my data a clear correlation emerges: the poor are much more likely to become addicts. Only 13 percent of my sample village smokers could be considered well off, the remainder are rather poor. Beside this, the better-off addicts manage their habit rather more carefully than those who are determined to seek oblivion. They are more likely to smoke unadulterated opium. They are less likely to lace their opium with chemical analgesics like aspirin which distend the blood vessels, enhance the absorptive capacity of the lungs and stimulate circulation.

The question then arises, "Have I posed the question the wrong way around? Are people poor because they are addicts?" It is extremely difficult to state with any confidence a response which would hold true in all cases. A vicious circle of poverty and addiction provides a much more realistic explanation. To identify the cause as one or the other is to hopelessly simplify the issue.

In Table 2 the socio-economic situation of the two groups, addicts and non-addicts is summarised; It provides a crude measure of industriousness. Clearly, on average, non-addicts cultivate larger fields of all crops including opium, commit more labour to agricultural tasks and get higher yields. Non-addicts are more likely, on average, to engage themselves for longer periods in off-farm work. The non-smoking population also secures a higher average income, 133 baht as against 104 baht per month.

Table 2 Comparison of the Agricultural Effort and Production of Lahu Non-addict and Addict Farmers (1983/84)

Activity	Non-addict		Addict	
	Ave.	Households involved (%)	Ave.	Households involved (%)
Opium Poppy				
Area Cultivated (rai)	1.6	67	1.4	71
Labour input (man/days)	90		70	
Yield (grammes)	1,334		889	
Dry-rice				
Area Cultivated (rai)	4.5	86	5.0	76
Labour input (man/days)	200		128	
Yield (kilogrammes)	240		108	
Maize				
Area Cultivated (rai)	3.0	77	2.6	84
Labour input (man/days)	140		120	
Yield (kilogrammes)	768		500	
Red Kidney Bean				
Area Cultivated (rai)	1.7	79	1.2	76
Labour input (man/days)	79		46	
Yield (kilogrammes)	210		104	
Wage and Forest Employment				
Number of working days	129	56	97	74
Income per household (per month in baht)	133		104	

Note: Total number of non-addict households surveyed was 52, and addict households 38.
Source: Field survey 1983/84

This is not to say that addict households do not try. A larger proportion of such households establish opium fields, cultivate maize and enter wage labour. They also tend to be more unrealistic about maintenance work. What is not shown in the Table is that they are ambitious starters, clearing larger fields than their available labour can cope with. They start on a large scale but finish with lower yields from poorly managed fields.

This background information to the problem does not enter into hill tribe responses when asked why they took up smoking. Their answers are quite specific to their personal experience. Professor Charus Suwanwela in a review of the reasons why people start with opium lists these as the principal causes: release from pain, as a medical sedative and for pleasure. To these I might well add, as a result of my study of the Lahu, imitation of elders and escape from depression. Table 3 summarises responses I was given.

When I review my field notes a qualitative profile can quickly be built up.

The relief of pain was given by 29 percent of my sample as a reason for starting. A young man, Leh Kui, of 20 told me that two years ago he first took opium to cure a bad stomachache and although his father had forced him to give up smoking on three different occasions, his friends insisted that he join their smoking parties as a non-paying guest. A well-to-do married man of 30, Ai Lu, addicted for four years told me that he had once taken some medicine from which he suffered a bad reaction. This caused him so much discomfort he started smoking to relieve the symptoms. Although he knows he cannot afford to smoke and often complains about the high price of opium, because of a serious skin disease he has tried to give up without success. As addicts lose their appetite and spend money on opium in preference to food, various form of malnutrition appear. Deteriorating ill health often provides a rationale for addiction.

Table 3 Reasons for Smoking Given by Addicts

Village	Number	Causes Given (%)				
		Imitate Elders	Join Spouse	Group Pressure	Sickness	Depression
— Huai Pong	36	25	30	10	31	4
— Huai Nam Rin	22	18	27	12	26	17
— Doi Mod	21	31	28	4	31	6
Total 3	79					
1	26	25	28	9	29	9

Source: Field survey 1983/84

Lahu Opium Addiction

Many start smoking as a consequence of emotional trauma. A widower fifty years old told me he began when his wife died early in their marriage. A young woman reported that she had taken up the pipe to relieve her sorrow on the death of her husband. Another because she was deserted.

Most gave the reason that they simply followed their spouse or parents. Over 50 percent of those questioned reported that they were either subject to peer pressure or copied others because it seemed to be the thing to do. Only 9 percent stated that they started simply for the pleasure it gave them.

More often than not it is combination of circumstances which leads to addiction. Ca Ku is a typical case. He comes from a family which smokes but avoided opium until after he was married. Following a domestic dispute with his wife, he sought the comfort of friends who were smokers. Within a short time he had become an addict. This story is repeated by many.

Opium treatment: does it work?

Over 70 percent of the addicts interviewed have undertaken cures. Most treatments currently in use do not work. Some 23 percent of those interviewed were not interested in considering treatment. As far as they were concerned opium gave them the strength to work and they felt that their indulgence was not a problem. Table 4 summarises their answers.

Table 4 Opium Treatment Experience

Village	Number	Treated	Never	Place of Treatment						Totals	
				Lam Pang	Chiang Mai	Tham KraBok	Chiang Dao	Fang	Village	Others	Treatments	Cost (baht)
Huai Pong	36	31	5	9	26	4	1	1	23	2	66	16,950
Huai Nam Rin	22	16	6	5	16	4	4	2	20	1	47	13,000
Doi Mod	21	14	7	8	14	–	4	–	18	1	45	13,620
Totals	79	61	18	22	56	8	9	3	61	4	158	34,570
Average											2.6	567
											1	218

Source: Field survey 1983/84

PROBLEMS

Treatment has been available since 1967 when a special facility was set up at Lampang public hospital. Many went many times. In 1970 an additional servicing clinic was set up at Suan Dok hospital in Chiang Mai. Many of those who had undergone treatment at Lampang tried Suan Dok. Again many went many times. Eight of those in my sample are veterans of such cures and have gone as far afield as Tham Kra Bok in search of the perfect cure. They are still awaiting a guru with the magic answer. Some have even attempted a cure by running away into the forest and providing their own treatment. My small sample has tried an average of 2.6 cures at an average personal cost each time of 218 baht.

It is widely reported by veterans of curative courses that although they stop while in hospital as soon as they return to the village it is extremely difficult not to take up where they left off. Some say that the physical discomforts which they relieve by smoking, such as stomach ulcers, persistent headaches, bad backs and the like are not taken seriously while they are undergoing treatment and as soon as they leave the hospital reassert themselves. Many do not like the way they are treated by medical staff and say that returning to the pipe is a way of forgetting their humiliation.

Table 4 lists "village" as the venue most often used for treatment. This is misleading in two ways. First in a general sense because treatment in situ is uncommon; and second, because the two courses of treatment conducted, although they attracted many participants, were superficial and too brief to be ranked as serious attempts at amelioration. The in-village treatments, presided over by a monk, Phra Pricha Atiwatano, lasted for only three days. These were sponsored by a well meaning group of the Bangkok National Womens Association of Thailand who could only afford to subsidise the cost of treatment for a total of ten days for each of the two sessions. In the seven days after Phra Pricha's departure one can only assume that the addicts were supposed to consolidate the cure that had already been achieved. Those who are addicted to another socially approved drug, tobacco, and have experienced the strength of dependence in the withdrawal symptoms will readily concede that neither three nor ten days is enough to effect a cure.

This is not to say that the village is the wrong place in which to attempt treatment. With community support, a well run programme could enjoy a much higher rate of success.

From this brief review of my Lahu data it can be stated with confidence that there is a close relationship between poverty and addiction. A more careful study conducted by a true master of social science could argue a strong case like Durkheim in his classic study of the close relationship between alienation and suicide. The problem of establishing causative factors is naturally different. There can be cumulative cycle of social events which lead to the final solution of suicide whereas addiction to opium can be viewed as part of an attempt to adapt to intolerable conditions.

As such, opium addiction must be seen in a category of drug dependence alongside alcoholism. If medical arguments that alcoholism is a physiological as much as a psychological illness hold true, perhaps the same argument can be used for opium addicts. In fact, many reformed opium addicts resort to alchohol as a substitute panacea and in doing so exchange one type of addiction viewed unfavourably by a dominant world culture for another just as damaging to those who are unable to manage it, but which happens to be culturally condoned. After all, what government would dare to deny the Russian proletariat their shot of vodka or insist on urine alchohol tests for State Department diplomats expected to attend what most Moslems and Hindus consider to be barbaric cocktail parties. In an anthropological sense, "drug addiction" must be seen for what it is: a culturally defined value judgement. The negative value judgement is muted in the case of socially accepted drugs of addiction such as tobacco and alcohol on the increasingly suspect grounds that those who habitually ingest them do not endanger the well being of the community at large.

It is not possible to state unequivocally from my small sample that material poverty is the sole cause of opium addiction. Nor is it possible for me to assert that addiction is a cause of poverty. Clearly though these two causative factors are related in more than a casual way. It appears that a relationship of mutual dependence does exist but is difficult to establish because more than a simple measure of material wealth ought to be examined to evaluate the case properly. The highlanders environment also contributes to a general malaise which makes it more likely that people will become addicts. This perhaps has just as much to do with the problem of working class alchohol abuse in the USSR and the USA as it does with the specific situation of the highlanders. It has a great deal to do with their relative social position, lack of control over their own destiny and their subject status in modern, bureaucratic state systems. This then extends the concept of poverty to include mental health in the wider sense of the term. We should not be surprised that the members of minority cultures subject to powerful pressures and demands to conform to a new world order feel fundamentally threatened.

It is personal fortunes and mostly misfortunes which best account for addiction. It is those who are least able to cope with the circumstances of daily life who are most likely to become victims. The sample study also has something to tell us about opium cures. So much attention is given to detoxification and suppression that the socio-economic and psycho-social context in which the problem occurs is virtually forgotten. In a broader sense a balanced development policy such as that suggested by Chupinit in this book would do much to alleviate the situation. But unfortunately such an approach seems a long way off. Although it would be unrealistic to expect anything to be done about the wider political context, the local setting should not be ignored when attempting cures. Treatment within the village has much to recommend it, especially if it is mounted in such a way that it addresses underlying and endemic problems of poor health (stomach ulcers etc).

Highlanders, like people all over the world, use drugs to lighten the drudgery of their daily existence. Modern Thailand has deemed that smoking be stopped but because of the availability of opium and the depressing nature of life in the mountains, it continues to be widely used. This opiate of the masses is a medication which has retained its popularity as a cure for the malaise of modern times, the need for which is usually reinforced by quite specific pyschological and physical injuries.

References

Charas Suwanwela, Vichai Poshyachinda, Prida Tasanapradit and Ayut Dharm-krong-at
(1978)

"The hill tribes of Thailand, their opium use and addiction" **Bulletin on Narcotics** Vol. XXX, No. 2, April-June: 1-19.

Paiboon Suthasupa, Sanit Wongsprasert and Yuthapong Kumudom,
(1982-86)

Agricultural Extension Strategy for Highland: a study of extension methodology to eliminate opium poppy cultivation Faculty of Agriculture, Chiang Mai University and Tribal Research Institute, Chiang Mai, Progress Reports No. 1-7 June 1982-February 1985, and Final Report, August 1986.

Further Reading

Berridge, Virginia & Griffith Edwards (1987) — *Opium and the People: Opiate Use in Nineteeth-Century England* Yale University Press: New Haven and London (Highly recommended study of the social context of drug taking in Victorian England and the rise of medical and legal control)

Vichai Poshyachinda (1986) — Information and Considerations on Opium Poppy Cultivation *Journal of Anti-narcotics* Vol. 1 (1): 1-27.

Vichai Poshyachinda (1981) — *Opium Cultivation on Ya-Po-Kee and Mor-Jor-Lor-Ku* Drug Dependence Research Center, Institute of Health Research Chulalongkorn University, Bangkok (pp. 16).

Westermeyer, Joseph (1982) — *Poppies, Pipes and People: Opium and Its Use in Laos* University of California Press, Berkley (pp. 336). (Highly recommended. Humane, intelligent and particulary well informed)

Williams, I.M.G. (1979) — UN/Thai programme for drug abuse control in Thailand—a report on phase 1: February 1972-June 1979. *Bulletin on Narcotics*, Vol.XXXI, No.2 April-June: 1-44, (First UNFDAC Thailand director's final report)

Anarchists of the Highlands? A Critical Review of a Stereotype Applied to the Lisu

Prasert Chaipigusit

> "It is difficult now, back in civilization, to evoke the sense of freedom that comes upon a man when he stands on a mountaintop and looks out over tens of thousands of acres of fertile and unexplored land in the valleys below. It is only then that a man knows that, given the wit and will to survive, he need not bow his head to any government, to any ideology, to any small-minded men who feel that they control the essentials of his existence. I understood more fully ....the Lisu."
> Eugene Morse **Exodus to a Hidden Valley**
> [1974: 64-65]

The Lisu are often characterised as strong individualists, to the extent even of labelling them as anarchists. This paper will find out where such a decidedly provocative stereotype originated and its basis in fact, briefly touch on the problem of pejorative labels used in reference to the hill tribes and discuss at some length why the nature of Lisu culture and social structure does not lend itself to such a description.

I will argue that while the Lisu display an individuality which is typical of highlanders, it is difficult to take this observation much further. Like all highlanders, their households are relatively independent and provide the foundation for a socio-economic and political framework which mediates day to day activities. They may meet Spencer's definition of an anarchist in that they are proud of a long standing tradition which, "denies the right of any government....to trench upon [their] cultural ideology [which could in difficult circumstances place] them in opposition to the rule of law and central government" but opposition is not a position they prefer to adopt: they are much too pragmatic.

In fact the stereotype becomes dangerous when, because of their long association with the Yunnanese (a few of whom make their living trading in opium and manufacturing heroin), they are seen to be engaged as partners rather than employees in illegal activities. Lisu villages appear to have been the hardest hit by deliberately intimidating or poorly disciplined, punitive army raids on opium growing communities.

Such a misunderstanding, built on years of cultural development marked by a high level of mistrust between lowlanders and highlanders, can do little good today. The ironic truth of the matter is that most Lisu, like hill people in general, are anxious to become Thai citizens. How then to reconcile the image imposed on them and the identity or legal status to which they aspire?

Stereotypes and stereotyping

It is quite normal for people to form impressions of the places they visit. We are often advised that first impressions count, that they mean something which is worth remembering. Visitors to Lisu villages most often first remark on the fierceness of the dogs and then on the proud egalitarian bearing of the people. Once it is discovered that others hold to a similar opinion the observation takes on a weight that makes it acceptable. Once part of an acceptable body of popular or consensus knowledge, the information and the labels used appear to take on a life of their own. People entering a Lisu village come expecting to see fierce dogs and a proud people so much so that they do not see the sleeping dogs but remember the one dog in a hundred that leaps, teeth bared in display; they do not see people sitting quietly in the shade of their houses embroidering or mending tools but only the well dressed man proudly leaving the village with a rifle slung over his shoulder.

Where does this take us? A broad discussion of the labels and mythology promoted by tour companies would make a study in itself. The type of advertising which appears on bill boards around Chaing Mai (See Plate) are enough to illustrate this. However the broader problem of the sociology of knowledge concerning the highlands and addressed in one way or another by most contributors to this book is perhaps best left for a more academic publication. Here let me limit myself to labels attached to the Lisu.

Forming a popular opinion about a highland group is not just something left to wide-eyed travellers. Missionaries returning to the USA and elsewhere explaining their work to congregations, who provide them with the means to continue their work in their field, indulge in romantic terms to describe "their people".

Paul Lewis, for example, is a Baptist missionary who has worked in Burma since 1947 and northern Thailand since 1968. His colourful book, *Peoples of the Goden Traingle,* is one of the most popular and frequently cited studies of the highland people, and its accounts often resort to stereotypes to distinguish the six different groups he describes. The chapter on the Lisu is headed "Desire for Primacy" and first describes children competing to wear the most beautiful New Year costumes. He concludes the section by saying "A Lisu always wants to be first" [Lewis, 1984: 241] and develops the theme into a portrayal of a people predisposed to a strong sense of competition and assertion of individual rights which can lead to violence. Lewis says it has been reported that village headman have been killed after adjudication against an aggrieved party and asserts that killings are probably more frequent among the Lisu "than any other tribal group" [Lewis, 1984: 270] although he gives no evidence to support this. The chapter concludes "For every Lisu wants to excel" [Lewis, 1984: 271].

The missionary, Eugene Morse, in his account of his family's adventures in the fascinating journal *Exodus to a Hidden Valley* presents very few generalisations about the Lisu and these are quite different from those of Lewis. Morse sees the Lisu as "a very independent people" [Morse, 1974: 39] and rather than given to violence writes that to avoid offence "The Lisu do not hold with the common democratic concept of majority rule. They feel that the losing minority is bound to be unhappy.... problem(s are) discussed and discussed until an obvious answer emerges". In the following paragraph Morse goes on to note,

> It seems only logical that, in a situation where man almost literally holds his life in his own two hands, each individual should be granted as much participation as possible in the decision-making process.... there is no set perogative, status or authority among individuals. Many times Robert and I — and our wives as well—had to instantly obey orders from our children unquestioningly and instantly (Morse, 1974: 199-200).

The extent of the identification of Lisu ways as a functional and natural response to the environment is also reflected in the quotation offered at the beginning of this Chapter. It is remarkable how closely in approximates to Spencer's definition of an anarchist.

Lisu as Anarchists

The picture which is built up by exposure to such observations may largely depend on what one thinks of the writer rather than who the Lisu really are. Missionaries are notoriously defensive of "their" people and it is interesting to note that Lewis has specialised on the Akha and Lahu. How to get out of this opinion trap? To what extent can anthropologists lead us to a more objective view?

In fact the anthropologist Dessaint offers comments not too dissimilar to those of Morse when he states that the Lisu highly value the exercise of equal rights [Dessaint, 1972: 96]. Durrenberger also points out that "There are no headmen to make decisions for the villagers, and Lisu loath assertive and autocratic headmen and that this amongst other characteristics are hallmarks of an egalitarian society" [Durrenberger, 1983: 218].

It is in the work of anthropologists that we are most likely to meet ourselves coming the other way. As outsiders do we foist an identity on ethnolinguistic groups or do we merely promote behavioural cultural characteristics of which we approve? One Lisu adage which has always appealed to me is the enigmatic saying that all people are the same height at the knee. I have observed that young people are encouraged to speak at meetings and a strong response must be expected from anybody slighted by word or deed.

However, it is a long behavioural leap from egalitarianism to anarchism. When the government asks a Lisu village to appoint a village headman, the community will readily respond even though they might not feel the need to make a formal appointment in the absence of a request. Their sense of social order runs deep and their pragmatism is readily mobilised to maintain peace. For a society with a reputation for independence, we should not be surprised to learn how remarkably obedient they are and how strictly they maintain the rules which support their social structure. Let me review the main institutional components of their society.

The Family and Lineage

Both the nuclear and extended family are known in Lisu society. When young people marry and bring their spouse into their family of origin, the household becomes an extended family. When a married couple decide to set up their own house, the process begins again.

Lisu are largely monogamous. Although they do not forbid a man to have more than one wife, the practice is uncommon. If a man has enough money to pay the bride price and the first wife allows it, he may take a second wife. This only works for men - women are not allowed to take another husband.

Lisu prefer to marry within their own society with lineages maintained through the male line. After marriage the husband usually lives with his wife's parents until he has paid off the bride price when he usually moves back into his own parents' house, bringing his wife with him.

Each of these changes provides an opportunity for the couple to set up their own house but this wish for independence cannot always be fulfilled. The husband must discharge his matrimonial debts before he is free to do as he chooses. Even when a couple set up their own household, they usually choose to make their home in the village of their parents. Parents continue to provide support for their married children and it is advantageous for the couple to remain in a village in which lineage support is available and reciprocal labour exchange easy.

The lineage is by far the most important broader matrix of Lisu social structure. Although according to the stated ideal that any one lineage is supposed to be the equal of all others, it is considered best to keep numbers up by encouraging cross cousins to marry and remain. This helps to maintain their strength and therefore their bargaining position within the community.

There are more than 30 Lisu lineages but the Lisu claim that only five to six of these are strictly of Lisu origin, the remainder are considered to have been initiated by Chinese marrying into their society. These are still however regarded as equally valid and operate along the same lines. Although lineages are important, within lineages the relationship between sister and brother is much closer than that between cousins. All relatives have to some extent an obligation to help and care for one another.

In small villages perhaps only two to three lineages will be represented but in a big village it is not unusual to have more than ten resident lineages.

The difference between lineages is most clearly marked by the spirits worshipped at the household shrine. Each family maintains its own offering bowls and the number varies from household to household.

Family names are important in indicating whom one can court. Those with the same family name (lineage) or who are in the same sub-lineage cannot, in strict terms, even consider marriage. However, although this is a taboo held to quite strictly, even this can be negotiated if the man has wealth enough to purchase an exception.

In summary we can say that relationships between sisters, brothers and close cousins are strongest. Second order relationships include all other members of the same

PROBLEMS

lineage. Last in order of priority come one's obligations to the community.

Educating Children

Lisu train and encourage their children to use their ability to reason and express themselves in front of elders. Children are expected to speak in a forthright manner, not to give in easily and if they feel they are right, to keep after a point until it is accepted or shown to be suspect or false. Both boys and girls speak their minds especially on matters concerning values and rights. They do not readily admit that one of their peers is more important than they; everybody is supposed to be equal. Within the family children are taught not only to which lineage they belong but what they can expect from it as well as their duties towards others. They learn who belongs to their lineage and to treat these people as family and give support where needed.

Social hierachy: Headmen and Elders.

Lisu are expected to show respect for their elders, especially those within their lineage, but village headmen and administrators are less likely to be treated in the same manner. Like most highlanders, their relationship with holders of administrative offices is much more circumspect. Senior villagers of good reputation will be shown respect regardless of their lineage but a young headman with whom they have few dealings will largely be ignored. If they experience difficulties, they will in preference turn to their family first. This is always the case. Although they know a headman has an important relationship with the government, the family comes first.

Whether they hold the position formally as a government headman or informally by consensus, community leaders are accepted more for proven personal qualities than wealth, trading connections or government friends. Such people must be knowledgable, competent and trusted both to respect and exercise the rights and concepts of freedom held by Lisu society as a whole. They are ethically bound not to hold themselves higher than others. Acceptance of headmen neither makes is necessary to show respect towards them at all times nor to listen to and follow all the orders they might give. Each office holder must establish his own community credentials.

Each lineage in a village has one or two senior people, usually older men who are acknowledged for their wisdom and ability to influence others. As many as five to eight elders may make up a traditional village committee. When conflicts arise, this group has the duty of arbitrating and settling the dispute through consultation. If they believe it will help, they do not hesitate to approach government officials or development workers who may be asked to help out by offering another opinion. This committee is also expected to schedule and participate in cultural activities such as the new year ceremony, new rice festival, new corn festival and burial ceremony.

Mo muang.

Ideally each village also has a *mo muang*, a religious leader. It is only in Christian villages that such a person cannot be found. Lisu believe in spirits, as do most Buddhists, but their belief system demands that greater respect be shown to them than in lowland society. To become a *mo muang,* a man must pass a selection test conducted in front of the village spirit shrine. The candidate is expected to throw two sticks to the ground three times in a row and have them both land face up each time. If he is able to do this he is acknowledged as a *mo muang*. In fact the selection process is not quite as casual as this. Candidates are usually married men with children and have other family responsibilities. Before they become candidates they must already have a good knowledge of ritual. The position cannot be inherited and for as long as a *mo muang* is resident in the village where he was "chosen" he cannot give up the post. His duties only end when he leaves the community.

The *mo muang* is responsible for fostering religious knowledge, playing a leading role in the performance of ritual and looking after the spirit shrine. He must go to the village spirit shrine every 15 days to change the water and it is he who announces what days are auspicious and hence when people should stop work. The *mo muang* is also a member of the senior committee. If the village does not have either a village headman *(phu yai ban)* or an assistant headman, the *mo muang* is expected to fill this role.

Nei pa.
The *nei pa* medium is a kind of spirit doctor who acts as a contact between the spirit world and the everyday world in which we live. People have many reasons to contact spirits, whether to seek out reasons for sickness or to have their fortunes told. Lisu respect spirits because they believe that they know the rhyme and reason of life which is hidden from humans. When consulted about the cause of sickness or other troubles, the *nei pa* usually indicate that some form of propitiation is necessary to secure their support. Those who follow his advice believe it will solve their problems.

Only men can be mediums, and although there is no rule regarding this, a disproportionate number of the sons of spirit doctors become *nei pa*. The expectation placed on him is stronger than that placed on *mo muang*. Once a medium, always a medium. The spirit doctor cannot quit or withdraw even if he moves away from the village where public acknowledgement was first made of his skills: he remains a *nei pa* until the end ot his life. When he grows old, he becomes a very special person, whose knowledge is greatly revered.

Lisu as Anarchists

Disputes and Nepotism

If two sides in a dispute cannot reach a settlement, the case is brought to the generally acknowledged leader of the village for a hearing. If his judgement is considered to be unfair and the litigants are not satisfied, it is usually because the successful party is closely related to the village committee of elders or that the village leader has a family interest in the affair. People in positions of authority usually help their relatives first, a bias which is strong in all highland minority communities and reflects the importance of kinship.

Even though Lisu have a first obligation to those in their family or the same lineage, they are also expected to respect and cultivate relationships with others. When they feel slighted by an unfair judgement, they resort to speaking their minds in private or gossiping against those who won the case or provided the judgement. Although they usually attempt to save the face of the leader by not making their opinion too public, they will nevertheless have much to say of an unflattering nature: that the committee was made up of people with little intelligence and less than average common-sense and so on. This response and manifestation of discontent, sometimes described as "anarchistic", is clearly not a monopoly of the Lisu.

Migration and Settlement

Oral tradition has it that throughout history the Lisu have been brave warriors. Their oral history records numerous battles fought against enemies, especially Chinese. Their defeat and movement south is also remembered. Their independence has been tested.

Not all migration has been forced upon them by war. The way in which Lisu move to a new village site is quite different from other mountain people. The matter is discussed fully with other members of the lineage and relatives. The arguments for moving must be convincing and the purpose clear because people will only choose to move if more fertile land is available for settlement or greater economic opportunities can be secured. When a group moves, it is not a follow-the-leader affair but a matter well thought through. New villages are usually set up with lineage clusters in which each hamlet can keep to its own tradition and style of life.

When Lisu come into lasting contact with the Thai administrative system, they are quite willing to accept more formal government guidelines. Their cultural ideology for all its strong statements of independence is distinguished by its pragmatism.

Attitude to other mountain people
The Lisu rank each of the ethnic groups with whom they have contact on a vertical scale. For instance they consider the Hmong and Mien as intelligent, diligent and possessing an admirable ability to make money. The Lisu say that the Meo (Hmong) are particularly clever when it comes to finding new land to cultivate. Many of the sites occupied by the Lisu were formerly worked by the Hmong. They admire the Yao for their literacy.

The Lahu, Akha and Lisu are linguistically closely related, classified as Lolo speakers in the Tibeto-Burman family of languages. They usually communicate with each other in Lahu and it is the Lahu with whom the Lisu seem closest, regarding the two groups as related. While many Lisu can speak Lahu, few Lahu speak Lisu.

Many Lisu men marry Lahu women and bring them home, the brideprice being much less expensive than when marrying a Lisu.

Lisu as Anarchists

Their attitude towards the Lahu, then, is usually friendly; the economics of the two groups are very close and in some villages Lisu and Lahu live quite happily side by side. Although there are many differences in tradition and culture, their style of cultivation is the same.

As for the Karen and the Akha, they are considered by the Lisu as being less than diligent and are seen as being on a lower level than themselves. Nevertheless, the Akha are acknowledged as people with linguistic ability, largely because they can speak Lahu. Some Lisu men marry Akha girls and some buy Akha children for adoption. Lisu do not choose to marry Karen women because of the considerable differences in tradition and custom. Many Karen opium addicts work for Lisu and this does little for their reputation.

In contrast the Chinese Yunnanese, or *haw* as they are known in Thai, are held in high regard as a people who belong to a much higher culture. Again literacy is a quality much admired and many Lisu are interested in learning to read and write and also to speak Yunnanese, the highland lingua franca. Most Lisu welcome Chinese Yunnanese who choose to set up houses in their villages. As traders and farmers they bring scarce skills and new knowledge. Many Yunnanese marry Lisu women and when children are born they may take their father's family name but perform the rituals necessary to remain within Lisu society. Many of the children of such unions become fully Lisu within a generation or two.

There are Chinese Yunnanese in most Lisu villages and if we trace back family lineages far enough, we eventually find that most have Chinese ancestors. Although we might expect a spiritual rift between Lisu animism and *haw* Taoism, the beliefs are not incompatible and can complement each other quite well. This is in fact one of the reasons why Chinese Yunnanese are able to live peacefully in Lisu

PROBLEMS

communities. The Yunnanese are even more pragmatic than the Lisu and it is usually they who adapt to the Lisu way of life.

A few Thai, especially Northern Thai, also live in Lisu villages, working as traders and farmers. A few have married Lisu partners.

This ethnic openness is not so much tolerance in the sense that they consciously put up with outsiders they would rather not accept, but is an established way of life.

Although in their rating system some ethnic groups are given high marks and others low, individuals must first and foremost be themselves. Nobody is accorded a dignity which rests on their ethnic origins any more than their political affiliations. This respect for individuality and independence is what is interpreted by some as a deeply structured anarchism but it is not an explicit part of Lisu ideology. Observers may project an image they want to see but for the Lisu individuality is commonplace, something that most sensible human beings are expected to exercise. Their deep suspicion of individuals who enjoy the exercise of authority and seek power over others may not be held in high regard by some but hardly constitutes anarchism.

The term "anarchist" then must be regarded with suspicion. Clearly, the cultural ideology of the Lisu occupies an important place but a strong sense of individuality and independence should not be confused with Spencer's "opposition to the rule of law and central government". They do not seek to place themselves in opposition to government, to the contrary, as is pointed out by the French social anthropologist Yves Conrad in this book Chapter 8, they are exceptionally pragmatic even in matters regarding identity. Only if their survival were placed at risk by the state would

Lisu as Anarchists

they embark on the dangerous course of defensive action. The problem with the term "anarchist" is that it is so often used in a pejorative sense, as a synonym for irrational opposition to all authority, that it has become a word of abuse. Strong emphasis on the negative aspect as opposition to all authority is taken as its sole meaning. As such, its use is misleading and dangerous. Lisu culture acknowledges authority in many forms and there are quite specific role responsibilities attached.

Lisu participation in development work
When compared with the enthusiasm expressed for ritual celebrations, the support given to development work is relatively muted. This is especially so in such cases where projects are initiated by outsiders on the understanding that village labour will be "volunteered" to carry out the work. Communical activities of this nature are new and the formal relationships that command such participation are not well developed. Although social arrangements exist which make it possible to call on cooperation from villagers, the response is usually poor.

The Lisu attitude towards being called to help is to ask who is doing the requesting. Development workers should eschew any hint that an order is involved which admits the right of one member of the community to exercise authority over another. It is here that the stronger ideological content of Lisu individualism is evident. Any activity of a formal nature that may involve communal work always faces problems. It is a quality development workers ought to understand rather than too readily label as uncooperativeness. A task well prepared and well understood by the participant-beneficiaries will receive full support. A task for which cooperation is demanded will always fail.

Pejorative terms are commonly used by development workers when talking about highland ethnic minorities. Chupinit (Chapter 3, this volume) reports Karen being called "asphalt," to describe them as "slow and sticky" and Baffie (Chapter 15, this volume) shows that in comic strip form hill tribes come off rather badly when used as objects onto which writers and artists project unconscious content for readers' entertainment. Is the term "anarchist" then just another projection, a more intellectual version of a well established bad habit?

In practical terms we should know that if we would like to work with the Lisu, we ought to know their customs, beliefs and character and also the traditional style of village administration. If an approach is made which is sensitive to Lisu practises and culturally informed, the consequence of any request is likely to be successful. Whatever the rules a people might state, their pragamatism and willingness to contribute to a common beneficial end will easily bypass cultural ideology and lineage differences. If cooperation or participation is not forthcoming it is usually not because they are in principle opposed to working together but because they do not see how the undertaking can be useful to them.

In such a situation we need to come to development work ready to ask such questions such as, "How many lineages are there in the chosen villages? Are there any outstanding conflicts between them? What are the causes of disputes and how entrenched are they?" We ought not set our expectations too high. The important idea of popular participation will only work on the basis of trust and a good cultural understanding. We ought also to be aware of the overall political structure of the village and beware of nepotism so that outside resources are made available to those who will serve community needs and not divert assistance to their kin's exclusive use.

The essence of the Lisu heart is a deeply held spiritual perception of the natural order, and the family has a central place in this. Their perception of Thai government intervention is still being formed but they are strongly aware that they can fit if given the chance to belong within the Thai milieu. Modern lines of communication, education and development make it much easier for them to accept that they are part of the Thai family.

Development workers and researchers are always made aware that they are agents of change: representatives of the outside world. When we understand the Lisu, it is not difficult to come to terms with their individualism and pride. The formal demands of modern administrative systems can annoy us all and arbitrary demands made by officious or patronising officers leave a bad taste in the mouths of all who must deal with them. The Lisu rejection of such people is a reminder of how we should behave. Lisu beliefs and behaviour are not cast in a mould which places them in permanent opposition to either contemporary bureaucratic procedures or life in a democratic state but they have yet to accept obligations and duties which lowlanders take for granted.

The term "anarchist" when applied to the Lisu without clarification is very misleading. Their own social structure allows for some to exercise more power than others: The authority of elders and village leaders is recognised everywhere. The Lisu are indiscriminately opposed neither to government intervention in their communities nor to being incorporated into the Thai state: on the contrary most are anxious to acquire Thai citizenship. Lack of participation in development related project activities is not evidence of lack of loyalty but of lack of understanding as to how they will benefit. Age old ceremonies which accompany such calendric events as the new year or which mark births and deaths, for example, have a stronger cultural context and meaning than the mysteries of contemporary development ideology. Lisu ideas regarding egalitarianism, individualism and pride should not be viewed as negative qualities but rather as positive characteristics of a people who, if given the chance, will easily find a place in Thailand's plural society.

References

Dessaint, Alain Y. (1972) — *Economic Organization of the Lisu of the Thai Highlands* Unpublished Ph.D. dissertation, University of Hawwaii: Honolulu

Durrenberger, Paul E. (1983) — "Lisu: Political Form, Ideology and Economic Action" in *Highlanders of Thailand* eds. McKinnon & Wanat Bhruksasri, Oxford University Press: Kuala Lumpur.

Lebar, Frank M.; Hickey, Gerald C; Musgrave, John K. (1964) — *Ethnic Groups of Mainland Southeast Asia* Human Relations Area Files Press: New Haven.

Lewis, Paul & Elaine (1984) — *Peoples of the Golden Triangle* Thames and Hudson: London.

Prasert Chaipigusit (1983) — *Leadership of the Lisu* (in Thai) Tribal Research Centre: Chiang Mai.

Tribal Research Institute (1986) — *Hilltribes Data in Thailand* (mimeo) Hill Tribe Research Institute: Chiang Mai.

Morse, Eugene (1974) — *Exodus to a Hidden Valley* William Collins & World Publishing: Ohio.

Lisu Identity in Northern Thailand: A Problematique for Anthropology

Yves Conrad

This paper presents a contemporary case study of the problematique of ethnic identification and identity in the multi-ethnic context of the highlands of north Thailand. Some of the theoretical and methodological issues explored here were first raised a few decades ago by Leach in his study of the Kachin. Since then a handful of scholars have made significant contributions to our understanding of what is a difficult and controversial matter.

Here I will attempt a brief and balanced synthesis of the main ideas and suggestions concerning the definition and use of ethnicity in an "ethnically" heterogeneous society. Because some of the "same" ethnic groups are represented in Burma, South-West China and Thailand, my discussion will rest on the literature dealing with this region.

With this outline in mind and with reference to both my own fieldwork and existing literature I will explore the question of Lisu identity in Northern Thailand.

The Root of the Problem

The following considerations stem from a basic empirical fact: the readily noticeable cultural diversity of the peoples inhabiting the mountainous border area between Thailand and Burma.

Apart from Thai and Chinese highlanders, six main "hill tribes" live in the uplands and are distinguished from each other by language, dress, customs, rituals and beliefs, art forms and economic and social organization.

An inventory of their distinctive characteristics can be found in the compilation of Lebar, Hickey and Musgrave's *Ethnic Groups in mainland Southeast of Asia* (1964). A remarkable photographic illustration of the cultural distinctiveness of some of these groups is also provided in Paul and Elaine Lewis's *Peoples of the Golden Triangle* (1984)

Some authors, going beyond the conventional dichotomy between lowland and highland societies and cultures, have associated the various groups with distinct ecological niches and subsistence systems. (e.g. A.Y. and W.Y. Dessaint 1982).

Still other levels of differentiation can be found in the structures and forms of social organization; some are said to function with patri, matri or bilineal kinship systems; some to have strong leadership, others to be rather egalitarian (eg. Durrenberger 1971; Prasert, Chapter 7).

This cultural multiplicity and diversity raises a methodological problem with profound theoretical implications: how to account for it?

The very enterprise of attempting to differentiate peoples in a systematic way rests on the implicit postulate that they are significantly different from one another. This focus on differences ensures that differences will be found and implies that their relevance should be taken for granted. This logic leads to an incorrect interpretation and understanding of empirical reality.

Lisu Identity

To record the existence of cultural differences between units of population is one thing. To attempt to list for each group an inventory of unique, distinctive and characteristic traits is another. This latter approach is the outcome of a particular conceptualization of a given society and its culture seen as an immutable historical entity with clear cultural boundaries. (On this issue, see Leach, 1954 and 1960; Maran La Raw, 1967; and particularly Lehman, 1967 and 1979; but also Keyes 1979; and Kunstadter 1979). It is only one step further along this road to consider the members of a group as having a common ethnic origin, a view that happens to be very much in agreement with the mythologies of these groups. (About the confusion between scientific classification and native category usage see Moerman, 1967). It is thus assumed that these groups have, through a long march over the centuries, come from a distant historical homeland, and their recent arrival in Thailand is the latest leg in a long journey.

What these groups (with the exception of the Yao) have in common is the absence of a written language. This makes a reconstruction of their past history very much guesswork. Scattered mention in chronicles is often of little help particularly those written by Westerners who viewed highlanders as "ethnic minorities" quite different and distinct from each other as well as from "majority" populations.

The main reason why these groups are perceived as such is that they speak different and mutually unintelligible languages. Cultural differences which can also be observed are then treated as concomitant and serve to reinforce the idea that language boundaries correspond to culture boundaries. Thus are defined ethnic groups, each one supposedly living in a sort of splendid isolation with a language and a culture peculiar to itself. Membership in such an ethnic category is seen as exclusive and determined by "participation in a particular historical tradition". The "ethnicity" of a group is, therefore "seen as depending on the origins of that tradition and of the people bearing it" (Lehman 1967: 102). According to the theory that the origin of a language is likely to be located in the area where most of its family branches are concentrated, groups such as Lisu and Lahu, whose languages are, on the basis of linguistic similarities sometimes classified as Tibeto-Burman would ideally originate in Tibet.

Leach calls these speculations "fables" and denounces the "myth of philological origins", stressing that "language groupings are of sociological, rather than historical significance" In Leach's view the ability to speak a language as a mother-tongue "has no necessary implication for the historical antecedents of the individuals concerned" (1951 : 51). There are linguists who have worked in the region who would apparently agree with him (Bradley, 1983 : 46-55).

This does not mean though, as Lehman points out, that we should therefore underestimate the importance of historical evidence in helping to define "not perhaps a common history, but the context of ethnogenesis" (1979: 216).

Besides the few valid historical inferences that can be drawn from language distributions, languages as a criteria for defining ethnic groups and cultural intergroup differences appears to be equally inadequate, if not irrelevant.

Le Bar et.al. confronted with "the problem of the identification of units for the purpose of ethnographic description", although conceding that language is "not always in agreement with the realities of cultural identification and cultural dynamics", still consider that it constitutes "the only consistent and complete basis for the selection and arrangement of units" (1954 Preface). Yet in the course of the subsequent descriptive summaries, "a whole range of other cultural elements is treated as if they were co-variant with language" (Hinton, 1983: 158) explicitly showing that the authors cling, de facto, to the idea that somehow it must be possible to establish a proper taxonomy of actual groups together with their respective cultures.

Lisu Identity

The idea of a systematic correspondence between ethnic identity, language and culture is challenged by ethnographic facts reported by several authors.

On one hand, groups identified as sharing a common ethnic identity may speak different languages. The most well documented example for South-East Asia is the case of the Kachin (Leach, 1954; Maran La Raw, 1967) an ethnic group, or rather category, which includes people speaking up to forty mutually unintelligible languages and dialects and displaying marked cultural variations. This is also the situation of the well-known Karen (Lehman, 1967 and 1979; Keyes et.al. 1979). In Kachin state alone at the lower level of the group(s) labelled Lisu (Maran La Raw, 1967: 132) three dialects have been identified.

On the other hand, these very groups that are linguistically defined as different may follow, despite their respective cultural singularities, an overwhelmingly homogeneous common cultural pattern. Again it is the case of the Kachin,

> who all share notions of common ancestry, practice the same form of marriage system, have an almost homogeneous customary law and social control system, use only Jinghpaw for ritual purposes, and are largely polyglots...Genetically the languages are divergent; culturally and bilingually, the groups of speakers converge (Maran La Raw, 1967 : 133).

Before proceeding to examine other interpretations offered in the attempt to account for this ethnically complex situation, it is necessary to review concepts in wide general use and provide a contemporary definition.

- **Ethnic group:** a set of individuals with similar consciousness and mutual interests centred on some shared understanding of common values.

- **Ethnic category:** a class of people or groups, based on real or presumed cultural characteristics (e.g. the categories "Kachin","Karen" etc.....)

- **Ethnic identification:** process of assigning an individual (including oneself) to a group or category, and thus implicitly recognizing boundaries of community of interests and predicting a set of behavioral traits appropriate to the members of the group or category (Kunstadter, 1979: 119-20).

It is a corollary of these definitions that ethnicity has nothing to do with ancestral racial-like origins and that an "ethnic group" is not necessarily ethnic in this sense. Ethnicity, like other social categorizations, functions as a means of differentiation between groups and is defined, not in absolute terms, but by reference to these other groups. "Ethnicity is a matter of the conceptual organization of intergroup relations" (Lehman, 1979: 216). The proposal, first formulated by Leach, to view ethnic groups as social, rather than cultural entities, whose definition is a function of structural opposition to other such social groups provides a starting point for discussion. This structural opposition fundamentally depends on differential access to productive resources, fecundity of women, political power etc...(Keyes, 1979: 3).

In Lehman's terms,

> When people identify themselves as members of some "ethnic" category...they are taking positions in culturally defined systems of intergroup relation...In such systems, ethnic categories are formally like (interdependent and complementary) roles (Lehman, 1967: 106).

It follows that an ethnic category may be defined as corresponding to a social, culturally defined role in an ethnic role system. This cultural definition is found in these "symbolic formulations of ethnic identity" (Keyes, 1979: 4) which includes myths, beliefs, rituals, folklore, art etc. That ethnic distinctions presuppose linguistic and cultural differences does not require that these differences be totally unique. Moerman has questioned the triviality and superficiality of the "distinctive" traits of Lue ethnicity and pointed out their similarity to those people from whom they wish to distinguish themselves (Moerman, 1965: 156).

As Lehman stresses,

> One cannot ascribe aspects of cultural inventory to membership in such a low level entity as an ethnic category, when it is objectively so much more widely distributed among historically related groups...and can often be shown to be most relevant to higher order social structures (Lehman, 1979: 325).

Thus,

> What counts in the cultural definition of and ethnic category is not possession of a unique common cultural "heritage", but the use of a set of cultural elements (language included, possibly) in a claim to membership of the category" (Lehman, 1979: 233).

The point is that this set is perceived as distinctive and characteristic of this identity.

It is probably in this sense that Barth sees the sharing of a common "assemblage of traits" by members of ethnic groups as "an implication or result" of their claim to the same ethnic identity, the determination of group membership being a function of "ascription and identification by the actors themselves" (But for a possibly controversial interpretation of this position see Keyes, 1979: 4). What Barth could have stressed here is the distinction between an ethnic identity as a cultural model, and the actual individuals or groups who may at some point claim this identity. Social and cultural systems are reference systems which are used selectively in specific environments where other groups use such systems (Lehman, 1967: 105). In such an environment ethnic categories are defined, not in absolute terms, but by "role complementation"(Ibid: 108). That is, an ethnic category does not correspond to some discrete ancestral group, but to a group or groups of people who assume a social role whose definition is a function of the environmental context of other such roles. The necessary condition for the existence of an ethnic group as such is not its linguistic/cultural distinctiveness, but its structural opposition to other groups in relation to different resources. Ethnic identities appear then to serve as adaptive strategies for people in a certain social conjuncture. As circumstances change, so do strategies change. Leach (1954) has shown the inherent ambivalence and flexibility of the *gumsa-gumlao* system operative among the Kachin of Burma where Kachin "become" Shan by adopting a type of Shan social organization. (For a critique and reformulation of Leach's theory see Maran La Raw, 1967: 138:40). A consequence of this is that ethnic groups, identities and categorizations are not permanent, and that their applications often depends on social context (Kunstadter, 1979: 120). This implies changes in ethnic identity: some groups or individuals may, alternatively or even concurrently, claim different identities.

The Case of Northern Thailand: what is it to be Lisu today?

I will now turn to the case of the Lisu in Northern Thailand and probe the specific nature of their social organization, particularly regarding these fundamental aspects: systems of kinship and affinity and of intergroup relations. This is explored as part of an attempt to delineate the Lisu role and identity in the ethnic mosaic of Thailand.

Lisu along with other major groups (e.g. Hmong, Mien, Akha, Lahu, Karen) are globally referred to by Thai authorities as *"chao khao"* (literally mountain people) and by English speakers as "hill tribes".

Lisu Identity

In South-East Asian ethnology, some societies have been labelled "tribal" when they "are not congregations for a great religion, have little supra-village political organization, and are only superficially involved in a cash economy" (Moerman, 1967: 153). A "tribal" society is defined as such in contrast to a "civilized" one (Leach, 1954 & 1960; Lehman, 1963; Moerman, 1965) and although Leach's initial distinction between the two on the basis of ecological and social organization differences has since been considered to be too drastic and simplistic, it is still widely used (e.g. Lehman, 1967; Maran La Raw, 1967).

A similar inter-dependence presides over the politically defined relations between a "minority" and a "majority", which cannot exist as mutually exclusive entities and must be viewed as related systems (Maran La Raw, 1967: 134).

These definitions call for some precision regarding their use in Northern Thailand. The groups encompassed in the category *chao khao* are called "hill tribes" to differentiate them from other "minorities" or "ethnic groups" such as Chinese or Shan, who also live in the hills.

Here I will deliberately leave aside a discussion of the Lisu as a minority within the Thai state polity and limit myself to a definition of their position in the local system of inter-ethnic relations.

Lisu Social organization

Lisu society in Thailand is divided into clans. Six of these clans are said by Lewis (1984: 258) to be "traditional" Lisu clans (this notion will subsequently be questioned), while others are Chinese-Lisu clans resulting from intermarriage with Yunnanese Chinese, known in Thailand as *haw*.

Descent is unilineal: membership in a clan is in principle inherited from the father. If the founder of a lineage is Chinese his descendants will bear a Chinese clan name. Intermarriage with Chinese creates no problem because Lisu and Chinese descent systems are similar. In the case of residence in Lisu society, the Chinese origin of a clan name is thus identifiable. Actually, in Chiang Dao and Pai areas (Chiangwat Chiang Mai and Mae Hong Son), such Chinese-Lisu clan names number more than twenty and most appear to have been fairly recently incorporated, with the memory of a *haw* ancestor often as close as the third generation. Similarly, this process of assimilation into Lisu society is fairly common. Sometimes it may be only temporary, given to either *haw* couples or families temporarily resident in a village or fixed as in the case of single males who marry a Lisu bride and take up residence in her village. Then again *haw* brides may be "imported" into Lisu communities.

My collection of genealogies also reveals a high frequency of incorporation involving Lahu men and women. Lahu do not have a clan system like the Lisu. If circumstances do not make it necessary to claim Lisu descent, the descendants of a Lahu man are called Lahu Na or Lahu Nyi according to the Lahu subgroup into which he was born. The question of whether these people are really Lahu or Lisu simply does not have much relevance for the people themselves. I did not come across a specific term for a special category of people who might have been called Lahu-Lisu as there apparently is one (according to Lewis and Durrenberger) for Chinese-Lisu (Hypa-Lisu).

If marriages with *haw* and Lahu are, in order of precendence by far the most numerous (at least for Chiang Mai and Mae Hong Son provinces) there is also evidence for intermarriage with members of other ethnic groups. Where Lisu and Akha live in close proximity they can also intermarry. In Chiang Rai province, there is at least one case of a village, Doi Chang, where the two ethnic groups live in one community. In Mae Hong Son there are a few Lisu villages which include distinct *haw* communities.

In a somewhat less typical situation I have witnessed the progressive integration of two Shan *tai yai* brothers into a Lisu village. These two came from Burma to harvest opium and remained to become residents. Two years later they spoke and dressed like Lisu. The older brother succeeded the head of the household with whom he was living after his host and employer was killed in a vendetta. He married the widow. His younger brother (17 years of age) would most probably also have married a Lisu girl had he not been arrested while guarding an opium pack-train for which he was subsequently imprisoned for life. It is significant that when interrogated by Thai police the unfortunate young man alternatively claimed both Shan and Lisu identity.

In contrast, apparently no marriages are entered into between Lisu and Hmong, Mien or Karen. This is not due to lack of geographical proximity. In the Pai area for instance, Lisu are often in contact with Karen; they go to Karen villages to buy locally distilled alcohol, pigs, and other supplies. Some Karen periodically work for Lisu as wage labourers but not the other way around. Lisu boys may be sent to live and study in Karen villages where there is a school. Lisu often pass through Karen villages which lie along the way from clusters of Lisu villages to the nearest market-town. Despite these opportunities for developing a degree of familiarity I am not aware of marriages taking place.

The same rule holds for the Hmong of whom there are many in the Pai district. Relationships between Lisu and Hmong are weak and virtually non-existent. One reason for this may be that Lisu villages tend to be grouped in clusters which occupy and control the upper part of a mountainous area; Lisu and Hmong thus would mutually exclude each other in their competitive search for possession of a similar ecological niche.

It is interesting to recount a Lisu explanation for this Lisu-Hmong separation. A Lisu man told me it was based on "cultural" incompatibility: Hmong men, he said, are polygamous, opium addicts and lazy, while Lisu men are monogamous, do not smoke opium and are hard-working; therefore, no Lisu girl ever wants to marry a Hmong.

It should also be noted that I have not come across any cases of a resident Northern Thai *(yuan* or *khon muang)* settled in a Lisu village and married to a Lisu woman, nor of a *yuan* woman married to a Lisu man, although direct contacts between the two groups are common.

So far I have only considered changes in ethnic identity resulting in the assimilation of outsiders into Lisu society. It is reasonable to assume that if some people may become Lisu the opposite may also occur that individuals may cease to be such. This is obviously more difficult to trace in a systematic way. I can however provide a few examples which help cast light on the process of ethnic identity changes.

Study villages
To illustrate the "fluidity and ambiguity" (Lehman's terms) that characterize Lisu society, it is necessary to adopt a diachronic perspective. I had the opportunity to probe some of the major changes that have taken place in a cluster of Lisu villages over the past eight years. A selection of examples illustrates the specific dynamic at work.

Within my study area, the number of settlements has remained approximately the same but one third of the villages have either moved a short distance, some several times, or been abandoned while new ones have been built on new sites.

Similarly, but not necessarily synchronically, the composition of each village population has undergone modifications. Some families have moved from one village to another; others have left the area (some only to come back later) and a few newcomers have moved in.

These changes had been dictated by a variety of significant circumstances which are too involved to report in detail in this paper but a brief summary of the history of one village and its population provides an illustration of a broader trend.

In 1967 Mahisu had fourteen houses. Analysed in terms of the ethnic origin of each household head, the village revealed a remarkable heterogeneity: Lisu, Lolo, *haw* and three varieties of Lahu (Na, Shi, Nyi). The village was recorded as a Lisu village by malaria teams and the pattern of settlement followed a ritual Lisu layout. All the women, girls, young men and children wore Lisu dress; some older men did not; one of them could not speak Lisu.

Ten years later all of the older men still lived in Lisu villages, the majority in the same area, some of which were in Pai. But, as a significant example, two sons of one household head (the same one who could not and still cannot speak Lisu) live nowadays in a *haw* community. Another son (from a different family) has married into his grand-father's Lahu village.

Nowadays the village of Mahisu does not exist as a Lisu village; it was abandoned a few years ago and taken over by *haw*. In some cases financial compensation was paid to the former owners for the fields they had cleared.

On the basis of this set of information let me underline a few points and attempt to set them in their day to day context.

What the ethnic label "Lisu" primarily describes is a shared life style. The matter of ancestral origins is clearly not important. Basically, to be Lisu is to live and work in a Lisu community and to be recognized as such by other villagers. In other words, it is to be part of a specific network of social relations. This network fundamentally consists of kinship and affinity relations. Lisu in everyday life do not address or refer to each other by names but use terms which describe their position in a kinship or affinity relation. These complementary terms correspond to status and sets of associated rights and obligations. Thus the kinship and affinity system appears to be the fundamental structure of the social organization and the privileged means of social recruitment.

In a village, individuals are (truly or fictitiously) related to each other within this frame of reference. Such relationships also link individuals in different villages, and in various ethnic groups. As a direct consequence of intermarriage this reference system extends beyond the limits of a single ethnic group. This last point is of particular help in accounting for the fluidity and ambiguous nature of ethnic groups in general, and of Lisu society in particular. There is evidence of constant movement in and out, one privileged aspect of which, when observing the evolution of the composition of a Lisu community is the continuous assimilation of "outsiders". But these outsides are not strangers. To understand the nature and the modalities of this general process, assimilation must be viewed as only one side of the coin. One is compelled to give up what Leach called the Mac Mahon conception of boundaries between separate contiguous territories and their distinct populations. This static interpretation of ethnic multiplicity is definitely misleading.

Ethnic groups are not closed, isolated and independent population units living in autonomy in "remote" areas. On the contrary it is evident that relationships between ethnic groups are multiple, albeit differential and circumstantial. An important feature of these various relations is that many of them are defined, not in terms of ethnic criteria but in different non-ethnic hierarchies (on this particular point, see Marlowe, 1979), for instance, patron-client relations not based on ethnicity.

What the system of intergroup relations points out is a general state of ebb and flow, a tidal flow of individuals in and out of the ethnically defined social alternatives which ethnic groups represent. This movement is channelled through different interlinked networks. What characterizes the system of relations of the Lisu with the *haw* and the Lahu, by contrast to the type of relations Lisu have with other groups, is that its structure is a network of kinship and affinity connections.

This has several important implications. The attempt to circumscribe a Lisu entity outside a given context is futile. Various Lisu groups or sub-groups must be primarily viewed as contextual categorizations.

Who makes the categorization, how and why?
An attempt to answer this question must, if only briefly, examine ideas discussed in the literature on the Lisu concerning ancestry, place of origin and the origin of both the name Lisu and clan names.

The implications are quite radical. If an ethnic group is not ethnic at all in the usual sense; if individuals, depending on circumstances actually circulate between ethnic categories and, by doing so, take up available alternative social roles, then it is apposite to reject the deep-rooted idea of ethnic entities based on ancestral origins. What is remarkable is that scholars continue to try to retain this notion. Lewis for instance observes for the Lisu of Thailand that:

> Six clans are traditionally Lisu, and have Lisu names.... There are further nine principal clans which have evolved from inter-marriage with Yunnanese (Lewis, 1984: 258).

This statement is of particular interest but unfortunately Lewis does not elaborate and we are left to debate what it means "to be traditionally Lisu". This is particularly tantalizing because according to Lewis's formulation it clearly does not rest solely on bearing a Lisu name.

In the absence of an explicit elaboration a tempting interpretation presents itself. Are there in Thailand two kinds of Lisu: the "pure" ones, so to say, and the "mixed" ones; a sort of authentic Lisu hard-core whose ethnic integrity would have been partially lost through the progressive assimilation of Yunnanese outsiders? One wonders how such a view could be convincingly substantiated: existing documentation (ancient chronicles, travellers observations, missionaries accounts etc) tend to suggest a different interpretation.

A survey of the literature such as Dessaint's **Lisu Annotated Bibliography** reveals that descriptions of Lisu by various authors at different times and at disparate places can be quite at odds with each other regarding anything from physical features, possible origins, behaviour, habits, dress, etc to types of social, economic and political organization. One constant feature however, reported by several authors in Burma as well as in China is their hybrid character, their mixing and intermarrying with local neighbours. This explains why different and sometimes contradictory opinions may have been arrived at regarding, for instance, the location of a hypothetical homeland believed by some authors to have been in eastern Tibet, by others in northwest Yunnan; or, as another example, the linguistic affiliations noted between the Lisu and the Lolo, the Moso, the Lutzu, the Atzi Kachin, the Burmese, the Lahu, the Akha, etc (Dessaint: 72).

There is no reason to question the accuracy of the observations, and even the validity of some of the speculations of various authors on the basis of their disparity. On the very contrary, it is precisely this disparity which gives the clue to what may ultimately turn out to be the truth of the matter, the actual process operative from time immemorial.

To take up again the matter of an original homeland. The conflicting answers to this alone indicate that the Lisu themselves are unable to answer, at least not in terms that make sense to those who ask the question.

Lisu Identity

Fraser writes,

> The origin of the Lisu race...is uncertain. The uniform testimony of the people themselves, from widely separated districts, is that they come from the "head of the river", which they refer, very vaguely, to either the N'Mai Hka, Salween, or Mekong rivers...As it can be observed that even the present tendency of Lisu migration is in a southerly direction..hence we may suppose that their original home is in or near Eastern Tibet (Fraser, 1922; i).

Enriquez reports,

> The Lisu speak of the birth-place of their race as the "Moon Rocks" of Rgha-hanpa...It is difficult to arrive at any definite conclusion with regard to the origin, history or migrations of the race (Enriquez, 1923: 72).

and elsewhere

> Many (Lisu) say (that they come) from the Upper Salween: some mention Hsiang hsiang (near Hpimaw): and others speak obscurely of the Wa Ba district in Upper Mekong. It seems more than probable that they came down from Eastern Tibet. (But he also warns) "the whole fabric is guess work (and) the argument is mainly philological and cannot be regarded as conclusive, seeing, as we do, **races around us who change their speech and identify without apparent effort** (my emphasis) (Enriquez, 1921: 72).

Both authors acknowledge the argumentation is rather weak and tentative, based on guesswork rather than historical verification of southward migration.

Enriquez, in his attempt "towards explaining the occurrence of the various races, whose distribution at first appears incomprehensible", is at a loss to account for the directions of the migrations, and in one single page (1923: 80) three times invokes the "strange instinct" that is "urging the people to the south". Then, he notes for instance that,

> Driven north, the Pyu founded a new capital at Pagan, consolidated, amalgamated with other tribes, and subsequently, **vanished, emerging again** (phoenix wise) to new life as Burmans" (1923: 79)... "The ancient Sak may have turned round in their tracks and **reappeared again** as Kadus" (1923: 80)....a generation ago, the Kuki Chins left the Chin Hills, settled in Maniput, and since 1877 have re-entered Burma again in the Somra Hill Tracts at a point considerably to the north of their original settlements (1923: 80).

Leach states quite explicitly (1954) that the Lisu may live with and marry non-Lisu, and may change ethnic identity. Consistent with these observations, two remarks help put things in proper perspective. Commenting on the Kachin-Lisu, Lehman stress that "Despite the fact that some kind of Kachin are Lisu, it would be meaningless to ask whether the latter are a "kind" of Kachin since everywhere else, Lisu are in no way Kachin." (1979 : 231). As for Durrenberger, he quite cleverly reflects that to be Lisu is perhaps first of all not to be "Karen, Akha, Lahu or any other ethnic group in the network of such groups" (1971 : 14).

What all these observations point to is quite clear. No socio-cultural homogeneity nor specificity whatsoever can be claimed for the Lisu "tribe" as a whole. What the Lisu of Burma, China and Thailand have in common is that they resemble their immediate neighbours rather than their distant "kinsmen". What remains is an ethnic label whose significance and relevance is local and contextual. It is therefore quite naive to consider that these people known as Lisu nowadays are the direct descendents of the ancient inhabitants of an original homeland that cannot be located with any certainty. **Lisu do not come from nowhere; they come from everywhere within an area that in-**

Lisu Identity

cludes eastern India, northern Burma, south-west China and, recently, Northern Thailand.

What does the name "Lisu" mean?

It is often claimed that the proper name for the "group" is Lisu. The Lisu refer to themselves and are referred to by others by this name just as they in turn refer to other groups like the Akha, Lahu, Hmong, Mien, Karen etc. with whom they share a similar life style.

According to Dessaint,

> They are known to the Chinese as Li, Liso, Lisaw, Lihsaw, Lishaw, Lishu, or Lip'a. The northernmost Lisu along the Salween are called Lutzu (not to be confused with the true Lutzu, further north and west), or Yehjen. The latter term is probably related to the Kachin terms for Lisu: Yawyin, Yawyen, Yaoyen. Lisu in Burma who have been less influenced by Kachin are sometimes called Shisham, while those more influenced are called Lasaw. The Maru refer to them as Lasi. The Lolo (Yi) call them Lip'o, and call those living along the Salween La-u-p'o. Shans and Northern Thai know them as Khae Liisoo, Liisaw or Lisshaw (Dessaint, 1971: 71).

Enriquez notes that,

> The Chinese call these people Lisaw, except in the east and central parts of Yunnan, where they give them their proper title of Lisu. Just there, perversely enough, the Lisu call themselves Lihpaw. The Naru and Lashi call them respectively Lasi, and Leurseur. The Chinese call the Kachin races generally Yejen or Ye-ren (Savages), and the Kachins have passed the same name on to the Lisu, changing it slightly in Yawyin. The Chinese never speak of the Lisu as Ye-ren (Enriquez, 1921: 72).

What these various remarks reveal is that: first, people considered to be Lisu by outsiders may actually call themselves by different names; second, each dominant group makes distinctions between various Lisu, usually on the basis of their dress styles which also reflects the extent to which they are locally influenced by the dominant culture. Kachin distinguish between Shisham and Lasaw; Lolo between Lip'o and La-u-p'o; Chinese between Pe Lisu, He Lisu and Hwa Lisu. Needless to say, these categorizations are local and contextual; it is irrelevant and pointless to ask Lisu in Thailand whether they belong for instance to the Pe, He or Hwa "subgroup".

Let us now consider the alleged meaning of the name Lisu. Here again they are multiple and have little in common except that they usually fit the view of those who use them.

Dessaint signals that the first radical of the Chinese term means "dog", which would explain why "wild dog" has been suggested. This is an appellation commonly used by Chinese in reference to "barbarians". According to Enriquez, the meaning of the name Yawyin given to the Lisu by the Kachin means "savage". For Fraser Lisu means, "People who have come down" and for Ta'o (1984), "Born from the stone". Dessaint, or rather some of his informants, claim it is a combination of *ili* "custom", "law" and *isu* "one who runs from", hence "outlaw, rebel". Last, but certainly not least, a Thai social worker suggested "Loser" (Khun Duanchai; personal communication). As for me, I never succeeded in getting any Lisu to volunteer a meaning.

To end this review, let me now examine the question of clan names.

Fraser is once again helpful,

> Many Lisu have Chinese surnames and claim Chinese origin. Though all Lisu clan surnames have their Chinese equivalents, some have Chinese surnames without Lisu equivalents: these are usually descendants of Chinese adopted into Lisu families. But even Lisu with ordinary Lisu clan surnames will

sometimes claim to be of Chinese extraction, averring that their ancestors originally came from eastern China, usually from the province of Kiangsi - the ancestral home of most of the Chinese living near the Burma frontier. Such Lisu do not, however, boast of their Chinese origin. No Lisu is ashamed to own his race, whereas the aborigines of Eastern Yunnan, where Chinese influence is stronger, are often ashamed to admit that they are not Chinese, and, indeed, tend to become absorbed in the latter race (Fraser, 1922: ii).

Enriquez writing on the same question observes that,

> The main subdivisions of the Yawyin race appear to be called Tawn Kya, Hgwa Hpa, Ngaw Hpa, Naw Kya, Gu Hpa, Lair Mair, Bya Hpa, Dzi Hpa, Waw Hpa (level tone), and Waw Hpa (descending tone)....All however do not occur in British territory. Those which do are known to the Kachins by Kachin names, **though there seems to be some inconsistency in the identification** (my emphasis). Thus, lists obtained from Kachins and Yawyins at Pajua (Sima) do not agree exactly with lists obtained in Sadon...Since we always communicate with Yawyins in the Kachin language, the clans are usually known to us by their Kachin names. Thus the Tawn Kya are spoken of as Mitung in Kachin; the Ngwa Hpa and Ngaw Hpa as Marip; the Zaw Kya as Lahpai; in Myitkyina, the Lair-mair are known to the Kachin as N Hkum, but in Bhamo as Lassang; and at Pajau the Zaw Kya were identified most positively as Labya.... The Yawyin families appear to have been named after individual peculiarities, or after animals. Thus the Ngwa Hpa means Fish People; Ngaw Hpa, Joined People etc...." (Enriquez, 1921: 73).

Ch'en who conducted field research in the Hsik'ang province on Lisu and Shui-t'ien groups who had migrated from Yunnan, reports the following:

> The Li-Su and Shui-t'ien have adopted Chinese surnames (hsing). All families belonging to the She-tsu group of the Li-su bear the surname Ho; those of the Mai-tsu group have the surnames Chang, Wei, Ku, Li, Lan, Chi, Yang and others. But under the Chinese surnames their original clan names can be observed. The She-tsu group has the Li-su name Hai-tsu-p'a. "Tsu-pa" means "surname"; hai means "rat". In other words, the Li-su surname is "rat". The word "hai" is similar in pronunciation to the Chinese character "Ho". Therefore, the Chinese surname Ho was adopted. There, however, exist in this group twelve clans which take their name from twelve different kinds of rats. (Some say that the Li-su in Yunnan have as many as twenty or thirty different clan-names, all of them being surnamed Ho, but most observers agree that there are twelve in number)...the surnames of the Mai-tsu group are also derived from different clan-names. (Plum, millet, bear, sheep, wolf etc....). It is quite clear that a Li-su clan always adopts the Chinese translation of his clan name, in order to serve as its Chinese surname" (Ch'en 1947: 25 6).

These various reports highlight a number of points and call for comments. First, wherever they are, Lisu adopt a lingua franca translation of their Lisu clan names which, as Enriquez notes, leads to some inconsistency in labels of identification. The same process can be observed in Northern Thailand today where Ngwa Hpa are called Lao Yipa or Sae Li, Bia Hpa Saemi, Li Kya Sinli or Saenli etc...It is also interesting to discover that clan names on both of the lists provided by Enriquez for Northern Burma and Ch'en for Southern China can be found in Northern Thailand. But, as Fraser stresses, if there are Chinese surnames

Lisu Identity

without Lisu equivalents, there are also Lisu with ordinary Lisu clan surnames who sometimes claim to be of Chinese extraction. So much for the idea that the origin of a clan could be traced through its name alone. Fraser quoted by Enriquez, (1921: 73), further says about these names that he "did not even regard them as clan, but just family surnames like our own or the Chinese, and that is all they amount to in districts where they are scattered". An observation which is corroborated by P. Durrenberger who writes:

> Most of the lineages are not exclusively Lisu Lineages. Some are Chinese, Lahu and other groups as well. That is, one has to specify both lineage and ethnic label to identify a particular lineage as Lisu, so this can be no measure of the groups to be called Lisu" (Durrenberger, 1971: 8).

It appears that these genealogically defined references to clan and lineage names cannot be systematically associated with a given ethnic identity. To the contrary, some clan and lineage names can be found in groups with different ethnic identities. In other words, there is not necessarily a connection between ethnic origin and identity. It is in this sense that such categorizations as the so-called "Chinese-Lisu" ultimately lack pertinence, except perhaps for policy decision-makers and immigration law enforcement agencies. As I observed earlier, although there is evidence of substantial inter-mixing of Lisu and Lahu in Northern Thailand, I could not confirm the existence of a special Lahu-Lisu category. I strongly doubt that these types of categorizations have the racial-like connotations and implications projected onto them by outside observers. For a Lisu, to be of Lahu or Chinese descent does not affect his claim to being Lisu.

But for those who see a difference it means a lot. The construction of a distinction has clear implications. The *haw* of Northern Thailand have no legal status as immigrants thus they are clearly distinguished from the *"chao khao"*. Until very recently opium cultivation, although illegal since 1957 was not subject to the severe repression that is now taking place. To many observers, opium-growing tribal groups basically were, and still are, upland farmers whose meagre subsistence depends on hard work and what they can harvest from difficult mountain fields. The ethnic category *"haw"* does not correspond to the same image. Anthropologists (Motte, 1967; Maxwell Hill, 1983) have unsuccessfully researched the etymology of this *"haw"* appellation (but on this subject, see Ch'en (1947; 257) quoted above). In Northern Thailand, this ethnic label is applied, on the presumption of Yunnanese origin to a variety of people as different as farmers, peddlers, traders, irregulars of the K.M.T., bandits, smugglers and traffickers. The remarkable disposition and ability of the Chinese to trade at all levels of society is identified as a characteristic of *"haw"* and as this group is seen to play a prominent role in the narcotics trade, it therefore takes a strong pejorative connotation. In the context of Northern Thailand this provides a compelling incentive for ethnic identity change. In this respect, a Lahu-Lisu category has little or no particular significance: they are just *"chao khao"*. But a Chinese-Lisu category indeed tells another story.

This point needs to be stressed: for the people concerned, to be "Lisu" is a matter of life style, not of ancestral origins. What then are the specific characteristics of the Lisu way of life? Due to the necessary brevity of this paper, allow me to limit myself to a succinct delineation.

Here again, it is vain to adopt an empirical approach and try to explain it through genetic like traits of character and mental characteristics (e.g. Lewis 1984), even if this sometimes appears to succeed in describing the empirical reality. Thai extension workers and contact teams of various development projects unanimously agree in calling the Lisu the most individualistic, even the most selfish and troublesome people they deal with when it comes to implementing measures designed to benefit the community as a whole (constructing drinking and irrigation water systems, organizing road maintenance, setting-up village committees to administer revolving loan funds etc...). I have myself witnessed behaviour apparently displaying a considerable lack of cooperation or concern at the village or intervillage level but such considerations are of no help in clarifying the structural components of the social reality which these behaviours exemplify.

It is at this point that theoretical suggestions of authors like Lehman generate observations of particular concrete value. Ethnic categories must be viewed as defined, not in absolute terms, but by "role complementation" and that the necessary condition for the existence of an ethnic group as such is its structural opposition to other groups in relation to different resources. This is to say that the social specificity of a given group can only be elucidated by comparison and through its relations, or absence of relations, with other groups. Ideally, to be able to define and characterize every group would require an equally in-depth knowledge of each, per se, and in its differential relations to the others. A sort of knowledge that few anthropologists, if any, can claim because most research is conducted within the prevalent conception of a rigid separation between groups. This leads scholars to limit the range of their research and focus their expertise on a particular group: an approach which by definition precludes the formation of a global view of the actual nature and function of ethnicity.

There is no doubt though that this specificity can be found in the structure, forms and modes of the social, economic and political organization. I indicated earlier that the fundamental structure of Lisu society is the kinship and affinity system which determines and controls social recruitment, organizes the process of production, defines and forms the allocation of power and authority.

Historically, wars in this part of the world were conducted to gain control not so much of territory as populations. People were the essential resource. For groups to survive they needed to control the fecundity of their women and the rules that regulated and controlled access to women were fundamental to the constitution of a group. This still holds: each groups' kinship and marriage system is a particular pattern followed in the exchange of women. Intermarriage associates different groups in this process and link them through privileged affinal ties.

Lisu specificity first resides in the structure of the kinship and marriage system. It is the study of matrimonial practice which enables us to analyze Lisu social organization and reveals a complementarity with the Lahu and *haw*.

What makes the kinship and affinity system the fundamental structure in Lisu society is that it also models the organization of the process of production, distribution and circulation of goods. Lisu social organization is adapted to the production of what was until very recently, the main cash crop: opium, and still fundamentally depends on it. The value of the bride-price for instance is directly indexed to the price of opium on the local market. The attitude towards the consumption of opium in Lisu society is notably different from that of other groups including the Lahu and *haw*. The structural complementarity which connects the Lisu with the Lahu and with the *haw* is differential and made up of compatible as well as opposing characteristics.

Lisu specificity also resides in the particular political organization of the group. I have indicated that the structure of power and authority follows that of the family household. The perceived individualism of the Lisu is part and parcel of a code of behaviour which is functional and consistent with the structure, forms and modes of the social organization.

Conclusion

In these pages, I have delineated a problematique concerning Lisu identity and indicated an interpretation of ethnicity which integrates and accounts for both the information provided in the ethnographic literature and my own fieldwork. I have invoked arguments and observations made by scholars whom I believe have contributed most to clarification of the question of ethnic identity. In doing so I have also called into question the views of those working within an empirical tradition whose writings obscure or mask the actual nature and function of ethnicity in a multi-ethnic context. I strongly doubt the validity of the concept of "rigidly defined" groups (Hinton, 1969: 4) constituted on the basis of alleged loyalty to an ethnic identity (but for a significant change in Hinton's approach to the problem see Hinton, 1983: 155-68). This concept is still very popular among scholars engaged in research work in northern Thailand and I dare say that it not only proves to be wrong and misleading but also to be an obstacle to a diachronic as well as synchronic understanding and clarification of the social mechanisms at work in the multi-ethnic context of Northern Thailand.

References

Barth, Fredrik (1969) — ***Ethnic Groups and Boundaries*** F.Barth (ed.) Boston; Little, Brown and Co.pp.9-38.

Ch'en Tsung-Hsiang (1947) — "The Dual System and the Clans of the Li-Su and Shui-t'ien Tribes" ***Monumenta Senica*** 12: 59-259.

Dessaint, Alain Y. (1971) — "Lisu Annotated Bibliography" ***Behavior Science Notes*** Volume six, Number Two, Human Relations Area Files: New Haven.

Dessaint A.Y. and W.Y. (1982) — "Economic Systems and Ethnic Relations in Northern Thailand" ***Contributions to Southeast Asian Ethnography*** No.1, Setember: 72-85.

Durrenberger, Paul E. (1971) — ***The Ethnography of Lisu Curing*** Unpublished Ph.D. dessertation, Univ. of Illinois, Urbana-Champaign.

Enriquez C.M. (1921) — "The Yawyins or Lisu" ***Burma Research Society Journal*** Vol. 1 II: 70-73.

Enriquez C.M. (1923) — "Story of the Migrations" ***Journal of the Burma Research Society*** Vol.XIII, Part II: 77-81

Fraser, James Outram (1922) — ***Handbook of the Lisu (Yawyin) language*** Rangoon, Superintendant, Government Printing, Burma.

Hinton, Peter (1983) "Do the Karen Really Exist?" McKinnon & Wanat Bhruksasri (eds) *Highlanders of Thailand* Oxford University Press: Kuala Lumpur, pp.155-68.

Hill, Ann Maxwell (1983) "The Yunnanese: Overland Chinese in North Thailand" McKinnon and Wanat Bhruksasri (eds) *Highlanders of Thailand* Oxford University press: Kuala Lumpur, pp.123-34.

Keyes, Charles F. (ed.) (1979) *Ethnic Adaptation and Identity* Institute for the Study of Human Issues: Philadelphia, pp.1-23; 25-61.

Kunstadter, Peter (1979) "Ethnic Group, Category and Identity: Karen in Northern Thailand" in *Ethnic Adaptation and Identity* Keyes, C.F. (ed.) Institute for the Study of Human Issues: Philadelphia, pp.119-63.

Leach, Edmund (1954) *Political Systems of Highland Burma* Bell, London.

Leach, Edmund (1960) "The Frontiers of Burma" *Comparative Studies in Society and History:* 49-68.

Lebar, Frank; M., Hickey; G.,. Musgrave, J. (1964) *Ethnic Groups of Mainland Southeast Asia* Human Relations Area Files Press: New Haven.

Lehman, F.K. (1967) "Ethnic Categories in Burma and the Theory of Social System" in Kunstadter, P.(ed.) *Southeast Asian*

Tribes, Minorities and Nations pp. 93-124 Vol. 1

Lehman, F.K. (1979) "Who are the Karen, and If So, Why? Karen Ethno-History and a Formal Theory of Ethnicity" in Keyes, C.F. (ed.) *Ethnic Adaptation and Identity* Institute for the Study of Human Issues : Philadelphia, pp. 215-67.

Lewis, Paul and Elaine (1984) *Peoples of the Golden Triangle* Thames and Hudson: London.

Maran La Raw (1967) "Towards a Basis for Understanding the Minorities in Burma: the Kachin Example" *Southeast Asian Tribes, Minorities and Nations* Vol.1, P.Kunstadter (ed.) Princeton: New Jersey, pp.125-46.

Marlowe, David H. (1979) "In the Mosaic: The Cognitive and Structural Aspects of Karen-Other Relationships" Keyes C.F. (ed.) *Ethnic Adaptation and Identity* Institute for the Study of Human Issues: Philadelphia, pp.165-13.

Moerman, M. (1968) "Being Lue: Uses and Abuses of Ethnic Identification" *Essays on the Problems of Tribe* June Helm (ed.). Proceedings of the 1967 Annual Spring meeting of the American Ethnological Society, Univ. of Washington Press: Seattle, pp. 153-69.

Motte, F.W. (1967) "The Rural 'Haw' (Yunnanese Chinese) of Northern Thailand" in Kunstadter, P. (ed.) *Southeast Asian Tribes, Minorities and Nations* Princeton: New Jersey, pp. 487-24.

49. Akha child (Ralana)

50. Food demonstration (Connell)

51. Akha mother (Hobday)

52. Akha boy and baby (Vienne)

53. Poppy field (Vienne)

54. Opium smoker (Supachai)

55. Harvesting opium (Connell)

56. Lisu farmers (McKinnon)

57. Lisu tomato harvest (Hobday)

58. Lisu women (Connell)

59. Lisu children (Hobday)

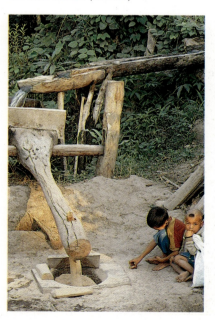
60. Hydraulic rice pounder (McKinnon)

61. Lisu girl (Vienne)

62. Mlabri victim of malaria (Vienne)

63. Mlabri women (McKinnon)

64. Karen woman cutting melon (Kampe)

65. Lahu Sheleh farmers (Supachai)

66. Lahu Sheleh farmers (Supachai)

67. Lahu Sheleh field ceremony (Supachai)

68. Karen wedding (Connell)

RESETTLEMENT: INFORMATION & INTERPRETATIONS

Perhaps the most controversial policy to emerge out of current thinking has been the willingness of the government to consider moving ethnic minorities out of areas in which they are seen to present either a danger to the environment or a risk to national security. As of August 1988, some 5000 people had been involuntarily moved out of national parks but it is not yet clear whether it is the intention to extend this strategy and include highlanders living in special watershed areas. Where people have settled near the border and it is believed that they entered the country relatively recently (since the mid 70 s) repatriation may be reconsidered.

One of the leading factors in this policy decision appears to be a concern to preserve what primary forest remains. The strategy outlined in Appendix V, entitled "Target Areas for Prevention of Forest Destruction by Hilltribes", provides the most succinct statement of intent available. The strategy of relocation is clearly seen as part of a need to protect recently declared national parks (eg Khlong Lan, Kamphaeng Phet). If this type of intervention is extended to areas in the upper north, highlander communities found in locations in which approximately 60 percent of the land remains under forest, may well be moved.

In locations where the forest has already gone, villages may also be clustered under project development work. Such consolidation, ostensibly designed to "reinforce administrative systems obligation, and faith in the institutions of Nation, Religion and Monarchy among the hill tribes" appears to be a part of national policy (Summary of the Plan for the Coordination of the Development of the Area Bordering the Doi Tung Development Project). This particular undertaking is being managed by the Centre for the coordination of Hill Tribe Affairs and Eradication of Narcotic Crops (COHAN 3rd Army) and the Internal Security Operations Command, Region 3 (ISOC) working in Mae Chan, Chiang Rai, along the Thai-Burmese border.

The idea of moving highlanders to sites deemed to be more suitable is not new. In 1960-61 the Hill Tribe Welfare Committee took a decision to set up resettlement areas in Tak, Chiang Mai, Chiang Rai and Petchaboon provinces. At this time little was known about highlander cultures, agricultural systems and even the number of people living in the hills. Quite soon after an administrative structure was set up, the idea of planned resettlement was abandoned. Following 1967, the outbreak of fighting between government forces and communist guerrillas based in the highlands created a need to provide centres to and in which hill people could be evacuated and settled. Both of these occasions provided learning experiences which underlined the administrative and financial problems which come with large scale resettlement including the difficulty of finding enough suitable land.

Whether the government of today is better prepared to provide the necessary resources to ensure a reasonable livelihood, for those who may be resettled is still under discussion, if not under question, and forms the main thrust of issues raised in this section.

Mr Wanat Bhruksasri's paper, couched in the liberal and humanitarian terms of earlier policy makers, provides an argument for making a generous accommodation, advocates voluntary as opposed to involuntary relocation and positive national integration rather than forced assimilation. Ardith Eudey, a primitologist from the Riverside Campus of the University of California who accidentally witnessed the resettlement of a Hmong village in Uthai Thani province provides a first hand account of how these operations are conducted.

Information & Interpretations

Cornelia Ann Kammerer, a professional anthropologist trained at the University of Chicago has prepared a comprehensive interpretation based on the imperatives of state formation and several years research conducted amongst the Akha. John McKinnon, a geographer from Victoria University of Wellington working with the TRI-ORSTOM Project builds on the broad analysis of his ORSTOM colleague Bernard Vienne and questions, amongst other things, the ecological thinking which provides the rationale for what he terms the current "get tough" policy.

Problem Solving Through Understanding: A Personal Opinion on How to Approach Development Problems in the Highlands.

Wanat Bhruksasri

In 24 years of continuous work in hill tribe affairs, I have never seen a conference more important than this. Five principal ministries and departments are represented and all in attendance have come to explain policy, planning and other activities under their responsibility. It is regrettable that provincial governors could not join this meeting but because of administrative tasks generated by the forthcoming election [July, 1986] their absence is understandable.

I am of the opinion that we are considering two to three issues which boil down to the one thing: dangers presented by highlanders. There are many aspects of this danger, many issues, but all of them have some bearing on the question of national security. It is important to assist hill people to settle and so protect the forests. Agreement on this point is a good place to start.

With this agreement in mind I would like to suggest a creative and practical approach to hill tribe problems in the

**This paper is an edited version of an address presented to the Seminar on the Prevention and Suppression of Intrusion into and Destruction of the forest by the Hill Tribes held at Government House Santi Mitre 15-16 July, 1986.

hope it will not only be acceptable but also have less negative impact than other methods proposed.

I would like to point out that when we consider problems associated with highlanders we often find ourselves talking as though we intended to wage a war in which there are only two sides: the enemy and us. In actual fact the situation is not so simple. There is a clear conflict of interests between highlanders and us but when we talk of hill people it is important to remember that we don't have a real enemy. We ought to admit this to ourselves before we get into a fight by default. Government policy has for years accepted in principle that all hill people are potential Thai citizens and that the state will grant citizenship to all those who qualify on the basis of existing regulations. This policy is based on a long established regulation first promulgated a decade ago (Cabinet resolution, 6 July 1976). Let me be quite explicit: we are not fighting the hill people but we are fighting their problems. They are our allies with whom we should join forces, shoulder to shoulder or at least in the same company.

What do I mean by this, that we are "fighting their problems"? How many here realise that the highlanders current situation is fraught with difficulties which they would certainly change for the better if they could? If we maintained a better relationship with them and we all understood the problems of the highlands from our different perspectives in a communicable way, would there be a war? If we expect to win the war against the problems of the highlands we must bring the Chinese principle of Zun Wu to our deliberations, that we need to know both them (the enemy) and ourselves.

For as long as we insist on considering differences rather than similarities, the judgements impacted in our discussion will themselves serve as obstacles to development and problem solving. A good example of how such thinking leads us away from solutions rather than towards them is contained in statements like this, "Hill people are not Thai, they are foreigners". Such an observation is at best a half-truth. If to be Thai means to share a belief in the same ethical system, then we have half the truth. However, if such a statement refers to an ethnolingistic reality, we had better watch our step. In a paper presented to the International Congress of Anthropology at Rome, Italy (1966), a Japanese historian announced that in ancient times the Meo-Yao group maintained close ethnic relationships with the Tai, a tribal group refered to as Pai in Chinese chronicles. The American linguist Paul Benedict (1975 and 1976) has argued convincingly for a language Superstock known as Austro-Thai which places Tai-Kadai and Meo-Yao in the same family. This has been accepted by the University of California linguist Jim Matisoff of Berkeley (1983). Then again we can draw a lesson from the late distinguished Professor Phaya Anuman Rajadhon, who long ago (1961) told a workshop of hill tribe survey workers that, "Although the Meo and yao are now forest mountaineers, do not look down on them because we might share a common ancestry".

As for the ethnic category "hill tribe" (*"chao khao"* in Thai) and all associated with the term, we had best remember that the word only came into official use in 1959 following the formation of the Hill Tribe Welfare Committee. When we count back this is just 30 years ago but hill people have been here much longer than that. Historical and archaeological evidence documents the fact that in some parts of the North, the Lua and Karen were here before Thai language and culture came to dominate daily life. Many people in the north are descended from these original inhabitants.

The term "hill tribe" is not well defined even in government regulations. From documents and established usage we can assume that what is meant is strictly this: the ethnic minorities residing in the highlands such as the Meo,

Yao, Lahu, Lisu, Akha, Karen, Lua, Htin and Khamu who moved from Laos to take up residence in Thailand before 1975 and before 1974 if they came from Burma. According to regulations those who migrated into Thailand after those years are illegal migrants who ought to be arrested and arraigned before the courts or repatriated. Even though such migrants may belong to resident ethnic groups they cannot legally be called hill tribes. The term "hill tribe" has a quite specific interpretation. Hill tribe people are part of the Thai population, a section of the community who, it is widely acknowledged, qualify for special attention if they are to develop the skills and knowledge necessary to become first class citizens. According to this classification, hill tribes are not foreigners at all in the sense that they either lack nationality or are the citizens of other countries.

Some look down on hill tribe people as though they deliberately engaged in illegal activities such as growing opium poppy, felling forests and so forth, as though they wanted to annoy clean living, honest Thai citizens. How can people see positive qualities when they are so well conditioned to see highlanders as both dangerous and inferior?

It would be difficult to attempt to correct all the negative highlander references in use, but working just with data and information concerned with the issues at hand, it is possible to straighten the record on a few.

First, highlanders have a record of giving assistance to the nation. All of us here remember the troubled times commencing in 1967 when a few small groups of hill people emerged in armed opposition to the state. This uprising took more than 15 years to bring under control. It was not until 1982 that enough mutual trust was reestablished to bring the rebellion to an end. The crisis was damaging in more ways than one. The trouble makers suffered, Thai citizens working in close proximity to the combat zone suffered and for a long time the life and property of all officials and villagers in the areas affected were exposed to serious danger. But how many know that from the time when these troubles first began until the situation was brought under control, many highlanders fought on the side of the government and gave their lives fighting against communist insurgents or provided information which helped the loyalist cause? Many military and Border Police Patrol officers know this. Some civil servants, who were able to go into hiding just before attacks were mounted, were warned by highlanders to whom they came to owe their lives.

Second, the picture of the hill tribes which most of us carry in our minds is that of opium growers. This is only partly right and that right part is quickly diminishing. Not every hill person grows opium: most have never grown opium simply because not every ethnic group has made this a part of their agricultural system. To speak loosely of highlanders as opium growers is to set a classification into which most people do not fit and where the category is foisted upon them anyway, we should realise that it makes for considerable misunderstandings.

In fact only Meo, Yao, Lisu, Lahu and a few Akha grow opium. Altogether these people make up only one third of all hill people. The Karen, Lua, Htin and Khamu in common with Thai farmers do not traditionally grow opium and nowadays the few villagers who do remain the exception.

Overall, fewer and fewer villagers are growing opium than in the not too distant past. If we compare the amount of opium produced in Thailand as estimated by UN experts in 1967 with what we know is produced today, the hill tribes of Thailand are producing at least 100 tons less than they did twenty years ago. Surely this is a measure of the success of problem solving whether directly or indirectly aimed at cutting back production? In 1967 the estimated yield was 145 tons. ONCBs production estimate for the 1984/85 season was only 34.6 tons.

This is an impressive result from twenty years work. Although there is no single comprehensive study on which I can base the observation, clearly the achievement is the consequence of many factors, such as efforts in educational development, public health, agricultural extension, opium crop replacement and suppression, road construction, market influences, religious teaching by Buddhist monks under the Dhammacarik programme and well publicised campaigns supported by radio and the mass media to highlight the dangers of opium smoking and addiction. There is also a widespread shortage of land suitable for growing opium because of both population increase and intervention on the part of government agencies concerned with watershed conservation.

All of these factors have contributed to the drop in opium production. But this doesn't mean that we are out of the woods. I would like to remind you of the words of Mr. Jorgen Gammelgaard the UNFDAC senior field advisor, "A one-sided approach to opium poppy emphasising only eradication of cultivation may have unwanted side effects which are so common in the history of drug abuse control. One is to convert Thailand into an opium importing country. Another possible effect may be to pave the way for heroin dependence in hill tribe villages"(Gammelgard, 1985). To keep the level of opium production dropping, it is necessary to cure addicts and encourage growers to voluntarily decrease production. I believe there are now suitable models available which could be widely applied.

Third, there is the stereotype of the swiddener as an itinerant gypsy. Some people believe that there is nowhere in the world where swiddeners have settled down to take up permanent residence. Perhaps we ought to take more care with our words? The term "swidden" itself cames from Anglo-Saxon and dates from a time, less than two thousand years ago when the ancestors of modern Europeans were swiddeners. In

Resettlement & Understanding

the contemporary world, those who insist on seeing the hill tribes as gypsies are reluctant to look at the facts and prefer to step across the mundane details that abound in our lives. As the proverb has it, "It is just as hard for the elephant to see the mite as it is for the mite to see the elephant" or as is said in English, "It's difficult to see the woods for the trees". In fact Thailand has examples of permanent settlements established by each hill tribe group and it is not necessary to look for examples elsewhere.

The truth of the matter is that the hill tribe way of life is quite different from that of gypsies. Gypsies are not agriculturalists but work as musicians, small-scale traders and do odd jobs. Their way of life is adapted to moving quite frequently from place to place. The situation of the highlanders is quite different. Their main occupation is agriculture. Their swiddening farming system makes extremely efficient use of energy and requires that they clear, dry and burn the natural vegetation before sowing seeds. The system does not require a knowledge of soil conservation and nourishment necessary to maintain permanent fields. Most highland soils are of low fertility and without very intensive care (eg. terracing) are not suited to permanent cultivation. Farmers rely on nutrients released from the biomass rather than those already present in the ground and if they attempt to extend the period of continuous cultivation beyond one or two years, they must face a weeding problem and falling fertility. It makes more sense to abandon the land and either allow the vegetation to regenerate before using it again (rotational farming or cyclical bush fallow) or go in search of new land on which the vegetative nutrient bank is well established (pioneer swiddening, or primary shifting cultivation). Some highland farmers, then, clear land and plant it for only one to two years before allowing it to return to fallow. Others use their fields for as long as possible, basically until it becomes too difficult to farm because of weeds, declining yields and low fertility.

Of these two methods, primary shifting cultivation has the most dramatic impact on the landscape. Virgin forest is destroyed on an ever-increasing front by people in search of land on which they can grow rice. The Lua and Karen however use a rotational system which is ecologically informed. As long as the fallow period is of sufficient duration to allow the vegetation and nutrient levels to recover, land can be used continually over many years. Some Karen villages for instance have been established for over 200 years.

Dr.Sanga Sabhasri and his colleagues studied this rotational system very carefully. They found that the method under which fields are used in a cyclical fashion over a set period has much to recommend it. Settlements are permanent. The boundaries of village estates are clearly known to all. Villagers supplement the product of their swidden fields with rice grown on irrigated terraces. Farmers keep strictly to their land and neither intrude into nor destroy virgin forest. They also possess a very strong tradition of looking after the forest because it provides so much they need to keep themselves alive.

It surprises me that some people consider such rotational farming as a waste of land. This is an issue we should look at carefully and analyse before we act. If there is an urgent problem it has more to do with primary shifting cultivation than rotational swiddening. It is the primary swiddeners who are constantly attempting to bring virgin forest land under cultivation, who wish to continue their pioneering life without having to take into account either new techniques or the new political situation in the highlands.

In my opinion, it is possible to solve the problems which come in the train of shifting cultivation and to protect the forest against further intrusion. I will base my argument on the following assumptions:
- the pattern of agriculture influences the duration of

Resettlement & Understanding

settlement;
- if the pattern of agriculture is shifting then the associated settlements will be of a temporary nature;
- if the pattern of agriculture is permanent the associated settlements will also be permanent.

I might well use the formula, agriculture commands residence rather than residence commands agriculture! Today it is not uncommon to find highlanders who set their village in one area but work in another. To do so they simply travel by small pick-up trucks which they obtain under hire purchase agreements. People can live where they like but they cannot live too far away from where they work. We can readily appreciate that permanent agriculture could well serve as the heart or foundation of any strategy designed to prevent people from intruding into virgin forest. The forest must first be felled before a farm can be set up. When the agricultural possibilities of the site are exhausted, farmers must move on. As they move, the forest is destroyed. If they grow opium at high altitudes (900-1000 metres), at the very top of the watershed, then forest destruction also means destruction of the watershed.

Primary shifting cultivation is a cause of the destruction of natural resources. including forest, soil, water and even wildlife. The sensible solution is to bring such shifting cultivation to an end by replacing it with a new model of agriculture.

When we are able to promote a new model of permanent agriculture, it can be expected that highlanders will themselves take up permanent residence. Just as Thai farmers base their communities and household stability on permanent rice paddies: hill tribe people will come to see their future from the same perspective and be happy to maintain stable communities.

RESETTLEMENT

It is my opinion that the best way of solving the problem of natural resource destruction by the hill tribes is to settle them on permanent sites well serviced by the administrative and socio-economic infrastructure. The appropriate government offices involved should be assigned to identify areas suitable for settlement. Settlement on land where it is possible to earn a living and gain access to agricultural extension services should receive the recommendation of all concerned officials. By this I mean that it is the suitability for sustaining agricultural production and long term residence which is the main point. The Royal Forestry Department is authorised to give permission for using land and could readily assign the Department of Land Development to check suitability with the appropriate criteria: slope, soil type etc. This Department is well qualified to decide whether land is best suited for use as watershed forest, commercial forest, orchards or farming. It seems to me that promotion of a settlement policy should be accompanied by optimum development of land use, especially establishing of trees which take a long time to grow. Hill people now understand the financial significance of trees and have always appreciated the availability of timber for building, firewood and other uses. Villages now located at some distance from forest have to pay for firewood to be brought to them. Forestry development for watershed protection and commercial plantations could well follow the establishment of villages and provide a source of income to the settlers while they build up their farms. Highlanders should certainly be more involved in community forest development just like lowlanders. Farmers could be encouraged to plant trees at recommended spacings throughout their farms. There is no reason why they could not take the benefit of this participation in agro-forestry.

In considering the question of how to identify the best way for hill people to earn their living from the land, the first consideration must make full acknowledgement of the need for them to cease practising primary shifting cultivation and

Resettlement & Understanding

to change to perennial gardening or permanant agriculture. We must not only think in terms of watershed classification but also permanent residence, sustainable production and the impact this is likely to have on both forest and watershed resources. The Karen and Lua who have maintained permanent settlements for centuries have shown that this is possible. Those living in this manner have also developed a very strong sense of land tenure which involves ownership (Chantaboon, Chapter 4). Ownership is hardly relevant to swiddeners who plant then move on. Such people are willing to welcome newcomers to their village, especially those who belong to the same lineage. After farmers come to base their livelihood on irrigated rice fields, grow perennial shrubs such as tea, coffee or fruit trees and see what their labour invested in the land can do, they become increasingly interested in protecting their holdings with a widely accepted form of land tenure including outright ownership. In a Ph.D dissertation prepared by the Englishman Bob Cooper, the broader social impact of this trend from shifting to more permanent forms of agriculture is explored. The kinship system of the Meo village he studied underwent considerable change.

Where land becomes a more valuable and scarce resource, several things happen. People are less likely to want to share. A Karen village in Mae Hong Son faced with a Government order to make room for other Karen pushed out of Burma in the course of fighting was most reluctant to do so. They fully realised that the availability of land was decreasing and that the fallow period was being foreshortened by natural population increase without exacerbating the problem by trying to help others. Over-use of land slows the rate of regeneration, reduces both nutrient build-up and release, and places farmers at risk. The weakest point of border control is that those already settled within Thailand do not report to officials when new people move in.

RESETTLEMENT

Increased awareness of land shortage can be used as a tactic to discourage immigration from neighbouring countries and the support of those already here could easily be secured by acknowledging their rights to land. If the status of hill tribe citizens was clearly distinguished from that of recent immigrants, their rights could, if necessary, be defended by the armed forces and the migrants expelled. Where it is decided to settle hill people and undertake agricultural development these people will, as citizens, identify closely with Thailand's interests. When such a situation holds, it will be much easier to undertake systematic development work rather than treat highland communities as a buffer against disaffected elements in neighbouring countries who have to engage in illegal trade in arms and drugs to survive. The state of anarchy which prevails at the moment is a real obstacle to setting up administrative procedures as well as adding to the problem of instrusion into the forest and its destruction.

To carry out effective develoment work implies that all aspects of the highlander's life would be taken into account. Plans would have to be prepared to deal with agricultural production as well as those things which can make such a difference to the quality of life, such as public health services, education, community work, attitudinal development, paid employment opportunities and an infrastructure of roads, water and so forth. Implementation must attempt holistic planning, what can truly be called integrated planning. In such planning, the people most affected by the outcome must be fully consulted. They must participate in every aspect of the operation and be encouraged to enter into the programme enthusiastically. Such participation should be aimed at providing learning experiences for individuals to pursue self-help, which is also an objective of current rural development policy.

There is a real need to call a forum where a free exchange of opinions on holistic and integrated development can take place. How development should be conducted ought

Resettlement & Understanding

to be settled in advance of action. Once resettlement areas are selected, the next question will be how to get the cooperation from the people who are to be moved. This can either be done in harmony with our hearts beating as one or with all the misunderstandings that come from being out of rhythm with the times.

This is not a matter to play with. We have every reason to be as one mind in this and enter both seriously and sincerely into a programme of common understanding. There should be a uniform approach to public relations, administration, application of the law and development policy. Let me discuss each of these in turn.

Public Relations

Once a strategy has been identified it should be clearly explained to all of the hill people concerned. Farmers should be told in quite precise terms the exact intention of the government: what land will be taken, where it is forbidden to settle (as this applies from province to province), how much support the government will give to development, and so forth. Statements must reflect a good understanding of the history of existing villages, some of which have been established for a hundred years or more. It is not enough to say out of the blue that such and such an area has been declared a public forest or national park or wild life conservation refuge. People have an intense sense of belonging to areas where their families have lived for centuries. It is reported for instance by some anthropologists that many Karen hold land to which they were given title by the Prince of Chiang Mai well before Bangkok established suzerainty over the North. If the government is to announce that the historic arrangement under which they hold the land is null and void then it ought to pay compensation for all of the improvements made by farmers such as: fruit trees, other commercially valuable perennials, permanent fields and existing structures. If under current law this cannot be done, then the law should be changed so that justice is not only seen to be done but really done.

Public relations workers should explain that it is not the intention of the government to deprive them of their livelihood but to provide support in special development areas set aside for them. Many highlanders face real problems concerning land shortage and currently attempt to secure a living from land which is already exhausted. These people are looking for new land and would be interested in responding to and cooperating with the government. Many government agencies maintain good relations with hill people who often make requests for land. If land was set aside for settlement, they could be shown it in their own good time. They could send representatives to look at it, bring information back to their homes and consult widely with others in their communities. Such a strategy has much to recommend it over exhortation and persuasion.

Where it is necessary to announce that it is forbidden to live in such and such an area, people should be told that full compensation will be paid to those who must move out. It is also essential to warn people well in advance of the move to give farmers time to prepare themselves. Provision should be made for settlers to move as they are ready and the authorities should be in a position to provide psychological and educational support. The use of force is a last resort. There is neither a real need nor a widely acknowledged emergency that justifies armed intervention.

Administration
An efficient administrative system should be staffed by those competent in cross cultural communication, assigned to keep their eyes open and their ears close to the ground, make contact with local leaders and do their best to avoid a situation that might provoke a hostile response.

Law

The law regarding forest protection should be rigorously enforced. However, not only those cutting trees should be punished but also those who support such activities. This is especially important when it comes to the issue of stealing commercially valuable timber. An example needs to be set to show how serious the government is about protecting the forest and to demonstrate how the law works.

Development

The commitment and readiness of government officers charged with responsibility for carrying out development work should be demonstrated. This will make the government's intention very clear. If farmers are to stay in the areas to which they have been assigned they must be given serious and sincere support in development activities, especially those which promote self-help. This strategy is recommended because if there are no differences between settlements where help is given and areas beyond the reach of help, farmers will be most reluctant to remain. The positive attraction of the assisted settlements should, in their own right, serve as an incentive to resettlement.

We could legally use direct force as a way of solving the problem and move people down at gun point. This may ensure that people will shift but such action would be totally opposed to retaining the best wishes, support and loyalty of our friends in the highlands. Surely the use of force is only justified when all other methods have been tried and failed? I sincerely believe that if force is used against the hill people they may well quickly form alliances with those along our borders and on the other side of our borders who owe nothing to Thailand. This could well evolve into armed rebellion. Highlanders have traditionally been prepared to rise in defence of what they believe are their own best interests.

RESETTLEMENT

Hill people who are forced to migrate are almost certain to be angry with the government. Some may move as far away as they can, out of reach. Others may well take a lesson from the many other minority people in neighbouring countries who are fighting to unite their fellow ethno-linguistic brothers and sisters and establish independent states. Alienated from the Thai government, they may well get into the rhythm of opposition, roll over and sleep, shut their ears to anything good which might come their way and close their eyes in case they see something which might contradict their prejudice. For such people the fruit of discontent, bitter though it may be, will be eaten as a natural act of defiance. Those unwilling to resettle will establish their communities on the basis of such bitterness that they are likely to harbour resentment against the injustice of their treatment for a long time to come. They will not forget how they were treated when they came in contact with government officers. They may well harbour feelings of hostility and resentment which they will pass on to their children and grandchildren.

We only need to look at our community of minorities to see what a huge impact relocation has had on both the number of people present in Thailand and their distribution. Highlanders are currently found in 21 to 22 provinces. If they were pushed together and came to share a common resentment, this would present a huge obstacle to integration and assimilation. If they came to consider it necessary to group together to form their own unitary state, such a move would challenge Thailand's unity as a nation. There can be only one unitary state and this ideal would be fundamentally compromised if we established special areas for highland ethnic minorities. We would end up with a type of mosaic integration, instead of the process of natural integration which prevails at present. Our nation is a plural society made up of many different ethnic groups. Is not the variety and complexity of this ethno-linguistic mix and consciousness the very basis of the richness of our culture?

Resettlement & Understanding

On this last point I would like to outline what I consider should be the principles on which the problems presented by the hill tribes should be approached, especially those concerning the conservation of forest and water resources.

First principle. I am confident and optimistic that if we work together with hill people and secure their full co-operation we will be able to win the war against "hill tribe problems". I am confident of this because I firmly believe that the main "hill tribe problems" arise from ignorance. However, ignorance is a condition well known to mankind for centuries.

Although we may be confident of our modern knowledge concerning the environment, we must be realistic. This knowledge is new, has not been available for very long and we cannot yet claim to have mastered it.

To solve "hill tribe problems," we ought to provide only relevant information about which we can be confident. To know what is relevant we need to know them thoroughly, including the factors which condition people's behaviour. I believe that most hill people have the ability to learn just the same as the members of any other ethnic group. To use the Lord Buddha's designation for homo sapien, we are all *venaya satawa*, trainable animals. There will be a few who stubbornly refuse to change. Such people can be found in every society. Sometimes these people make it necessary for strong measures to be used against them otherwise they refuse to learn. However, the disincentive of punishment will teach them to behave. After the appropriate lesson, they will cooperate and make the necessary changes.

Second principle. Although highlanders are able to learn from others, they still do not understand the environmental inter-relationships, especially between soil, water and forest, which together constitute the main renewable resources in the highlands. It is an urgent matter to instruct the hill people about this matter in an appropriate way. Today they are much better prepared to understand than in former times. This is because they are aware that resources have diminished. They lack timber for building and firewood. Ground water resources have dried up. Wildlife is greatly reduced and some species have disappeared from some regions. Many products that were once gathered from the forest can no longer be found. An explanation which traces the root cause back to shifting cultivation would have a salutary effect. It would not be difficult for them to accept their responsibility and be more willing to take up permanent agriculture based on irrigated rice, permanent gardens or orchards in place of shifting cultivation. I dare say that the hill people will readily accept permanent cultivation over swiddening. At the moment, they lack knowledge of the methodology, tools and labour as well as the land suitable for this. As long as there is no hurry to transform the problem of intrusion into, and destruction of, the forest overnight, then in due course, when the fields of their old farms no longer provide the yields they need and the soil is exhausted, they will prove to be students willing to listen to a better alternative.

I am of the opinion that it is an urgent matter to start making provision for wide scale adoption of permanent agriculture. Land suitability surveys should be got underway. The promise of long term settlement ought to be used as part of a strategy to protect and conserve highland resources. An example should be made of law breakers to discourage others. However, although some hill people will be arrested, this should be done on the basis of individual wrong doing rather than to approach all highlanders as if they were criminals.

Third principle. I believe that the corner stone of hilltribe welfare and development policy is the Cabinet Resolution promulgated 6 July 1976, specifically with the objec-

Resettlement & Understanding

tive of making "hill tribe people self-reliant, Thai citizens". These words reflect the highest wishes of government. The objective clearly serves the cause of building a united nation made up of many ethnic minorities who are not a socio-economic burden to the administration. If we take this one step further, we can say that the intention of this policy is to both establish national solidarity and continuing socio-economic growth.

This intention might well serve as another important ideological component of current policy in which both sides, the state and the individual, in this case citizens and highlanders, would willingly participate in a common effort to reach the stated goals. In practice, pursuing this collective and co-operative ideology concerning ethnic minorities makes it necessary to clearly distinguish between what we call "hill tribe problems" and ethnic minorities who are not satisfied that their interests are served by the policy and activities of the government to the extent that they identify their "best interests" with others similarly dissatisfied in neighbouring countries. If this happens and security problem emerges, it will make it much more difficult to solve our "hill tribe problems". It is most important that our current concerns for the environment do not generate a security crisis. Stability should remain uppermost in our minds and if highlanders remain loyal and can understand actions undertaken by government officials, we will be given the time necessary to solve the issues that most concern us.

Fourth principle. Social action that attempts to change the status quo always provides a challenge to humanitarians. It would be best if everything went smoothly but if there is to be some suffering, the pain should be minimized. If the transformation is well managed the change we are asking for may be willingly accepted or at least tolerated. The change may be compared to the fear and worry with which a mother faces the birth of her first child. The process of giving birth is naturally painful but the reward of producing a healthy child is a joy which makes suffering worthwhile.

Social action of this kind need not be conducted blindly, social science has provided us with experience and theories which can guide us. There are no formulas similar to those of physical science. There is not the certainty that two parts of hydrogen and one of oxygen will produce water but by conducting ourselves sensibly and allowing time for adequate reflection, theories of social action can guide us through the change with full participation at all stages. Social action is like a journey; the destination is known but there are many ways to reach the goal. I would select a safe path and intelligent companions who can be consulted along the way. It may not be the most direct way, it may not offer any short cuts but if we meet any obstacles, we will have companions with whom we can share the hardships, we would not expose ourselves to loneliness and we would eventually reach our destination together.

To sum up, I believe that there is no need for us to make a hard struggle out of "hill tribe problems". The hill people are not our enemies. The main strategies we must keep in mind concern realistic land classification and land allocation for both the hill tribe people and the many Thai who earn their living from the highlands. This is principally a question of making provision for the permanent settlement of farmers on agricultural land, a settlement of people who have lived for millenia in this kind of environment. We should use a wide range of strategies all designed to meet our most important goal: the accelerated promotion of stabilized agricultural systems to replace shifting cultivation as a cause of environmental degradation. To do this we must utilize techniques that support the overall strategy. We must face up to the ecological ignorance of the hill tribes and educate and train them in the scientific interelationships between natural resource conservation and the need to sustain agricultural production. The participation of the hill tribes and others should be based on a firm alliance that eschews the use of violence and is regulated by a psychologically informed approach, including public relations, payment of compensation and resettlement grants to reduce the inconvenience of relocating and enable them to reestablish their communities, houses and fields with a minimum of hardship. Administrative arrangements should avoid a situation in which the hill tribes become welfare dependants. Law enforcement should be conducted so that justice is done and that punishment is handed out on a case-to-case basis. Provincial authorities should identify resettlement areas and set up a public relations system designed to persuade highlanders reluctant to move to migrate voluntarily to designated areas.

Land set aside for agricultural development in resettlement areas should be classified to facilitate implementation of good ecological and conservation principles. Land classification should be carried out from the lowlands right through to the mountain tops. Resettlement itself should be entirely infused with the idea that the participation of the hill people in area development will guarantee that they receive the full benefit of their own labour and grants made in assistance. The farms, paddy fields, crops, orchards and trees which they plant will protect the watershed and there should be no need for them to destroy new forest. Management of new forest could well incorporate local labour in such a way as to provide additional income. If social action is managed with considerable skill, perhaps the hill people may volunteer their labour in a manner not unknown in the past.

The sort of strategies and tactics outlined above and supplemented by common sense may well serve to win hill tribe support and participation to protect the forest without any risk to national stability which might otherwise lead to a security crisis.

14 April 1986: Eviction Orders to The Hmong Of Huai Yew Yee Village, Huai Kha Khaeng Wildlife Sanctuary, Thailand

Ardith A. Eudey

Introduction

On 14 April 1986, I witnessed the first encounter between the Hmong of Huai Yew Yee (or Yooyi) village and officers of the Third Division of the Army and officials from the Royal Forest Department in Bangkok (Plate 74). Most of the adult members of Huai Yew Yee had reached the village site by foot about 19 years earlier. I had taken more than one day to hike into the village from my base at the Khao Nang Rum Research Station to the east in Huai Kha Khaeng Wildlife Sanctuary. Three helicopters, in time best measured in minutes, had transported the various Government agents to this remote village at the western boundary of the sanctuary in Uthai Thani province in west-central Thailand.

In 1973 I initiated what has become a long-term field study to work out the distribution and habitat preference of the five species of macaque monkeys (Primates: *Macaca*) that are broadly sympatric in Huai Kha Khaeng Wildlife Sanctuary. My search for macaques was expanded in 1982 and 1983 to the lower montane or hill forest inhabited by Hmong in the western most region of the sanctuary. This research has been carried out in cooperation with the Wildlife Conservation Division of the Royal Forest Department, and workmen and rangers from the Khao Nang Rum Research Station have been my field companions.

RESETTLEMENT

Following my first brief expedition to the Hmong area in 1982, I was informed of the intention of the Royal Forest Department to remove the Hmong from Huai Kha Khaeng Wildlife Sanctuary and contiguous Thung Yai Naresuan Wildlife Sanctuary to the west in Tak province. The intent of my research in 1986 was to conduct a demographic and land use survey of the Hmong residing in Huai Kha Khaeng Wildlife Sanctuary and to record the presence of all primates in the immediate region. The resulting data would function as baselines to study the status of the forest and primate populations through time.

Background

During the initial period of field work in the Hmong region (7-18 March, 1986), I was able to census their villages: Huai Yew Yee, the only Hmong village in Huai Kha Khaeng Wildlife Sanctuary and probably the most traditional village in the region, and Huai Nam Kheo and Bao Wai Dam in Thung Yai Naresuan Wildlife Sanctuary. On 14 April 1986, the population of Huai Yew Yee consisted of 176 people living in 19 households. Forty per cent (70) of the population was 10 years of age or younger, and 26 percent (46) of the population was five years of age or younger. Seven percent (12) of the population was between the ages of 60 and 80. Household size ranged from two to 22, with the mean being just over nine. The larger households were extended families containing married sons and their off-spring.

With the exception of two households, all 17 heads of household (89%) had established residence in Huai Yew Yee 18-19 years before the time of my study and about four to five years before Huai Kha Khaeng Wildlife Sanctuary was declared in 1972. Most of these people formerly lived in Pa Ka in Phop Phra King Amphoe (subdistrict), Tak province. This appears to have been a communist stronghold about 20 to 10 years ago, during which time the Hmong of Huai Yew Yee left the area at the request of the government. Hmong now living in Pa Ka,

Eviction Experience

who total at least 1400, have saturated the area which they appear to have entered about three to five years ago, after it was brought under the control of the government.

Until 8 April 1986, the village of Hai Yew Yee was accessible only by foot. Its residents were self-sufficient and grew short-grain rice and corn. Most households had additional fields of sugar-cane and/or bananas, and some had gardens with fruits such as papaya and pineapple. All grew a variety of vegetables. In addition, the people maintained large numbers of chickens and pigs (and some cattle) for food and kept cattle as beasts of burden. Opium poppy was also grown in the area, but the amount of land *(rai)* allocated to this cash crop was small in comparison to that devoted to rice and corn. The larger households had anywhere from 30-50 to 100 *rai* planted in corn and rice but, at a maximum, only four to six *rai* planted in poppy. Smaller households tended to cultivate only two *rai* of poppy. One acre (or 4,047 square meters) is the equivalent of 2.5 *rai*. The rolling plains cultivated by the Hmong are surrounded by forested mountains crowned by rocky outcrops, and macaque monkeys and other wildlife such as barking deer *(muntiacus muntjak)* were observed adjacent to both fields and the village of Huai Yew Yee. During the course of my study, articles appeared in the English-language Thai press to the effect that the Hmong had encroached on Huai Kha Khaeng Wildlife Sanctuary and were supporting themselves by growing opium and poaching wildlife eg. **Bangkok Post**, 24 March and 14 April 1986).

The illness of one of the workmen made it necessary for me to return to the Khao Nang Rum Research Station on 19 March. Before I was able to resume my study, the Chief of Huai Kha Khaeng Wildlife Sanctuary informed the residents of Huai Yew Yee that they had to abandon their village by the 15 of April or face arrest. He also declared the Hmong region to be a sensitive zone and ordered no-one to enter it. As a consequence, on

RESETTLEMENT

26 March, I travelled northward to Tak in an effort to obtain information about the proposed relocation site for the Hmong.

I was able to obtain permission to travel to Pa Ka in the Phop Phra subdistrict of Tak province and was able to inspect the proposed relocation site. Some 3000 - 5000 Hmong from Huai Kha Khaeng and Thung Yai Naresuan Wildlife Sanctuaries (and perhaps others from the north) are scheduled to be relocated in an isolated community, analogous to an "American Indian reservation," in a lowland area at kilometer 48 to 45 on the Mae Sot - Umphang road. The area was devoid of water and denuded of vegetation and may require the equivalent of US$600,000 - $1,000,000 to develop, if such development is feasible (Plate 72) Following the completion of my study, I was informed in Bangkok that before the Hmong from the sanctuaries are relocated in Phop Phra subdistrict they will be kept for as much as one to two years at a "temporary" holding site at Krakakee village, an area of degraded forest adjacent to the road leading northward to Umphang from Thung Yai Naresuan Wildlife Sanctuary. Here, in an "intermediate zone" they may begin to undergo a programme of forced cultural assimilation. The argument for this proposed relocation scheme is summarized in a document entitled **Target Areas for Prevention of Forest Destruction by Hilltribes** (See Appendix V), a copy of which was given to me at the Royal Forest Department in Bangkok on 18 April by the Chief of the Watershed Survey and Planning Sub-Division.

Events Preceding Confrontation
On 6 April, with permission from the Royal Forest Department in Bangkok, I returned to the village of Huai Yew Yee. At the time the mood of the people was more one of excitement than apprehension. I noticed that the trail linking Huai Yew Yee with the village of Bao Wai Dam had been widened during my absence, and on 8 April the first automobile, a Japanese minitruck driven by a Hmong from further north, ar-

Eviction Experience

rived in Huai Yew Yee. The Hmong in villages in Thung Yai Naresuan Wildlife Sanctuary had extended the "temporary road" to Huai Yew Yee. This road was built by the Army from Umphang to just inside the northern boundary of the sanctuary to facilitate the removal of hill tribe people. The arrival of the first of three minitrucks was celebrated with the consumption of local corn whiskey. Many of the women and most of the children of Huai Yew Yee had never before seen an automobile, and the horn, lights, and windshield wiper immediately became objects of fascination for them. The minitrucks began to move the belongings of the Huai Yew Yee Hmong and some of the more elderly members of the village to Bao Wai Dam. The drivers of the minitrucks may have been recovering their expenses by selling fruit such as mangoes and oranges and other items such as cigarettes, at prices far below those charged by ethnic Thai merchants who first appeared in the region following my 1983 study when they transported their goods in by pack horses. Contrary to assertions in the press that women and children would be taken out by helicopter (**Bangkok Post**, 14 April 1986), the Government was providing no assistance, but other Hmong were helping the people of Huai Yew Yee to evacuate their village.

Beginning on 11 April, more than 30 heavily-armed members of the Volunteer Army *(thahaan pran)* began to arrive in Huai Yew Yee by pick-up truck, in anticipation of the arrival of officers of the Third Army three days later. Minor misconduct toward the young women of the village and considerable discharge of automatic weapons, including possibly the shooting of birds and small mammals in the vicinity of the village, characterized their behaviour. The excitement was heightened by the Hmong conducting a two-day ceremony commemorating the 14th anniversary of the death of a "Mother" in which the *thahaan pran* freely participated (Plates 69 and 70) Finally, on the afternoon of 13 April, the Chief of Huai Kha Khaeng Wildlife Sanctuary and 17 of his men reached the village on foot.

Confrontation

A military helicopter bearing a Lt. - General from the Third Division of the Army and the Deputy Director-General of the Royal Forest Department was the first to arrive on the morning of 14 April (Plate 73). The ***thahaan pran*** had cleared a landing pad outside the village, and, as the Government contingent walked toward the centre of the village, they were met by the men of Huai Yew Yee, who had assembled at the house of the village headman (Plate 71). I clearly remember a young Hmong woman coming out of her house to throw a stick at a dog growling menacingly at the approaching strangers.

The Lt. - General conducted all discussion with the Hmong men. With vigour, the first question that he asked the men was where they hunted gaur *(Bos gaurus)*, a wild cattle, which led them to believe that they were being evicted from Huai Yew Yee so that the Army could come in to hunt wildlife. The Lt. - General seemed surprised that Huai Yew Yee had been occupied for 19 years, while other members of his contingent expressed surprise at the diversity of Hmong agriculture and the number of children in the village. One man kept repeating in English that the villagers did not practice birth control. When the Lt. - General stated that to be a good citizen one must comply with the decisions of the Government, each Hmong man raised an identity card indicating that he was a Thai citizen.

The men of Huai Yew Yee asked for permision to remain in their village through the monsoon season in order to harvest the rice crop. Instead, they were given an extension until 15 May to evacuate the village but were allowed to continue to work their old rice and corn fields in Huai Kha Khaeng Wildlife Sanctuary. In Bangkok, the Army and Royal Forest Department had decided to move the people to Huai Nam Kheo, a village that may have had fairly extensive contacts with ethnic Thais, but the men requested and received permission to stay with relatives in nearby Bao Wai Dam. The monsoon had already begun in the area, with heavy rains in the afternoon, sometimes extending into the evening, lasting from two to five hours daily. The Lt. - General offered plastic to the Hmong to make tents or temporary shelters if they did not have sufficient: the 176 residents of Huai Yew Yee would have to be accommodated among the more than 240 people already in residence at Bao Wai Dam.

The military helicopter had already departed when two small (Ministry of Agriculture) helicopters arrived with more officials from the Royal Forest Department, including the Chief of the Watershed Survey and Planning Sub-Division. Someone with a television camera accompanied them. This was my first encounter with this group of officials, who were unaware of my presence in Huai Yew Yee, but it appeared that they were responsible for the eviction of the Hmong from Huai Kha Khaeng Wildlife Sanctuary and ultimately from Thung Yai Naresuan Wildlife Sanctuary. I was informed that a development project in situ for the Huai Yew Yee Hmong was impossible because others would move in to take advantage of the project, but no effort had been made to study their patterns of land use and other economic activities. Likewise, I was told that although forest destruction in the region had been relatively minor, a new policy of "preventing forest destruction by hill tribes" was being initiated in the two sanctuaries because they were contiguous with Kamphaeng Phet province, where one of the highest rates of forest loss had been recorded in northern Thailand. The idea that to receive government assistance the hill tribes must become "Thai," to the extent that they must abandon their own culture, including their distinctive dress, and adopt Thai culture, repeatedly came up in our discussion.

In front of the men of Huai Yew Yee, I questioned the Chief of the Watershed Survey and Planning Sub-Division about the feasibility of relocating the Hmong in Phop Phra subdivision. He had never inspected the proposed site. However, he stated that USAID Thailand had offered to assist with the relocation of the Hmong and that a request would be submitted for assistance only in transporting the Hmong to the relocation site and developing an irrigation system there. Subsequently I learned that the Royal Forest Department never followed through by submitting any form of proposal for consideration by USAID.

Aftermath

Even before the last two helicopters had departed, and before it was necessary for me to return to the Khao Nang Rum Research Station, I met with the men of Huai Yew Yee in the house of the headman. As a woman, even a foreigner or *farang*, it was a profound experience for me. The men had been terrorized by, in their own conception, being singled out for eviction and relocation in Phop Phra subdivision. Several stated that they were being sent to Phop Phra to die or that it would be better to die than to go to Phop Phra. Their primary concern was that they would not be able to plant rice to feed their families. One of the most articulate men in the village said that if they could remain in Bao Wai Dam or even Bhekhee, the largest village in Thung Yai Naresuan Wildlife Sanctuary, they would be able to carry on their subsistence activities. At no time did they threaten to resist relocation, but they were attempting to come up with a reasonable alternative to Phop Phra. And during this intense discussion, a younger man could not refrain from running out of the house to watch the helicopters, a wonder of modern technology, fly over the village and disappear behind the nearby mountains.

Afterthoughts

The Royal Forest Department appears to have taken the position that the Hmong in Huai Kha Khaeng and Thung Yai Naresuan Wildlife Sanctuaries are adversaries or enemies - "encroachers" causing the destruction of forest and wildlife. One junior officer even informed me that the Hmong entered Thailand deliberately to destroy the forest and that ethnic Thais practice slash-and-burn agriculture only because of the example of the hill tribes. As a consequence, the potential for using the Hmong to stop forest destruction, through the promotion of permanent land tenure has been overlooked. In 1982 the headman of Huai Yew Yee village, for example, expressed interest in methods or technology that would permit his family to cultivate their fields for longer periods of time.

The eviction of the Huai Yew Yee Hmong necessitated that the Chief of Huai Kha Khaeng Wildlife Sanctuary, as an ad hoc response, establish a new ranger substation at the former village site in anticipation of increased hunting pressures in the area. My observations made during searches for primates suggest that they and other wildlife may have been hunted out of some areas frequented by ethnic Thais and Karen, especially a trail leading southward to Ban Rai at the southern boundary of the sanctuary. Huai Yew Yee village may have acted as a deterrent against the extirpation of wildlife in its vicinity. In addition, an apparently thriving business in the horns of protected wildlife such as gaur, supposedly obtained from Burma but more likely obtained from south of Umphang, already occurs in Tak province at the border town of Mae Sot. Such trade probably will increase as a consequence of the road constructed within Thung Yai Naresuan Wildlife Sanctuary. There is no indication that any effort was made to establish the relative benefits and costs to conservation efforts of evicting the Hmong from Huai Kha Khaeng and Thung Yai Naresuan Wildlife Sanctuaries.

Postscript

The first of almost 5000 Hmong scheduled to be removed this year from Thung Yai Naresuan Wildlife Sanctuary, a "batch" of 270 from Phap-hueng village on the sanctuary's boundary were reported to have been moved directly to the resettlement area in Phop Phra subdistrict on the 3 May 1987 (**Bangkok Post** 4 May, 1987). A 7 July, 1987 communication from the U.S.A Embassy in Bangkok identified the United Nations Fund for Drug Abuse Control as providing some "development assistance" for the resettlement project. According to this communication, "Every effort is made to resettle people on a voluntary basis although the promise of Thai Citizenship for all those who agree to be resettled is used as a persuasive measure". The communication describes the land of the resettlement area as being "the most arable in Tak province and....located near good water sources".

In early October, 1987 the United Nations Fund for Drug Abuse Control announced that at this time it was no longer associated with the resettlement of the Hmong in Phop Phra subdivision because of the failure of the Thai Government to establish an independent panel under the auspices of the Human Rights Division of the United Nations Economic and Social Commission for Asia and the Pacific to review the resettlement project.

Acknowledgments
Field work in 1986 was supported by a grant from the National Geographic Society, and in 1982 and 1983 by a grant from the New York Zoological Society. I wish to thank the Wildlife Conservation Division, Royal Forest Department for sponsoring my research in Thailand.

69. Hmong mother, Huai Yew Yee (Eudey)

70. Mock assault (Eudey)

71. Village officials 1982 (Eudey)

72. Phop Phra relocation area (Eudey)

73. Soldiers, Huai Yew Yee (Eudey)

74. Soldiers & Hmong confer (Eudey)

75. Raising the flag (Eudey)

76. Akha bride (Ralana)

77. Akha ceremony (Vienne)

78. Akha thatching roof (Ralana)

79. Lahu felling a tree (Supachai)

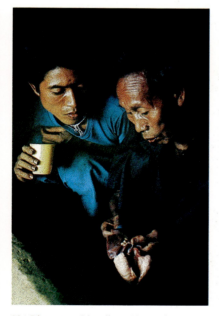
80. Lisu consulting liver (Conrad)

81. Lahu field ceremony (Supachai)

82. Htin mother and child (Connell)

83. Akha children (Hobday)

84. Mien women (Connell)

85. Karen mother (Connell)

Territorial Imperatives: Akha Ethnic Identity and Thailand's National Integration

Cornelia Ann Kammerer

> *Cultural identity implies, and fundamentally presupposes, a sense of territoriality.*
> --Remo Guidieri and Francesco Pellizzi (1980)

> *In the modern conception, state sovereignty is fully, flatly, and evenly operative over each square centimetre of legally demarcated territory.*
> -- Benedict Anderson (1983)

With the emergence of modern nation-states in peninsular South-East Asia in the post-colonial era, the structure of the hill/valley conjuncture altered fundamentally. The territorially bounded states in the Western mode that emerged through the colonial encounter replaced the centre-oriented "galactic polities" of traditional Indianized principalities whose "borders were porous and indistinct" (Tambiah 1976; Anderson 1983:26). Today, these new nations challenge the legitimacy of highlanders' cultural *cum* territorial existence in a way unknown under the older order.

Anthropological research among both hill-dwellers and valley-dwellers in Burma and, to a greater extent, Thailand has focused on processes of ethnic differentiation and identification since the publication of Leach's iconoclastic-turned-classic monograph, *Political Systems of Highland Burma*. Drawing mainly upon this now substantial literature, I attempt to formulate an analytical approach towards ethnic identity that I hope will illuminate the current confrontation of mountain minorities and the consolidating nation-states of continental South-East Asia. Ethnic identity here designates explicit self-definition which is cultural but not coterminous with culture. Applying this approach to the case of Tibeto-Burman-speaking Akha in the hills of northern Thailand, I argue that Akha identity is based upon common clanship and shared "customs," and presupposes a duplex concept of territory not shared by the lowland Thai majority. In the concluding section, prospects for Akha and other highlanders are considered in light of efforts by the central government of Thailand to integrate "hill tribes" into a territorially bounded nation.

Ethnic Identity in the Mainland South-East Asian Context

Ethnographic fieldwork, by its very nature, impels questions of ethnic likeness and difference to the fore (Moerman 1968:165-66); not only does each observer seek a monograph-sized sociocultural entity, but observer and observed encounter one another as strangers. Yet the emphasis on ethnicity in anthropological accounts of mainland South-East Asia cannot be written off as a true reflection of the anthropologist's interests and methods and a distorted image of the anthropological object. In the South-East Asian context, concerns of anthropologists and natives coincide. Most, if not all, researchers who have worked in upland South-East Asia would, I believe, echo Moerman (1968:165) in claiming that "ethnic identifications...have high priority to the people I studied." Stories and myths often include characters from other ethnic groups and frequently explain social and cultural differences between groups. For example, Akha, Chin, Karen, and Lahu all relate tales that account for their lack of writing and its presence among neighbouring cultures in the valley.

To students of South-East Asian sociocultural systems, Leach bequeathed a structural model of group definition through opposition, which demands that social groups be viewed relationally rather than as stable isolates. By demonstrating that Kachin speak mutually unintelligible languages and display significant cultural differences, by documenting that individual hill-dwelling Kachin become valley-dwelling Shan and vice versa, and by establishing the interdependence of Shan and Kachin political systems, Leach (1954:281) challenged "conventions as to what consitutes *a* culture or *a* tribe" shared by colonial administrators and social scientists alike. In **Political Systems of Highland Burma**,Leach (1954:43) simultaneously undermined the evolutionist/biological view that "race" is "a synonym for language" and that the inhabitants of British Burma are representatives of successive waves of migrations of diverse races, as well as the structural-functionalist conception of a tribe as a discrete, homogeneous social unit in equilibrium.

Beginning with Lehman's (1963) study of Chin as a "subnuclear" tribal people adapted to Burman civilization, students of the hill/valley conjuncture have built upon Leach's lead. Whereas Leach's aim is to show *that* valley neighbours influence hill sociocultural systems, Lehman's aim is to show *in what ways* they do so. Two recent works expand and refine Lehman's focus on the moulding of highlander cultures through opposition to dominant lowlanders: Alting von Geusau (1983) examines dialectical oppositions such as upslope versus downslope developed in Akha oral tradition in response to the presence of stronger valley-dwellers, and Radley (1986) investigates Mong (Hmong) tiger myths as embodiments of attitudes toward the powerful Chinese. In a complex dialectical process, patterns of social interaction and adaptation shape cultural traditions and definitions of identity among hill and valley neighbours, which in turn influence patterns of social interaction and adaptation.

Uplanders are well aware of both the material advantages and the greater political power of lowlanders, but they also demonstrate deep respect for the traditions handed down by their ancestors. Commentators since Lehman (1963) have drawn attention to the double ambivalence displayed by mountain people. Attitudes toward valley civilization combine admiration with distrust; attitudes toward their own customs combine pride with feelings of inferiority. Distrust toward valley-dwellers can be interpreted, following Hinton (1979:85-86), as a consequence of longstanding oppression, and feelings of inferiority can be viewed not simply as reactions to the obvious inequality in material resources between hill and valley, but also as the internalization of opinions of those politically and economically dominant.

It should be pointed out that hill/valley is always a significant axis for self-definition among highlanders, but it is not the only one, and, furthermore, that self-definitions may recognize similarity as well as contrast with others. For example, Karen, whose perceived place within the sphere of the valley state is an essential ingredient in their self-identification, consider Lua to be different but nonetheless akin on the basis of their common residence between plains and mountain tops and their similar positions vis-a-vis traditional valley principalities, at the same time that they feel no affinity with hillmen of the higher slopes (Kunstadter 1967, 1969, 1979; Marlowe 1969, 1979). Karen, and by analogy Lua, represent the "'hills' as an extension of the 'sown'" whereas the true highlanders such as the Akha, Hmong, and Lisu represent the "'hills' qua 'hills'" (Marlowe 1979:196). These hill-dwellers distinguish themselves one from the other, yet recognize more affinity among themselves than with inhabitants of the valleys below: Akha acknowledge a basic likeness among "mountain people," and the Mien creation myth recounts the emergence of "hill people" and "plains people" (Kandre 1967:621). Content and consequences of ambivalence as well as axes of contrast and affinity must be established through research and cannot be assumed to be stable through time.

Ever since Moerman (1965) posed the question "Who are the Lue?," anthropological attention has focused on native

Akha Identity

definitions of group affiliation. As an ideological formulation, ethnic identity is cultural, but it is not coterminous with culture. To my knowledge, no ethnographic case has yet been reported in which the set of attributes included within a culture's definition of ethnic identity is coincident with the total culture of people claiming that identity, nor should such a case be expected. I would argue that isomorphism between ethnic identity and culture is impossible because ethnic identity is explicit and self-conscious whereas much of culture is implicit and unconscious. Accordingly, in the perspective adopted here not all sociocultural change entails change in ethnic identity. Ethnic change is here understood as either a claim to membership in a different group (e.g., Lua becomes Karen or Northern Thai [Kunstadter 1983a: 151]) or as an alteration in self-definitional criteria for membership in a particular group (e.g., Lua remains Lua but differently defined [Kunstadter 1983a:151])

Since criteria for group self-identification are not uniform or universal, "it therefore becomes the ethnographer's task to discover, in each instance, which features are locally significant for purposes of assigning ethnic labels" (Moerman 1965:1220).

To understand the degree of resilience or vulnerability of ethnic identity in the context of shifting patterns of inter-groups relations, it is necessary not only to determine the content of ethnic self-identification but also its configuration. Besides differing in content, ethnic identities exhibit greater or lesser degrees of systematicity and complexity. For instance, the cultural features Thai Lue consider markers of their identity include the female sarong, a recessed fireplace, a village spirit house, and a style of folk songs (Moerman 1968:156-58). On the other hand, Mien define themselves as Mien on the basis of adherence to a named "socio-economic-ritual system" (Kandre 1967:584-85).

The ethnospecific cultural subsystem is called by native informants "The Custom" *(lēi nyèi)*, which corresponds to the Chinese concept of *Li* [good customs, rites and ceremonies...] (Kandre 1976:172, brackets in the original).

Some self-definitions, like that of Mien, take the form of interlocking networks of cultural attributes. Others, like that of Thai Lue, are loose sets of traits akin to anthropological trait lists of a bygone era. Definitional sets may also be implicational or hierarchical with traits logically ranked one with respect to another. For example, there appears to be an implicational relationship among the criteria of Karen-ness cited by Kunstadter (1979:125) in that knowledge of the Karen language is a prerequisite for knowledge of Karen folk tales. Indeed, Kunstadter isolates language as the most important criterion. In the case of loose sets, it is possible that one element might be dropped or replaced without threatening the viability of the definition. In the case of implicational or hierarchical sets, perhaps an element of lesser rank might be abandoned without the definition collapsing. Self-definitions, like that of Mien, which isolate a specific cultural subsystem rather than an inventory of traits as distinctive of group membership, appear to be more fragile by virtue of greater internal coherence; however, the presumption of fragility rests upon the questionable assumption that ideas and practices belonging within a named cultural domain, for instance "The Custom" of Mien, are themselves immutable. A label may be retained while that to which it is applied alters considerably. The amount and kind of change a specific cultural subsystem can absorb is a subject for research in each particular ethnographic case.

Beyond looking at the content and configuration of self-conscious definitions of group membership, it is also important to explore connections between identity and other explicit and implicit aspects of culture. If a self-definition does not incorporate all the conditions necessary to meet standards of group membership, identity can be threatened by change affecting those conditions that are presupposed by the self-definition but not

Akha Identity

directly included within it. To give one illustration, although the Mien language is not included in definitions of Mien-ness, one cannot follow "The Custom" without knowing the Mien language (Kandre 1976:173). For Mien, then, a loss of language would entail a loss of identity (as presently defined), despite the fact that language is not an explicit element in self-identification. Thus self-conscious bases of identity need not coincide with the effective bases of identity.

The first epigraph at the beginning of this paper proclaims that "cultural identity...presupposes a sense of territoriality" Although "a sense of territoriality" is often an explicit element in ethnic identification, either tangibly as a particular parcel in possession (an occupied homeland) or intangibly as a memory (a former or mythic homeland), it need not always be self-consciously incorporated into ethnic identity. If not explicit, a conception of territory is in many, and perhaps all cases, implicit. What is at issue here is not territory as tract but territory as idea. I hasten to add that this does not mean that territory as tract is of no consequence to the fate of ethnic minorities. Territory as idea cannot be tilled. Since nation-states in the modern mode themselves presuppose a single conception of territorial legitimacy that, as the second epigraph indicates, admits no alternatives, I believe that it is important to unravel the explicit or implicit "sense of territoriality" in highlander identities in order to understand the current minority-majority conjuncture in the nations of peninsular South-East Asia.

An argument made in connection with language can, I believe, be applied to ethnic identity to help account for differential kinds and rates of ethnic change. Hymes (1971:116) contends that "the role of language may differ from community to community." Transposing his argument to the question of ethnic identity, I contend that the role of ethnic identity may differ from community to community. Whereas one community may show little tendency toward ethnic change whether from one label to another or in the content ascribed to a continuing label, another community may change readily either by adopting a new label and all that it entails or by altering the definitional criteria of the label retained.

Since Leach (1954) first drew anthropological attention to the phenomenon, shifts in claims to group membership have concerned students of mainland South-East Asia. As Dentan (1976:78) observes,

> multi-culturation in Southeast Asia provides many people with a series of identities which they can don and doff as particular interactions dictate. Goffmanesque models of self-presentation and interaction ritual are adequate to describe this behavior, often with only tangential reference to notions of ethnicity.

In keeping with Dentan's own emphasis on the potential dangers of scholarly research and writing on ethnicity in South-East Asia given the existence of real ethnic tensions, I would like to draw attention to a potential danger of the recurrent stress in the anthropological literature on the "donning" and "doffing" of identities. It is one thing for a person to choose to alter her/his behaviour to suit the situation (as perceived by that actor), and it is an entirely different thing for alteration to be demanded by another person (or government) to suit the situation (as perceived by that other person [or government]). Willingness to adapt one's behaviour to a particular context should not be interpreted as absence of attachment to an identity not then in play.

Andrianoff (1979:77), Hinton (1969:4-5), and Kunstadter (1983b:38) observe that not all ethnic groups in Thailand are assimilators to the same degree. As Hinton (1969:4) notes,

> it is probably significant that researchers who have been preoccupied with changing cultural identity have

been students of the ... Karen, Lua', Thai Lue and Shan peoples. The identity of some other groups seems to be rather more rigidly defined.

The other groups to which he refers are Hmong and Mien, speakers of related Austro-Thai languages (Matisoff 1983:65), and the three Tibeto-Burman-speaking groups, Lahu, Lisu, and Akha. Andrianoff (1979) and Geddes (1967:568) support his view concerning Hmong, Kandre's (1967, 1976) work echoes him on Mien, and my ethnographic experience certainly corroborates him on Akha. Conrad (this volume) provides data on shifts between Lisu and Lahu identity. Partly on this basis, he rejects Hinton's notion that there are "rigidly defined" groups. Interestingly enough, Conrad's data, which include no examples of shifts from Lisu to Thai identity, tend to support the view that members of some groups are less willing than those of others to assimilate to the dominant lowlanders. It seems then that Hinton is correct in asserting that among the first set of peoples loyalty to identity is not as strong a cultural value as among the second. I hasten to add that it is not my intention to indicate that the cultural evaluation of ethnic identity is the sole variable in determining the speed and direction of ethnic change, or to convey the impression that this evaluation is independent of historical circumstances. The cultural weighting ascribed to group identity is but one factor among many to be considered in the study of ethnic change, but it is a factor that should not be ignored.

The content, configuration, and evaluation of ethnic identity are products of history, which in turn pattern perceptions of change and channel change itself. Hmong, Mien, Lahu, Lisu, and Akha are all groups to which Alting von Geusau's (1983) characterization "perennial minority" applies; all are marginalized people who have historically withdrawn from and/or resisted pressure posed by dominant valley-dwellers (Radley 1986). Though their ethnic identities differ as do the cultures of which they are part, members of these groups appear to share a positive evaluation of allegiance to ethnic identity. All live in highland villages interspersed with those of other ethnic groups, and none has a tradition of stable, patterned political connections with powerful lowlanders. They define themselves in relation to valley neighbours, but, unlike more ready assimilators such as Karen and Lua, (former) dependence upon a (former) valley-principality is not internalized into self-identification.

The mountain minorities have for centuries, even millennia, been in contact with more powerful valley-dwellers. Consciousness of their relative weakness is not new; it is part of tradition itself. It may well be that self-definition through opposition is a feature of all cultural systems and that autonomous cultural systems are a myth of the tribe of anthropologists.

> Membership in a group, incorporation within it, is dependent upon a category of the excluded, a sense of otherness....The Outside, then, is necessary to the Inside (Murphy 1964:848).

For highlanders in mainland South-East Asia, the dominant other is an age-old counterpart. Yet during this century a fundamental transformation is evident: traditional ethnic self-consciousness has in some cases metamorphosed into political ethnic self-consciousness. Assertive, politicized ethnic self-consciousness seems to incorporate aspects of the Western notion of the bounded territorial nation-state. While Weber (1978) and Keyes (1976,1981) suggest that ethnic self-consciousness can be considered a form of "descent," I suggest that politicized ethnic self-consciousness can be considered a form of dissent. Whereas the first claims to differ, the second differs to claim.

The general approach to ethnic identity presented here demands that in each ethnographic case the content as well as the configuration of the self-definition of group membership be investigated. Unraveling links between the self-conscious bases of identity and other explicit as well as implicit aspects of culture exposes sources of resilience and vulnerability, and of flexibility and rigidity, in the face of changing intergroup relations and politico-economic circumstances. Of particular importance in the context of today's world of nation-states is the "sense of territoriality" either explicit or implicit within definitions of ethnic identity. Finally, a culture's evaluation of allegiance to group membership provides a clue to differential rates and kinds of ethnic change. Applying this approach to a particular ethnographic case, the bases of ethnic identity among Akha in northern Thailand are examined, and the confrontation between Akha as well as other highlanders and the national government is explored.

Akha Ethnic Identity

Akha as an ethnic group are here distinguished not on the basis of any objective criteria, but rather as the people who identify themselves as Akha. Population statistics for mountain minorities in South-West China and South-East Asia are notoriously unreliable. Suffice to say that there are between three and five hundred thousand Akha residing in Yunnan and in the highlands of South-East Asia stretching from Burma's eastern Shan States through northern Thailand and western Laos, apparently into the north-west corner of Vietnam. The first Akha settlement in northern Thailand was founded just after the turn of the century (Alting von Geusau 1983:246). Through both natural growth and immigration from Thailand's politically troubled neighbouring states, the population of Akha and other highlanders has increased substantially since the 1960s. In 1964 there were under 7,000 Akha (L. Hanks, J. Hanks, and Sharp 1964:facing p.5); in 1986 there were more than 33,000 (Appendix I). Most reside in Chiang Rai, the northernmost province; the remainder reside in Chiang Mai, Kamphaeng Phet, Lampang, Phrae, and Tak, other northern provinces (Appendix I).

In the ethnic mosaic of the highlands, autonomous Akha villages are scattered among those of other ethnic groups. Like other hill-dwellers, Akha cultivate swiddens in a belt of land surrounding their community. Dry rice is the main subsistence crop and the focus of required calendrical rituals. Every traditional settlement must have a village founder-leader *(dzoema)*, who is responsible for leading community-based ceremonies. The position is restricted to men and is often hereditary, but the village founder-leader is in no sense a ruler. Disputes are settled through discussions among male household heads, and fines are paid at the village founder-leader's house. Descent is patrilineal and residence patrivirilocal. The effective unit in the regulation of marriage is the exogamous, unnamed sub-lineage, rather than the named patrilineage. A woman joins the household and lineage of her husband at marriage. Although there is no indigenous supralocal political organization, Akha in geographically dispersed communities are bound by ramifying ties of consanguinity and affinity.

The ethnographic research (1979-81) from which data are drawn was conducted in Chiang Rai Province among self-designated *Jeug'oe* Akha traditionalists. With Alting von Geusau (1983:246) and Lewis (1968:viii) and contra Feingold (1976:91-92), I consider *Jeug'oe* to be a native classification corresponding to a dialect group. Based upon the comparability of Lewis's findings in Burma and both Alting von Geusau's and my own findings in Thailand, I believe it likely that the ethnographic information presented here is of general applicability to those *Jeug'oe* speakers who have not abandoned their inherited "customs" in favour of Christianity. They recognize that members of other subgroups are also Akha, and they can detail variations in practices between subgroups. My suspicion is that comparative work among other subgroups will reveal that various sorts of Akha define themselves as Akha in a similar manner. After all, the mode of self-identification described below acknowledges likeness and allows for differences among Akha.

Ethnic group as clan. From the Akha point of view, their ethnic group is what is called a clan in anthropological parlance.

Akha Identity

Akha believe themselves to be lineal descendants of a single apical ancestor, "Main Sky, Middle Sky" *(Mmamg'ah)* below whom there were nine generations of spirits before the first man, *Smmio,* appeared. The various named, unranked patrilineages to which all Akha belong segment below *Smmio.* The Akha genealogical system is described as "universalistic" by Feingold (1976:88) because a person can add his name below that of a specified ancestor and thereby become an Akha. Although it is true that non-Akha may become Akha in this way, the genealogical system is not universal in the sense of embracing all people. As descendants of *Smmio,* Akha are set apart from non-Akha. The system is universal in that it encompasses all Akha; "it pronounces that all Akha are brothers" (J. Hanks 1974:126).

A child becomes a member of its father's patrilineage not at birth but shortly thereafter at the naming ceremony. The genealogical name given at this ceremony follows the Tibeto-Burman pattern of patronymic linkage in which the last one or two syllables of a father's name become the first one or two syllables of his child's name (Lo Ch'ang-p'ei 1945). Thus, for example Liba's child might be named Bado. Through her/his genealogical name a person is linked to the chain of patrilineal ancestors stretching back sixty or more generations to the apical ancestor. Every Akha has both an everyday name and a genealogical name. Use of the latter is restricted to contexts that are included within the domain of "customs." During curing rituals the patient is addressed by that name and thereby identified to ancestors whose aid is sought. The recitation of the deceased's genealogy is central to the funeral ceremony (J. Hanks 1974; Hansson 1983:280-81). A woman who dies before marriage is buried following the recitation of her father's lineage; a woman who dies after marriage is buried following the recitation of her husband's lineage. Akha say that every man should be able to recite his genealogy. Some men have neither the gift nor the inclination to commit the sixty plus names to memory, but at least one older man in each sub-lineage must know it. Reciters *(phima),* ritual specialists whose grasp of the branching genealogical system is particularly extensive, as well as other knowledgeable elders can readily identify the critical point of segmentation not only of their own lineage but also of others.

Ethnic identity as customs. In addition to defining themselves as descendants of a single apical ancestor, Akha also define themselves on the basis of their adherence to a specific set of "customs" *(zah)*. To be an Akha is to uphold the prescriptions and proscriptions for action which constitute Akha customs (Lewis 1969-70:24). According to Akha traditions, long ago the various peoples were differentiated at the bestowal of customs. In Bradley's (1983:52) phraseology, "the source of ethnic distinctions is cosmologized" in the myth which relates that Northern Thai, Chinese, Lahu, Akha, etc. were called together and given customs. The Northern Thai, Chinese, and Lahu all went carrying loosely woven baskets. In some tellings, not only were these baskets woven with wide spaces between the bamboo strips, they were also broken and torn. Unlike the others, the Akha went to fetch customs carrying a tightly woven sack, the kind in which rice is brought back from the fields so that not one precious grain is lost. The Northern Thai, Chinese, and Lahu put customs into their baskets and returned home. On the way customs fell through the holes and were lost. The Akha, on the other hand, placed customs inside the sack and on the way home not one piece fell out. This is the reason that the customs of others are few while those of Akha are many. The story permits the addition or deletion of other groups depending on both current and past intergroup relations, and on the inclinations of the teller. Akha in northern Thailand do not live near Shan, but many older Akha who used to live near them in Burma include Shan when recounting this story.

Not only do Northern Thai, Chinese, Lahu, Akha, etc. all have their own customs, so too do different sorts of Akha. A particular ritual may be performed differently by members of one named lineage than by members of another. For example, all Akha coffins are made from hollowed tree trunks, but deceased members of the *Anyi* lineage are placed with their feet towards the base of the trunk, whereas deceased members of other lineages are placed with their heads towards it. A common expression is "Everyone has their own customs," which may be said with reference to groups such as Northern Thai and Lahu or with reference to individual Akha belonging to different lineages. Akha accept and are tolerant of variations in customs at either the ethnic or the intra-ethnic level, since Akha assume that customs at all levels are legitimated in the same manner, that is, by being handed down from the ancestors.

Akha customs include the plethora of rituals crowding Akha life: calendrical ceremonies, life cycle rites, curing ceremonies, rituals concerning rice cultivation, and corrective rites of numerous sorts. In addition, customs encompass much that anthropologists generally label kinship, such as rules concerning lineage segmentation, permissible marriages, and affinal responsiblities. Also included in customs is patterned behaviour not part of ritual performances or kinship relations, for instance, activities permitted and not permitted on various days of the Akha week. Many customary injunctions concerning everyday behaviour are the obverse of ritual injunctions. To give one example, hanging washing out to dry on the porch as sunset approaches is normally prohibited because during a funeral a blanket belonging to the deceased must be hung out to dry there late in the afternoon following burial. An action permitted, indeed required, in its appropriate ritual frame is prohibited on any other day. As a system of rules, customs stipulate not only actions, actors, recitations, and ritual paraphernalia for all ceremonies, but also proper and improper behaviour in many non-ritual contexts.

The well-known highlander self-reflexive ambivalence is evident in two often quoted sayings: "Akha customs are many" and "Akha customs are difficult." These two are pronounced with self-deprecation, with pride, or with both. On one occasion, an Akha man was prompted by his long description of the proper procedures for a short segment of the elaborate funeral ceremony to recount the story of receiving customs. He concluded by declaring that the Akha who fetched customs in a sack was stupid. Another time, after an old man finished the tale, a young woman turned to me and only half-jokingly said, "Go ahead and tell him that the Akha was stupid." However, Akha also proclaim their customs to be many and difficult when their importance is being stressed. The old learning which has been handed down from the ancestors must not not be allowed to disappear. As a fragment of ceremonial song emphasizes, "in father's footsteps on the earth, a son should walk; in mother's footsteps on the earth, a daughter should walk."

The many customs are difficult in being both complex and costly. Minutely specified procedures must be followed precisely; an offering incorrectly performed must be repeated. To enact annual rituals, curing rites, and ceremonies of the life cycle each household must sacrifice a great number of animals. In Thailand today customs are becoming more difficult because many Akha are increasingly hard pressed to raise or to acquire the necessary sacrificial animals. Highlanders are numerous and hill land is scarce; lowlanders, themselves impoverished, cut swiddens on mountains slopes; and government reforestation programmes reduce upland farmland by planting trees while, at the same time, licensed and illegal logging removes trees. Akha who convert to Christianity often do so because they can no longer afford to make the sacrifices demanded by the many and difficult customs of their forebears.

The legitimacy of customs rests, as noted above, on the authority of the ancestors. Since customs were originally received, they have been passed down from one generation to the next; however, it would be a mistake to assume that they are static. Customs can and do change. The following example is chosen because it is relevant to the discussion in the next section of the "sense of territoriality" implicit within Akha ethnic identity. Besides the village founder-leader who is responsible for internal village affairs, there is a second official who is responsible for matters concerning hill/valley relations. This man is the village headman (called *phuujajbaan* in Thailand), who is appointed or confirmed by valley political authorities. According to customs, men who have held this position are the only Akha eligible to receive a horse at their funerals. Not so many years ago, in order to offer a horse, more than one buffalo also had to be sacrificed. Buffalo are expensive and it is now difficult for a family to provide even a single buffalo for a funeral; therefore, the procedure for a horse funeral was recently changed by male elders after discussions among themselves. Now the sacrifice of one buffalo suffices to permit the offering of a horse at a village headman's funeral. Customs, then, can be altered in response to changing circumstances, including the deteriorating economic situation of mountain minorities. Newer practices share with older practices the same stamp of legitimacy. By virtue of being labelled customs, inherited traditions and innovations are invested with the authority of the ancestors. The adaptability of customs has been and continues to be crucial to the survival of Akha as an ethnic group; yet the limits of adaptability of customs as a coherent, cosmologically-grounded cultural subsystem could well be reached in the not so distant future.

Implicit duplex "sense of territoriality." Each Akha community is identically structured according to the dictates of customs. The boundary between a community and the surrounding forest is demarcated by two village gateways renewed annually at a ceremony presided over by the village founder-leader. No fence encloses the community, but the dividing line separating the domain of people within the settlement from the domain of spirits in the encircling forest is no less real for being intangible. Portions of many rituals, especially curing rites, must be enacted at a village gate; it is not necessary, however, to go to one or the other gateway. Although there are only two gates with wooden uprights and crossbeams, a certain point on every path leading away from the residential compounds is labelled by the same term applied to these two gates. From any such point, the wandering soul of a sick person may be called back from the forest, the domain of spirits. In the ordered Akha universe, people, ancestors, rice, and domesticated animals belong to the village realm, while spirits and wild animals belong to the forest realm.

One of the many segments of ritual text recited during three nights of chanting at an elaborate funeral as well as during various other rites is called "Descent of the Dwelling Places". This text recounts the Akha journey southwards over lands and rivers from China to Thailand. Akha deem their past and present dwelling places to be tokens of a single type, replicas of a single cosmologically-grounded model. Villages are united through their shared structure despite being geographically separated. Not only are living Akha, wherever they reside, linked by common community order, so too are the living and the dead. Ancestors reside in a village structured like villages of the living. Just as the first house to be built in a new settlement is that of the village founder-leader, so the first grave to be dug in a community burial ground is that of the village founder-leader of the ancestor's village. The apparent emphasis in the Akha conceptualization of the historical branching of villages in the descent from China is not on a social genealogy, with one village the parent of the next, but upon the structural identity of each village as a microcosm.

Akha villages are identical islands surrounded not only by forest, but also by hills, valleys, and rivers as well as by villages inhabited by members of other ethnic groups (Plates 9 & 10). Among *Jeug'oe* Akha in Burma and Thailand, the "Offering to Lords of Land and Water" follows the renewal of the village gateways in the annual ritual cycle. Lewis (1969-70:256-57) reports that Akha in Burma acknowledge that this rite was borrowed from Shan some two generations ago. The recitation is done is Shan, in a combination of Shan and Akha, or in Akha alone. Features of the ceremony are similar to two Shan rituals described by Durrenberger (1980:51-54): the rite for spirits of valleys and hill fields and the rite for the ruler of the country. Elements of the

Akha Identity

Offering to Lords of Land and Water such as popped rice, burning candles, and white umbrellas are clearly Shan (-Buddhist) and do not appear in other ceremonies belonging to Akha customs. At the required time each year, a procession of men headed by the village founder-leader goes to an altar in the woods beyond the confines of the community. There two chickens and a pig are sacrificed while the village founder-leader or another knowledgeable male elder begs the "owners" of nearby mountains and rivers and the "Lords of Land and Water" for abundant harvests and for healthy people and domesticated animals (Plate 33). According to Alting von Geusau (1983:251), the dominant valley-dwellers' control over the land is acknowledged in the performance of the Offering to Lords of Land and Water. I would argue that it is not the political order of the dominant valley-dwellers which is acknowledged so much as it is the special relationship between the dominant group and the spirits of the land in the region.

Customs, then, presuppose a duplex conception of territory: every village as an identical moveable microcosm and each village as situated within a specific geographical sphere that includes more powerful ethnic groups. Correspondingly, the Akha polity has a dual nature: within a community the village founder-leader represents the ordinating principle of the village as microcosm, while the village headman links the village to the dominant political authorities in the region. These orientations of polity, like both conceptions of territoriality, are implicit within customs. The village founder-leader, who is indispensable to the enactment of customs, is mentioned frequently in the ancient ritual texts of the oral tradition. Although the village headman is not mentioned in these texts, customs decree that he alone is entitled to a horse offering at his funeral. Since both the practice of Offering to Lords of Land and Water and the position of village headman are fairly recent innovations, it may well be that Akha conceptions of territory and of polity were each simplex rather than duplex a few generations ago. But the duplex "sense of territoriality" and the duplex orientation of polity are important implicit aspects of the ethnic identity of Akha in Thailand today.

Mountain Minority Identity and Thailand's National Integration

The ethnic identity of Akha in northern Thailand is based upon shared lineal descent from an apical ancestor and adherence to common customs inherited from the ancestors. The Akha ethnic group as clan has persisted for generations and appears likely to continue for generations to come. The shared "socio-economic-ritual system," here glossed as customs, is a strikingly intricate and complex cultural subsystem. Structured relations between living and dead, between humans and spirits, and between wife-givers and wife-takers that are encoded in customs generate and maintain order within the Akha world. Though adaptable, customs are not infinitely flexible. A central axis of customs is rice, which is the focus of special calendrical ceremonies and annual ancestor offerings. Having reached the end of the mountain ranges extending southwards from China, Akha are well aware that, given their present technology, expanding highland population, and increasing competition from valley farmers and loggers for scarce hill land, their economic situation will continue to deteriorate. They are eager to adopt agricultural innovations provided these do not jeopardize their subsistence base. Any development schemes which ignore rice cultivation in favour of cash crops will not only endanger the subsistence base, but will also threaten the core of Akha customs and thereby threaten Akha ethnic identity. Akha in the mountains of northern Thailand see their southward journey at an end and consider Thailand to be their home. Their duplex conceptions of territoriality and polity permit them to respect their inherited traditions at the same time that they participate in the Thai nation-state.

Of all the nations in mainland South-East Asia, Thailand may well have entered the post-colonial era with the brightest prospects for successful national integration. Whereas in Burma the Burman majority resides in a minority of the land and in Laos the Lao majority is the numerical minority, in Thailand

Akha Identity

the highland region is a bare one fifth of the national territory, and the highland population is perhaps one percent of the national total. Unlike Burma and other neighbouring countries, Thailand has no legacy of the direct colonial rule that accentuated divisions between hill-dwellers and valley-dwellers (Kyaw Thet 1956:161). Thailand also has no legacy of politicized ethnic self-consciousness like that which has fractured the Union of Burma. Furthermore, Thailand's kings skillfully withstood colonial pressure, and the traditional monarchy has remained in constitutionalized form to serve as a symbolico-political center for majority and minorities alike. I would, however, argue that the sources of Thailand's potential success in fostering the integration of lowlanders and highlanders may prove instead to be the seeds of its failure.

Akha are one of the so-called "six tribes" of Thailand, that is, one of the six major mountain minorities. Five of these, including Akha, have already been characterized as reluctant assimilators. These five--Hmong, Mien, Lahu, Lisu, and Akha--are relatively recent immigrants into the territory now constituting Thailand. Only members of the sixth and by far the largest highland minority, the Karen, were in the area prior to the colonial era. Traditional relations between Karen and northern principalities, like those between Lua and these principalities, were severed early this century with the commencement of the bureaucratic and symbolico-religious integration of the northern region into the emerging Thai nation-state (Keyes 1971; Tambiah 1976). As the periphery was consolidated into the centralized Thai kingdom, in large measure in response to jockeying by colonial powers, "the gulf between the hill people and the representatives of lowland authority" widened (Walker 1979-80:428; see also Keyes 1979b:53). Not until the 1950s did the central government begin to fill the vacuum which resulted from its very creation.

Present and prospective relations between the national government and highlanders in Thailand can be approached with the aid of an analysis concerning the transformation of the

Burmans' relations with peripheral peoples in the post-colonial era. According to Lehman (1967:103),

> Throughout the pre-colonial period of history the Burmans had a reasonably correct tacit understanding of the nature of their relations with bordering peoples, tribal and non-tribal. That Burma seems to have lost this understanding today is almost certainly directly attributable to the importation of very explicit European ideas about nations, societies, and cultures, and the kinds of phenomena that they are taken to be.

Hinton (1983:167), who has done field research among Karen, contends that in Thailand an appropriate "tacit understanding" remains. That I take exception to his conclusion is, I believe, directly attributable to the fact that I worked among Akha, one of the more recently arrived groups.

Among officials in Thailand, Karen (and Lua) society is apparently taken to be significantly different from the societies of the remaining five "hill tribes". According to a publication of the Tribal Research Centre (now Institute) (1967:6) of the Department of Public Welfare,

> The Yao [Mien], Meo [Hmong], Lisu, Akha and Lahu are all shifting cultivators who farm land above 3,000 feet. Rice and corn are their main subsistence crops, with opium poppy, miscellaneous vegetables and jungle products being chief sources of cash income. Because shifting agriculture dictates periodic change of residence, all...tend to be widely distributed through the hills. The numerous Karen, and similar groups such as Lawa [Lua]...and [Thai] Lue have more or less sedentary agricultural economies, cultivating terrace or lowland rice fields. Consequently, they tend to be concentrated in particular regions.

The first five groups mentioned are lumped together not only as residents of higher elevations, but also as the "opium-growing tribes" (Patya Saihoo 1963:37) even though many among them live below 3,000 feet and many cultivate no opium.

As recent arrivals, Hmong, Mien, Lisu, Lahu, and Akha are considered immigrants with no historical or legal claim to the land. All the land upon which highlanders reside is government property (McKinnon and Wanat Bhruksasri 1983:xii). The Land Code, which prohibits damaging land in the hills by fire, essentially outlaws their traditional slash-and-burn agriculture (Sophon Ratanakhon 1978:18-49). Although their illegal method of cultivation is generally tolerated by officials, it is widely regarded by Thai both within and outside government as destructive to forests and watersheds, and floods in the lowlands are attibuted to swidden practices in the highlands **(Bangkok World** 1970:3). Swiddening practiced properly with sufficiently long fallow periods is, in fact, the most productive system of cultivation in upland forested areas and is not destructive to the land (Race 1974:89n.6). The problem in the mountains of northern Thailand is not slash-and-burn agriculture itself, but the limited size of land relative to the population to be supported by this mode of agriculture. Many farmers in the hills swidden improperly not through ignorance or preference, but because they must eat. In contrast to the five recently arrived mountain minorities, Karen are taken to be more benign: their agricultural methods are familiar, their settlements reassuringly stable, and their crops comfortingly legal. Furthermore, recognition of the historical depth of their presence in Thailand provides them with a legitimacy denied the other "hill tribes."

Mountain minorities of the higher slopes are alien and intrusive in the eyes of government representatives, while the Karen, though "hill tribe," are nonetheless akin and indigenous. Not all Karen are descendants of residents; some are recent immigrants from turbulent Burma. Nevertheless, the history of some bestows an aura of legitimacy on others. Thai authorities have consistently underestimated the length of residence of members of the five remaining major mountain minorities. Akha, for example, had been in Thailand almost seventy years when it was declared that they had arrived "no longer than 30-50 years" ago (Tribal Research Centre 1967:6). Such underestimates are not surprising given the vacuum that existed between the turn of the century and the reestablishment of official contact in the 1950s. These underestimates are, however, unfortunate because they inhibit the extension of the type of "tacit understanding" which continues to be operative in Karen-Thai relations to relations between the so-called "opium-growing tribes" and the Thai. Instead, understandings derived from "very explicit European ideas about nations" determined the nature of initial contacts with these highlanders in the 1950s and have profoundly influenced government policies and programmes concerning hill-dwellers since then.

Reestablishment of offical contact with peripheral peoples in the north was the consequence of efforts by the newly founded Border Patrol Police (BPP) to secure and safeguard the national frontiers. Not long thereafter, the BPP programme expanded to include social welfare projects in highland villages, notably Thai-language schools. It is interesting and perhaps significant in the overall development of modern highlander-government relations that the BPP mandate did not extend to the Karen (Moseley 1967:406). Since 1959 the National Tribal Welfare Committee, headed by the Minister of the Interior and composed of representatives from the Department of Public Welfare and the Ministries of Agriculture, Education, and Public Health, or its 1974 successor, the National Tribal Committee, have been responsible for overseeing the many government agencies and programmes concerned with the approximately 500,000 hill people in the nation's north. The objectives of the central government in its relations with highlanders were summarized at a 1967 symposium at the recently established Tribal Research Centre (Suwan Ruenyote 1969:13).

1. To prevent the destruction of forest and sources

Akha Identity

of natural streams by encouraging stabilised agriculture to replace the destructive shifting cultivation...

2. to end poppy growing, by promoting other means of livelihood;
3. to develop the economic and social conditions of hill tribes...
4. to induce the hill tribes to accept the important role of helping to maintain the security of national frontiers, by instilling in them a sense of belonging and national loyalty.

Each year Thailand's government, with aid from numerous international agencies and foreign governments (especially the US), has spent ever-increasing sums on ever-mushrooming programmes to realize these objectives. The so-called "hill tribe problem" was originally defined, as numerous commentators have noted, in terms of national interests and needs rather than in terms of the interests and needs of highlanders. Despite humanistic attitudes towards highlanders on the part of the present monarch King Phumiphol, and other members of the royal family as well as of some representatives of the national government, this original emphasis continues to predominate. Indeed, the four objectives listed above were tellingly reduced to three with the deletion of the third by one high official interviewed in the mid-1970s (Bo Gua 1975:76). This same official equated the maintenance of the security of the national frontiers (objective 4 above) with "combating communist terrorism among the hill tribes" (Bo Gua 1975:76).

I believe the image of the highlander as insurgent that is pervasive among government officials, rather than the small number of highlanders who have resisted or might resist government pressure by force, is the most dangerous element in the present hill/valley conjuncture. This dangerous image of largely imaginary danger results from the application of the "Red Meo" model to highlanders generally. A brief look at the origins of this model is revealing. The first armed clashes between highlanders and the government in 1967 did not involve the few Hmong (Meo) communist ("Red") cadres. Rather, they arose "in response to extortion by Thai officials for so-called 'illegal' agricultural activities [i.e., slash-and-burn cultivation]" of Hmong villagers (Turton 1974:339; see also Bo Gua 1975:71; Cooper 1979:326; Race 1974;98-99). Nowadays any highlander who so much as questions government corruption or policies is liable to be labelled a communist. Many government officials are so preoccupied with suppressing communism that they ignore economic and social conditions. Rather than asking whether highland villagers have enough rice, they ask whether there are any communists in the area.

Although Geddes (1967:556), an Australian anthropologist who served as the initial foreign advisor to the Tribal Research Centre, advocated a policy of "open-ended integration" to the Royal Thai Government, the thrust of numerous programmes is obviously assimilationist. For example, schools established in the highlands are taught exclusively in the Thai language, and the Public Welfare Department supports an extensive programme under which missionary monks propagate Buddhism among highlanders (Keyes 1971; Tambiah 1976:434-54). The philosophy underlying the resettlement programme initiated in the late 1960s was "accelerated integration," and the aim was to transform "former hilltribe villages" into a "normal Thai village" (Krachang Bhanthumnavin 1972:23, 31). This programme was operated by the Communist Suppression Operations Command (CSOC), which has since been renamed the Internal Security Operations Command (ISOC). It was initiated in response to the massive refugee population created by the Royal Thai Army's bombing and napalming of suspected insurgent strongholds, particularly in Nan Province, and developed into an evacuation programme aimed at removing highlanders from areas of suspected communist influence (Thomson 1968). (See Hearn 1974 for a critical study of this programme).

Akha Identity

Not all Thai supported this resettlement policy. For example, in an article entitled "The Hilltribes: Who Should Do the Moving?" which appeared in the English-language newspaper the **Bangkok Post,** Suthichai Yoon (1970) urged that "instead of moving them to the officials, the latter should move closer to the hilltribesmen both physically and psychologically." Yet the policy of evacuating highlanders to the lowlands was abandoned not because their right to remain in the hills was recognized, but because it was feared that additional highlanders from neighbouring Laos and Burma would simply move in and fill the void. The wisdom of the position advocated by Suthichai Yoon has been recognized by the Department of Public Welfare, which now concentrates of delivering agricultural, educational, and medical aid to hill people through a system of selected core and satellite villages rather than by continuing to follow its original programme of creating "'settlement areas' *(nikhom)*" in the highlands and "encouraging tribes to migrate to these settlement areas" (Manndorff 1967:531-32).

It is both ironic and significant that the resettlement programme was touted as "the first time officials have faithfully carried out government policy in treating the tribesmen as full Thai citizens" (Krachang Bhanthumnavin 1972:23). The irony is that most highlanders today remain non-citizens. The government, it is argued,

> cannot ease regulations [concerning conditions for registering as a citizen]too much or quicken registration, for fear that this would serve to further encourage already substantial immigration (McKinnon and Wanat Bhruksasri 1983:xii).

The significance is that a full citizen is envisaged as indistinguishable from an ethnic Thai. Some officials see national integration not as the incorporation of distinctive parts into a united whole but as the homogenization of disparate parts into a uniform whole. What such officials seek is not the identification of mountain minorities with the nation but their identity with the national majority.

This monolithic notion of national identity held by some Thai officials as well as by some Thai not in government seems to represent the coupling of a European conception of a bounded territorial state with an older conception of Thai identity. Not only is just one "sense of territoriality" considered legitimate, so too just one sense of identity is considered legitimate. Both should be "fully, flatly, and evenly operative" over the entire nation (Anderson 1983:26). The pre-colonial "tacit understanding" of hill/valley relations permitted peripheral peoples to retain an identity different from those at the center. Now many Thai do not recognize the possiblity of dual identities or loyalties; the extreme position is that "To be Thai is to speak only Thai, to be Buddhist" (Keyes 1979a:19). As the overwhelming majority and as the residents of most of the land, Thai are not forced to realize that "bilaterality of integration" is required (Maran La Raw 1967:143). Not only must minorities adapt to the nation, the majority must accord them an equal place within it. Lacking assertive, politicized ethnic identity, mountain minorities have not persuaded the Thai government to redefine its objectives so that the highlanders' problems replace the highlanders themselves as the "hill tribe problem."

The highlanders' problems are likely to become more severe. Continued economic marginalization appears inevitable given an expanding population in a limited area dependant upon an agricultural technology predicated upon the availability of either sufficient land for swidden rotation or new land for settlement. Government programmes have paid little attention to stabilizing the subsistence rice economy, and none of the many cash crops such as coffee and decorative flowers initially introduced to replace opium poppies has had wide-spread success. More recently, crops like cabbages and tomatoes have been highly lucrative but have exacted a heavy toll from the land, in the form of increased erosion, and from the people, in the form of side-effects from pesticides and fungicides. The subsistence economy is collapsing at the same time that its long-term companion, the cash crop economy, is not expanding rapidly enough to fill the gap. Highlanders are increasingly forced to join the wage-economy of the northern hills. A small but growing number of Akha, for example, live in leaderless hamlets on the outskirts of market towns. Hanks and Hanks (1975:75) found that in these abject, amorphous aggregates "collective life within the Akha tradition had shrunk near a minimum while hungry householders struggled to find something to eat".

Although all mountain minorities will face increasing economic hardship, Karen overall will probably experience less cultural disruption than others provided that Thai continue to grant them a legitimate place within the nation by virtue of their history and do not further assimilate them to the "hill tribe" model (Keyes 1979a, 1979b; Kunstadter 1979). Unlike Karen, members of the remaining five major highland groups-- Hmong, Mien, Lahu, Lisu, and Akha--are not permitted to retain their traditional identity and to be Thai simultaneously. If members of these groups who are strongly attached to their respective ethnic identities are allowed to slip into Thai identity only by default, through gradually abandoning their inherited identities because poverty prevents them from fulfilling the demands of those identities, they will never gain the "sense of belonging and national loyalty" the government claims to desire for them. I do not share Bradley's (1983:54) confidence that "positive group identity" alone is sufficient in the context of modern nation-states for preserving ethnic identity, either as traditionally defined or as consciously refashioned by the people themselves to meet changing circumstances. As the economic situation continues to deteriorate, the role of those in government who recognize that dual identity and dual "sense of territoriality" are possible and who believe that it is imperative that national integration be forged within diversity will become increasingly crucial.

RESETTLEMENT

Since this paper was written (1983-84), it has become increasingly likely that the sources of Thailand's potential success in fostering the integration of lowlanders and highlanders will instead prove to be the seeds of its failure. There is growing evidence that rather than moving "closer to the hilltribesmen...psychologically," as Suthichai Yoon (1970) urged nearly twenty years ago, officials have moved away. In Thailand today the territorial imperative of the nation-state is clearly dominant. Now that the uplands are riddled with roads connecting them to the lowlands and all villages have been pulled into the orbit of the centralized bureaucracy, concern with incorporating the highlands and highlanders administratively has been eclipsed by concern with controlling the utilization of mountain land in what is perceived to be the national interest. And the highlanders themselves are seen to have no share in that national interest and indeed are deemed to be inimical to it.

It is not the image of highlander as insurgent that now pervades official thinking. Largely because of the collapse of the Communist Party of Thailand in part due to the government's amnesty programme initiated in the late 1970s, this image is no longer at the fore. In its stead is the image of highlander as destroyer of the nation's forests and watersheds through slash-and-burn agriculture and log poaching and as destroyer of the nation's international reputation through cultivating opium poppies and trafficking in illegal drugs. Recent statements by the deputy secretary-general of the National Security Council and by the commander and the chief-of-staff of the Third Army Region (covering the North) confirm the prevalence of these stereotypes (**Bangkok Post** 1987; Sinfah Tunsarawuth 1987; **The Nation** 1987a, 1987b).

A two-pronged policy has begun to be implemented to remove highlanders from mountain land. Involuntary resettlement is designed to relocate uplanders into more low-lying areas, and involuntary repatriation is aimed at driving illegal immigrants into either Burma or Laos. Given that resettlement

Akha Identity

was abandoned as policy some two decades ago after being effectively challenged by Thai within and outside the government on both humanitarian and pragmatic grounds, its recent resurrection is particularly disheartening. Like resettlement, repatriation must be questioned on similar grounds. In late September of this year (1987), Akha and other highlanders expelled from thirteen villages in Chiang Rai Province were left at the Burma border with neither food nor shelter. Since many highlanders, even those born inside Thailand to parents who were themselves born inside Thailand, do not have citizenship papers, it is difficult to distinguish between legal residents and illegal immigrants. It is also hard to determine from official statements the basis upon which legal residence is determined. In fact "repatriation" is a misnomer because many highlanders are stateless persons who are not accorded citizenship either by Thailand or by its neighbours. Moreover, no provision is made for due process to allow those scheduled for expulsion to argue against the claim that Thailand is not actually the country of their birth or is not the country in which they have a right to citizenship. From a political perspective, forcible expulsions of the type carried out in September can only serve to create fear and antagonism towards the government on the part of those highlanders who can legitimately claim membership of the Thai nation.

While forest conservation and watershed preservation are important for all Thailand's peoples, highlanders and lowlanders alike, there is little scientific support for the view that the only way to achieve these aims is to remove highlanders from the hills. Development workers argue that agriculture can be practiced on steep slopes in a manner (for example, strip farming) that prevents erosion and soil depletion. In addition, recent projects in social forestry enlist the support of uplanders and lowlanders in the revitalization of overworked areas for their mutual benefit. Even in these critical days there is hope that policy-makers will heed those inside and outside government who see the current crisis in the mountains of northern Thailand not as "the hill tribe problem" or even as the problems of the hill tribes but rather as the problems of the entire nation which can only be solved by highlanders and lowlanders in cooperation.

Acknowledgements. The full version of this paper appeared in *Ethnicities and Nations: Processes of Interethnic Relations in Latin America, Southeast Asia, and the Pacific* edited by Remo Guidieri, Francesco Pellizzi, and Stanley J. Tambiah (1988, Houston: The Rothko Chapel, distributed by the University of Texas Press, Austin). My thanks to the Rothko Chapel for permission to publish this abridged version here and to Mrs. John de Menil, originator and sponsor of the Rothko Chapel colloquium, for financial support during writing. I gratefully acknowledge research permission from the National Research Council of Thailand and research grants from the Fulbright-Hays Doctoral Dissertation Abroad Program, the International Doctoral Research Fellowship Program of the Social Science Research Council (New York), and the Joint Area Committee on Southeast Asia of the Social Science Research Council and the American Council of Learned Societies (with funds provided by the Ford Foundation and the National Endowment for the Humanities). More complete acknowledgements accompany the original published version of this paper. For helpful comments on a draft, I would like to thank John Bowen and Joan Vincent, whose names were inadvertently omitted from those acknowledgements.

References Cited

Alting von Geusau, Leo (1983) "Dialectics of *Akhazan:* The Interiorization of a Perennial Minority Group" *Highlanders of Thailand* John McKinnon and Wanat Bhruksasri (eds) pp.243-77. Kuala Lumpur: Oxford University Press.

Anderson, Benedict (1983) *Imagined Communities: Reflections on the Origin and Spread of Nationalism* London: Verso.

Andrianoff, David I. (1979) "The Effect of the Laotian Conflict on Meo Ethnic Identity" *Nationalism and the Crises of Ethnic Minorities in Asia* Tai S. Kang (ed.) pp. 77-80. Westport, Conn.: Greenwood Press.

Bangkok Post (1987) "Tribesmen Forced Back into Burma". 26 September p. 5.

Bangkok World (1970) "Ravaged Earth Blamed in Chiang Rai Floods". 6 July p. 3.

Bo Gua (1975) "Opium, Bombs and Trees: The Future of the H'mong Tribesmen in Northern Thailand" *Journal of Contemporary Asia* 5(1):70-81.

Bradley, David (1983) "Identity: The Persistence of Minority Group" *Highlanders of Thailand* John McKinnon and Wanat Bhruksasri (eds.) pp. 46-55. Kuala Lumpur: Oxford University Press.

Cooper, R.G. (1979) "The Tribal Minorities of Northern Thailand, Problems and Prospects" *Southeast Asian Affairs* 6:323-32.

Dentan, R.K. (1976) "Ethnics and Ethics in Southeast Asia" *Changing Identities in Modern Southeast Asia* David J. Banks (ed.) pp. 71-81. The Hague: Mouton.

Durrenberger, E. Paul (1980) "Annual Non-Buddhist Religious Observances of Mae Hong Son Shan" *Journal of the Siam Society* 68:48-56.

Feingold, David A. (1976) "On Knowing Who You Are: Intraethnic Distinctions among the Akha of Northern Thailand" *Changing Identities in Modern Southeast Asia* David J. Banks (ed.) pp. 83-94. The Hague: Mouton.

Geddes, W.R. (1967) "The Tribal Research Centre, Thailand: An Account of Plans and Activities" *Southeast Asian Tribes, Minorities, and Nations,* Volume II. Peter Kunstadter (ed.) pp.553-81. Princeton: Princeton University Press.

Guidieri, Remo, and Francesco Pellizzi (1980) "Ethnicities and Nations: Contemporary Reinterpretations of the Problematic of Identity" (Ten Themes of Reflection for a Colloquium). Ms.

Hanks, Jane R. (1974) "Recitation of Patrilineages among the Akha" *Social Organization and the Applications of Anthropology:*

Hanks, Lucien M., and Jane R. Hanks (1975)

Essays in Honor of Lauriston Sharp. Robert. J. Smith (ed.) pp. 114-27. Ithaca: Cornell University Press.

"Reflections on Ban Akha Mae Salong" *Journal of the Siam Society* 63(1):72-85.

Hanks, Lucien M., Jane R. Hanks and Lauriston Sharp (1964)

A Report on Tribal Peoples in Chiengrai Province North of the Mae Kok River Bennington-Cornell Anthropological Survey of Hill Tribes in Thailand. Bankok: The Siam Society (Data Paper Number 1).

Hansson, Inga-Lill (1983)

"Death in an Akha Village" *Highlanders of Thailand* John McKinnon and Wanat Bhruksasri (eds.) pp. 278-90 Kuala Lumpur: Oxford University Press.

Hearn, Robert (1974)

Thai Government Programs in Refugee Relocation and Resettlement in Northern Thailand Auburn, N.Y.: Thailand Books.

Hinton, Peter (1969)

"Introduction" *Tribesmen and Peasants in North Thailand: Proceedings of the First Symposium of the Tribal Research Centre, Chiang Mai, Thailand, 1967.* Pp. 1-11.

(1979)

"The Karen, Millennialism, and the Politics of Accommodation to Lowland States" *Ethnic Adaptation and Identity: The Karen on the Thai Frontier with Burma* Charles F.

Keyes (ed.) pp. 81-94. Philadelphia: Institute for the Study of Human Issues.

(1983) "Do the Karen Really Exist?" **Highlanders of Thailand** John McKinnon and Wanat Bhruksasri (eds.) pp. 155-68. Kuala Lumpur: Oxford University Press.

Hymes, Dell (1971) "Two Types of Linguistic Relativity (With Examples from AmerIndian Ethnography)" **Sociolinguistics.** William Bright (ed.) pp. 116-67. The Hague: Mouton.

Kandre, Peter (1967) "Autonomy and Integration of Social Systems: The Iu Mien ("Yao" or "Mien") Mountain Population and Their Thai Neighbours" **Southeast Asian Tribes, Minorities, and Nations,** Volume II. Peter Kunstadter (ed.) pp. 583-38. Princeton: Princeton University Press.

(1976) "Yao (Iu Mien) Supernaturalism, Language, and Ethnicity" **Changing Identities in Modern Southeast Asia** David J. Banks (ed.) pp. 171-97. The Hague: Mouton.

Keyes, Charles F. (1971) "Buddhism and National Integration in Thailand" **Journal of Asian Studies** 30:551-67.

(1976) "Towards a New Formulation of the Concept of Ethnic Group" **Ethnicity** 3:202-13.

(1979a) "Introduction" *Ethnic Adaptation and Identity: The Karen on the Thai Frontier with Burma* Charles F. Keyes (ed.) pp. 1-23. Philadelphia: Institute for the Study of Human Issues.

(1979b) "The Karen in Thai History and the History of Karen in Thailand" *Ethnic Adaptation and Identity: The Karen on the Thai Frontier with Burma* Charles F. Keyes (ed.) pp. 25-61. Philadelphia: Institute for the Study of Human Issues.

(1981) "The Dialectics of Ethnic Change" *Ethnic Change* Charles F. Keyes (ed.) pp. 4-30. Publications on Ethnicity and Nationality of the School of international Studies, University of Washington, Volume 2. Seattle: University of Washington Press.

Krachang Bhanthumnavin (1972) "Overcoming the Problems of Resettling Hill Tribes" *South-east Asian Spectrum* (SEATO) 1 (1): 23-34.

Kunstadter, Peter
(1967) "The Lua' and Skaw Karen of Maehongson Province, Northwestern Thailand" *Southeast Asian Tribes, Minorities, and Nations* Volume II. Peter Kunstadter (ed.) pp. 639-74. Princeton: Princeton University Press.

(1969) "Hill and Valley Populations in Northwestern Thailand" *Tribesmen* and *Peasants in North Thailand: Proceedings of the First Symposium of the Tribal Research Centre, Chiang Mai, Thailand, 1967.* Pp. 68-85.

(1979) "Ethnic Group, Category, and Identity: Karen in Northern Thailand" *Ethnic Adaptation and Identity: The Karen on the Thai Frontier with Burma* Charles F. Keyes (ed.) pp. 119-63. Philadelphia: Institute for the Study of Human Issues.

(1983a) "Animism, Buddhism, and Christianity: Religion in the Life of Lua People of Pa Pae, North-Western Thailand" *Highlanders of Thailand* John McKinnon and Wanat Bhruksasri (eds.) pp. 135-54. Kuala Lumpur: Oxford University Press.

(1983b) "Highland Populations in Northern Thailand" *Highlanders of Thailand* John McKinnon and Wanat Bhruksasri, (eds.) pp. 15-45. Kuala Lumpur: Oxford University Press.

Kyaw Thet (1956) "Burma: The Political Integration of Linguistic and Religious Minority Groups" *Nationalism and Progress in Free Asia* Philip W. Thayer (ed.) pp. 156-68. Baltimore: Johns Hopkins Press.

Leach, E.R. (1954) *Political Systems of Highland Burma: A Study of Kachin Social Structure* Cambridge, Mass.: Harvard University Press.

Lehman, F.K. (1963) ***The Structure of Chin Society: A Tribal People of Burma Adapted to a Non-Western Civilization*** Illinois Studies in Anthropology, Number 3. Urbana: University of Illinois Press.

(1967) "Ethnic Categories in Burma and the Theory of Social Systems" ***Southeast Asian Tribes, Minorities, and Nations,*** Volume I. Peter Kunstadter (ed.) pp. 93-124. Princeton: Princeton University Press.

Lewis, Paul (1968) ***Akha-English Dictionary*** Southeast Asia Program, Data Paper Number 70. Ithaca: Cornell University, Department of Asian Studies.

(1969-70) ***Ethnographic Notes on the Akhas of Burma*** Volumes I-IV. New Haven: Human Relations Area Files.

Lo Ch'ang-p'ei (1945) "The Genealogical Patronymic Linkage System of the Tibeto Burman Speaking Tribes" ***Harvard Journal of Asiatic Studies*** 8(3-4): 349-63.

McKinnon, John, and Wanat Bhruksasri (1983) "Preface" ***Highlanders of Thailand*** John McKinnon and Wanat Bhruksasri (eds.) pp.ix-xii. Kuala Lumpur: Oxford University Press.

Manndorff, Hans (1967) "The Hill Tribe Program of The Public Welfare Department, Ministry of Interior, Thailand:Research and Socio-economic Development"

Southeast Asian Tribes, Minorities, and Nations, Volume II. Peter Kunstadter (ed.) pp. 525-52. Princeton: Princeton University Press.

Maran La Raw (1967) "Towards a Basis for Understanding the Minorities in Burma: The Kachin Example" *Southeast Asian Tribes, Minorities, and Nation* Volume I. Peter Kunstadter (ed.) pp. 125-46. Princeton: Princeton University Press.

Marlowe, David H. (1969) "Upland-Lowland Relationships: The Case of the S'kaw Karen of Central Upland Western Chiang Mai" *Tribesmen and Peasants in North Thailand: Proceedings of the First Symposium of the Tribal Research Centre, Chiang Mai, Thailand, 1967.* Pp. 53-68

(1979) "In the Mosaic: The Cognitive and Structural Aspects of Karen-Other Relationship" *Ethnic Adaptation and Identity: The Karen on the Thai Frontier with Burma* Charles F. Keyes (ed.) pp. 165-214. Philadelphia: Institute for the Study of Human Issues.

Matisoff, James A. (1983) "Linguistic Diversity and Language Contact" *Highlanders of Thailand* John McKinnon and Wanat Bhruksasri (eds). pp. 56-86. Kuala Lumpur: Oxford University Press.

Moerman, Michael (1965) "Ethnic Identification in a Complex Civilization: Who Are the Lue?" *American Anthropologist* 67:1215-30

(1968) "Being Lue: Uses and Abuses of Ethnic Identification" *Essays on the Problem of the Tribe: Proceedings of the 1967 Annual Spring Meeting of the American Ethnological Society* June Helm (ed.) pp. 153-69. Seattle: University of Washington Press.

Moseley, George (1967) "Voices in the Minority" *Far Eastern Economic Review* 55(9): 405-7.

Murphy, R.F. (1964) "Social Change and Acculturation" *Transactions of the New York Academy of Sciences* Series 2, 26(7): 845-54.

The Nation (1987a) "Illegal Border Immigrants Will Have to Go" 15 October, p. 5.

(1987b) "Repatriation of Illegal Highlanders: Senior NSC Offical Denies Using Violence" 13 October, p. 3.

Patya Saihoo (1963) "The Hill Tribes of Northern Thailand and the Opium Problem" *Bulletin of Narcotics* 15(2):35-45.

Race, Jeffrey (1974) "The War in Northern Thailand" *Modern Asian Studies* 8(1):85-112.

Radley, Howard M. (1986) *Economic Marginalization and the Ethnic Consciousness of the Green Mong (Moob Ntsuab) of Northwestern Thailand.* Unpublished Ph.D. thesis. Institute of Social Anthropology, Oxford University.

Sinfah Tunsarawuth (1987) "Govt Pushes out Illegal Burmese Immigrants" **The Nation** 26 September, pp. 1-2.

Sophon Ratanakhon (1978) "Legal Aspects of Land Occupation and Development" *Farmers in the Forest: Economic Development and Marginal Agriculture in Northern Thailand* Peter Kunstadter, E.C. Chapman, and Sanga Sabhasri (eds.) pp. 45-53. Honolulu: The University Press of Hawaii for the East-West Center.

Suthichai Yoon (1970) "The Hilltribes: Who Should Do the Moving?" **Bangkok Post** 7 September, p. 7.

Suwan Ruenyote (1969) "Development and Welfare for the Hill Tribes in Thailand" *Tribesmen and Peasants in North Thailand: Proceedings of the First Symposium for the Tribal Research Centre Chiang Mai, Thailand, 1967* Pp. 12-14.

Tambiah, S.J. (1976) *World Conqueror and World Renouncer: A Study of Buddhism and Polity in Thailand against a Historical Background* Cambridge, Eng.: Cambridge University Press.

Thomson, John R. (1968)	"The Mountains Are Steeper" *Far Eastern Economic Review* 60(15): 139-41.
Tribal Research Centre (1967)	"Introduction" *Social Scientific Research in Northern Thailand* Bulletin Number 1 of the Tribal Research Centre, Chiengmai, Thailand (Department of Public Welfare, Ministry of Interior, Government of Thailand) pp. 5-7.
Turton, Andrew (1974)	"National Minority Peoples in Indo-China" *Journal of Contemporary Asia* 4(3):336-43.
Walker, Anthony R. (1979-80)	"Highlanders and Government in North Thailand" *Folk* 21-22:419-49.
Weber, Max (1978)	"Ethnic Groups" *Economy and Society: An Outline of Interpretive Sociology,* Volume I. Guenther Roth and Claus Wittich (eds.) pp. 385-98. Berkeley: University of California Press.

Structural Assimilation and the Consensus: Clearing Grounds on which to Rearrange our Thoughts

John McKinnon

> ...It is enough to observe that actual men do not **behave:** they **act** with an idea in their heads, perhaps that of conforming to custom. Man acts as a function of what he thinks, and while he has up to a certain point the ability to arrange his own thoughts in his own way, to construct new categories, he does so starting from the categories which are given by society; their link with language should be a sufficient reminder of this.
> (Louis Dumont, *Homo Hierarchicus* 1970:6)

Contemporary Thai policy towards highlanders is not the product of current scientific knowledge, it is largely formed out of an older cultural and historical position informed by modern ideas about what constitutes progress, development and national territory. This consensus is part of a broader socio-political structure which has enabled the Thai state to internationalize its economy while promoting a hierarchical and technocratic ideology of modernization which is not too much at odds with the past. It is as a microcosm of this construction that development intervention in the highlands precludes careful scientific consideration and qualitative evaluations of specific environmental and social conditions and commits national and foreign development agencies to activities which by default, primarily serve to ensure their own survival. The technical bias of development keeps government activities within what I will attempt to identify as a domain of structural assimilation.

In using this term, "structural assimilation", I wish to draw a distinction between stated policy and affective action: between what is said and what is done.

As outlined in the discussion of policy in the first chapter of this volume, a liberal and humane policy is aimed at integrating highlanders into the mainstream of national life, as speakers of Thai willing to abide by Thai law and subject to all other conditions accepted by the community. Then as first class, self-reliant people they will be granted citizenship. From this it is generally understood that they will be able to practise their own religions, customs and retain their own languages for as long as they find it rewarding to do so. In this sense integration does not mean that they must involuntarily reject their identity as members of minority cultures but rather that they will adopt an additional range of knowledge, skills and loyalties which will enable them to better adapt their lives to the way life is lived on the lowlands.

It is my impression that this process is well under way. Highland communities have been greatly assisted to acquire these qualifications and have spontaneously accepted these ground rules. Their continuing survival has come to depend on increasing participation in the national economy and cooperating with government officials, both of which require them to speak Thai. The profound affection and regard in which they hold the Royal Family implicitly states a loyalty which leaves little doubt about where their genuine interests and sympathies lie.

The beliefs and actions of those engaged in planning and carrying out this integration are, however, inconsistent with the policy itself. The more deeply structured configuration of practical and urgent interests, such as the elimination of opium production, environmental protection and maintenance of security, have a far greater impact, and combined with the contemporary state of knowledge form an affective mode of intervention which overrides the stated policy.

The matters which best illustrate this problem are to be found in popular opinion and received knowledge which does not seriously challenged a paradigm which places highlanders in a marginalised and subordinate position in relation to the mainstream of Thai society. This deeply structured consensus is reinforced by law, which makes it difficult for highlanders to secure official recognition as residents and the documentation this requires such as identification cards, citizenship and so forth as well as legal land rights. Strictly speaking, in a purely formal sense, most highlanders have no right to occupy the land they cultivate and as long as they are seen as interlopers who lie outside the law there is little incentive to prepare a substantial reinterpretion of their position. As a consequence, most scientific work on the highlands tends to preclude full consideration of the highlanders position in favour of a conformist view, consistent with the law rather than the reality of what can be seen in the field or what can be gleaned from scientific literature. The point is that a more cautious and disciplined approach might raise serious doubts about what passes for information. It is from such a careful point of view that this paper has been written as an attempt to better align both stated and affective policy with the scientific facts about the highlands and their inhabitants.

My discussion is limited to a review of current popular knowledge and more substantial information that appears to both reflect and strongly influence official thinking on policy matters. The Chapter first addresses the matter of widely shared opinions about the highlanders as a subordinate group within an established social hierarchy and the idea of "consensus" developed by Vienne in Chapter 2 of this volume. As a geographer I have documented questions concerning the urgency of the ecological problem in the highlands more thoroughly. In the interests of keeping the text to a reasonable length not all of the issues raised are discussed in the same detail. The discussion focuses principally on empirical data including a brief comment on the role played by foreign funded development projects in supporting the current paradigmatic structure. The Chapter concludes with reference to observations made by General Saiyud Kerdphol on the issue of "enforced assimilation" and how the largely unintended consequences of this may lead to disaster (Saiyud, 1986: 102; Saiyud, **Bangkok Post** 4 January, 1976: 9-10)

Ideology and knowledge

In Bangkok society any mention of the words "hill tribes" is sure to elicit a confident response. Academics, teachers, business people, civil servants, everybody who is anybody knows something about the highlanders. They are an object of pity, people whose poverty qualifies them as a suitable target for charity. They are a tourist attraction for an industry which has come to contribute a major part of foreign earnings to the national economy. Then again they are also seen to be dangerous. They practice slash and burn cultivation, destroy the forest, spoil the environment, endanger the watershed, grow opium, migrate from place to place and constitute a security problem. Depending on who is speaking, mention may be made of how certain groups practise "free love", never wash and live a terribly primitive life and must therefore be enlightened by development aid, or how their rapidly increasing mumbers must be checked: according to a prominent official to "really end this hill tribe problem, they must be sterilized by force" (**Siam Rath** 27 February, 1987).

Thailand is, as General Saiyud has pointed out, a society with a tolerant pluralist tradition (Saiyud, 1986: 97-111) but the extent to which this tradition is extended to highlanders is clearly in doubt. The newspaper statement quoted above poses a profound ethical question for social science. Just as the medical profession is expected to do something about illness and disease, and architects and engineers are expected to design buildings and other structures that will not pose a hazard to those who use them, social scientists have a professional responsibility to point out how an impoverished sociology of knowledge is likely to lead to social and political problems which might otherwise be avoided.

Calling Names

As language presents us with the problem, the relevant nomenclature is as good a place to start as any. In Thailand highlanders are known as *"chao khao"*. Literally translated this means hill or mountain people but the English colonial practise in Burma was to call highlanders "hill tribes" and this subsequently came into general use and is now the standard translation. Unfortunately, today the word "tribal" conjures up a picture of primitive and backward people who live outside the state system.

It is misleading to call highlanders "tribal". Mountain people who are said to belong to set ethno-linguistic, cultural groups neither occupy or lay claim to coherent territories nor act as if they belonged to independent political communities. Their long standing relationship with lowland peoples, mediated through trade and tribute in historical systems of interaction so well described for neighbouring Burma by Leach (1954), should long ago have put to rest the idea of a tribal identity formed in isolation and fixed and frozen for all time (Conrad Chapter 8).

As to their supposed primitive and backward state, in a scientific sense their culture or language is no more or less complex or sophisticated than that of any other in the world. The term is pejorative, misleading but so firmly established in daily speech that mention of "hill tribes" leaves no doubt about who is being named. The title of this book acknowledges this reality. Even where both editors deny the descriptive validity of the term, in contradistinction, they also acknowledge its place in everyday language.

A name is more than a label. The contradiction embedded and obscured in the title points out the difficulty. What happens when we extend our consideration to the use of language? What sort of reality does language convey? If highlanders are thought of as "tribal" and found to be poor and living in houses constructed of bamboo and grass thatching, does it then become possible to treat such people in a manner considered to be consistent with their ascribed identity? Regretably a recent involuntary relocation reveals a distressing historical coincidence between the past and the present. After several hill tribe villages had been cleared of residents, an official, faced with the task of defending the use of a practice established in the last century of "firing villages... to show a claim of ownership" (Anon., 1895; 58), claimed that houses were not burnt down because what the people "lived in could not be called houses but only huts" **(Bangkok Post 15 October, 1987: 5).**

Such a comment, offered partly as an explanation of an action indistinguishable from the burning of Ban Mae Khum, Chiang Rai, by Siamese officials in 1889 is disturbing in its implications (Anon., 1895: 58). Such a statement identifies, after 98 years of modernization, a remarkably intact and unaltered attitude, the survival of a social distance, the existence of a class distinction and a belief that those who have no legal rights or social position can be treated in an arbitrary manner. The evidence of language, what is spoken spontaneously, cannot be ignored as an idea that was just plucked out of the air. In these post-Freudian days we must admit that the origins of any such statement lie deeply embedded in both the mind and the cultural ideology of the speaker.

The extent to which historical coincidence and manifestation of the subconscious can be used to reflect on the state-of-knowledge on the highlands and highlanders is another question. Conscious deliberations fall into a quite different category of thinking which lends itself to much more careful management and discipline.

Scientific method is the most systematic and careful way of assembling knowledge. If science plays a role in policy formation, can we then expect to entirely escape subjective psychological or socio-political influences on our thinking? History tells us that this is to expect too much. What we choose as individuals to investigate scientifically is already limited, for the average researcher in any society, to a range of options considered to be useful by those in positions of authority. If the sociological imagination of decision makers is limited to the domain of their principal administrative concerns, and/or research is structured into a belief system that demands conformity or reassurance and does not welcome any challenges, the pressure to conform to opinions generated as a function of received knowledge is quite strong. If scientific research is dismissed as academic and rated below that of opinions expressed by social superiors, then under such an ideological regime, government personnel must be under severe constraints to behave as expected rather than act as they think fit. Are not researchers caught in such a conservative milieu forced to choose self-censorship to survive?

But the commentary runs ahead of the evidence. What reasons are there for maintaining that the observations offered as examples of misinformation are actually wrong? Some matters such as nomadism and "free love" can be challenged at a relatively high level of confidence and, in the context of this essay, put aside. Other issues such as population increase, security, opium production, slash and burn agriculture, deforestation, and land degradation which are invoked in support of a wide range of views in opposition to highlander interests warrant, closer examination.

Nomads

In strictly scientific terms the people farming in the hill country of the North are not nomads; they do not circulate between set destinations and if by nomadic or semi-nomadic commentators mean that they migrate frequently, what does this mean? That they migrate more frequently than Thai farmers who occupy a similarly marginal ecological niche or that they move their households more often than a North American executive, a Thai civil servant appointed up country as a provincial governor, district officer or public prosecutor? On both counts comparative research would most probably document that highlanders are no more or less sedentary than any of these people whose occupations makes it necessary for them to move from time to time. Only the social status of their role, like the difference between a bus driver and an airline pilot makes it acceptable to draw a distinction. Hill tribes migrate: public officials are transferred.

    When we search the literature for sociological explanations as to why people move and how this fits into an intelligent strategy of survival, we are likely to be disappointed. Here we run into another problem, how social research is conducted. Quantitative, empirical research which starts with the idea that migration is, ipso facto, a problem that only needs to be documented, adds little or nothing to our understanding. The most recent study that I was able to locate employed very sophisticated statistical methodology in which amongst many other things we are told that according to a regression model the frequency of Hmong migration based on the "number of times in memory that a family head has moved from place to place" is "-.01930 (standard error) .12733 " (Benchavan, 1987: 459) but in the absence of any discussion of the cultural context, what have we been told? Such a writer will go on to assert, tautologically, that migration remains a problem because the authority of the consensus demands it.

"Free-love"
    No scientific, anthropological work prepared by a professional social scientist documents or identifies the existence of any such practice in the highlands of North Thailand. Courting is a highly socialized procedure in all communities and subject to an etiquette of reasonable behaviour and strong social mores.

Science and the Consensus

To impose a western concept of the sexual act, performed with no further expectations or obligations, as if it had no indigenous social significance is quite misleading. Such observations say more about the nature of the unconscious projections of the minds of those who venture them than about the behaviour of those to whom they are ascribed. The exotic and the erotic should not be confused.

Population Increase

The unavailability of reliable demographic data collected for a large population has been a serious impediment to demographic knowledge. Although this lacuna is currently being corrected with a comprehensive population survey, widely held beliefs centred on the role played by high birth rates being a major contributing factor to rapid population growth are already so firmly entrenched that they are difficult to reform or place in a more enlightened context. Reference solely to figures, a characteristic of the literature on this specialised subject, does not help although no intelligent discussion can ignore them. The results of early research, such as that carried out by L. and J. Hanks as part of the influential Bennington-Cornell Survey (1964, 1969), provided an estimate of natural population increase amongst the Akha of 6.2 percent per annum (Lewis, 1973: 4). This is far and away the most extravagant claim made by any social scientists and there is reason to believe that their data, collected under difficult circumstances, must be treated with caution. More recent studies report rates of natural increase much lower than this. Sanit, working with a small Lahu population, reports approximately three percent (Sanit, 1977). As for the Karen, who make up approximately 50 percent of highlanders, Kunstadter reports that dependable studies show them to be increasing at a similar rate (Kunstadter et. al., 1987b: 19). The highest figures that can be credited to a reliable researcher are those presented by Kunstadter for the Hmong, 4.34 percent (Kunstadter, 1983:24).

In a recent survey of a highland population of 400,914 conducted by the Task Force on Hill Tribes and Minority Groups, Ministry of Education, the highest natural increase recorded for any highland group is once again given for the Hmong, 4.3 percent. The remainder indicate the danger of venturing a general figure: Mien, 3.5; Akha, 3.1; Khamu, 2.7; Lua, 2.5; Karen, 1.9; Htin, 1.1 (Prachuap et. al., 1987: 4). It appears that the Hmong rate of increase is consistently higher than that reported for other minority groups but this figure cannot be used as typical of the hill tribe population as a whole.

Several observations need to be made. First, that it is simply not realistic to extrapolate a general figure for the natural increase of population in any one district or for any specific population and apply it to highlanders as a whole. Not only do cultural attitudes play an important part in natural population increase but local variations in living conditions must also be taken into account. The extremely low figure for the Htin is a case in point. Whether the figure is correct or not, it clearly does not lend itself to wider use. It is also misleading to apply a high of 4. + percent, which on the basis of inadequate current information appears to hold for the Hmong, to the highland population as a whole. Until it is proven to be wrong, a more realistic figure for natural population increase in the highlands must stand at three percent. This is so close to the rate of increase in materially poorer, more traditional, lowland communities as not to warrant special comment. As it stands, natural annual population increase in the highlands must be placed against high mortality rates, especially amongst infants, a relatively low life-expectancy and endemic poverty. The most effective prophylactic in family planning is prosperity plus the move away from production systems with a high dependence on manual labour.

Another aspect of population increase owing to both natural increase and migration, which is often quoted as a fact against the hill tribes, is the spectre of over-population. Neo-Malthusian ideas relating to a notional man: land ratio are used to explain the felling of forest, shortening of fallow cycles and general pressure on the land leading to land degradation. Proper investigation of the matter must include consideration of both

Science and the Consensus

administrative intervention, which prevents highland farmers from clearing suitable land by placing it beyond their reach in national parks and wildlife reserves, and also the spread of commercial cropping, which introduces a new idea of maximizing use of labour and capital. The overall situation of the communities for which data is collected must be considered before adequate explanations of what is happening can be advanced.

Security

Compared with the situation ten years ago, there appear to be few reasons for promoting a concern for security. Highlanders are anxious to acquire citizenship. The activities of development projects may have made few inroads into the endemic poverty of the highlanders but road construction, the extension of health services, education and the presence of an increased number of government officials have made highlanders very much aware of the power of the state and the authority of the administration. They are willing to cooperate. There is no active insurgency which constitutes a threat to the safety of Thailand. Highlanders have nothing to gain by challenging the over-whelming superiority of the Royal Armed Forces. If they were to be badly treated under policies of repatriation and programmes of relocation, they might in desperation feel compelled to retaliate. Such a reaction, though, would surely be self-destructive since they would certainly be defeated. The disruption caused by any such armed protest would certainly constitute a security crisis.

Opium

For various reasons efforts to suppress cultivation of the opium poppy have been remarkably successful. Overall production is down from the high of the late 60s of approximately 150 tons to just under 26 tons in the last season (1986/87). The proportion of highlander households growing opium has dropped from 45 percent to 20-25 percent. It is not yet clear how many of these growers may only be producing enough for themselves or a highly localised market. Opium cultivation is no longer an activity restricted to ethnic minorities. Northern

RESETTLEMENT

Thai now form the largest group of farmers cultivating the opium poppy in the Mae Chaem District of Chiang Mai.

It is my subjective impression, based on many visits made to a considerable number of villages in the years 1975-78 and between 1986-88, that decreased production appears to have been achieved alongside growing addiction rates among highlanders, at a rate consistent with their increasing poverty. Anthropologists in the field privately report alarming rates of heroin addiction amongst highlanders.

What Thailand produces is of little relevance to the international market. Ann Wrobleski, the US Assistant Secretary of State for International Narcotics Matters was recently reported as saying the "opium production had almost doubled in Laos during the past year to 700 tons of the heroin-base from 400 tons" (**The Nation** April 14, 1988: 3). Although the actual figure is most probably well below this (regional experts estimate about 70 tons) it is still high but not as high as production in the Shan States where estimates vary between 200 and 1,000 tons. Thailand is already a net importer and there appears to be no purely clinical answer to the problem of addiction. Dick Mann, a veteran of crop substitution projects has said that, "in five years opium production could drop to 'maybe five tons, maybe six tons,' being grown for local consumption." He went on to say,

> Thailand was already a net importer of opium and heroin since it had some 40,000 addicts, each consuming about one kilogramme of opium a year, or a total of about 44 tons (**Bangkok Post** 13 November, 1987: 4).

Given this qualified success and the declining number of growers, why the continuing ease with which hill tribes are stereotyped as opium growers?

Science and the Consensus

As noted in a recently reprinted book on opium use in Britain in the last century, "Opiates still have particular symbolic meaning for national activity and international crusade..." (Berridge & Edwards, 1987: 239-240). The fact that Thailand is the only country in the region prepared to host what can loosely be described as foreign-funded opium crop replacement projects ensures that the public will be constantly reminded. As has been rather cynically pointed out by Chao Tzang Yawnghwe (Eugene Thaike)

> I sometimes wonder whether the opium problem has not become a goose that lays golden eggs... enriching, on one hand, the drug syndicates and the traffickers and on the other providing multinational and international bureaucracies with more jobs, funds and good living (Thaike, 1987: 268).

Swiddening

"Slash and burn" is another name given to shifting cultivation or swiddening. For a wide variety of reasons-such as the spread of commercial farming, increased pressure on land, administrative intervention which has limited access to virgin forest-fewer than half of all highlanders are still able to practise such farming (Fig.1) According to estimates made by Sanit Wongsprasert for the province of Chiang Mai, "shifting cultivation is practised by only three percent of the highland population; land rotation, 70 percent of the population; and crop rotation by 27 percent" (Sanit, 1986, personal communication). Chantaboon Sutthi also provides a discussion of the extent to which other farming systems have come into use (Chantaboon, Chapter 4).

Forest Destruction

To witness the destruction of forest is a distressing experience (Plate 37)and there are good ecological and economic reasons why the government must take steps to put a stop to wholesale felling. However, to answer the question, "Who is

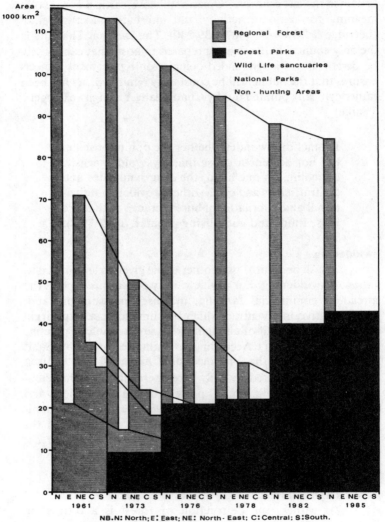

Fig. 1

Source : Anat, 1987

Science and the Consensus

responsible?" it is necessary to be objective and point out that most of the destruction has been carried out not by highlanders but lowland settlers. As the forests have declined the role of timber merchants has become more apparent.

Between 1978 and 1982, more forest was felled in the province of Nan than in any other area in the North, some 152,600 ha. (Suree, 1986: 9). E.C. Chapman who was working there at the beginning of this period credited this to the fact that Nan was a,

> "poverty corner" of Northern Thailand, with more than 50 percent of farm holdings under 6.0 rai (just under 1 hectare) are mean rice production per farm holding of 1,715 kg which was the lowest for all 23 provinces in northern and northeastern Thailand, despite rice yields per rai much above the average for the kingdom. That the situation has certainly deteriorated considerably since 1963 is reflected in the steady expansion of swiddening, as farmers endeavour to compensate for the relatively static situation in wet-rice cultivation...In an extensive sample survey of villages made in B.E. 2509 (1966) made by the Department of Land Development, it was found that four-fifths of rural households had swiddens, usually to supplement their rice production from irrigated fields (Chapman, 1973: 223).

Chupinit Kesmanee of the Tribal Research Institute has gone so far as to point out that on the basis of available information it is "possible to argue that 'because of the hilltribes, the Northern region has more forests left than the other regions' " (Chupinit, 1987: 28)

This rather enigmatic statement is best explained with reference to Figure 1 showing the Regional Decline of Forests and the National Increase in Forest Parks. The Figure shows that before any National Parks were declared (1961) the North had the largest area covered by forest (approximately 115,000 km^2 followed by the Northeast (approximately 71,000 km^2). In the twelve years between 1961 and 1973 the northern forests declined by at most 3 percent (some 2,500 km^2) and the forested area in the Northeast by nearly 30 percent (21,000 km^2). Since 1973 the clearing of the northern forest by the gradual settlement of perhaps four million thai farmers followed the same pattern observed in areas further to the south like Pichit, which had been cleared much earlier. In Kamphaeng Phet, in the lower North, forest destruction was particularly severe. In the Northeast, over the brief period between 1973 and 1976 more than half the forest remaining in 1972 was cut down. In the North, where a similar area of forest was cleared the rate of destruction remained relatively low (8 percent). In subsequent years up until 1982, by which time most forested land in the Northeast suitable for arable farming had been cleared, the total area of forest felled annually exceeded that of the North. Chupinit's remark serves to draw attention to a fact that is often overlooked in the concern to name "outsiders", highlanders, as being responsible for the destruction of Thailand's forests.

Another aspect of forestry interest in the highlands shown in Figure 1 is the recent rapid increase of areas declared special parks, Wild Life Sanctuaries, National Parks and Non-Hunting Areas. I do not wish to question the long term ecological objectives behind this but the added weight this gives to the authority of the Royal Forestry Department should also be noted for the way in which it limits access to land. Highlander population growth and continuing immigration are often presented as sole reasons for land shortage in the highlands. Such observations need to also take into account how administrative intervention has exacerbated this problem. Highland farmers, whatever their ethno-linguistic affiliation, are caught in a scissors movement: over-intensive use of fragile upland soils leads to a likely adverse environmental impact but the farmers have nowhere to go because access to alternative sites has been blocked by administrative and legislative intervention.

A further reason for the recent decline of forests is the rapid rate at which commercial farming has grown in the highlands under the sponsorship of prominent traders, mostly well-placed people who can secure the administrative and political support necessary to move in settlers, clear the land and grow crops for which the big man knows there is a ready market. This is widespread but I will restrict myself to one example from Mae Chaem. In 1988 a local politician settled over 100 families mostly Thai but including some 30 Hmong households who cleared over 5000 rai of forest. It is extremely difficult for the government to maintain any credibility in this matter when those who are seen to be authorities, themselves abuse their power.

Land degradation
The first words in a book on land degradation recently prepared by Blaikie and Brookfield states that "Land degradation should by definition be a social problem. Purely environmental processes such as leaching and erosion occur with or without human interference, but for these processes to be described as 'degradation' implies social criteria which relate land to its actual or possible uses" (Blaikie and Brookfield, 1987: 1). Any statement about land degradation is then a comment which is based on a distinction between processes and perturbations known to occur in nature and those changes which are a direct result of human intervention. Any investigation of land degradation must then be established by reference to our scientific understanding of what natural processes are at work.

In Thailand the issue of environmental degradation attributed to highlanders focuses on forest destruction. In a recent publication prepared by the Thailand Development Research Institute this is said to result in

> denuding important watershed areas. Forest reserves, which are protected for conservation purposes, are continually encroached. Soil erosion increases, as does sedimentation in rivers which originate in the highland areas, promoting downstream flooding and, by accelerating run-off, aggravating drought problems in the dry season (Anat et. al. 1987: 80).

In the light of the Blaikie and Brookfield position, we must be cautious in our approach to statements which maintain that, "If (the Royal Thai Government) wants to protect the highland watersheds, it will be forced to institute widespread resettlement of hill farmers from (the highlands), protecting the watersheds thereafter with force, if necessary" (Anat et. al., 1987: 80). Deciding what the ecological imperatives of such a situation are then becomes much more than an academic matter. If the experts like Dr. Anat et. al. are correct, and that the national watershed is in immediate danger, a case can be made out for urgent intervention "with force if necessary" but if this is not the case then there is time for more accommodating long term plans to be drawn up.

When we turn to the appropriate experts for guidance any hope for a clear and unequivocal answer to what is true and what is false soon eludes us. In a recent publication of the Environment and Policy Institute, East-West Center, D.S. Cassells, M.Bonell, L.S. Hamilton and D.A. Gilmour all known for their work in forestry felt it necessary to repeat observations made in other publications that,

> Perceptions of the impacts of development activities on the hydrological behavior of tropical forest lands are frequently based on myths, misinterpretations, misinformation, and misunderstanding that recently characterized the perceptions that many forest managers held about the hydrological

Science and the Consensus

behavior of forests in the humid latitudes (Hamilton, 1983 & 1984 quoted by Cassells et. al., 1987: 32).

Some of the myths they address enjoy a wide following in Thailand. On the popular proposition that the felling of the forest reduces rainfall the Thailand Development Research Institute publication notes that,

> By maintaining the humidity in the atmosphere, forests probably increase the amount of rainfall, though to degrees which vary from place to place and which are not yet predictable (Anat et. al. 1987: 93)

This cautious statement is much more confidently countered by Cassells and his colleagues with reference to Lee, one of the most widely quoted authorities on forest hydrology.

> The natural coincidence of forest cover and higher precipitation has undoubtedly caused, or at least reinforced, the popular notion that forests increase or "attract" rain and other precipitation forms. Acceptance of the forest as a causal factor leads naturally to the conclusion that forest cutting will reduce precipitation, or that afforestation will increase it; this conclusion played a major role in the development of forest policy in the United States and elsewhere and is still the basis of considerable concern among environmentalists. Objectively, however, the arguments in favor of a positive forest influence are severely weakened when the alleged mechanisms for the influence are critically examined. (Lee, 1980: 101, quoted by Cassells et. al., 1987: 30).

A leading Thai forestry researcher Dr.Suree Bhumibhamon appears to cautiously agree with this position when he noted in a recent publication that "There has been no significant change (in the amount of water vapour carried into the atmosphere) in northern Thailand during the past decade (Suree, 1986: 67). The period during which the forest has been felled at a higher rate than ever before.

On the subject of the belief that floods are more likely to occur if the forest is removed, accepted knowledge in Thailand has it,
> ...that forest cover alleviates flooding in the rainy season by holding back some water and returning some to the atmosphere through evaporation and transpiration. Precipitation is also increased in mountain forest through condensation on leaf and twig surfaces. Forest cover holds rainwater and may facilitate recharge of underground aquifers which supply water after the rainy season. Forested watersheds provide water of higher quality for household use and aquatic life than do deforested watersheds. In these ways, the benefits of nature conservation reach virtually everyone in the kingdom (Anat et. al., 1987: 93).

There can be little doubt that a higher quality of water is discharged from forested watersheds. Unfortunately this benefit is restricted to those few fortunate people who live immediately below forested areas. The authority of established "knowledge" (or is it myth?) is particularly strong. Without offering any proof or documentation Dr.Suree Bhumibhamon asserts that,
> Deforestation has promoted flooding in the rainy season, as caused by watershed degradation and is directly related to the surface run-off problem and soil erosion. In the deforested areas, soil moisture dries up in the summer and thus causes drought in the summer (Suree, 1986: 72).

On the substance of the preceding statements Cassells et. al. quote Lee again,

> The popular notion that forests tend to "retard and lower flood crests and prolong flow in low-water periods"... was still in vogue amongst foresters until the middle of the current century. It is true to a degree, that forests "lower flood crests", but some of the largest floods on record have occurred in forest drainages...The attractive notion that the existence of forest cover will "prolong increased flow in low water periods is clearly false". (Quoted by Cassells et. al 1987: 43).

In the course of their review they note that in fact "planting trees in non-forested catchments will tend to decrease the water yield" (Cassells et.al., 1987: 50). The argument that the presence of trees (any sort of trees) is absolutely necessary to maintain good watershed characteristics is difficult to maintain with reference to total water yield. In fact in countries like New Zealand, granted under quite different climatic conditions, trees are planted to reduce soil moisture because figuratively speaking, they pump water into the atmosphere (Hathaway, 1986: 39).

Soil erosion

In the highlands, as for Thailand as a whole, soil erosion is clearly a problem that cannot be contested (Anat et.al., 1987: 38-39; also see Plate 91). In the upper North studies of upland areas, old alluvial terraces and fans with relatively acid soils and on slopes greater than five percent, cleared of forest by Thai farmers practising shifting cultivation, soil loss has been measured at 16 tons per rai (approximately 96 tons per hectare) (Marston, 1984; noted by Anat et.al., 1987: 38), some 20 times above recommended tolerable soil loss. Chomchan and Panichapong (1986) report that soil loss in the Ping and Nan river basins averages about two to ten tons per rai per year and estimate that "If land use changes from forest to row crop cultivation without soil and water conservation measures, soil loss will increase about 6 to 10 times" (Chomchan and Panichapong, 1986 quoted by Anat et. al., 1987: 38).

These general estimates of erosion are one thing and clearly indicate that there is a problem. Specific studies provide another perspective. If a reliable figure is to be obtained for erosion directly attributable to farming activities, many factors must be taken into account: farming system, cultivation method, conservation practices, soil type, slope, aspect and so forth and as Sangha Sabhasri notes, "Erosion occurs every year no matter whether the forest is disturbed or undisturbed. This is a natural phenomenon in any forest community" (Sangha, 1987: 170).

Scientific measurements prepared from an analysis of fan deposits under Lua swiddens at Pa Pae carried out by Paul Zinke, Sanga Sabhasri and Peter Kunstadter led them to conclude that "an approximation of the depth of erosion may be 1.15 mm per 10 years, or 11.5 cm per millennium" (1987: 153). Tolerable losses. Then again, estimates based on data gathered for one year (1968-69) by Sanga Sabhasri for the same area using a different method averaged between 10.33 mm and 12.02 mm (1978: 169). The methods alone produced estimates that differ by a factor of 10. In other words erosion calculated from fan deposits was 10 percent of that estimated from a stake-out method.

Highlanders know that if they seriously mismanage the land they will be the first to suffer the conseqences. Their cultures are ecologically informed and have ensured their survival over millennia. This is not to say that the relatively stable agricultural system of the Karen and Lua is easily replicable, that their cyclical swiddening method is not susceptible to population pressures, that the introduction of commercial crops has not impact, that the situation at Pa Pae is the same today as it was in 1968-69 when the study under discussion was carried out but it is worth remembering that over half of the total number of highlanders draw their agricultural wisdom from this tradition. An impartial reassessment of the traditional agricultural knowledge of all farmers in the highlands would go a long way towards correcting the negative impression harboured by most government officials. Perhaps then, rather than stereotyping highlanders as ignorant spoilers of the environment, they could be seen to be doing their best to come to terms with an increasingly difficult situation and in most cases, doing so in a sensible manner.

The case needs to be balanced. It is not possible to argue that there is no problem at all. If for the moment we put aside considerations critical of the methods used to obtain estimates of soil loss, those readily available show that in many areas erosion rates run at unacceptably high levels. Micro-studies in which sedimentation tanks have been constructed directly beneath farmers fields show high rates of soil loss. In the Mae Sa watershed just north of Chiang Mai, Sheng measured soil loss from control plots at 24.1 metric tonnes per hectare (t/ha) (Sheng, 1979:60). Recent work carried out by an Australian consultancy group with an interest in promoting their work in the highlands, monitored over a single cropping season, a loss of 45 t/ha from fields cultivated under "traditional methods" (Hoey, 1987: 10). Sheng recorded a dry soil loss of 12.3 t/ha from bench terraces (Sheng, 1979: 60) while the Australian's working in a different area produced a figure for the same method of conservation farming of 1.7 t/ha (Hoey et al, 1987: 10).

It is interesting to compare Sheng's findings with Hoey's because the exercise illustrates the difficulty of comparing different sites for the same season but in different years. The absence of detailed descriptions of exactly what kind of "traditional" farming was being used and using results gathered over a relatively short study period does not inspire a high level of confidence. The added eccentricity presented by researchers who make use of different methods of measurement and present data at different levels of generalization also adds another difficulty.

Given these difficulties in getting a clear picture of what is happening, it appears that not all the news concerning highland farming methods is bad. Neither the worst predictions for likely soil loss given above by Marston (96t/ha) nor the pessimistic estimates provided by Chomchan and Panchapong (120-600t/ha) have been measured in or recorded for the highlands. If it holds up to the scrutiny of wider testing, the remarkably low loss of soil from fields contoured with grass strips (1.3t/ha), a strategy, indentified by an Australian team of consultants and now being promoted by the Thai-German Programme has provided support for the opinion that permanent cropping may be possible (Hoey et al, 1987: 10) but as discussed below, there are good reasons to be cautious about the unintended implications of such claims.

Sedimentation
Sediments originating in the highlands and entering water ways as distinct from those entering at lower elevations is another issue that is more difficult to document with the opinions of experts. The problem is to find studies of a relevant scale which address the issue on an appropriate regional level.

The measure of interest to us here is the amount of turbidity and sediment per unit of water being carried in streams out of the highlands. In a normal stream profile the amount of material carried in suspension down water courses should be higher in the mountains where the water runs faster and lower on the plains where it slows and can no longer carry heavier debris. If highlanders make a significant contribution to the sedimentation of Thailand's major rivers, it can be expected that higher than normal loads are being carried in mountain streams. In fact the only reliable case study carried out in the North with which I am familiar shows that the "normal" pattern was, under land use disturbances current in 1979 clearly inverted. The sedimentation load carried by the Mae Ping was found to be much higher than that of a typical tributary.

Science and the Consensus

In 1979, T.C. Sheng the technical officer in watershed management and conservation farming referred to above and employed by the UNDP/FAO as an expert on the Mae Sa Integrated Watershed and Forest Land Use Project presented the results of a five year study of the principal waterways in the Mae Sa catchment just 20 kilometers or so north of Chiang Mai town. The area was originally chosen as a sub-catchment typical of the region and one of the principal objectives of the undertaking was to attempt to identify a development model for the relatively newly formed Watershed Division of the Royal Forestry Department. His preliminary results indicated "that the Mae Ping Basin has very serious erosion problems and the Mae Sa is probably better than the average watershed in the region. However this merits more detailed study and investigation" (Sheng, 1979: 68).

The upper reaches of the catchment was farmed by Hmong highlanders. Beneath them were to be found northern Thai farmers who maintained irrigated rice fields and on the margins of the forest, cleared swidden fields for upland crops. When the study was conducted, the government had put though 143 kilometers of mostly unsurfaced roads.

His principal findings of interest to us here were as follows,
1) The sediment load carried in the Mae Ping river (the main river which runs through Chiang Mai) is higher than that carried in the Mae Sa river (Sheng, 1979: 68).
2) Government road building activities alone accounted for 30 percent of erosion in the Mae Sa catchment (Sheng, 1979: 52).
3) Turbidity in the Mae Sa Mai stream in a subcatchment worked by Hmong swiddeners was less than that found in the Mae Sa river (Sheng, 1979: 68).

Several observations can be made on the basis of his findings.

First, if the Mae Sa sub-catchment watershed area is typical of the upper North, the higher turbidity of the Mae Nam Ping clearly indicates that erosion and other earth moving activities which contributed to this load originate at elevations below the highlands and that hill tribe farmers cannot be held to be responsible for aggradation of this major waterway.

Second, that badly formed highland roads built by the government may well be responsible for a large proportion of the total amount of debris entering streams in the highlands (Plate 90).

Third, erosion from land worked by highland swiddeners does not enter water courses with the frequency that is widely assumed. The relationship between erosion measured immediately below fields and sediments entering streams has yet to be established.

The study of land degradation in the highlands requires reference to far more work than that on which I have reported in this brief survey and serious readers engaged in research on the matter would be well advised to consult literature on the region other than that which I have quoted (Benchaphun, 1985; Gibson, 1983: 318-385).

It appears that enough critical and informed opinions have been published which raise serious scientific questions about whether highlander farming activities pose an urgent ecological threat to the lowlands. The facts about hydrological deterioration and land degradation have yet to be established.

Land Classification

It is on the basis of this less than satisfactory information base that the Office of the National Environment Board has prepared a watershed classification for the North. Under this project all major catchments have been zoned into six categories, class A1, B1, 2, 3, 4 and 5. According to the director of the Watershed Management Division, Mr.Preecha Ob-eye,

> Class A1 is the existing forested areas on the most steep slopes on the upper part of the basin and this class is considered as the most important part of the watershed area. The government, by decision of the cabinet, has declared this class as the protected area, all kind of development activity will not be allowed....our target area for forest protection is the area of class 1A (Preecha to McKinnon, 7 August, 1980 (sic 1987).

As land classes have been mapped at a scale of 1: 50,000 the areas identified as A1 are very generalized and encompass a considerable number of highland communities including Karen who have farmed some of this land for many generations. As it stands, under current policy, it is the government's intention to involuntarily resettle all occupants of these areas under a strategy outlined in Appendix V.

Resettlement

If implemented, the policy will make it necessary to move a considerable number of people. Given current provisions, there is little hope that they will be adequately resettled. A study of the relocation of 5557 highlanders from Khlong Lan National Park (Kampaeng Phet, 1986) lists the following short comings: advanced warning was given; the costs of moving were largely borne by those relocated; resettlement sites were inadequate; subsistence support for villagers (food, water and shelter) did not approach the standard of what they had lost; and that it created internal refugees some of whom tore up their Thai identity papers so they could enter Ban Kae refugee Camp in Chiang Kham (Chupinit, 1987: 37-38). Between 15 April and July, 1986 the number of highlanders registered as evacuees declined from 5,087 to 3,701 people (Chupinit, 1987; 10).

Specific studies are available. Eudey (Chapter 10) provides a case study of Ban Huai Yew Yee and Chupinit Kasmanee provides interviews with farmers from six villages in Kampaeng Phet (Chupinit, 1987: 13-25). The field visit I made to a resettled village in Kampaeng Phet left me with little reason for optimism. Yao informants for whom settlement arrangements were made by the authorities had little for which they could be thankful.

Why this get-tough policy?
If natural population increase is not too rapid, if opium production is falling, if there is no urgent ecological or security crisis looming, why is the government apparently launching a stronger policy? Why is it that intervention threatens to become tougher than actual conditions appear to justify? From this review of the current state-of-knowledge, much that is widely accepted as "facts" about the highlands and highlanders is open to question. As far as policy is influenced by research and surveys, it appears that Thailand is not being well served by scientists, engineers and other technicians working in the hills. Is this the case or does the inverse apply? Is Thailand served all too well by the experts at its command, both foreigners and nationals who see that their best interests are more easily secured if they conform to an unsatisfactory state-of-knowledge rather than if they challenge it?

Before we can broach such contentious question, a normal perspective needs to be established. Scientific information only rarely plays an important and discrete part in policy formation. Policy is formed by politicians and administrators who consider interests and information presented as a consensus and allocate funds for research and development along lines which they believe will, for the greater good, be most effective. Such is the normal hierarchical arrangement of government decision making. Professional scientists, researchers, engineers and technicians, however, do not only play a passive role in such a configuration. Rather than just applying their skills to tasks defined by others, it is part of their responsibility to raise questions, exercise an independent set of skills and identify work which will generate a better understanding of phenomenon.

To make such an abstract statement of principle is one thing, to act on it in a concrete and objective situation is quite another. To transcend the tension, the opposition which exists between the citizen who would prefer to thrive and needs to survive in a specific set of work relationships on which society is built *and* to act as a professional scientist and exercise his intellectual responsibilities is far from easy. In a society in which critical thinking is not always acceptable, where the sociology of knowledge is focused on a technical role, where people lack confidence to exercise independent judgement which requires that they deviate from officially proscribed guidelines, the space left for lateral thinking is seriously limited. If those who deviate too far from their expected role experience difficulty in securing funding or finding employment, the matter is no longer just imagined. The practical and pragmatic response is simply to avoid issues, opinions and matters considered to be contentious by those who control the purse strings. In such a conservative milieu the tendency is for those employed within it to act as savants, to confine themselves to officially condoned activities and avenues of research within the existing framework of knowledge and intellectual paradigms, to conform to the consensus: in such cases everybody loses. If the consensus is not challenged decision makers also remain trapped in what may be described as a kind of involutionary state of mind. Then administrators respond to calls for action (because they, unlike researchers, must act rather than investigate) and *"act with an idea in their head"* that may be at odds with reality. What is seen to be necessary to undertake, because the information on which this imperative is based precludes the possibility of a broad, objective and scientific understanding, must be increasingly undertaken by force.

That such a situation has come about is partly a legacy of decisions made in the very early days of modernization. As Dr.Anan Ganjanapan observes in his comprehensive review of the history of anthropology in Thailand, when the country opened itself to new academic disciplines, subjects such as sociology and anthropology which encompass the potential for a broad, interdisciplinary research, because they "did not provide conceptual tools of direct relevance to administration were not acceptable" (Anan, 1986: 68). The small group of administrators and intellectuals who decided what should be taught "were not interested in understanding the people and societies that would participate in development...(because they were)...confident of the effectiveness of the established mode of administration which had been practised for a very long time ...(and as a consequence)...gave their attention only to technical and applied science to secure the advantages this knowledge provided to western administrative and economic systems" (Anan, 1986: 68)

As Dr. Anan might well agree, this legacy does not provide a completely satisfactory explanation to the problem identified here. Dr.Chayan Watanaphuti, also on the faculty of Chiang Mai University, points out that in the field of social science, "most of the research (in the highlands) has been carried out by expatriates" (Chayan, 1987: 5) who are not subject to the same constraints placed upon their Thai colleagues. The current unsatisfactory state-of-knowledge on the highlands and highlanders is not the specific product of a Thai consensus but a function of a wider issue in which foreign researchers, engineers, technicians and project administrators must accept a large part of the responsibility. But to return to the tough questions posed at the beginning of this section, does the focus on individuals provide a way of understanding the matter? Many foreign researchers who have enjoyed the privilege of working in

Science and the Consensus

Thailand have prepared and/or published critical and informed commentaries. (Bo Gua, 1975; Cooper, 1979; Gia Yia Lee, 1982; Kammerer, 1987; Radley, 1986; Tapp, 1985 & 1986; Walker, 1979-80). The attempt to generate an explanation solely with reference to ethical shortcomings (i.e. Chambers, 1985;Kerr, 1984) cannot be sustained. We must look elsewhere.

Pejorative influence of foreign intervention

A much more difficult problem emerges which cannot be resolved solely with reference to either the state of scientific knowledge in Thailand or the individual professional responsibility of national and international researchers. Foreign geopolitical intervention has had a profound impact on policy formation.

A proper analysis would require a full historical discussion of the nature of western intervention in Thailand and the manner in which this has been managed. Such a task is well beyond the scope of this paper. To arbitrarily state a starting point marked by the French withdrawal from Indochina (1954) and the engagement of American military interests begins to tell a story. In recent years the surveillance and development effort focused on the task of eliminating the production of opium has taken centre stage. Both military and "development" interests placed a heavy emphasis on dealing with highlanders as if they were less than full human beings who could therefore be manipulated at will and cajoled into doing whatever outsiders thought best. Unfortunately this reinforced

> the dialectic of the relationship between dominant rice growing lowland society undergoing a process of cultural homogenisation through state formation involving opposition to a mosaic of politically acephalous, minority settlements which must be recognized as a de facto reality (Vienne, Chapter 2).

Foreign intervention emphasized the structural opposition between lowlanders and highlanders in a manner which suited the former but worked to the disadvantage of the latter. This dialectic lies at the very heart of the sociology of knowledge concerning the highlanders and presents the most profound obstacle to the construction of a proper scientific understanding of the situation.

This experience of deleterious foreign intervention on the drug issue alone has not been restricted to Thailand. In his book *Poppies, Pipes and People,* the medical anthropologist Westermeyer documents the empirical reality for neighbouring Laos. Peter G. Bourne's Foreword to the same work states the case succinctly.

> Perhaps the most important lessons from this study relate to the remarkably adverse impact of various foreign policy decisions made in the United States that were based in part on misinformation and misunderstanding, geared toward dealing with the drug problem as it affected Americans, and had very little regard for the impact they might have in Laos (Peter G. Bourne in Westermeyer, 1982: xv).

It appears that little has changed since the decade in which Westermeyer carried out his study (1965-1975). The Americans have been joined by a host of western, industrialized nations whose failure to deal with their drug problem at home has led to a major, technocratic effort in Thailand to end the cultivation of opium. Conceived as a police and military problem, rationalized in part as development aid, built on an inadequate understanding of the highland situation this effort has exacerbated an already difficult and tense situation and pushed the Thai government into precipitative action.

From the very start strategic and military interests have exercised a great deal of influence. Thailand has a highly differentiated economy, a literate and skilled work force and spends a larger proportion of total public expenditure on education (25.35 percent) than any of 30 other countries in the Far East (FEER, 1987: 8-9), plus a form of parliamentary democracy. However, agencies run on other than democratic principles still exercise a great deal of influence. The Armed Forces still claim 32.43 percent of public expenditure (FEER, 1987: 8-9) and their authority is reflected in the composition of government.

It is not surprising that the international concern for narcotics production has become aligned with the type of operational efficiency associated with military competence. The recent decision to give authority to the Third Army to set up an administrative centre for hill tribes and minorities in the upper North clearly has antecedents. Current preparation of a new master plan "which de-emphasizes control on narcotics cultivation and focuses more on improving living conditions of hilltribe people and environmental conservation" (**The Nation** 28 November, 1987: 1) does not, under the current state-of-knowledge, promise any liberalisation of the style of intervention.

Although still under discussion, it appears that under this plan two national committees will be set up under the existing Committee for Solving National Security Problems Related to Hill Tribes and Narcotics Cultivation. The new coordinating subcommittee is likely, for the first time, to be headed by the secretary general of the National Security Council and a fund-seeking subcommittee is to be headed by the general secretary of the Office of the Narcotics Control Board.

Structural assimilation
The foregoing description of professional ethical and institutionalized security, narcotics and ecological interests provides a perspective on policy formation which makes it easier to understand the constraints placed on research and development work in the highlands. A brief review of some aspects of

foreign assistance illustrates the product of this configuration. The concern of the state and international development agencies provide the most authoritative vehicle on which the current consensus is carried. As shown above, the principal objective of policy has always reiterated the principle that the hill tribes are to be integrated into the state as first class, self reliant citizens but the way both national and international concerns come together precludes the need to take highlander interests into account. Amongst officials, the absence of both a good understanding of highlander cultures (their separate identity is often treated as an obstacle to becoming Thai, because citizenship is perceived to be more than a legal matter) and any authoritative acknowledgement of their social, political and agricultural management systems is taken to mean that there are too few reasons for the government to go out of its way to accommodate highlanders within a policy of integration: integration becomes rhetoric in the face of structural assimilation, what Vienne has called "a process of cultural homogenisation through state formation" (Vienne, Chapter 2).

Foreign Assistance and Highlanders

Foreign assistance is provided for a wide range of activities undertaken by the Royal Thai Government. This effort, as stated above,is primarily aimed at eliminating the growing and trading of opium and ranges from the welfare work of the Norwegian government funded Church Aid to the police suppression activities conducted as a joint operation between the Royal Thai Government and the United States, with personnel assigned from the Central Intelligence Agency, The Drug Enforcement Agency and the State Department coordinated by the Narcotics Assistance Unit (NAU) headquartered in the US Embassy, Bangkok.

The representative sample of foreign funded development projects listed in Table 1 address a broad set of socio-economic issues and the magnitude of their investment alone indicates the strength of their position. Figure 2 locates the areas in which some of these bigger projects work.

Table 1
Project Partly Funded by Foreign Donors Listed by ONCB as Primarily Committed to Opium Crop Replacement (August, 1986)

Name	Number villages	Pop. served	Thai budget (US$)	Financial support (US$)
Thai-German (1981-1994)	135	22,092	1,182,665.5	6,121,058
Thai-Norwegian (1985-89)	43	7,250	1,612,162.5	5,600,000
USA-NAU * (1981-1986)	129	16,512	1,012,188	4,004,702
Doi Pae Per UN Agencies ** (1986-1991)	141	14,122	1,082,195.5	1,852,000
Sam Mun Canada & Sweden (1987-1991)	56	9,574	not available	2,000,000
Doi Vieng Pha Italy (1987-1991)	88	12,919	not available	2,000,000
TOTAL	592	77,969	4,889,211.5	21,577,760

NB. * US Narcotics Assistance Unit.
  ** UNDP, UNFDAC, UNFAO, UNICEF
   An updated assessment (November, 1988) of the total foreign funds currently committed under the management of all the agencies engaged in the highlands (excluding the King's Project) provides a figure of US$ 83 million.

Source: Office of the Narcotics Control Board (ONCB) and Department of Technical and Economic Cooperation (DTEC). Paper on "Arrangements for Solving the Problem of Opium Production", presented to the *Seminar on Suppression and Control of Hill Tribe Intrusion into and Destruction of the Forest,* 15-16 August, 1986: 1-15. The updated figure was compiled from project documents and a wide variety of sources. Although it is not an official estimate it is reasonably accurate.

RESETTLEMENT

Although Table 1 ignores the multitude of small government and non-government projects recently added to the list (those located at Pha Mon and Doi Tung), it should be noted that in a directory of development activities prepared by the Department of Public Welfare some 3,947 projects operating in nine provinces were listed as serving 1,298 villages (Department of Public Welfare, 1983). Neither the scale nor the quality of intervention can be measured solely by a review of the foreign contribution.

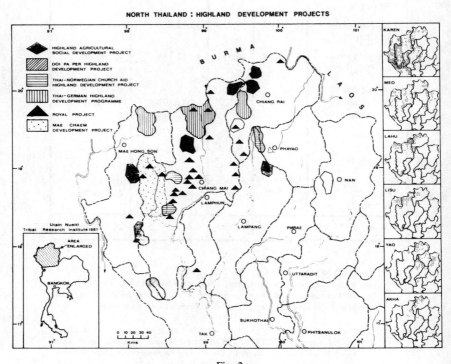

Fig. 2

Clearly, the larger share of the funding is provided by foreign donors but as agencies working with the Thai civil authorities, they have a responsibility to fit their activities as much as possible within the framework of national planning and policy guidelines. Through their institutional affiliation with the ONCB, it is assumed that opium production remains the underlying concern.

This is not, however, a role in which many foreign development workers like to see themselves. Most believe they are engaged in a humanitarian undertaking designed to improve the living conditions of the mountain people and few project documents make explicit reference to the task of eliminating opium production. The Thai-German Highland Development Programme, for instance, does not identify this as a high priority in their project documents. The Project prefers to be seen in a helping role, assisting in the extension of government services with roads, water supply and buildings, strengthening associated medical, agricultural and administrative skills. Projects like the unlisted Highland Agricultural and Social Development Project, working with the Department of Public Welfare, serviced by a team of bilaterally funded Australian agricultural consultants and until recently funded by the World Bank has long been guided by policy in which matters of welfare and agricultural production predominate. The information booklet of the unlisted Mae Chaem project attached to the Ministry of Agriculture and Agricultural Cooperatives and funded by a USAID grant of 9.2 million US dollars also makes no mention of opium crop replacement.

The subjective humanitarian preoccupations of project personnel are genuine but it would be naive to assume that their best intentions either enable or encourage them to extend their activities beyond the structural limitations placed upon them by the current state-of-knowledge and the way in which this consensus is institutionalized. They are primarily committed to servicing a technical-managerial and planning function and as outsiders they see it as their job to work within this reality. The value they place on local knowledge, the knowledge of the people with whom they work, does not extend much beyond rhetoric. As technicians and managers, they believe they can find answers to problems of agricultural production which are quite independent of indigenous systems and where they want cooperation from villagers they know this can be secured with incentives and/or the willingness of highlanders to demonstrate their support for the government. They employ those whose technical expertise can be relied upon and whose professional discipline and commitment to the enterprise will not cause embarrassment. They have been known to divest themselves of experts whose local knowledge leads them to question the efficacy of field strategies.

Although the greatest contribution made to change has been in the field of agricultural extension, project work has been effective on a wide front. Projects have put considerable effort into training government officers to undertake work in agriculture; built schools, health stations, water systems; set up revolving banks which make fertilizer and other agricultural inputs available as well as rice banks to provide a source of food to households whose rice consumption needs periodically exceed supplies. They also help out with marketing to the extent that in many villages production is heavily subsidized and farmers are dependent upon continuing project support. The decline in the production of opium which can be measured as a success by outsiders is a profound source of concern to those who are no longer able to grow it. Such farmers are rarely better off as a result of cooperating with the government. The social impact experienced by the Lisu and described by Hutheesing as a "loss of repute" (Hutheesing, 1987) is one aspect of this. The Hmong farmers who have spontaneously and successfully adapted their agricultural activities to the market economy, who use tractors and the like, provide another example. They have attracted serious criticism from leading civil servants for their destruction of the environment. This then provides an argument with which to justify relocation (Vithoon Chapter 13).

Given that foreign donors are inclined to view their contributions to the development effort as part of the war against poverty, one would expect that the poor and most needy would figure high on the list of beneficiaries. This is clearly not the case. The Karen who form the largest and most deprived group, who have not ever been heavily involved in opium production, are not well serviced by the bigger foreign donors (see Fig.2). A count of smaller projects carried out as part of a survey conducted by the Office of Special Activities, Ministry of Education, showed that Shan and displaced Burmese top a list of recipients on which the Karen score lowest of all (Prachuap et.al., 1987: 13).

State formation, citizenship and land rights
The political impact of development work has been most profound. Foreign funds have enabled the state to administratively pioneer remote areas by extending a wide range of government services. The infrastructure of roads and services has enabled highlanders not only to gain access to medical centres, schools and markets on which to both sell produce and purchase manufactured goods but also greatly enhanced their awareness of the authority of the Thai administrative system. The investment provided by foreign donors must be seen as a contribution to state formation.

The effect this has had on indigenous social structures, agricultural and land tenure systems has largely been ignored: increased socio-economic participation and integration has not been accompanied by positive political incorporation within the state structure. For highlanders this is not an abstract matter of principle; political integration means simply legally documented acknowledgment of their presence, as citizens with legal title to land. In the absence of any real power to transcend this situation, cooperation with the government on both ceremonial occasions and with approved projects, remains, apart from a polite subservience, the only avenue in which they can demonstrate their loyalty. The tension and concern this generates in highland communities is manifest in an anxious willingness to go along with what is asked of them even where they are not convinced that cooperation will materially improve their situation.

Foreign project and civil servant development specialists perceive the social and political realities of highland communities as lying outside their responsibility if not their understanding but the issue of citizenship and land titles is not an issue of which they are unaware. What have they done about it? Unfortunately the short answer is "very little". A fair and longer answer makes it necessary to briefly review the situation.

To secure title to land the farmer must be a citizen. To obtain citizenship he must live in a dwelling registered with the local authority. The householder must be able to establish that he was born and reached maturity in Thailand, and be able to secure the support of a government official from the Ministry of the Interior, military or some other reputable agency, must have lived in one place for at least five years and not have a security or criminal record. As long as the individual entered Thailand before 1975 (if they entered from Laos) and 1976 (if they entered from Burma) they can then become citizens.

The record for registration and granting of citizenship for that proportion of the population which falls under the direct supervision of the Department of Public Welfare indicates that delays are endemic. Of the total 278,858 people under DPW administration (1985) the following had secured the following documentation.

Document	Number of People	Percent of Total
ID cards	67,663	24%
House Registration	166,759	60%
Citizenship	157,431	56%

As the granting of citizenship was made a policy objective in 1974, the Ministry of Interior cannot claim to have made a seriously concerted effort to provide highlanders with proper documentation.

Science and the Consensus

The vast majority of highlanders occupy land illegally and work it under either customary land tenure or informal rights of purchase. Under customary tenure, the land must be worked continually. Unless periodically cultivated, this right lapses and the land can be claimed and used by another cultivator. Depending both on how local rights of usufruct are defined and whether the original claimant is still in residence, a fee may be paid to secure the transfer. Land which has been purchased as distinct from that relinquished for a fee, appears to provide for outright ownership. A fully monetized system of land transfers operates on what can be called a black market. It exists outside the law but is fully acknowledged in contemporary local practice. The system, as a rational accommodation to their situation, appears to work quite well.

In strictly legal terms this means that the rightful owner of the land, the state, as represented by the Royal Forestry Department can impinge on the land occupied and worked by highlanders, carry out reforestation work or establish boundaries on the land worked by highland famers and evict them at will. Title to land is an important issue in establishing farmer security. Even though adequate provisions is made in law to allow farmers to secure land under Article 16 of the National Reserved Forests Act (1964) and special arrangements can be made to implement this Act by Cabinet resolution (as in the case of the Mae Chaem Project, 11 May, 1982) little has been done to legalize the highland farmers position.

Figures collected in the recent survey carried out by the special Task Force of the Ministry of Education are instructive.

> Of the 75,632 families surveyed, 68.93% still have no legal right to the land they work, while 11.01% possess a document showing legal ownership. The remaining 20.06% did not understand land ownership under the law (Prachuap et.al., 1987: 7).

RESETTLEMENT

These two profound issues of citizenship and secure land tenure are matters of vital concern to highlanders and yet most development projects have done little or nothing to use their bargaining position to help farmers secured proper documentation. Where the bigger highland projects as official undertakings have promoted coffee plantations, village woodlots as a source of firewood and encouraged farmers to build bench terraces, practise a form of rotational farming on stable holdings divided by contour grass strips, there can be little doubt that the work has been carried out by farmers on the understanding that they will retain the product of their labour. Yet, the legal status of their holdings remains in doubt.

Any foreign donor seriously concerned for the welfare of highlanders would be well advised to negotiate mandatory legal acknowledgment for the farmers they are supposed to help before they commence work. Such an agreement should include citizenship and the granting of land rights to those who follow conservation recommendations. Without this assurance, the farmers with whom they are working may well be subject to resettlement or repatriation and the development effort lost altogether.

Although donors may be reluctant to enter into what is a political domain, this is a matter which cannot be ignored as a peripheral issue. The USAID funded Mae Chaem Project has been particularly active in this respect and the concessions they have won from the Royal Forestry Department could well serve as a model for other projects, which have largely failed to face up to the problem. From the outset.

> the Mae Chaem Watershed Development Project made the issuance of Land Use Certificates a condition precedent to project implementation...Fulfillment of this condition required nearly two years and required a decision by the Cabinet, resulting in the first and only time that official

permission has been given for people anywhere in Thailand to reside and farm within a national forest preserve (sic) (Kampe, 1986: 1).

Although the size of the holdings recognised by the titles is inadequate (average 2.25 rai),
> These (Type I land use Certificates) entitle the holder to reside and farm the prescribed plot(s) of land for a period of 5 years, provided they meet the conditions stated therein (e.g. land can not be sold, opium can not be grown, no adjacent lands can be farmed). This document...gives the bearer the "privilege" to use up to 6 acres of land (Kampe, 1986: 2).

By the end of 1986, some 3,464 people were scheduled to hold 4,203 certificates which would give them legal access to 3,774 acres. The original objective set by the project was to issue 4,000 titles and the fact that they have succeeded in securing more than this in such a sensitive and highly politicised area where other projects have barely got off the ground is worthy of the highest praise. The fact that the project document was drafted by two consultants with considerable experience in highland villages is also worthy of note.

The road to hell is paved with good intentions
This success raises another more general question which reflects on the manner in which projects are drawn up and the way they adjust their activities to limitations imposed by the configuration of the consensus. As long as project experts design field strategies primarily to fit within the information and structural constraints placed upon them, rather than attempting to develop a scientific understanding of the objective enviromental, social and economic situation, they remain in danger of promoting extension models which may build in too many compromises to survive the withdrawal of project support. Liberal and humane intent is no substitute for hard thinking.

Project planners faced with a stituation in which they are aware that the position of farmers is being questioned, that plans are afoot to relocate communities, may in their efforts to secure a place for their clients, actually expose them to considerable risk. Take for example the issue of optimum or viable farm size.

Highlanders traditionally practise an extensive form of arable farming. This is particularly well adapted to fragile mountain soils. On a farm of 50 rai, depending on the size of the household, only 10 to 20 rai may be under cultivation at any one time. Fields are usually scattered and cultivated in rotation. This not only enables them to grow their household crops and market needs on the most suitable land available but also fallow land when, either weeding becomes a problem, or the availability of plant nutrients falls below acceptable levels. The fact that most fields are small, even where formed on relatively steep slopes, ensures that erosion is kept to a minimum. In long settled highland villages like the Mien village of Pha Dua, Mae Chan, because farmers know that they cannot extend their holdings, they have evolved in negotiation with local, resident government officials, not only a quite satisfactory if entirely illegal system of land tenure but also an environmentally informed system of land use which includes a woodlot on steep sloping land in close proximity to the village from which they can gather bamboo shoots, take bamboo for building and collect firewood. The practical incentive this provides for limiting family size, diversifying economic activities and promoting education as a necessary prerequisite to more successful integration for the next generation provides an example of adaptation worthy of study.

The project approach outlined in several documents is quite different (Hoey, et.al.,1987; Schubert et.al.,1986; Salzer, 1987) and from a critical point of view personnel may be considered as sociologically naive as they are confident of technical solutions. This is not to say that they are unaware of the political

Science and the Consensus

attitudes founded on the current state-of-knowledge. They know what concerns the government, the large amount of land under periodic cultivation, the clearing of further forest and plans to relocate and consolidate villages and establish pine plantations. Rather than challenge the consensus, they argue an adaptive case, that permanent cultivation on the highlands is possible on small permanent holdings (18 rai). The underlying assumption postulates a view that if the system can be shown to work, this will provide a technical argument in favour of allowing highlanders to remain in the highlands.

However technically correct and demonstratively practical under project guidance, farmers may lose long term flexibility and in the absence of project patronage, maintenance of conservation measures such as grass strips, may well prove to be impractical. Consolidating holdings to fit a Royal Forestry Department preference that highland farmers be concentrated into smaller areas could well result in further marginalization of their position as well as increased pressure on land in areas of resettlement leading to the higher rates of erosion that the system is designed to avoid. As noted by Dr.Benchaphun Shinawatra, following a review of research undertaken by Thai scientists, the use of intensive, modern agricultural practices, in the absence of proper conservation measures, poses a greater potential erosion hazard than traditional methods of farming (Benchaphun, 1985: 125).

Foreign projects prefer technical solutions which enable them to bypass complex structural problems because this also enables them to acknowledge the consensus and meet government expectations consistent with development ideology and avoid coming inside the highlanders situation. However as Peter Kunstadter, the eminent anthropoligist who has worked in the mountains of north Thailand for more than 20 years, recently stated,

> By now we should have learned from numerous examples that there is no **magic bullet** of technolo-

gy so cleverly designed that it has only desirable, expected and immediately recognized consequences...In engineering as in medicine, our intervention usually carries unintended and undesired side effects, including implications for cultural values" (Kunstadter, 1987a: 10).

The job of identifying an optimum size for farms is extremely difficult. In a highly dynamic milieu such as the highlands where sensitive political issues complicate the matter even further, one of the first steps must be to evaluate project suggestions against indigenous systems and here the absence of relevant and reliable information on an appropriate scale makes it necessary to mount special research designed to investigate the problem. Land use studies currently being conducted by the Tribal Research Institute have been designed to clarify the matter but unfortunately events have a way of running ahead of research. To fulfill the expectations of the sociology of knowledge within which they work, development projects and organizations like UNFDAC must be seen to be doing something. Identifying plausible undertakings, securing funding and, in negotiation with the government, assigning responsibility to implementing agencies. When expenditure runs ahead of understanding, project work can be expected to become increasingly concerned with internally generated rather externally checked strategies. The end result may culminate in the physical integration of the highlands under central government but what will be the social and political costs of this if, in the process, highlanders become even more seriously disadvantaged and possibly alienated? This is a real challenge.

The current state-of-knowledge on the highlands and about the highlanders, the manner in which this serves as a basis for action, the way in which this is institutionalized within both the administrative system and the type of strategies undertaken by development projects can only be seen, if it is to be properly examined, as structural assimilation. The consensus appears to

Science and the Consensus

serve neither the best interests of Thailand nor the highlanders. As has been pointed out from a contemporary historical perspective by General Saiyud Kerdphol,

> ...we should not blind ourselves to the side-effects of (the state's) central premise, which is the penetration of a highly centralized bureaucracy to the remotest reaches of the national territory. It has led to high levels of domestic tension, to political disruption and protest, to regional revolts, and ultimately, in our own time, to the weakening of the very state it was intended to support. When applied to non-Thai areas such as those occupied by hilltribes in the North, the policy has triggered a disastrous tribal revolt...

> The history of this region suggests that there is only one successful way to bring national unity out of the ethnic heterogeneity. The way is not forced assimilation, which only increases tensions. Nor is it isolation and exclusion from the body politic, which thus far has been our attitude towards the peoples on the periphery of our nation. The only method which has worked is a genuine sharing of power and responsibility (Saiyud, 1986: 101-102).

Assimilation is not a systematically elaborated policy and the structural assimilation named here is not a secret agenda, drawn up in some geopolitical think-tank hidden away in a bureaucratic bunker. This Chapter has been written as an attempt to identify as a social fact and a problem for research, the political aspect of the consensus that can only be dealt with if it is named and brought into language. The discussion represents a preliminary attempt to construct a new category, a different way of looking at the situation so that those charged with the responsibility for reseach and planning or in a position to influence the future of the nation can arrange their thoughts in a rational and scientific way, consciously using categories given by society: categories which include all those who make up the multi-ethnic society which is modern Thailand.

What is new is not necessarily best or most appropriate. To succeed, intervention in the highlands need not depend on the deliberate introduction of new technology, new crops and new forms of credit and marketing; the response which follows the building of roads and the manner in which this allows farmers access to new economic opportunities, better medical care and education is enough to ensure that integration will take place spontaneously. What matters is the way in which the situation is interpreted and the categories imposed, for this will determine what information will be taken into account and what activities will be given priority. If poorly informed, critical attitudes are constantly imposed, which preclude the possibility of a better understanding of the manner in which highlanders are rapidly adapting to national life, and categories of concern continue to focus on disembodied aspects and muddled interpretations of issues like opium production, security and land degradation, serious obstacles will remain on the path to integration. Under such conditions, highlanders will be subject to the increasing suspicion, dislocation and alienation which accompany structural assimilation as a policy by default. If a humane paradigm is chosen, current trends towards spontaneous integration will be assessed to provide a basis on which the full advantage of the social, political and economic impact of this can be secured and with highlander citizenship and land rights assured, the remaining issues will, with cooperation and trust, be relatively easy to resolve.

The hard issue is what should come first: "hill tribe problems" as this term is currently understood or the problems faced by the highlanders? To me there appears to be no choice at all. The most important information we have about the highlands is that these lands are occupied by minority peoples. This fact should take priority over all other considerations. These are the grounds on which I believe we should rearrange our thoughts.

References

Anan Ganjanapan (1986) — "Status and Methodology of Thai Anthropology 1947-1985" (in Thai) *Thai Sociology and Anthropology: Status and Direction* pp. 68-102. Faculty of Social Science, Chiang Mai University.

Anat Arbhabhirama, Dhira Phantumvanit, John Elkington, and Phaitoon Ingkasuwan (1987) — *Thailand Natural Resources Profiles. Is the Resource Base for Thailand's Development Sustainable?* Thailand Development Research Institute: Bangkok.

Anon., (1895) — *An Englishman's Siamese Journals 1890-1893* Facsimile of *Report of a Survey in Siam* Siam Media International Books: Bangkok.

Benchaphun Shinawatra (1985) — *Highland-Lowland Interrelationships in Northern Thailand: A Study of Production, Distribution and Consumption* Unpublish PhD dissertation Michigan State University: Michigan.

Benchavan Tongsiri (1987) — "Fertility and Migration of the Hilltribes in Maehorngsorn Province". In Suchart Praisith-rathsint (ed) *Population and Development Projects in Thailand* Field Studies Steering and Review Committee Microlevel Studies Program on Population and Development Interactions in Thailand.

Berridge, Virginia & Giffith Edwards (1987)
Opium and the People: Opiate Use in Nineteenth Century England Yale University Books: New Haven & London.

Blaikie, Piers & Harold Brookfield (1987)
Land Degradation and Society: Defining and Debating the Problem Methuen: London & New York pp. 1-26.

Bo Gua (1975)
"Opium, Bombs and Trees: The Future of the H'mong Tribesmen in Northern Thailand" *Journal of Contemporary Asia* 5(1):70-80.

Cassells, D.S., (1987) M.Bonell, L.S. Hamilton, D.A. Gilmour
"The Protective Role of Tropical Forests: A State-of-knowledge Review" in Vegara, Napoleon & Nicomedes D. Briones (eds.) *Agroforestry in the Humid Tropics: Its protective and ameliorative roles to enhance productivity and sustainability* East-West Center: Honolulu.

Chalermrath Khambanonda (1972)
Thailand's Public Law and Policy for, Conservation and Protection of Land The National Institute of Development Administration: Bangkok.

Chambers, Robert (1985)
"Normal Professionalism, New Paradigms and Development" Paper presented to the Seminar on Poverty, Development and Food: Towards the 21st Century held in honour of the 75th Brithday of Professor H.W. Singer, Brighton, December 13-14.

Chapman, E.C. (1978) "Shifting Cultivation and Economic Development in the Lowlands of Northern Thailand". In Kunstader, P., E.C. Chapman & Sanga Sabhasri (eds) *Farmers in the Forest: Economic Development and Marginal Agriculture in Northern Thailand* East-West Center: Honolulu.

Chayan Watanaphuti (1987) "The Study of Minorities in Lan Na" (in Thai) *Bulletin of Lan Na Studies* 2(2):5-11; 57-59.

Chupinit Kesmanee (1987) *Hilltribe Relocation Policy: is there a way out of the labyrinth? A case study of Kampaeng Phet* (mimeo) Tribal Research Institute: Chiang Mai.

Cooper, R.C. (1979) "The Tribal Minorities of Northern Thailand: Problems and Prospects" *Southeast Asian Affairs* 6:323-332.

Department of Public Welfare (1983) *A Directory of Development Activities in the Opium Poppy Cultivation Areas of Northern Thailand* Appendix I & II, (mimeo) Ministry of Interior.

Dumont, Louis (1970) *Homo Hierarchicus: An Essay on the Caste System* The University of Chicago Press: Chicago.

FEER (1987) *Asia 1988 Yearbook* Far Eastern Economic Review: Hongkong.

Gar Yai Lee (1981) *The Effects of Development Measures on the Socioeconomy of the White Hmong* Unpublished PhD dissertation, University of Sydney: Sydney.

Gibson, T. (1983) "Toward a Stable Low-input Highland Agricultural System: Ley Farming in *Imperata cylindrica* Grasslands of Northern Thailand" *Mountain Research and Development* Vol. 3 No. 4:378-385.

Hanks, L.M., J.R. Hanks & L. Sharp (1964) *A Report on Tribal Peoples in Chiengrai Province North of the Mae Kok River.* Bennington-Cornell Anthropological Survey of Hill Tribes in Thailand Data Paper No.1. Siam Society Bangkok.

Hathaway, R.L. (1986) "Plant Materials for Slope Stabilisation" in *Plant Materials Handibook" for Soil Conservation* Vol.1 *Principles & Practices* pp 39-40, Soil and Water Miscellaneous Publication No.93. Government Printer: Wellington.

Hoey P.M., S. Tepsarn & S. Thuamcharoen (1987) Results and Recommendations for the HASD Fieldcrop Programme *Proceedings Farming Systems Seminar 18-19 June 1987* (mimeo) The Highland agricultural and Social Development Project: Chiang Mai.

Hutheesing, Otome (1987) "The Degeneration of Lisu Repute" Paper presented to the International Conference on Thai Studies ANU, Canberra 3-6 July.

Kammerer, Cornelia Ann (1987) "Minority Identity in the Mountains of Northern Thailand: The Akha Case" *Southeast Asian Tribal Groups and Ethnic Minorities Prospects for the Eighties and Beyond* Cultural Survival Report 22, Cultural Survival Inc.: Cambridge, MA.

Kampe, Ken (1986) "Land Use Certificates in the Mae Chaem Watershed Development Project" (mimeo) Unpublished occasional paper "For the Record ...12" Mae Chaem Watershed Project: Chiang Mai.

Keer, Donna H. (1984) *Barriers to Ingegrity; Modern Modes of Knowledge Utiliztion* West View Press: Boulder, Colorado.

Kunstadter, Peter (1987a) "The End of the Frontier: Culture and Environmental Interactions in Thailand". Unpublished typescript. To be published in edited form in the *Proceedings Siam Society Symposium on Culture and Environment in Thailand, 15-22 August* Chiang Mai.

Kunstadter, Peter, Chupinit Kesmanee & Prawit Pothi-art (1987b) *Hmong and Karen Health and Family Planning: Cultural and Other Factors Affecting Use of Modern Health and Planning Services by Hilltribes in Northern Thailand* Ministry of Pulbic Health: Bangkok.

Kunstadter, Peter (1983) "Highland Populations in Northern Thailand". In McKinnon & Wanat" (eds) *Highlanders of Thailand* Oxford University Press: Kuala-Lumpur.

Kunstadter, P., (1978) E.C. Chapman & Sanga Sabhasri *Farmers in the Forest: Economic Development and Marginal Agriculture in Northern Thailand* East-West Centre: Honolulu.

Leach, E.R. (1954) *Political Systems of Highland Burma: A Study of Kachin Social Structure* Harvard University Press: Cambridge, Mass.

Lee, R (1980) *Forest Hydrology* Columbia University Press: New York.

Lewis, Paul (1973) *A Proposal for the Development of a Family Planning Program Among the Akhas of Thailand* Department of Anthropology, University of Oregon.

Luechai Chulasai et.al. (1985) *Profile of Northern Thailand* Chiang Mai University: Chiang Mai.

McKinnon, John (1987) "Resettlement and the Three Ugly Step-Sisters Security, Opium and Land Degradation: a question of survival for the Highlanders of Thailand". Unpublished paper presented to the International Conference on Thai Studies, ANU, Caberra 3-6 July.

McKinnon, John (1983) A Highlanders Geography of the Highlanders: mythology, process and fact *Mountain Research and Development* Vol.3, No.4:313-317.

McKinnon, John Wanat Bhruksasri (eds) (1983) *Highlanders of Thailand* Oxford University Press: Kuala Lumpur.

Prachuap Kambunratana et.al. (1987) *Survey of Hill Tribes & Minority Groups in Northern Thailand* Summary Report, Task Force on Hill Tribes and Minority Groups, Office of Special Activities, Ministry of Education: Bangkok.

Radley, Howard M. (1986) *Economic Marginalization and the Ethnic Consciousness of the Green Mong (Moob Ntsuab) of Northwest Thailand* Unpublished PhD dissertation, Cambridge University.

Saiyud Kurdphol (1986) *The Struggle for Thailand: counter-insurgency 1965-1985* S. Research Center Co., Ltd.: Bangkok.

Saiyud Kurdphol (1976) "Government Policy is Leading to Disaster in the Hills" *Bangkok Post* 4 January: 9-10.

Salzer, Walter (1987) *The TG-HDP Approach Towards Sustainable Agriculture and Soil and Water Conservation in the Hills of North Thailand* (mimeo) Thai-German Highland Development Programme: Chiang Mai.

Sanga Sabhasri (1978) "Effects of Forest Fallow Cultivation on Forest Production and Soil". In Kunstadter, Chapman & Sanga (eds) *Farmers in the Forest: Economic Development and Marginal Agriculture in Northern Thailand* East-West Center: Honolulu.

Sanit Wongsprasert (1977) *The Sociocultural and Ecological Determinants of Lahu Population Structure* SEAPRAP Research Report No.14, IDRC: Singapore.

Schubert, Bernd et.al. (1986) *Proposals for Farming Systems-Oriented Crop Research of Wawi Highland Agricultural Research Station in Northern Thailand* Technical University of Berlin: Berlin.

Sheng, T.C. (1979) *Management and Conservation Farming in Northern Thailand* Mae Sa Integrated Watershed and Forest Land Use Project, Working Paper No.11 (mimeo) (Tha/76/001) UNDP/FAO: Chiang Mai.

Suree Bhumibhamon (1986) *The Environmental and Socio-Economic Aspects of Tropical Deforestation: A Case Study of Thailand* (mimeo) Kasetsart University: Bangkok.

Tapp, Nicholas (1986) *The Hmong in Thailand: Opium People of the Golden Triangle* Anti-Slavery Society: London.

Tapp, Nicholas (1985) *Categories of Change and Continuity among the White Hmong (Hmoob Dawb) of Northern Thailand* Unpublished PhD thesis, SOAS: London.

Walker, A.R. (1979-80) Highlanders and Government in North Thailand *Folk* 21-22: 419-49.

Westermeyer, Joseph (1982) *Poppies, Pipes and People: Opium and Its Use in Laos* University of California: Berkeley.

86. Opium replacement crop (Kampe)

87. Highland land use (Connell)

88. Karen burnt swidden (McKinnon)

89. Reforested farmland (McKinnon)

90. Road erosion, Doi Thung (McKinnon) 91. Field (rill) erosion (McKinnon)

92. Road construction (McKinnon)

93. Two generations, Karen (McKinnon)

94. Mlabri *"talap manut"* (Baffie)

95. Lisu *pla ra wok* (Baffie)

96. Hmong *tao phu khao* (Baffie)

97. Akha *pu chong ai phi ba* (Baffie)

98. Tourist exotica (McKinnon)

99. Lahu Sheleh women (Connell)

100. Hmong seller: *farang* buyer (Connell)

101. Night bazaar, Chiang Mai (Hobday)

REFLECTIONS: FRAGMENTS & IMPRESSIONS

In some cases because of subject matter, and in others because of the approach taken, the chapters offered in this section provide a less formal and more personal treatment of information.

Vithoon Pungprasert, a reporter with **The Nation** who has a special interest in highland affairs demonstrates his competence by providing a particularly interesting interview with Suthee Argaslerksh, permanent secretary for the Prime Minister's Office during the Prem administration. Khun Suthee, as a principal figure on the Committee for the Prevention of the Intrusion into and Destruction of the Forest by Hill Tribes, is encouraged to speak directly and openly with little concern for the opinions of people working in other highland agencies. The reader senses his confidence in the primary importance of environmental protection and the will to carry through a more aggressive policy.

Mr Pravit Phothiart, a senior researcher at the TRI, is also a poet. Following a long established tradition in Thai culture where the literary man, may speak his mind, Khun Pravit chooses to use his experience as a researcher to provide an impressionistic account of over twenty years work with the Karen. This approach to his subject enables him to convey both a personal understanding as well as to present information based on formal investigation. There are many echos in this piece which match some of the more critical points made by Chupinit, Chantaboon and McKinnon. Pravit's road to hell though is paved not with good intentions but with chemicals and fertilizer. He tells us about the "jackfruit and mango tango" and closes with a question; "We, the development worker, are we part of a great merit making exercise or are we lost, and will the winds of change soon blow cold?

Jean Baffie, a French anthropologist attached to CNRS, has worked in Thailand for ten years. He has as much to tell us about "one baht" Thai comics in general as he does about how highlanders are portrayed in their cartoons. Clearly hill people are not a popular topic. Out of a random sample of 5000 texts only seven deal with highlanders, a mere 0.0014 percent of the total. What is of interest is what is chosen to entertain the reader. "Whilst violence, sex and the supernatural are common themes in popular Thai comics, films and literature, they are sometimes treated very differently in a highlander context. Hill people are seen to be devoid of any feeling of guilt with regard to the law, morals and official religion. Thus, the Mlabri husband who kills his wife appears to have the right to do so, and the old Hmong will not be questioned for having bumped off the four chinese *haw*. Amongst the Akha a stereotype of sexual freedom seems to be the order of the day".

Duangta Seewutiwong a research assistant with the TRI-ORSTOM Project, allows us to see village life from the perspective of a relatively habituated visitor looking at other strangers. Her existential honesty and the ease with which she indicates the complex manner in which villagers relate to each other as well as foreign tourists weaves a reality that is both convincing and amusing. The juxtaposition she pinpoints of *farang* material wealth and Akha poverty, Coca Cola and pig's blood, provides a subtle and humourous commentary on the comforts and dislocations of modern life. There are times when all we desire is a peaceful haven illuminated by an electric light bulb where we can read without interuption, at least for an hour or two.

Hill Tribe People Blamed for Deforestation*

Vithoon Pungprasert

A government working group in charge of formulating measures to stop hill tribe people from destroying forests in northern Thailand believes the problem has reached a crisis and the policy toward the hill tribes must now emphasize suppressing illegal activities, especially forest poaching, rather than accommodating them.

Suthee Argaslerksh, permanent secretary for the PM's Office, who heads the working group told **The Nation** recently that a large number of hill tribe people destroy forests for profits, and not just to make ends meet as most outsiders believe.

Many hill tribe people are in the business of cutting trees in national forests and selling the wood. They clear the forests to grow maize on a well-organized large-scale basis. "These are not innocent hilltribesmen who do the traditional slash-and-burn cultivation. They are more sophisticated, and I would say more dangerous, than you would think" Suthee said.

---

*This article was first published in **The Nation**, (Saturday, March, 7, 1987:2) and is reprinted here with their kind permission.

They grow maize to sell the crops in town. Some of them even have pick-up trucks to transport the crop into town and to take supplies back to their communities. In one community on Doi Inthanon, Chiang Mai, some hill people have bought 10 wheeled trucks, Suthee reported.

He said government attempts to stop forest destruction by the hill tribe people have failed because there are too many hill tribe people scattered over 22 northern provinces; the government does not know how many are there, the estimate is between 700,000 and one million.

While many of them have settled down, others still roam the northern region and they resist government attempts to confine them to any settlement areas, Suthee added.

Another senior official who is familiar with this problem told **The Nation** forest destruction in the northern region could chiefly be blamed on the hill tribe people. Moreover, they are also responsible for polluting water sources with residue from insecticides and other chemicals used in their farming.

The official who asked not to be named said soil erosion caused by the denudation of trees in the water source forests has muddied the water in Mae Ping, Mae Kok, and Nan rivers. This, coupled with the chemical residue, has made the water in these rivers unsafe for human consumption downstream.

He concurred with Suthee that a large number of hill tribe people clear forests to plant maize for commercial purposes. He cited as example Lao San who is headman of Ban Khek Noi in Lom Sak District of Phetchabun. He said Lao San is a well off and experienced farmer/merchant. Lao San grows opium poppy to make money, rice for consumption in his household, maize, coffee and lichee for sale. Lao San even **employs Thai villagers on his farm.**

Deforestation

The official said sophisticated tribesmen like Lao San do not have to depend on merchants in town. They can transport their crops and sell them in town. The merchants in town actually depend on these people to supply them with crops.

This official strongly disagrees with the Public Welfare Department in trying to accommodate the hill tribe people regardless of whether they are engaging in any illegal activities or not. "Instead of stopping the hill tribe people from encroaching on national forests, officials of the Public Welfare Department usually go in to help them settle in national forests," he said.

Highlanders are often recruited to serve as security guards for road construction crews in areas infested by communist insurgents. These hilltribesmen would see the richness of the virgin forests and return later to cut the trees. This was the case in Khlong Lan in Kamphaeng Phet, he added.

The Public Welfare Department is supervising about 350,000 hill tribe people. But the authorities believe that the actual hill tribe population is much larger. In Tak, for example, the population was initially registered at about 60,000. Several years later, another official survey found 500-600 new villages, and the tribal population in this northern province has doubled.

In Chiang Rai, Chiang Mai, and Phayao, over 1,000 new villages have been set up in recent years. They have been populated by tribal migrants from Burma and Laos.

These people have strong family ties. When one family manages to establish in one area, family members usually send word to invite their relatives to move across the border to join them in starting a new village. Thus, hill tribe people continue to trickle across the border from Burma and Laos into northern Thailand.

The growing population puts a lot of pressure on the national forests as well as on settlement areas prepared by the authorities. The policy of accommodation has caused resentment among Thai villagers in the lowlands who often clash with hill tribe people in competing for lands.

Many hill tribe people are dissatisfied when they are given only 15 rai of land for farming in settlement areas because each family usually clears over 100 rai of forest and claim it as their land.

Suthee said it is time for the authorities to change their view of the hill tribe people. "We used to think that they are helpless pitiful people. But now, we have found that they are also extremely destructive to our forests and we must stop them" Suthee said.

One top priority in this problem is controlling and confining people in settlement areas, and not allowing them to roam from one forest to another. Those who resist government control and those who destroy forests will be severely dealt with, Suthee said.

Those who have just migrated from Burma and Laos will be pushed back as soon as possible. But some of them may be allowed to settle in a hill tribe centre in Chiang Rai. Border security will also be improved to prevent new migrants from entering Thailand.

The hill tribe people will all be evacuated from water source areas. Those who live in national forests which have

Deforestation

not yet been completely destroyed will be moved as soon as suitable resettlement locations have been found. Those living in forests which have already been denuded of trees will be contained in their present locations until they too can be moved into resettlement centres.

Karen: When the Wind Blows

Pravit Phothiart

Before we start and step into my discourse let us remember.

Forests have trees, animals and people.
That nothing is fixed and reality is change.

That the factors of change are many and are manifest both directly and indirectly. The dialectic of change brings goodness as well as badness, change is a sharp, two edged sword.

To the point then, who are the Karen? How many are there? The Karen are the largest group of ethnic-minority highlanders in Thailand (270,803 Appendix I).

Karen live in the forest, high on the mountains. Trees are their closest neighbours, along with many kinds of animals. Life for them has been like this for centuries.

Karen are humans, people who live together in their own society in villages. But this does not mean that they live in isolation from the outside world. Just as the winds of change transform societies everywhere in the world so do these winds affect Karen. The most important changes have occurred in agriculture. The most direct impact comes from development projects supported by both government and private enterprise, Thai and foreign money. Changes of more indirect origin are structured into the nature of modern industrial society, which also alters the relationship between Karen and Thai lowlanders because it completely transforms the perception and use of resources. Modern transport and communication are so convenient and make it easy to reach markets and family and friends. New conflicts and problems are also brought in.

In the early days of this development game the Karen were always accused, like other minorities, of causing problems and of having no talent for the skills and knowledge required by the new age. Unfair accusations which would not survive investigation.

If they are so backward why is it that they have been able to survive in the mountain environment for so many centuries? Why have their numbers slowly increased? Surely this is evidence of success.

We, all who come from the huge capital of Bangkok, are able to perceive, study and see directly into Karen society. They are our equals are they not?

Cultivation: all for mouths and stomachs
Born as human beings, no matter where we live, we are captives of our ancient pasts, with memories of deep hunger and the search for food.

For the Karen the word "food" is synonymous with rice. Rice is the staple and forms the largest part of any meal. If they have sufficient land and labour, farmers will grow just enough for their own family needs and that's all. As for plants and crops, cultivated fields resemble the selected and reassembled conditions of forest, mountain, valley and stream. A modest type of agricultural intervention, engineered in a manner that harmonizes with nature. If nature is in a state of balance, we can talk of a certain type of perfection ; then life is happy. Yet even this balance is transitory, change is as inevitable as suffering.

The faster things change the greater the pressure added every minute, every hour to everyday life.

Rice farming is not forest destruction
Around the estate of each village stand clumps of trees which provide a home for the spirits of the land. These are not touched for they also stand as evidence of the respect one village holds for another. The law of the jungle is more gentle than we might imagine. It is an ancient law of conservation. The agricultural cycle is conducted with economy.

Fields cut before the end of winter-February.
Fields burnt before the end of summer-April.

Rice seeds sown before the coming of the rains at the end of April or May.

Weeding continually through the time of the rains.

Harvesting when the cold of winter once again visits - November till December.

This is the annual cycle in the everyday lives of Karen.

Several kinds of plants are established in the rice fields, all passed down from generation to generation. Rice dominates but is mixed with edible kitchen, medicinal and other plants of many kinds (see Chantaboon, this volume). In a good field the plants grow up nice and close together in an order set by the farmer but not boldly announcing in misplaced pride that they follow an exacting and complex system.

Some crops mature quickly and may be harvested for eating long before the others. Their early removal exposes the slow developers to more light. With more space available, they gradually take over.

In a rice field not only is rice grown. We may find maize, several types of bean, many types of melon and potato, taro, cucumber, pumpkin and gourd: all that plants which provide delicious food. Then let us not forget the extras that give taste and comfort to life ; chillis, sesame, cotton, tobacco and so the list goes on. All for the family.

One problem is linked to another in a relationship of mutual dependence. One of the biggest problems now is the shortage of hill land available for growing rice, well-watered valleys for constructing terraced paddy fields and so it goes. Rice fields are cultivable land, fields in which many food crops can be grown: agriculture is conducted for survival.

The size of the land is fixed. The forest still covers the land but the canopy stands lower. The biggest change from old times is the higher population. Fertility has always been controlled by late marriage and strict rules governing who may sleep with whom and when, but reproduction is a basic enterprise which must be successful for any society to survive and for their families to continue.

In the past when mortality rates were high, a lot of people died of diseases. Deaths often exceeded births. Natural increase at a steady rate is a contemporary phenomenon but surely it is not frightening.

As the number of people increases they will need more rice, more rice must be grown. How can this be done if the forest is also diminishing?

Forest: "Do Not Enter"

Almost everybody who doesn't know, accuses highland farmers of destroying the forest by slash-and-burn cultivation. Somehow critics forget to look at the parts of the country where there are no ethnic minorities and where the forest is disappearing even more quickly.

Who is responsible for this attack? Is it not the work of those who will accumulate more power by advocating the establishment of forests?

Afforestation activities extended onto land farmed by the Karen and Lua are not always justified. Sometimes planting is extended in disregard of household fences.

Karen people live peacefully and have never sought power to oppose the authority of the state. When all they have offered is cooperation, the bitterness they feel is understandable. The dignity of climax forest and all that it stood for has become a memory and now what remains is being taken away and placed under the care of a much more commercially minded hoarder.

Because of this, day and night, people worry about land and how to grow enough rice to eat.

While claims over land used for decades are abrogated, the number of people who eat rice increases. While the ability to extend fields is restricted, land normally left fallow for a decade or more must be used again before the nutrient fixing vegetation has recovered. As the amount of biomass felled gets smaller, fewer nutrients are released by the burn. As fertility declines and weeding becomes a problem, yields drop.

Nobody can complain that the system is not conservation minded. Some trees must be felled in the clearing process but most are just heavily trimmed. These trees survive the fires. When the rains come, they quickly recover and serve to provide a reservoir of seeds for the next generation of trees. Not only is the system of farming cyclical, the forest is also husbanded in a cyclical fashion.

If the forest still stands, if enough rice can be grown for household needs, then life can be good and the people happy.

If the number of people increases but the forest diminishes, then the good life and happiness can be expected to fade away.

Enter new materials
Current poverty among the Karen is frightening. There are many to whom help should be given. But fear not, several projects have come to the rescue. The objectives are clear, for sacred development's sake will the transformation take place. With these compassionate development plans come many new plant materials and industrial products.

The list is impressive. A new rice variety *hom mali* (which smells of sweet jasmine), and also *mei nong*. But not all places are good for all the new varieties. Some locations are too cold or unsuitable because of the prevalence of disease.

If Karen too readily believe what extension workers tell them and enter into what is really an experiment with too much optimism, too much hope in the promise of new

Karen World

plant materials, they may well find themselves expelled from paradise before harvest day.

It is always the cautious Karen who ask, "Is this an experiment or proper extension?"

And what is offered? New plants to replace rice. Cash crops are promoted with the advice that they replace crops grown for food. So all those plants on the list, cabbages, potatoes, rosemary, strawberries etc march in. They all come in the role of saviours, palliatives against poverty. They create a new dream, new hope for a future of plenty.

At the start there can be hope that the dream will come true.

Those who first accept the innovation will become rich. But this flame is blown out in a single breath, the same breath that carries the news from mouth to mouth, from mountain top to mountain top. The Karen breathe on the flame gently in the hope they share with other highland farmers that this sweet promise will come true. So they watch carefully for the rush of wind which will blow out the fire.

Yes, news of new crops spreads quickly like fire through straw. Farmers want to be better off and are prepared to adopt the use of chemical fertilizers, herbicides, new agriculture tools and machines which seem to jump up and say, "Hello!" to Karen and every passing highland farmer.

Traders with pick-up trucks come with their marketing skills and attractive bundles of goods. There is reason enough to earn more money.

Everything is money and gold, getting by, buying and selling. These are the days of the great hope to buy and the disappointment of sell-out. Modern urban clothes, whether jeans or jumpers: these are what people want. New rice and desserts, whether rainbow coloured or plain, are what everybody desires. All of these take money: liquid time, labour and land.

In the name of slaves and servants

Marketing is upbeat. Such really nice companies. Skilled advertisers can create the illusion of divinity and magic: violet or red banknotes can secure wishes and buy happiness. A new divinity: the money god.

In the past, no matter what was grown, it was principally grown for eating to sustain the lives of mothers, fathers and children. The surplus if any, specially of sesame or dry chilli, could be sold. At this time what was grown was an extension of what the household needed not what the dream merchants of the market required and told people would bring them a better life. When work in the fields is done for the siren of the market, ambitions seek new goals in a land full of opportunities in which it is difficult to reach your destination without running aground on the rocks of bankrupcy. Friends, can you not picture how Karen cabbage farmers feel uneasy, worried that their crop will not fetch a price good enough for them to buy what they want? Last week the price was 4 baht per kilo. This week it dived down to 4 kilos per baht where it sits in cold silence. The new divinity, the money god, like many gods before resides over the horizon in a land to which the Karen are strangers.

Still it lives. Some have said they have seen it. Some have visited the magic land to get a taste of plenty.

Irrigated rice terraces

For Karen rice is security. Security of rice is the possession and good management of irrigated rice fields. To control water is to free oneself from the unpredictable and capricious rain god, who too often passes in cloud and shadows. Still these sky shadows call to every farmer when it is time to cut, rake, plow and transplant. It is always like a competition between man and the elements to grow enough food. Never mind the number of mouths, this depends on fate. But to be able to grow more rice than required is an outcome that enables people to escape a cruel fate.

So best wishes to the Karen for a secure future. If it means they need only irrigated rice terraces either on the valley floor or slope, as long as water is available, which can be redirected through channels and pipes, then their lives will be rich and fulfilled. Unfortunately, sites with such development potential are not so easy to find. Those who first came to the mountains have already claimed the best spots and not left much for those who followed.

Sites which lack a source of reliable water are avoided because they have no potential. Terraces that cannot be flooded give low returns and present the farmer with considerable weeding problems.

So it is true that the development strategy which would have the Karen dig giant steps into the side of hills has not met with an enthusiastic response. This is so not because the Karen are unable to undertake such construction work but because they know what small returns they will get for their effort. What they know must often be kept to themselves because those who come to tell them what to do assume that they know better and the Karen stand back to allow development and extension workers freedom of expression; words to the winds.

Heritage and participation

Irrigated rice fields are only this, a heritage from grandparents. A small gift obtained by hard work largely in the absence of financial assistence, built when time was precious, in the service of a family's mouths and stomachs. Slow hard work with a hoe. And if there is enough for the generation of builders what of those who follow? Not good news. Those who follow must share the use of the land. A good tradition of sharing between all off-spring without favouritism or prejudice save for a little extra for the youngest daughter, who inherits more land because she looks after her parents until they die. But not without problems.

This nice tradition makes the Karen a little like the silk caterpillar that produces thread for a cocoon but must itself die because of this work. It is the same when land is shared out equally between all the children in a family. Viable holdings are fragmented into increasingly small pieces. Farms become smaller, the yield of rice also declines: the mundane reality of poverty.

But who is able to see these kinds of facts? Who is able to see through the idyllic rural scene beside the road? Beautiful green irrigated rice terraces so symmetrically arranged from the top to the bottom of the slope. Indeed a worthy subject for an expensive camera in the hands of one who has never touched poverty.

Signs of suffering

Where has all the water gone? But from where come these diseases and insects?

Water is needed for growing rice. Not just a little now and then, a lot of water from a generous creek, much more water than cản be caught on fields from the rain. A flow that continues day and night is the stuff of dreams. As the cold

Karen World

season advances into the hot, stream flow diminishes and dwindles to nothing. Farmers and the heavenly rains. They tie their hopes to the onset of the rains. If the water does not start to flow again, the forest will die but if the forest is gone and the rain continues can we then say that the forest and watershed has been destroyed by tribesmen? Trees still grow: the rain still falls.

What a reasonable observation you might say. How simple and easy to understand. We all want to have clear information.

But where does misinformation about destruction come from? Hill tribes use axes for felling trees not the powerful tools which others bring, such as electric saws, tractors, elephants and money to employ labour. Is it really true that there is less water in the highlands because there are fewer trees? If it is so, then responsibility cannot be pinned solely on the hill tribes, certainly not on the Karen. It is certainly not an outcome they want. If it is true, they are the first to suffer.

Farmers must wait for rain. Late rain is late rice. If there is not enough, rain there will not be enough food. Poverty comes hand in hand with drought.

With the vegetation degraded and its complex ecology impoverished and communications vastly improved, another route to suffering is opened which brings increasing difficulties. With development comes new rice with improved rice diseases and raiding insects flying in greater numbers. Perhaps these pests come with Land Rovers or on the soles of the comfort of shiny shoes. More hunger now than ever before.

Technology and rice

When a family depends on their own efforts to grow enough rice to eat and they can no longer do so, they are usually willing to crawl if necessary to find a solution that will ensure their survival.

Almost anything which may be suggested about ways in which to increase rice production will be received with eager interest by Karen and other highlanders.

So modern materials are taken into rice fields and onto farms reached by development workers. This means new rice varieties, new cash crops, fertilizers and chemicals. Success is the only expectation. Failure is a hazard nobody wants to face. They will accept any innovation that promises to lead to higher production. Alas, this outcome seems to lie beyond the power of this technology.

New rice varieties such as those recommended for Karen fields (*hom mali,* I.R 7, *muei nong,* and other numerous experimental varieties) have marched past the eyes of the Karen long enough for them to come to their own opinion. Some are successful such as the *muei nong* type grown at Mae Chaem, or the *siw mae chan* at Mae Taeng. But sadly this is glutinious rice when the Karen prefer to eat ordinary rice!

Many varieties have failed, such as *hom mali* at Mae La Noi, I.R 7 at Mae Chaem. Some varieties could not bear the cold highland weather, others have been attacked by the gall midge, an insect which greatly reduces yields and is, year by year, gradually pushing the Karen of Mae Chaem to the brink of poverty.

Behind this failure are the most sincere and dedicated agriculture development workers. Honest Karen farmers

Karen World

easily accept friendliness from outsiders. If they trust too much, in the end they become victims. In the optimistic circle of great hopes and expectations both sides do not always carefully consider whether the new rice varieties will be able to adapt to the local area. Few know whether adaptation trials have been held or not.

Paradise can become a nightmare. Green, green rice fields can be deceptive, all leaf and little or no rice. Pests are a dangerous enemy.

New rice varieties are not quite as resistent to pests and give new life to old diseases. So on comes the technology of better management, fertilizers and insecticides with their shiny new, unblemished qualifications. So impressive. Who would be so presumptuous as to ask for proof and explanations? It is easy for the Karen to accept. If somebody objects or asks questions they might be accused of being stupid or underdeveloped or the like. All opposition is abandoned.

The road to hell is paved with chemicals and fertilizer
Ignorance is a fertile ground on which to establish troubles. Until recently Karen used neither chemical fertilizer nor insectieide, which also means they have just recently come to the dangers of handling them and are still learning how to avoid bad side-effects. Bad results can follow when farmers are ignorant of how new things work. Some fields end up with only green rice leaf *sans* seed because too much fertilizer has been applied or treatments are attempted with the wrong qualities at the wrong time. All these errors may adversely affect the yield.

Insecticide is good when handled properly but it can also be dangerous. The farmer sprays into a breeze and the poison blows back. Those who work with uncovered abrasions expose themselves to the danger of contamination by osmosis. What happens to these people?

The Karen of Ban Mong, Mae Chaem district used to produce a surplus of rice but the gall midge insect has become established in all their rice fields over the past decade. Production has dropped from plenty to deficiency. Now there is poverty and suffering.

Both development projects and extension workers from government service and private enterprise came a decade ago along the broad and promising road of development to introduce new rice varieties, new cash crops, chemical fertilizer, insecticides, herbicides and so forth. When they came, everybody at Karen Ban Mong experienced hope and looked forward to progress. Nobody anticipated that with this effort would come their present troubles. The gall midge attacked local rice varieties as well as the new I.R. 7 Some sections of rice fields are now no good for rice production.

New agriculture technology in the form of insecticide and chemical fertilizer came too. But Furadan, a powerful chemical insecticide if used in the right way revealed its horrors when a farmer accidentally poured some on to a wound on his foot. He spent a very long time in hospital. Another farmer sprayed Furadan into the wind and he also became sick for a long time. Now everybody is too frightened to touch it.

Then there was another Karen who applied chemical fertilizer to his rice field when the rice was beginning to form (he simply wanted a bigger harvest). When the field otherwise appeared to be ready for harvest, the panicles of rice had still not matured. The harvest was lost through ignorant conscientiousness. Such things should not happen under development guidance.

Karen World

Training for success or failure?
Training is mounted to combat ignorance. But its success depends on many factors, particularly working in with different traditions.

Those who work with Karen must speak Karen or at least some Northern Thai. Good communication is not possible without one of those languages. To speak only central Thai to those who have never been to school is to speak over their heads. The resource people, instructors and the like will convey so little that they had better spend their time elsewhere.

Then again, where the training is held is also an important consideration. When training courses bring trainees to instructors in towns, participants find it difficult to concentrate because there are so many distractions. While they are away from their village, they worry about getting behind with their fieldwork because time and labour allocation must work within a tight schedule from the time swiddens are cleared and burnt. After the rice is sown, it is dangerous to get behind. Standing crops must be weeded and after harvest, stored. Time is precious.

Why not more demonstrations in villages on how to use fertilizer, spray insecticide and so on? These farmers are practical people. They learn things by doing them rather than reading or being told about them.

Development workers familiar with Karen traditions realized long ago that the Karen heart rests on rice. Enough rice to eat is almost all they want. When we hold village meetings about increasing rice production, everybody listens.

The audience or the outsider might think this is pretty simple stuff but it is vital to the Karen. An extension worker who understands this and can do something about it will soon win the hearts and minds of the people.

The night after a hard days training is the time when a resource person, if he or she is really interested, should visit homes and sit around the Karen hearth. This is the time to learn, when the teachers will hear Karen opinions, become acquainted with their attitudes and problems. A good teacher must learn from students, learn what issues they feel are important: this will make the teacher more effective in the future.

Only tea and salt will be provided by the hosts, not whiskey and a high time. Karen only drink whiskey on special occassions when performing rituals or ceremonies. They are not like lowlanders or other hill peoples who drink whenever the opportunity presents itself. When a Karen is drunk, he goes to bed. It is not often you see anybody drunk.

Any challenge to tradition threatens understanding. Psychologically this has a very strong impact even though it may only be shown in small ways. All this developers and planners should have learned a long time ago. If they knew, it would provide an excellent basis on which to learn more. When will a better understanding of hill tribe culture be demonstrated in training programmes?

Home garden
Beside distant fields Karen farmers cultivate home gardens. There you can find a wide variety of plants: chilli, eggplant, legumes, taro, potato, pumpkin, papaya, sugar cane and etc are planted together. Sometimes jackfruit or other perennials are also planted close by.

Most important of the condiments is chilli, which is an essential component of every meal. There is even a saying,

"A Karen who doesn't eat chilli is not a Karen". Even the chilli has been affected by the development invasion from the outside world. Whether leaf curl entered the mountains on the feet of that rare creature, a walking development official, or a motorcycle borne extension worker, a Land Rover riding, squeaky shod academic doesn't matter now. Leaf curl has arrived and production from all of the plants that catch it has dropped close to zero. All sorts of pests unknown to the Karen before development are now well established in the village. The white fowl lice and thrips to mention only two. It is not hard to get rid of these if you have access to the right modern technology but this costs money. Would it not be better if Karen could still grow their own chilli rather than have to buy it? Is this a matter which is too insignificant for extension workers to bother themselves with?

Orchards old and new

Traditional Karen orchards have jackfruit and mango. They are like markers. When groves like this are seen in the forest you can guess that a Karen village was once located there. The age of such trees can tell us how long the village has been established. Each family has its own jackfruit or mango. Tamarine, orange and lime are also grown depending on the preference of the householder.

Coffee and lichee are more recent comers and appear to have arrived about 15 years ago out of a growing preoccupation with markets! Coffee is an especially interesting crop and certainly catches the eye. Trees are planted in quite big plantations and promise a lot for future profitable returns. But don't be too optimistic. If they are to be grown successfully, they require good conditions. Frost and rust can destroy the promise of an otherwise healthy plantation. All the trees might die if heavy frosts occur and yields will be poor if rust gets the upper hand. This is a new crop and requires careful handling. Farmers who lack sufficient training can manage to achieve only low yields.

Lichee commands a better price than coffee. But much of the fruit is eaten by children who love its sweet-sour taste. Then there is the problem of getting the harvest to market.

Land tenure is a problem here. Everybody recognises ownership of irrigated rice terraces but the land on which orchards may be established is seen as public land, common if you like, and it cannot be permanently alienated for private use. To establish an orchard by up-rooting the big stumps left from the natural forest takes more labour than one household can muster.

Then there are the maintenance tasks necessary to keep coffee or lynchee orchards in good order. Terraces are formed, large holes must be dug and filled with the correct material, fertilizer must be applied, fences built, weeds cut and branches trimed. Every activity requires knowledge and understanding.

The choice of land is often difficult. Sometimes farmers plant through areas used in rotation for rice cultivation and this adversely influences the fallow period. When farmers want of grow lynchee, they are forced to make an opportunity cost measurement. If they plant where rice can be grown, how will this change the rice production cycle? Less land available for rice cultivation may mean hardship if the profit from the sale of fruit or coffee does not enable them to purchase enough to make up shortfalls.

The jackfruit and mango tango

Most Karen grow jackfruit and mango. They germinate seeds and plant them everywhere, in the household garden or far away. It is a long time before they bear fruit, six or seven years but it is not hard to wait. Jackfruit is used in cooking or eaten on its own, raw. Mango is something both children and adults enjoy. Why have these trees not received any attention from extension workers? Are there not better varieties available? Better methods of propagation? Why are these not as attractive to developers as coffee and (lichee?)

Tamarind and lime and other local trees which have adapted well to the cold mountain weather get the same treatment. Many Karen villagers grow those trees quite successfully, obtain good yields even in lowland off-seasons when the market price is high and urban residents are trying to forget about eating sour fruit for a while.

The trees are at fault? They are only ordinary local fruit trees and do not qualify for the dignified attention of extension workers, who much prefer to look to international markets to set their standards and provide them with prestige.

Then again perhaps responsibility for this oversight can be laid at the door of the wealthy nations who provide much of the finance for development. It is their experts who promote and propagate these trees in the highlands even though they are unfamiliar with either the capabilities of these trees or their popularity on local markets.

Self-reliance: towards zero
The environment of forest and mountain has changed a lot particularly in villages which have received attention from development projects. Traditional garden plants have diminished in number, especially chilli, tobacco and cotton. These used to grow quite well in home gardens and in rice fields. They were grown for domestic use and no money was spent on their purchase from markets or traders. Farmers were independent and untouched by price changes that lay beyond their ability to control.

REFLECTIONS

We must accept that as cash crops are successfully extended farmers are able to make more money even if this also means higher expenses. Sometimes expenses run too far ahead of income.

It's a pity we don't know more about how the relationship between production costs and selling prices fluctuates. We hear more about how the population is increasing than the rate at which production expenses are taking-off. The government's hill tribe problem is not exactly the same as the problems of the hill tribes.

The broad path to development and progress seems to have become rather narrow and rough. Rough not only for the Land Rovers of the development set but also for the trucks carrying project cash crops out, as well as for the small pick-up operators, motorcycle traders and big merchants too.

Those who bring modern necessities and luxury items from lowland markets up the ladder which leads into every Karen household, bring everything: the goods themselves, salted fish, canned fish, ready made noodles, crackers, cake, tomatoes, cotton and plastic mats, picture clocks and quartz watches; and the means with which to buy them on credit, hire purchase and etc. All the prices have to be higher than they are on the lowlands. "Buy on installment if you don't have the money". And the Karen are so honest that they're a low risk customer. They don't play games with their debts. They don't think to run away from those to whom they are indebted.

Rice mills and cooperatives have appeared in the neighbourhoods of many villages. People have abandoned the pounding of rice which preserved vitamin B complex, and now sparrow mouth disease is common. Village shops suck in coins from children wanting colourful, sweet candy. Then there is that insidious, carcinogenic additive, monosodium

Karen World

glutamate, and sweet fizzy water in bottles. How wonderful the bounty of development!

Seeking new roads

Change doesn't always mean movement towards what is better, particularly if what is being done lacks a deeper sense of virtue than just moving superficially with the times.

In a material sense Karen society is quite easily understood. It has four main interlocking concerns: clothes, house, food and medicine. Each of these can be produced from resources present in their environment using available skills and labour. If they are sometimes short of things for household use, they can borrow from friends even if they are not brothers. No security is asked for.

But direct and indirect development have insinuated their way into the Karen world view. They want more than what is offered by Buddhist missionaries preaching the four basic material conditions of life. Now a fifth factor of endless accumulating has emerged. The tranquility of a society based on a simple set of material needs has gone forever.

In the not too distant past all that the outside world had which Karen wanted was salt for cooking, which could be had for a very small amount of money. It was easy to find other things in the forest that could be sold on lowland markets.

But now all has changed, people demand more than fundamentals. Even the original four basic concerns of clothes, house, food and medicine have been transformed into complex sets of options, all of which can be purchased with money. Clothes used to be made from cotton grown in the field and spun into thread, dyed with a bark extract and woven by women as time was made available from other tasks: everybody was adequately clothed, carried shoulder bags, slept under blankets etc. But today few grow or spin their own cotton. They go to town to buy it or purchase ready made clothes just like lowlanders.

Clearly money is necessary for most transactions.

Why don't we encourage farmers to grow cotton for their own use? It is not too difficult to grow and extra training could be provided as part of an attempt to promote spinning. Why don't we train people in dress making? Many young Karen women who have completed primary school to Fourth or Sixth grade are ready to work. There are many shops run by various organizations which sell hill tribe products. Why not train Karen how to run such businesses?

This will take money, but is it not worthwhile?

Houses used to be set on piles or poles gathered from the forest with a superstructure built of bamboo and lined with dipterocarpus leaves. None of these products was ever bought. When anybody needed to build a house, all the villagers came willingly to help. To build a house today means expenses for employing labour to fell, saw, finish, erect and construct a building. Concrete tiles for the roof and sometimes even the wood for building must be bought from far away towns.

Money

Why do people stop living in bamboo cottages and borrow money from neighbours to build wooden houses? The hearth is moved to a special room which becomes the kitchen. Now the other rooms are visited by mosquitoes carrying malaria. In its original state the Karen house style is much more appropriate to its environment. Perhaps the old style houses could be a bit cleaner and better arranged to provide a more comfortable resting place but better to do that than spend so much money copying the life style of lowlanders. To have special rooms set aside for sleeping is only neceesary in Bangkok, isn't it?

In former times food could be found everywhere in the forest or on the mountain, now it must be hunted and gathered from shops both in markets in the town and in small shops in the village. If we look only at the surface, this seems to serve nutritional needs. But let us consider how difficult it has become to save money. Every day something is purchased. In the past they felt they must have many hundreds of baht before they dared go into town. Now one or two baht is enough to visit the village shop and those who have no money happily risk indebtedness for the dubious joy of eating colourful food just like their neighbours.

More Money
    The day when they might have chosen to improve their diet by gathering forest products or cultivating village gardens is gone. But there are more than ten types of Karen bean that can be cooked and preserved and eaten all year round. Why not encourage young women to make good quality food to maintain good nutrition?

Still, first among all foods is rice. Why is there no project that supports rice production instead of new crops that nobody really wants? Why don't we work seriously on training farmers to maintain soil fertilily or increasing the yield of food crops? Why not more revolving funds to assist the people over rough periods, rice banks to make up shortfalls in food supply. For deep in every Karen heart that is all they want: more rice to eat.

And medicine what has happened there? As belief in spirits loses strength, more people go to the hospital. They will have to buy more medicine; commercialisation of disease and curing increases very quicky. Can the production of cash crops keep up? Now when people are ill, especially in villages targeted by agriculture development projects, they will go straight to town, to the hospital if necessary and this means they must spend a lot of money for travel, food, accommodation etc.

Why don't we provide training to convey the practical knowledge of when is the proper time to go to the hospital? Why don't we help them to make best use of their own medicinal herbs?

Winds hot and cold
When the winds of change blow, they blow very gently at first but gather strength as they pass over the lowlands. The winds of change have reached every place in the highlands. Karen social structure is being shaken by both material things and new ideas.

Everywhere old ways of living and working have disappeared, in fields and in home gardens. The words and hands of development workers who have a mind to provide only good things to villagers, in fact, bring hardship to all Karen.

If development efforts eventually lead to real happiness, then roll on that day and congratulations to those who toil in the name of development.

But if the changes lead to counterfeit happiness which the new divinity, the money god, has dreamed up to lead us all astray, then having forgotten a more basic reality we are lost.

We, the development workers, are we part of a great merit making exercise or are we lost, and will the winds of change soon blow cold?

Highlanders as Portrayed in Thai Penny-horribles*

Jean Baffie

In 1979, a Dutch anthropologist deemed it necessary to rectify the image of the Akha who had been portrayed as rather barbarious people in Vichit Kounavudi's film: **khon phu khao** (The Mountain People)[1]. This was not the only film to feature the ethnic minorities of northern Thailand; as a result of the success of **khon phu khao** many more films of the same type were made, and in particular Phaitun Ratanon's *ido,* 1984, which offered an even more stereotyped vision of the same Akha people.

The Thai media have always attached importance to these ethnic minorities. Films featuring the highlanders are the Westerns of Thai cinema[2]. Many novels, works for the general public and numerous articles published in Thai newspapers and magazines have been devoted to them. One can include here the recent popularity of hill tribe singers, the Hmong in particular (or groups which dress in traditional Hmong costumes at any rate), like Noklae and The Hmong.

---

* The author and editors acknowledge, with gratitude, the assistance of Mrs. Diana-Lee Simon who translated this article from French.
1. Leo Alting von Geusau, "Akhas not Depicted Accurately on Screen", **The Bangkok Post,** 30 September 1979.
2. I found twenty-two Thai films featuring highlanders but since there is no existing repertoire of Thai cinema to date, one can assume that there are many more.

REFLECTIONS

One-baht comics in Thailand

In this article I will discuss one of the most neglected media in Thailand, the comic, and more precisely what the Thais call *nangsu katun lem la bat,* one-baht comics.

It is estimated that since 1979 at least five thousand one-baht comics have been published by about twenty-five publishers. Between 25,000 and 70,000 copies of each have been printed which means that perhaps two hundred million one-baht comics have been circulated throughout Thailand over the past eight years[3]. When one considers that each comic is read by several people and that there is a great demand for second-hand comics, the relevance of making a study of these comics goes without saying.

No survey undertaken up until now reveals exactly who the readers of these comics are. However, it is accepted that the readers are mainly children, but also vendors, workers, bus and *samlor* drivers, fishermen, agricultural workers, masseuses and prostitutes[4]. This indicates that a large proportion of the population reads comics, and in particular the poor and least educated. Many students and university lecturers are not even aware of their existence.

Comics measure 13 × 18.5 cm. They take the form of small, 16 – or 24 –page booklets, each page comprising between one and six drawings. The front cover which is always carefully designed, is in colour: generally speaking the main scene or scenes of the story are depicted here, in much the same way as on posters advertising films in Thai cinema See Plate 94,95,96,97[5].

---

3. *Phalong Num* July, 1979: 34 ; *Matichon* 22 June, 1980: 9
4. *Phalang Num* May, 1979: 52-53 and *Phalang Num* July, 1979:33.
5. With regard to comparison with the cinema, I would like to acknowledge the information furnished by M. Gerard Fouquet, who is working on a doctoral thesis on contemporary Thai cinema entitled "Le Cinema Thailandais Contemporain", at Paris 7 University.

Seven stories out of five thousand

A great many Thai penny-horribles (perhaps 40% of the total) are *phi* stories (about spirits, ghosts or genii). Next come stories of gangs, crime and vendetta. However, a great variety of different themes have been chosen, some dealing with historical subjects, others with popular tales and yet others about the very rich, or the *sethi,* drugs or prostitution. One would have difficulty in isolating a theme as yet untackled.

The ethnic minorities are no exception. Chinese stories are relatively abundant, but they very often take the form of historical tales. Sometimes one even comes across comics depicting Malays, Vietnamese, Burmese and Mons.

Out of all the comics we were able to find, only seven feature the ethnic minorities of northern Thailand. They are the following:

1 **khao mai liso** (The New Rice of the Lisu), illustrated by Phot Chaiya, vol. No.655, ed. Bangkoksan, 24 pages. As suggested by the title, the story is set in a Lisu Village.

2 **tao phu khao** (The Old Highlander), illustrated by "Lomnua", series No.8 ed. Aksonwiwat, 16 pages. The old highlander in question is a Hmong who comes to grips with the Chinese *haw.*

3 **doi phi fa** (The Mountain of the Genie of the Heavens), illustrated by Seri Rawi, series No.40, ed. Nakhonsan, 16 pages. The action is set amongst the Lisu.

4 **"talap manut"** (The Humans' Box), the first story in a collection titled **ruammit'tun** (sold for an exceptional five baht) illustrated by Raphi Phuwong, ed. Chakkarasan, 16 pages, The Mlabri, or *phi tong luang* are the heroes.

5 *pla ra wok* (The Monkey *pla ra*), illustrated by Ottanoi, series No.21, ed. Chakkarasan, 16 pages. The author chooses deliberately not to set the story in any particular group, but states that it could have taken place amongst any one of the ethnic minorities. However, the costumes remind one of those worn by the Akha, whilst the headdresses look more like those worn by Lisu women.

6 *pu chong ai phi ba* (The Mad *pu chong* Phantom), illustrated by Phot Chaiya, vol. No.544, ed. Bangkoksan, 24 pages. The *pu chong* is the young Akha girls' love instructor.

7. *sao doi tao* (The Maiden of Turtle Mountain), illustrated by Suwit Sitthichok, series No.21, ed. Siam Sarn, 16 pages. Although never directly stated by the author, the costumes worn are those of the Yao.

Seven out of several thousand is few indeed[6], and one cannot make out a case which credits these with having much of an influence on the reading public. I will concentrate simply on the tribal image portrayed through these comics.

Drawing Highlanders

It is not difficult to explain why the theme "highlanders" is so rarely chosen as a topic. Naturally if the author aspires to a certain authenticity, he is obliged to carry out some research in order to select the subject and the texts. Illustrations require even more research. This of course may not always seem profitable for a seventeen-page comic which will be sold for one baht.

A comic is usually defined as "a story told through pictures". However, as it is not my intention to examine the

---

6. I have chosen to exclude some comics depicting scenes which take place amongst imaginary tribes which sometimes resemble American Indians, Melanesians or West-Africans.

Thai comic in its own right, I shall concern myself with neither the quality of the drawings nor the techniques involved. It is worthwhile nonetheless to examine the ways in which the different authors have depicted the highlanders in their drawings.

The *phi tong luang* illustrated by Raphi Phuwong are almost nude (Plate 94). This no doubt facilitates the author's task, but corresponds to the image of the Mlabri as they appeared to Thai people in the series of photographs published in May 1984 by the press (in particular the daily **Thai Rath,** which has a turnover of 900,000 copies) and in the film *tawan yim chaeng* (The Grinning Sun) in 1985. Ngong-ngaeng, the Mlabri heroine of *"talap manut"* does, however, wear earrings and necklaces similar to those worn by the Lahu, Meo and Yao; and on the front cover she has a very light complexion and wears a panther skin draped around her hips. No iconographic research seems to have been undertaken for *doi phi fa.* The only detail which leads us to believe that the story is set amongst the Lisu is the pointed bonnet worn by Amiyo, the heroine, but this hat, which on the front cover reminds one of the head-dress of the Akha women with their characteristic coins, is not identifiable.

If one excludes *pla ra wok,* the story in which the author depicts an imaginary tribe by integrating certain details pertaining to existing tribes and inventing others, we are left with four comics which, from a graphic point of view, are relatively accurate. Strictly speaking, the young Yao girl's costume has been simplified, no doubt to facilitate the drawing, the Hmong bonnets in *tao phu khao* seem to have been borrowed from the Lahu or Yao, and the Lisu "witch-doctor"[7] is almost identical to the Akha "witch-

---

7. The Thai word *"mo phi"* literally means "spirit doctor". The word "witch-doctor" is used here in full understanding of its pejorative meaning because a "tribal magician of a primitive people" is what is meant by the authors of the comics.

doctor" in *pu chong ai phi ba,* both having been drawn by Phot Chaiya, but on the whole these liberties in no way detract from the reader's ability to recognise the characters as highlanders.

Violence, Eroticism and Ghosts

In the comics we have selected, we come across themes which are very common in Thai comics and also in films for the masses[8]. Bearing this in mind, setting the narrative amongst the Lisu or the Yao is simply a matter of changing the decor or finding a new setting for classical subjects.

Violence.

There are two heroes in *tao phu khao,* the old Hmong (Meo of course in the Thai text) and the M 16 rifle. It is a story about old Lao Tang's family. His son is killed in his poppy field. Then, his wife poisons herself in despair. Lao Tang and his daughter-in-law remain, the latter being pledged to a *haw* merchant in exchange for the money needed to harvest the opium. But when the harvest is over, four Chinese *haw,* armed with M 16 rifles come and steal the opium. Lao Tang cunningly thinks of a trick, snaps up the opportunity and makes off with one of the M 16s before killing the four thieves (Plate 91).

All in all, six of the seven covers depict an explicit act of violence. In *khao mai liso* a fight between two *phi* is depicted, in *doi phi fa* it is the fight between a Thai, versed in the art of Thai Boxing, and a Lisu armed with a knife. In *sao doi tao,* a Yao wields a sword, stabbing a man who has raped his girlfriend. On the cover *ruammit'tun,* of which *"talap manut"* is a part, the jealous Mlabri husband kills his young wife with a rock, and on that of *pla ra wok* the

---

8. These are mostly films for provincial people, Bangkokians' taste being apparently rather different in this regard.

massacre of the monkeys is depicted see Plate 95. As for the seventh comic, **pu chong ai phi ba,** whilst the author has chosen to depict themes of eroticism and ghosts, on the front cover, the theme of violence can be found on the first page of the story, which is in fact like a second cover: one sees a nasty ghost devouring the entrails of a young Akha virgin he had just disembowled. Three or four of the covers are bloody, and in each of the seven stories man or animals die. Violence and cruelty are the major themes in hill tribe stories in Thai comics. Needless to say this theme is not very original.

Eroticism.

Not many Thai comics are based on the theme of eroticism and in fact none of those surveyed feature highlanders. However, suggestive illustrations are commonly found. The covers of **pu chong ai phi ba** and *"talap manut"* feature an Akha woman and Mlabri woman half nude, and next to the scene of vengence depicted on the cover of **sao doi tao** there is a kissing scene between the two Yao heroes. Scenes of love and eroticism are totally absent only from **khao mai liso** and **tao phu khao.**

Quite frequently a rather "natural" eroticism is depicted. The Mlabri in *"talap manut"* are naturally very scantly clad (Plate 94),the very sexy mini-skirts worn by the *pla ra wok* women are evidently part of their ethnic costume (Plate 95) whilst in *pu chong ai phi ba* the author undresses the young Akha girls in order to explain one of the customs of this tribe to us (Plate 97). It is difficult not to draw a comparison with certain magazine articles like those published in **National Geographic,** which offer readers "ethnographic" nudes in an academic context and have thus contributed to the sexual education of generations of Americans.

Sao doi tao feature both themes of sex and violence. The story begins like a Yao version of "Romeo and Juliette". Meyfin is in love with Sali, but their fathers are arch enemies. One day two opium merchants who have come to talk business with Meyfin's father are struck by the girl's beauty. At nightfall, Meyfin goes into the forest to meet Sali with whom she has decided to elope. But on the way she passes the merchants' camp and they make off with her and rape her. Alarmed by her cries Sali comes running to her aid, but too late. He kills the two merchants (above). At the end of the story, Meyfin commits suicide, thinking that Sali would want nothing more to do with her. This comic seems to portray a particularly Thai conception of good morals as some of the less well informed books on the hill tribes likely to have been consulted by a conscientious author maintain that "Yao people are very free and open in sexual matters and such a word as "rape" has no place in their language"[9]

Ghosts.
The third theme represented in Thai penny-horribles is that of *phi* (ghosts, spirits or genie). *Khao mai liso* and *pu chong ai phi ba* are two ghost stories. Whilst *doi phi fa* (The Mountain of the Genie of the Heavens) is a story of love and jealousy, the author has chosen-no doubt to attract his readers-to place a *phi* both in the title and on the cover. Magic does come into it: the jealous Lisu goes to consult the *mo phi* ("witch-doctor") who gives him a small pieces of malefic leather to enable him to get rid of his rival.

Khao mai liso is the story of a rather individualistic Lisu who omits to bring the rice he has just harvested to the ceremony organised by the village for the rice spirit. The spirit punishes the Lisu who becomes half-man half-*phi*. During a fight with other Lisu, he bites a villager who turns into a *phi*. But the two possessed spirits end up by becoming men once again.

All three themes of violence, eroticism and ghosts are intermingled in **pu chong ai phi ba.** In some of the literature about the Akha, there is said to be a *pu chong* (or *khachirada*) whose role it is to deflower young virgins and to teach them the art of love. To establish the truth of this is another matter but in the village in which the story is set, the *pu chong* has just died a strange death. Mayo is chosen to take his place. He immediately gets down to work. But each time he goes into the forest with a young maiden, he becomes possessed by the spirit of the preceding *pu chong;* he then changes himself into a *phi*, kills the maiden, disembowels her and devours her liver and other viscera.

---

9. Preecha Chaturabhand, **People of the Hills,** Bangkok Editions Duang Kamol, (1980: 27). See also Samnakngan Saranithet, Kong Banchakan Tahan Sungsut, **chaokhao phao yao,** Krungthep, (2520: 31) and Gordon Young, **The Hill Tribes of Northern Thailand.** Bangkok: The Siam Society, 4th Edition, (1969: 50-51)

REFLECTIONS

Whilst violence, sex and the supernatural are common themes in popular Thai comics, films and literature, they are sometimes treated very differently in a highlander context. Hill people are seen to be devoid of any feeling of guilt with regard to the law, morals and official religion. Thus, the Mlabri husband who kills his wife appears to have the right to do so, and the old Hmong will not be questioned for having bumped off the four Chinese *haw*. Amongst the Akha a stereotype of sexual freedom seems to be the order of the day. The only religion referred to is that of the *phi*. The *mo phi* seems to be the most important member of the village. Setting the action amongst the highlanders, who are depicted as "innocent savages" of a pre-Buddhist era before censureship and the law, enables the authors of these comics to express fantasies which would otherwise be condemned by "modern" Thai society.

northern Thailand.

Illegality, Exotism and Acculturation

A few other themes are to be found in the comics selected, these being more directly linked to the position of the ethnic minorities of

Illegality.

The highlanders in the comics are involved in illegal activities. The Hmong in **tao phu khao** and the Yao in **sao doi**

402

tao produce opium, the Lisu in *doi phi fa* make a living from illegally felling trees in the forest, or are *mu pun* (hired gunmen). There are of course exceptions to these examples: the Lisu in *khao mai liso* simply cultivate rice. In *pla ra wok* we

are told that the mixed ethnic group in question used to make a living from opium poppy cultivation, but that nowadays in line with Thai policy, they cultivate pumpkins, melons, watermelons, cucumbers etc. But it is highly unlikely that the massacre of hundreds of monkeys by the villagers would meet with the approval of the Wildlife Conservation Division of the Royal Forestry Department. As for the Mlabri in *"talap manut"*, it is evident that they in no way conform to any legality outside of their group since they pack up and move out as soon as any foreigners are sighted.

Exotism.

Exotism describes the environmental landscapes, the costumes worn by the highlanders and most particularly the strange and sometimes imaginary practices and customs presented.

In *tao phu khao* we are shown in some detail how the Hmong cultivate the opium poppy and collect the opium before selling it. The beginning of *khao mai liso* is an illustrated manual showing how the Lisu cultivate rice in the mountains using a bamboo rod and their feet. The beautiful Mlabri heroine in *"talap manut"* climbs trees and hunts wild boars with a spear. We have already made mention of the custom pertaining to the *pu chong* (or *khachirada*), the Akha's love instructor, which is the subject of *pu chong ai phi ba*.

The funerary customs of the highlanders which are so very different from those of Thai Buddhists, are frequently described or alluded to. Amiyo, the young Lisu girl in *doi phi fa* is interred in the manner customary to her tribe. Chuni, the Hmong mother in *tao phu khao* is buried at the foot of a great tree. The funerary customs of the Mlabri are even more original: the body, wrapped in a rattan mat, is suspended from a tree. Once the flesh has completely decomposed leaving only the skeleton, the parents return to share out the bones which they preserve with great care.[10]

Few of the rites are described in detail; the Lisu ceremony in honour of the new rice spirit in *khao mai liso,* is an exception to the rule even if the mere glimpse we are given of it still leaves us guessing. As for the recipe in *pla ra wok* - the only "comical" comic - there is a chance that it has been invented. The *pla ra* is a sort of fish which has been fermented in saumure. It is a very popular dish in north-east Thailand and Laos. The author of *pla ra wok* explains that the highlanders who have difficulty in getting fish, prepare their *pla ra* using animals of the forest, and in particular monkeys. The story is about the cunning way in which the highlanders manage to kill hundreds

---

10. It appears that the author has imagined this custom. See Surin Phukhachon, *"kanfangsop khong klumchon phi tong luang"* (Mlabri burials) **Phuandoenthang** (February 2526) 4:38 pp. 77-9 and Surin Phukachon et.al. *chonklumnoi phao "phi tong luang" nai prathet Thai* (The Mlabri Ethnic Minority in Thailand). The Ethno-Archeological Research Project, Silapakorn University (2525-26: 53-55).

of mondys which periodically ravage their vegetable gardens. The preparation of the *pla ra* is described on the last three pages, the monkey skins being preserved as *pla ra* stock.

Towards Acculturation.

Only the Akha in *pu chong ai phi ba* and the Lisu in *kho mai liso* by the same author, Phot Chaiya, do not seem to have any contact with other ethnic groups. In *tao phu khao, sao doi tao* and *pla ra wok,* the foreigners are merchants and bandits who come to buy or steal the highlanders' opium and vegetables. In *tao phu khao,* they are quoted as being Chinese *haw.*

In *doi phi fa,* the foreigner is a young Thai of the Royal Forestry Department by the name of Rawin. He was been wounded by bandits whilst carrying out a survey on the illegal felling of trees when Amiyo, a Lisu girl, comes across him and falls in love with him. But Sime, Amiyo's cousin, a bandit, is jealous and feels threatened. He tries to eliminate the Thai in various ways, but in the end it is Amiyo who is killed by the bullet which was meant for Rawin.

Whilst the story of Rawin and Amiyo appears to be inspired by a Thai film[11], the subject of *"talap manut"* reminds us of the theme in the Botswanan film, "The Gods Must Be Crazy", by the South-African producer, Jamie Uys (1980) : an empty Coca-Cola bottle thrown by an aviator out of the aeroplane window over the Kalahari, disrupts the life of a Bushman family. In the *"talap manut"* story about the Mlrabri, a lady's powder-box takes the place of the coke bottle. A *phi tong luang* family is living quite peacefully until some smoke in the distance indicates the presence of strangers. The group decides to move further away, but while the men are away looking for a suitable new spot a young women Ngong-ngaeng, goes towards the smoke to see what these "humans" *(phuak manut),* so often spoken about by her husband and father, look like. When she gets there,

---

11. The film *suphaburut thoranong* (The Haughty Gentleman) by Phairot Sangworibut (1985) is a love story about a young Yao girl and a civil servant of the Royal Forestry Department.

the camp is deserted, but she finds a powder-box. She sees her reflection in the mirror and imagines that is where the "humans" are hiding. Some time afterwards, Ngong-ngaeng's husband takes his wife by surprise as she is laughing and talking to the powder-box. He snatches it from her and looks to see a man's reflection in the mirror. Thinking that it is his wife's lover hiding in the box, he kills Ngong-ngaeng (Plate 94).

In *"talap manut"* foreigners (members of another ethnic group, Thais, tourists, European ethnologists?) are the source of evil, even if they do not come into direct contact with the Mlabri. Ngong-ngaeng's father had already told his daughter of "a piece of metal which makes a noise" causing the death of several members of the tribe - the gun, which suggests the possi--

bility of a violent extermination, but the powder-box - another symbol of a foreign culture - shows that even the most banal objects can be mortal. The "Meechai" condoms which the *pla ra wok* vendor tries to exchange for a hill tribe woman's watermelons, introduce a peril of a different nature. If we add that the Lisu murderer in *doi phi fa* ends up in prison, one can only conclude that it is primarily the negative aspects of cultural contact which are evoked in comics.

Similar but Different

The *phi tong luang* in the comic *"talap manut"* of the same name, find that the "humans" have monkey-like faces, yet they concede that "humans" and *phi tong luang* have common origins. The reader of Thai comics is undoubtedly convinced that he is different from the highlanders. This enables the author to push violence, sex, immorality and the bizarre. In the same way, whereas Buddhism forbids the taking of an animals life hill tribe men, women and children who believe only in spirits, can take pleasure in the massacre of hundreds of monkeys.

As opposed to certain constraints imposed by the illustrations (not withstanding in fact that one can always, as is the case in *doi phi fa,* dress the Lisu like Thai peasants), the author gains freedom of expression in depicting violence, sex and exotism in particular in their various forms.

At an exhibition on the *phi tong luang* at the *"pata"* Commercial Centre of Phra Pinklao, Bangkok, featuring real Mlabri people brought all the way from Nan, a Thai commented aloud: "After all, they look like us, and if they were dressed like us they could be mistaken for Thais"[12]. Naturally enough highlanders do look very much like Thais, but creators of pennyhorribles are more interested in depicting their differences, and this no doubt provides the spice their many readers are after.

---

12. An observation made by a bystander, 19 October, 1984 during my visit to the exhibition.

Weddings, Wealth, Pigs and Coca Cola:
farang Tourists in an Akha Village*

Duangta Seewuthiwong

The village is not far from Chiang Rai city, only 20 or so kilometers but the distance seems much greater. There is a great gulf between this rural setting in which I work as an untrained teacher and student of Akha culture and that urban environment in which I was bought up. I have been working here for only three months. When I am here, I miss the comforts of city life and no matter how many times I tell myself that I am lucky to be wealthy amongst so many poor people I do not like to be cast in the role of the privileged. People are always asking me for things. Whisky for this or that celebration, thread, needles and beads. A constant stream of people come asking for medicine. The 3500 baht I am paid per month by the project marks me apart as a rich person, how can I refuse?

Ban Akha village does not have electricity. There is no Government office here. A Baptist missionary has set up a school with two teachers. One is principally a trader, who at the moment is busy with the rainy season business of buying bamboo shoots in the village and selling them on the city market. He lives in Chiang Rai and travels up to the village each day on his motorcy-

---

*This Chapter is based on observations made in the course of field work conducted under a Fellowship provided by the Mountain People's Culture and Development Project (MPCD) funded by NOVIB, The Netherlands. I am most grateful for their support and the encouragement of Dr. Leo Alting von Geusau to publish these beginners remarks.

cle. The other teacher is an opium addict. The women still dress in traditional Akha style and members of the community maintain their old customs.

This is a preferred isolation in which we live. The road has been sabotaged to make it difficult for police in search of people engaged in activities like smoking opium, distilling alcohol and so on. This way the residents are more likely to be left in peace. The village headman also supports this isolationist policy. He maintains the only guest house in the village. If pick-up trucks could come in easily, that would be good-bye to overnight guests and hello to hordes of day trippers.

This chapter is largely about these visitors, trekkers tourists, world travellers, who pay us visits. How do they behave? What impact do they have on the village? How are they received? How do they fit into the ritual life of the village?

To provide a professional social science answer to these questions is beyond my capabilities at present. I can't talk about the Akha in the way I have read about them or heard researchers talk about them. How I know them does not always fit with the experts' reality. True, I am an observer in this village sent to learn but I am constantly reminded that I am not Akha. I am their student who for a few months will stay and then most probably leave forever; my reason and their reasons for being here are quite different. I know only events that I can understand and to me these are facts. What I will write may be quite wrong. But my reader can feel confident that I am much more than an ordinary tourist. I already know these people as individuals. I know their names. I know from which household they come. I know their children who come to my bamboo house to learn to read and write and stay to draw and talk.

When I first came to the village I was wary of contact with anybody involved in the trekking business. I did not contact

Thai guides. I kept my head down when faced with *farang* and waited to see how I would be seen and treated. It became a game which my Akha hosts began to enjoy as much as I. Once at the washing place when I was taking a bath with a group of Akha women, a girl addressed my companion in recognizable Thai,

"Hello, I stay in Chiang Rai, understand? I can speak Thai, understand? I've come to rest in this village, understand?"

My companion could not understand and after dropping her head forward looked at me quietly. We smiled: a conspirators smile. It filled me with pleasure. I was at home. For a moment I could be Akha in the *farang* eye and share a place in common with the Akha around me.

Passing, passing. When I saw then with their cameras I sometimes hated them. "Do you not have eyes with which to see? Why do you have to take something?" The Akha seemed to be much more charitable. Then there was the patronizing, the humouring as if they were talking to fools, children or both. In those first few months tourists and all that came and went with them seemed to make-up the bizarre side of village life.

I can remember sharing the shock of one of the girls in my school when she looked out to see a *farang* making ready to leave. He took a hefty hunk of bread from his pack and threw it towards one of those low-slung pigs that are always scavenging around the village. She wanted that bread. She emitted a small, high pitched groan from the back of her throat to repress her real feelings. The visitor wanted the amusement of seeing the fight for the bread. As the pigs chased, chomped and chewed she drew her hands to her mouth, she was swallowing saliva. The *farang* laughed at the skirmish.

Who are these people? What do they expect and how are these expectations served in an Akha village? How are they received? These are questions I cannot answer from my own experience but according to the statistics they are reasonably well educated and most hold university degrees, they are young and males outnumber females. Clearly they are on an adventure. The chances are pretty high that they will try opium, stay only one night in any one village, leave with a lot of photos and some good stories. They'll recommend the journey to their friends.

The first day Ian and Gay came into the village I didn't take much notice of them. There had been so many tourists in residence when I got back from Chiang Mai that I played my old avoidance game until the *farang* quotient had thinned out and I was mentally prepared for them. This New Zealand couple I soon found out had come into the village with Amanda who turned out to be the *farang* who had accosted my Akha companion when we'd been taking a bath a month or two ago.

No resentment harboured. Amanda is a woman of enterprise and by that I don't mean anything bad. She has a jewellery business in Chiang Rai, she's trying to learn about the trekking business and already owns four MTX bikes for hire. She is guide and tourist in one.

The three of them Ian, Gay and Amanda were in Bot'u's house when I first met them. A wedding ceremony was in progress. Amanda was using her Thai to find out what was happening. She had made herself well known to the headman who also speaks business Thai. He is perfectly able to communicate on matters that are likely to have a profitable outcome. Amanda is on the look out for those who can help her establish her business. It's an arrangement that suits the headman. His guest house relies on people like her to bring tourists in. Last year he made a good profit, this year has been even better.

On the woman's side of the house a group of older women were sitting around a big bamboo tray waiting for the ritual to commence. On the other side of the house the elders, all men were also ready. The bride and groom sat down in front of the fire place set up between the two rooms. The bridegroom's mother split open a boiled egg and shared it out between the couple. The groom ate first then the bride. The son of the bride played in the circle of the old women.

The men in our circle talk casually of many things, about what was happening in the village. Occasionally one or two of the men turn to me and tell me what is happening and what is coming up.

Bot'u the groom looks at me and smiles shyly. He is wearing an earring in his right ear. He looks very smart. Yesterday he was in my house and it was then I learned that he was to be married today. I was surprised. Last month he often disappeared from my evening classes. Nobody told me he was courting. He spent the time getting over to a neighbouring village about four kilometers away. He was absent often. Now I understand. But not altogether. The girl he is marrying was also much admired by another of my students who had also planned to take her as his wife. Now, there she sits beautifully dressed in Akha finery, a mother who divorced her opium addicted husband, making a fresh start.

Amanda, Ian and Gay start to take photos. The sharp light of the cameras snaps again and again. The hosts are pleased. An old woman of 70 has tears in her eyes from laughing, "a flash light in her house". The owner of the household tries to tell the guests to place themselves in a better position but communication breaks down. Are they being told not to disturb the peace? They stop taking photos and for the first time I intervene.

"You don't have to stop. They like it. They're just telling you to put yourself in a better position"

And Amanda is amazed.

"You speak English very well, is your house here?"

Ian and Gay position themselves close to me and begin to ask questions about what is going on.

Once established communication becomes an asset to all. The man sitting in front of me suggests that it may be possible to ask these guests if they'd like to contribute two or three bottles of whisky so that they can participate more fully in the ceremony. I'm only too glad. Whisky is such an important element in all such celebrations. For once I am not being asked, now it is another guests' turn.

A vigorous squeal heralds that the pig is about to be bought in. When there is a young man in the household; parents tend it in preparation for just such an event as this. Gay is frightened. "Murder or worse is being done" is written on her face. She is pale and must be shaking.

Enter the pig well trussed up. Smmio, the elder who is playing an important role in the ceremony produces a sharp knife ready to make the offering. This is too much for Gay who retreats to the far side of the men's room and puts her hand over her eyes. What terror is she dreaming? Ian and Amanda are made of sterner stuff and continue to prepare their cameras for the kill.

The stage is set. The men is charge of the pig arrange a space so that the event can be properly recorded and wait for Amanda to lift the camera to her eye. Knife ready. Cameras ready. Action. Smmio plunges the knife deep into the throat of the pig. The screaming stops. Blood pumps and gurgles into an old cooking pot. The bride and groom sit quiet and calm in front of the hearth.

Tourist Impressions

A quivering liver is laid on a board to be read by the elders. Good omens. The couple's first child will be a boy. They will have good luck. It can be read plainly from the streaks of fat which run through it in three, or is it four directions?

The whisky has arrived. A bottle is broached and cups sent to everybody in the room. One cup and I feel like a fire breathing dragon.

Now everybody can relax. The first step is completed. The old men resume their talk and fill their glasses. After the hair is scraped off and the entrails removed, the pig is butchered. Gay tells me that copies of the photos will be sent back later, much later because they are headed for Kathmandu and other countries before they reach England, their first fixed destination on a long juourney.

Amanda remarks again on my English. I'm painfully reminded of some facetious remarks I made to a young Akha man who was slightly drunk and slurred some of his words.

"Your tongue has a mind of its own."

I had not thought he would be sensitive about his ability in Thai. When I recall his answer, it still hurts.

"My tongue is clumsy but make your mind clear before you speak."

The meal begins. People are still crowding into the house. There are three tables. The guests are invited to sit with the elders.

Now I have become an expert. I am asked to explain the proceedings. What can I say? Here I am a student. Should I be seduced into the pretense of knowing? I respond and feel uncomfortable in the role. Here, tonight we are strangers sitting around a small bamboo table. We are individuals who are eating together. We come from different cultures. How can we make sense of what is true for others?

When the meal is finished, the *phi'ma*, the ritual leader begins to recite a long text from the wedding *zang*, the name given to the corpus of oral literature, law and learning which lies at the heart of Akha culture.

The old women who sit on the other side of the house throw rice over the heads of the wedding couple and into the men's side. I am told to instruct the guests to follow suit. It is cooked, broken rice rolled into balls. It was borrowed from a lowland trader who must be paid back after the new rice is harvested. It is thrown again and again. The men throw to the women and the women throw it back again.

The host approaches Carol and Gay with the tips of his fingers smeared with soot taken from the hearth. He touches some on the cheeks of both girls and tells Ian to take soot from the fireplace and to touch the cheek of every woman present.

The *phi'ma*, continues to recite his prayer.
The faces of the bride and groom are darkened by the soot blessing of many people.
The headman talks louder and louder. He is drunk.

I run away.

The people say that this year more *farang* tourists have come than last year. Ten years ago when the first group came they were divided up and stayed in different houses. The headman was especially hospitable. He was wide awake to the commercial possibilities. He has the character of a *chin haw*, a Yunnanese Chinese. If there is anything going that looks

Tourist Impressions

profitable, he will be found there. He worked for the Baptist mission as a health worker. Later he was happy to joint the project I'm now working for. He is reasonably familiar with *farang* behaviour and he could see where hospitality might pay off. Seven years ago he made the right decision to build a guest house in his compound. Since then he's enjoyed a monopoly. He gets to know the guides. He adjusts his services and his price according to what circumstances dictate. The rate varies according to what is thrown in. The basic rate varies between 20 and 50 baht. Extras such as a pipe or two of opium (cooked or raw), massage, *ganja* or other products guests might ask for are charged separately.

Not everybody is happy. There are critics in the village, especially this year when so many visitors have come. The critics don't mind the guests sitting up late at night smoking *ganja* or opium as long as it doesn't attract policemen who would come and harass them. Besides, so many of the married men smoke opium what difference does it make if a few outsiders come in? They pay well. A *mu* of opium about the size of the end of a little finger costs 15 baht. This can be sliced into enough pieces for 10 small pipes (one *bao*). At 10 baht for one pipe it is good business. Then there are the guests who come for one night but stay for two or three. The headman told me that he often earns several hundred from such guests.

Most of those who criticize are put out by the fact that they don't get a fair share of the trade. But this is not to say that others in the village miss out altogether. Because *Ban Akha* village is the first settlement on most visitors itinerary, guides employ people as porters. The returns from this can be quite good, 50 to 70 baht a day.

This month my students are more eager than ever to study at night. Three months ago when I first came the young men and women who are literate in Thai expressed a wish to learn

English. Enough to enable them to speak to foreign visitors. It is remarkable how quickly they have developed their skill. In between my departure and arrival this time, an absence of ten days, they have added new words to their vocabulary. They come and ask me if this or that usage is OK. When they see the surprise written on my face they tell me they've been talking to *farang*. One new student has presented himself. These students are very serious.

Next morning I learn that Amanda has returned to Chiang Rai. Ian and Gay are still here and they will go to the Boqt'u family swiddens about 3 kilometers from the village to spend a day in the fields. This is the month of weeding (August) and it's a good thing to be doing. Everybody can work at their own pace. It's easy to see what ought to be done and avoid making a mess.

In the fields Boqt'u's wife is worried that the visitors will soon be exhausted.

"Tell them both, if they cannot work in the field then it's better to rest in the field hut."

When I tell Ian and Gay, they smile and reply that in New Zealand they both worked in apple orchards and potato fields. In their country there are also mountains like the North. They're used to walking up and down steep slopes.

As we work, pulling the grass from between the rice stalks, we talk and laugh. Gay works very well. Everybody has questions for them and I am the interpreter rather than the expert.

Boqt'u asks if there are mountain people in their country. Ian replies to the negative but adds that there are communities in the hills. People live and farm but they are not like the Akha.

Tourist Impressions

We all lunch together in the field hut eating fresh vegetables, pumpkin and corn. When it's time to return to the village Ian carries *saka,* Boqt'u's wife's field basket back to the village and she reciprocates by carrying his camera. These two *farang* emanate a sense that they are acting properly. A certain pride is being displayed. We, the people.

Next morning they leave and we say good-bye.

Tomorrow Saboq will be married. A second marriage ceremony in so few days. I feel well done by. Another chance to learn. This is not the usual time for weddings, not the optimum time. Other villagers say that it's quite strange how so many young men have decided to get married. People prefer to arrange weddings after the harvest. Everybody is agreed that it's regrettable that every year, about May-October, many households have to borrow poor, stale rice which must be replaced with good fresh rice. Still it is good to see weddings taking place. It is always useful to have extra labour in the household to help out in the fields.

Women are a great asset in any house. They do most of the work. Saboq's mother for instance works very hard. She feeds the pigs, carries the water, collects bamboo shoots and firewood, works in the field and household. As Saboq works alone in the field it would be good for him to have a partner.

A'ja, his father, told me with a laugh that the bride is a woman from Sa Laep village. The same village from which Bot'u took his wife. Like Bot'u's wife, Saboq's wife has been married before, in fact three times. She has divorced all of her husbands. The last was a Thai, an opium smoker. Saboq will be her fourth husband. Until last week she had two children living with her. She exchanged her three month old baby for a radio-tape machine. The three year old remains with her and will be brought into the marriage. A'ja is full of plans for his son. After the wedding he, his son and some other men in their lineage will build a guest house of their own in front of his house. He's sure that this year tourists will continue to come, especially after the rainy season finishes.

He seems to be asking for my opinion but he does not ask directly. I don't need to say anything. Their minds are made up. All the inhabitants of the village assume the right to do as they wish and as they are able. Perhaps there is some sensitivity here relating to the change this will bring by breaking the monopoly of the headman. How will the challenge be mediated through the village social structure and political situation?

It is another wedding day. A'sur, my best student and the younger brother of Saboq the bridegroom, is going to escort a couple of French tourists to a neigbouring village. Two new groups of travellers have arrived. Many are pleased to witness their arrival, especially A'ja who will host the wedding ceremony.

It is a replay. The bride and groom beautifully dressed in full Akha gear are photographed again and again. A guide who knows enough about me to make me part of his itinerary introduces me as a teacher, a runaway from civilization devoting my life to the service of the people.

Three months has become a lifetime. Am I already part of an instant mountain mystique? What can I say in the face of this projection? Tell everybody the truth that each morning I wake up and pray to any caring god who may be listening to send me back under the protection of the almighty electric light bulb in close proximity to a good bookstore.

I need not worry, nobody is interested. They are all watching with fascination the squealing pig which is being carried into the room. The knife is poised and drops. There is a gasp. A male guest has collapsed. He recovers and retreats with his right hand exploring his face as if in hope of finding a place where the experience has lodged and from which it may be wiped away. We will not see him again tonight. What will

Tourist Impressions

he dream?

These guides are cross-cultural entrepreneurs. They know how to turn their experience to profitable account. Most have a good knowledge of the cycle of village rituals. They know who is who, or make it their business to find out. At least they know when something interesting is going to happen. What is expected of them and so forth. But they are definitely not either anthropologists or sociologists or any other kind of "olies" or "ists" because if they were they would not be the guides I have overheard.

One of the most important obligations faced by guides is to provide answers to questions. They do not know the phrase "I don't know". Perhaps that would be a sort of betrayal. Betrayal of a guesswork conspiracy to the doubts of science. Only the ignorant can be confident for they have not learnt anything of much significance and therefore do not have any idea of how much they do not know. It is a pretentious role within which the mind flatters the ego. The all knowing preacher, teacher, guru steps out of the soul. A naive figure emerges full of false pride. They overflow. They bask in their own importance ordering villagers to do this and that like colonial masters I have seen, running Hollywood plantations from wooden verandas.

Michael, a 20 year old medical student from somewhere in the USA comes to my house to help me teach conversational English. He starts, "What is your favourite movie?" Nobody can answer.

In the morning the wedding is still going. The guides and their visitors have already departed. They have left a story behind. The guide got drunk. What a bastard. If the story is true, I wonder if he'll be welcomed here again. In the middle of the night he made a public announcement that if the bride would sleep with him he'd give her new husband 500 baht. I can only imagine what these quiet and patient people think of my fellow lowlanders. I am ashamed and angry and ask who he works for.

REFLECTIONS

I tell nobody but I intend to write to the manager with their complaint.

A'sur arrived back this afternoon. He looks tired but his eyes are bright.

The wedding at Saboq's is still going. Many more guests and more provisions than for Bot'u's ceremony. The elders, both men an women, remain ensconced in the house for the whole day.

A'sur tells me that he's done well. He was paid 200 baht for working as a porter for the guide and was given 500 baht by a French couple he had befriended. This is the first time he has had so much money in his pocket and he will give it all to his mother. Now many other young men have decided to take up the study of English seriously.

The day I left the village for a project meeting building materials were beginning to pile up outside A'ja's house. The materials look quite substantial. Wooden posts but mostly bamboo. I stop and talk about how three months ago they'd collected materials to build a house for me. That was before we were friends and I can't stop myself from saying that this guest house will be much better than my dwelling. I am assured that my next house will be well built and strong. I reply that it's too late, I'm already hurt. I need to be honest: I don't mean to be cruel.

It is still early morning when I walk the seven kilometers down the hill to catch a pick-up. It's the 12 August, a good day, no rain and the walk is easy. Coming down it's possible to see much more than on the way up.

In front of me a private movie. Hills running down to the Chiang Rai plain. All is green, quiet, calm.

Tourist Impressions

No, this is not a picture. I am part of what I see. I am also a tourist of sorts, a long-term guest visiting the highlands. I am glad a meeting has been called. I have had enough. I am tired and on an escape route. Where have I been living and why? What have I learned? The *farang* come in search of a reality outside the comfort afforded by their wealth, stumble when the knife falls, collect photos that will attest to their sense of adventure, make friends along the road. How different it is to live the daily reality of poverty. There is nothing romantic about life in an Akha village. No privacy, too much mud and everything is damp. My house is already yielding to gravity. I do not like fleas and sometimes I ache to be alone. Will I be able to face the return?

There is a new shop on the last ridge before the descent into the top northern Thai village. This must be the frontier to some other civilization for there are crates of Coca Cola and soda bottles piled up outside. Four minibuses are parked along the road. The drivers are inside eating. They invite me to join. They're waiting to pick up a group of tourists who are visiting a Mien village in the vicinity. I wait with them to catch a ride down to the bus stop. After one and a half hours the tourists begin to trail in. For ten baht they can get a ride back to town that will only cost me seven.

We're off. Many roads to many hill tribe villages. As we bounce down the road I look back at the Coca Cola bottles and think of pigs, weddings and wealth. I am looking forward to my book shop and comfortable nights spent reading under an electric light bulb.

Appendix I

ตารางที่ สรุปเกี่ยวกับชาวเขาในประเทศไทย - TRIBAL POPULATION SUMMARY

จังหวัด / Province		กะเหรี่ยง / Karen	แม้ว / Meo	มูเซอ / Lahu	ลีซอ / Lisu	เย้า / Yao	อีก้อ / Akha	ล้ว / Lua	ถิ่น / H'tin	ขมุ / Khamu	รวม / Total	แหล่งข้อมูล / Data Source	ปีที่รวบรวม / Year
กาญจนบุรี / Kanchanaburi	*	85	–	–	–	–	–	–	–	–	85	ศูนย์ฯ กาญจนบุรี	2530
	**	2,746	–	–	–	–	–	–	–	–	2,746	Provincial	1987
	***	15,194	–	–	–	–	–	–	–	–	15,194	H.W.D.C.	
กำแพงเพชร / Kamphaeng Phet	*	6	7	5	2	20	2	–	–	–	42	ศูนย์ฯ กำแพงเพชร	2529
	**	145	334	237	148	521	26	–	–	–	1,411	Provincial	1986
	***	701	2,667	1,132	1,107	4,022	142	–	–	–	9,771	H.W.D.C.	
เชียงราย / Chiang Rai	*	32	37	194	38	50	162	6	–	8	(736)1,526	โครงการสำรวจ	2529
	**	1,028	1,986	5,513	1,323	1,522	4,935	266	–	277	16,800	ประชากรชาวเขา	1986
	***	5,483	13,171	28,882	8,119	10,644	28,807	1358	–	1,691	98,105	H.P.S.P.	
เชียงใหม่ / Chiang Mai	*	730	64	172	58	6	24	12	–	–	1,066	โครงการสำรวจ	2529
	**	15,905	1,688	4,051	1,708	130	436	505	–	–	24,423	ประชากรชาวเขา	1986
	***	88,142	14,731	22,684	10,331	1,017	2,411	2,630	–	–	142,946	H.P.S.P.	
ตาก / Tak	*	421	35	7	6	7	1	–	–	–	477	โครงการสำรวจ	2528
	**	9,623	1,798	411	190	82	91	–	–	–	12,195	ประชากรชาวเขา	1986
	***	49,818	14,857	2,298	1,098	635	563	–	–	–	69,269	H.P.S.P.	
น่าน / Nan	*	–	29	–	–	40	–	–	146	20	235	โครงการสำรวจ	2530
	**	–	1,488	9	–	924	–	–	4,800	914	8,135	ประชากรชาวเขา	1987
	***	–	13,528	67	–	7,832	–	–	28,516	5,135	55,078	H.P.S.P.	
ประจวบคีรีขันธ์ / Prachuap Khirikhan	*	1	–	–	–	–	–	–	–	–	1	ศูนย์ฯ กาญจนบุรี	2530
	**	31	–	–	–	–	–	–	–	–	31	Provincial	1987
	***	186	–	–	–	–	–	–	–	–	186	H.W.D.C.	

พิษณุโลก Phitsanulok	* ** ***	— — —	8 766 5,100	— — —	— — —	— — —	— — —	— — —	— — —	— — —	6 422 4,638	โครงการสำรวจ ประปาการชนบท H.P.S.P.	2530 1987
เพชรบุรี Phetchaburi	* ** ***	14 459 2,293	— — —	— — —	— — —	— — —	— — —	— — —	— — —	— — —	14 459 2,293	ศูนย์ฯ กาญจนบุรี Provincial H.W.D.C.	2530 1987
เพชรบูรณ์ Phetchabun	* ** ***	— — —	10 1,118 8,039	1 56 342	3 6	1 35 176	14 76	—	2 8	—	11 1,193 8,471	โครงการสำรวจ ประปาการชนบท H.P.S.P.	2530 1987
พะเยา Phayao	* ** ***	— — —	9 607 4,295	— — —	— — —	1 35	36 891 6,481	—	—	—	46 1,533 10,912	โครงการสำรวจ ประปาการชนบท H.P.S.P.	2529 1986
แพร่ Phrae	* ** ***	14 1661 7720	4 140 1,406	—	—	—	—	1 50 252	—	—	—	19 1,351 9,378	โครงการสำรวจ ประปาการชนบท H.P.S.P.	2530 1987
แม่ฮ่องสอน Mae Hong Son	* ** ***	563 12,690 68,516	16 268 2,487	28 833 4,877	16 592 3,591	—	—	—	18 618 3,619	—	—	641 15,001 83,090	โครงการสำรวจ ประปาการชนบท H.P.S.P.	2530 1987
ราชบุรี Ratchaburi	* ** ***	26 868 4,537	— — —	— — —	—	—	—	—	—	—	26 868 4,537	ศูนย์ฯ กาญจนบุรี Provincial H.W.D.C.	2530 1987
ลำปาง Lampang	* ** ***	24 604 3,158	7 121 880	5 95 425	4 6 28	36 576 4,222	9 135 691	2 2	—	4 29 140	89 1,568 9,516	โครงการสำรวจ ประปาการชนบท H.P.S.P.	2530 1987
ลำพูน Lampun	* ** ***	62 4,314 21,280	— — —	— — —	—	—	—	—	—	—	62 4,314 21,280	โครงการสำรวจ ประปาการชนบท H.P.S.P.	2530 1987
เลย Loei	* ** ***	— — —	1 89 500	— — —	—	—	—	—	—	—	1 89 500	โครงการสำรวจ ประปาการชนบท H.P.S.P.	2530

		Karen กะเหรี่ยง	Meo แม้ว	Lahu มูเซอ	Lisu ลีซอ	Yao เย้า	Akha อีก้อ	Lua ลัวะ	H'tin ถิ่น	Khamu ขมุ	Total รวม
ยอดหมู่บ้าน/Tot. Villages	*	2,015	230	411	128	204	194	41	146	34	3,408
ยอดหลังคาเรือน/Tot. H/Holds.	**	50,778	10,459	11,152	4,103	4,814	5,673	1,440	4,802	1,274	94,495
ยอดประชากร/Tot. Persons	***	270,803	82,310	60,321	25,051	36,140	32,866	1,845	28,524	7,284	551,144
ร้อยละ/Percentage		49.13	14.93	10.94	4.55	6.56	5.96	1.42	5.18	1.32	100

ศูนย์ฯ : ศูนย์พัฒนาและสงเคราะห์ชาวเขา

H.W.D.C. : Hill Tribe Welfare and Development Centre

H.P.S.P. : Hill Tribe Population Survey Project

* **จำนวนหมู่บ้าน** : No. of Villages

** **จำนวนหลังคาเรือน** : No. of Households

*** **จำนวนประชากร** : No. of Persons

หมายเหตุ

1. ยอดรวมยกเว้นชาวเขาใน จ.เชียงใหม่ไม่รวมเผ่า "ปะหล่อง" ซึ่งเพิ่งอพยพเข้ามาจำนวน 4 หมู่บ้าน 90 หลังคาเรือน 485 คน
   The total population of Chiang Mai Province excludes the "Palong" who recently moved into Thailand and established 4 villages, consisting of 90 households and 485 persons.

2. ยอดรวมยกเว้นชาวเขาใน จ.น่าน ไม่รวมมะลาบิดองเหลือง จำนวน 138 คน
   The total population of Nan Province excludes 109 Mlabri who make up 26 households.

3. ยอดรวมยกเว้นชาวเขาในจังหวัดแพร่ไม่รวมมะลาบิดองเหลืองจำนวน 34 คนจอย 7 ครัวเรือน
   The total population of Phrae Province excludes 34 Mlabri who make up 7 households.

รวบรวมโดย : งานข้อมูลและแผนที่
ฝ่ายบริการและเผยแพร่
สถาบันวิจัยชาวเขา
จ.เชียงใหม่ 50002

กันยายน 2531
September 1988

Prepared by : Service and Publicity Section
Tribal Research Institute
Chiang Mai, Thailand
50002

Appendix II
List of Swidden Plants

SCIENTIFIC NAME	COMMON NAME	USE
F. ALLIACEAE (LILIACEAE)		
Allium ascalonicum L.	SHALLOT	vegetable ceremonial medicinal
Allium chinense G.Don	CHINESE CHIVES	vegetable preserved ceremonial
Allium porrum L.	LEEK	vegetable
Allium sativum L.	GARLIC	condiment vegetable
Allium schoenoprasum L.	CHIVES	vegetable
F. AMARANTHACEAE		
Amaranthus caudatus L.	GRAIN AMARANTH	animal feed
Celosia argentea L.	COCKSCOMB	ornamental ceremonial medicinal
Celosia sp.	COCKSCOMB	vegetable ornamental
Gomphrena globosa L.	GLOBE AMARANTH	ornamental ceremonial
F. ARACEAE		
Amorphophallus sp.	BOOG (LOCAL)	vegetable
Colocasia esculenta Schott	TARO	ed. root ceremonial

APPENDIX II

Xanthosoma sagittifolium Schott	COCOYAM	rice substitute animal feed ed. root rice substitute |ыш

F. BASELLACEAE
Basella alba L. — EAST INDIAN SPINACH — vegetable, medicinal

F. BROMELIACEAE
Ananas comosus (L.) Merr. — PINEAPPLE — fruit, medicinal

F. CANNABINACEAE
Cannabis sativa L. — HEMP — fibre, medicinal

F. CANNACEAE
Canna edulis Ker. — AUSTRALIAN ARROWROOT — vegetable, ed. root

F. CARICACEAE
Carica papaya L. — PAPAYA — fruit, animal feed, medicinal

F. COMPOSITAE (ASTERACEAE)
Carthamus tinctorius L. — SAFFLOWER — dye, ceremonial

Cosmos caudatus HBK — BURMESE MARIGOLD (LOCAL) — vegetable, ceremonial, ornamental

Cosmos sulphureus Cav. — COSMOS FLOWER — ornamental, vegetable, ceremonial

Helianthus annuus L. — SUNFLOWER — ed. seed
Lactuca sativa L. — LETTUCE — vegetable
Lactuca sativa L. var. asparagina Bailey — ASPARAGUS LETTUCE — vegetable

Spilanthes acmella Murr.	PARA CRESS	vegetable medicinal
Spilanthes sp.	——————	medicinal
Tagetes erecta L.	AFRICAN MARIGOLD	ornamental ceremonial
Tagetes patula L.	MARIGOLD	ornamental ceremonial
F. CONVOLVULACEAE		
Ipomoea batatas Lamk.	SWEET POTATO	ed. tuber animal feed rice substitute medicinal
F. CRUCIFERAE (BRASSICACEAE)		
Brassica alboglabra Bailey	CHINESE KALE	vegetable
Brassica chinensis L.	CHINESE CABBAGE	vegetable
Brassica juncea Czern & Coss.	CHINESE MUSTARD	vegetable preserved ceremonial
Brassica napus L.	SWEDISH TURNIP	vegetable
Brassica oleracea L.	CABBAGE	vegetable
Raphanus sativus L.	RADISH	vegetable
F. CUCURBITACEAE		
Benincasa hispida Cogn.	WAX GOURD	vegetable
Citrullus lanatus (Thunb.) Mansf.	WATER MELON	fruit vegetable
Cucumis melo L.	MELON	fruit vegetable
Cucumis sativus L.	COMMON CUCUMBER	vegetable fruit
Cucurbita moschata Duch.	PUMPKIN	vegetable ceremonial ed. seed
Cucurbita pepo L.	MARROW	vegetable ed. seed

APPENDIX II

Lagenaria siceraria Standl.	BOTTLE GOURD	
cv. large	BOTTLE GOURD	ceremonial utensil
cv. medium	BOTTLE GOURD	utensil vegetable
cv. small	BOTTLE GOURD	decoration
Luffa acutangula Roxb.	ANGLED LOOFAH	vegetable
Luffa cylindrica Roem.	SMOOTHED LOOFAH	vegetable utensil filter
Momordica charantia L.	BITTER GOURD	vegetable
Sechium edule Sw.	CHAYOTE	vegetable
Trichosanthes anguina L.	SNAKE GOURD	vegetable
Trichosanthes cucumerina L.	BAA NOI CHAA (LOCAL)	vegetable

F. DIOSCOREACEAE

Dioscorea alata L.	GREATER YAM	ed. root rice substitute
Dioscorea bulbifera L.	AERIAL YAM	ed. bulbils rice substitute
Dioscorea cayenensis Lam.	YELLOW GUINEA YAM	ed. root rice substitute
Dioscorea esculenta Burk.	LESSER YAM	ed. root rice substitute
Dioscorea opposita Thunb.	CHINESE YAM	ed. root rice substitute

F. EUPHORBIACEAE

Manihot esculenta Crantz	CASSAVA	ed. tuber
Ricinus communis L.	CASTOR BEAN	cash crop medicinal

F. GRAMINEAE (POACEAE)

Coix lachryma - jobi L.	JOB'S TEARS	cereal
Coix lachryma - jobi L. var. *stenocarpa* Stapf	JOB'S TEARS	decoration

Swidden Plants

Coix puellarum Bal.	JOB'S TEARS	decoration
Coix sp.	POP JOB'S TEARS	cereal
Cymbopogon citratus Stapf	LEMON GRASS	condiment
Eleusine coracana Gaertn.	FINGER MILLET	cereal
		liquor
		ceremonial
Oryza sativa L.	RICE	
cv. early, medium, yearly	NON-GLUTINOUS	cereal
		medicinal
		liquor
		ceremonial
		animal feed
cv. early, medium, yearly	GLUTINOUS	cereal
		liquor
		ceremonial
		animal feed
Saccharum arundinaceum Retz.	SUGAR CANE	ed. stem
Saccharum officinarum L.	SUGAR CANE	ed. stem
		sugar
		cash crop
Setaria italica Beauv.	FOX-TAIL MILLET	cereal
		cash crop
		liquor
Sorghum vulgare Pers.	SORGHUM	cereal
		liquor
		ceremonial
Sorghum nervosum Bess. ex. Schult.	KAOLIANG	ed. stem
		liquor
Triticum aestivum L.	WHEAT	decoration
Zea mays L.	MAIZE	
cv. early & yearly	NON-GLUTINOUS	animal feed
		cereal
		liquor
		ceremonial
		construction
		rice substitute

APPENDIX II

cv. early & yearly	GLUTINOUS	rice substitute cereal ceremonial
Zea mays L. var. *everata* Sturt.	POPCORN	cereal

F. LABIATAE (LAMIACEAE)

Isodon ternifolius Kudo	PAAK E LUEN (LOCAL)	cul. herb.
Mentha arvensis L.	MINT	cul. herb.
Mentha cordifolia Opiz.	KITCHEN MINT	cul. herb.
Mesona sp.	————	cul. herb.
Ocimum basilicum L.	SWEET BASIL	cul. herb.
Ocimum canum Sims.	HOARY BASIL, HAIRY BASIL	cul. herb. ceremonial
Ocimum sanctum L.	HOLY BASIL	cul. herb. medicinal
Perilla frutescens Britt.	SUTTSU	cereal

F. MALVACEAE

Grossypium spp.	COTTON	fibre ceremonial
Hibiscus esculentus L. (*Abelmoschus esculentus* Moench)	OKRA	vegetable

F. MARANTACEAE

Maranta arundinacea L.	WEST INDIAN ARROW-ROOT	ed. root

F. MUSACEAE

Musa nana Lour.	DWARF BANANA	fruit fibre medicinal
Musa sapientum L.	BANANA	fruit animal feed medicinal fibre

F. PAPAVERACEAE
Papaver somniferum L.   OPIUM-POPPY   cash crop
oil
medicinal
narcotic
vegetable
ed. seed
ceremonial

F. PAPILIONACEAE

Arachis hypogaea L.	PEANUT	ed. seed
Cajanus cajan Millsp.	PIGEON PEA	vegetable
		ed. seed
		animal feed
Dolichos purpureus (L.) Sweet		
cv. black seed	HYACINTH BEAN	vegetable
cv. white seed	HYACINTH BEAN	vegetable
		ed. seed
Glycine max Merr.	SOYBEAN	ed. seed, curd
cv. early & late		preserved
		condiment
		ceremonial
Pachyrrhizus erosus (L.) Urban	YAM BEAN	ed. tuber
		vegetable
Phaseolus lunatus L.		
var. *macrocarpus* Benth.	LIMA BEAN	ed. seed
		vegetable
Phaseolus vulgaris L.	COMMON BEAN	vegetable
		ed. seed
Pisum sativum L.		
cv. small pod	PEA	vegetable
Psophocarpus tetragonolobus DC.	WINGED BEAN	vegetable
Vicia faba L.	BROAD BEAN	vegetable
		ed. seed

APPENDIX II

Vigna mungo (L.) Hepper	BLACK GRAM	ed. seed
Vigna radiata (L.) Wilczek	GREEN GRAM	ed. seed
Vigna umbellata (Thunb.) Ohwi & Ohashi	RICE BEAN	vegetable ed. seed cover crop
Vigna unguiculata (L.) Walp.	COW PEA	vegetable ceremonial
Vigna unguiculata (L.) Walp. subsp. *sesquipedialis* (L.) Verc.	YARDLONG BEAN ASPARAGUS PEA	vegetable

F. PEDALIACEAE

Sesamum indicum L.	SESAME	oil ed. seed ceremonial

F. POLYGONACEAE

Polygonum odoratum Lour.	PAAK PAI (LOCAL)	cul. herb medicinal

F. ROSACEAE

Prunus persica Batsch	PEACH	ed. fruit medicinal

F. SOLANACEAE

Capsicum annuum L. var. *acuminatum* Fingerh.	CHILLI SPUR PEPPER	cash crop condiment vegetable
Capsicum frutescens L.	BIRD PEPPER	condiment cash crop utensil vegetable
Capsicum frutescens L. var. fasciculatum (Sturt.) Irish	CLUSTER PEPPER	condiment vegetable
Lycopersicon escutentum Mill.	TOMATO	vegetable

Swidden Plants

Nicotiana tabacum L.	TOBACCO	narcotic medicinal
Solanum aculeatissimum Jacq.	COCKROACH BERRY	vegetable
Solanum incanum L.	COCKROACH BERRY	vegetable
Solanum melongena L.	EGG PLANT	vegetable
Solanum torvum Sw.	SUSUMBER	vegetable
Solanum tuberosum L.	POTATO	ed. tuber rice substitute
Solanum sp.	BITTER EGGPLANT	vegetable

F. UMBELLIFERAE (APIACEAE)

Coriandrum sativum L.	CORIANDER	cul. herb vegetable
Cuminum cyminum L.	CUMIN	cul. herb medicinal
Eryngium foetidum L.	PAAKCHEE FAARAANG (LOCAL)	cul. herb
Foeniculum vulgare Mill.	FENNEL	vegetable cul. herb medicinal
Heracleum burmanicum Kurz.	MAA LAB (LOCAL)	condiment
Oenanthe stolonifera Wall. (O. javanica DC.)	ORIENTAL CELERY	cul. herb
Petroselinum crispum (Mill.) Nym. ex A.W. Hill	PARSLEY	cul. herb

F. URTICACEAE

Boehmeria nivea Gaud.	RAMIE	fibre

APPENDIX II

F. ZINGIBERACEAE

Curcuma domestica Valeton	TURMERIC	dye
		ceremonial
		medicinal
		condiment
Kaempferia sp.	WAAN (LOCAL)	medicinal
Zingiber officinale Rosc.	GINGER	vegetable
		ceremonial
		medicinal
Zingiber sp.	GINGER (SMALL)	ceremonial

Appendix III
List of Non-swidden Plants

SCIENTIFIC NAME	COMMON NAME	USE
F. ACANTHACEAE		
Baphicacanthus cusia Brem.	HOM (LOCAL)	dye
		medicinal
Graptophyllum pictum Griff.	CARICATURE PLANT	ornamental
Rhinacanthus nasutus (L.) Kurz	THONG PAAN CHAANG (LOCAL)	ornamental medicinal
Strobilanthes sp.	─────	ornamental
		medicinal
		weaving
F. AGAVACEAE		
Agave sisalana Perr.	SISAL HEMP	medicinal
Cordyline fruticosa Goppert.	MAAK POO (LOCAL)	vegetable
Cordyline sp.	─────	ornamental
Sansevieria trifasciata Prain.	BOWSTRING HEMP	medicinal
F. ALLIACEAE (LILIACEAE)		
Allium cepa L. var. *aggregatum* G. Don.	MULTIPLIER ONION	vegetable
Allium fistulosum L.	WELSH ONION	vegetable
F. AMARANTHACEAE		
Celosia argentea L. var. *cristata* Ktze.	COCKSCOMB	ornamental
		medicinal
F. AMARYLLIDACEAE (LILIACEAE)		
Crinum amabile Don	RED CRINUM	ornamental

APPENDIX III

Crinum asiaticum L.	CAPE LILY	ornamental medicinal
Crinum spp.	SPIDER LILY	ornamental medicinal
Haemanthus multiflorus Martyn	BLOOD FLOWER	ornamental
Hippeastrum johnsonii Bury	BARBADOS LILY	ornamental
Hippeastrum spp.	WAAN SI TIS (LOCAL)	ornamental

F. ANACARDIACEAE

Bouea oppositifolia Meissn.	MARIAN PLUM	ed. fruit
Mangifera indica L.	MANGO	ed. fruit
Mangifera lagenifera Griff.	MANGO	ed. fruit
Mangifera odorata Griff.	MANGO	ed. fruit
Spondias pinnata Kurz	HOG PLUM	ed. fruit vegetable medicinal

F. ANNONACEAE

Annona reticulata L.	CUSTARD APPLE	ed. fruit
Annona squamosa L.	SWEET SOP	ed. fruit

F. APOCYNACEAE

Adenium obesum Balf.	IMPALA LILY	ornamental
Allamanda carthartica L.	ALLAMANDA	ornamental
Catharanthus roseus G. Don	WEST INDIAN PERIWINKLE	ornamental
Ervatamia coronaria Stapf	EAST INDIAN ROSEBAY	ornamental
Nerium indicum Mill.	OLEANDER	ornamental
Plumeria acutifolia Poir.	FRANGIPANI	ornamental
Thevetia peruviana Schum.	TRUMPET FLOWER	ornamental medicinal

F. ARACEAE

Acorus calamus L.	SWEET FLAG	medicinal

Non Swidden Plants

Alocasia indica Schott	KRAADAAD, (LOCAL)	ceremonial medicinal
Alocasia lindenii Rod.	SAANEH CHAAN KHAO (LOCAL)	ornamental
Alocasia macrorrhiza Schott	ELEPHANT EAR	ornamental
Alocasia sp.	———	ceremonial
Anthurium andraeanum Lind.	ANTHURIUM	ornamental medicinal
Anthurium scherzerianum Schott	ANTHURIUM	ornamental
Caladium bicolor Vent.	BON SEE (LOCAL)	ornamental
Dieffenbachia seguine Schott	DUMB CANE	ornamental
Homalomena rubescens Kunth	SAANEH CHAAN DAENG (LOCAL)	ornamental
Lasia spinosa Thw.	PAAK NAAM (LOCAL)	vegetable

F. ARAUCARIACEAE

Araucaria bidwillii Hook.	BUNYA BUNYA	medicinal

F. ASCLEPIADACEAE

Calotropis gigantea R. Br.	CROWN FLOWER	medicinal
Gymnema inodorum Decne.	PAAK SHIANG DAA (LOCAL)	vegetable
Marsdenia tinctoria R.Br.	KRAAM THAO (LOCAL)	dye
Marsdenia sp.	———	dye
Telosma minor Craib	COWSLIP CREEPER	ornamental vegetable

F. AVERRHOACEAE (OXALIDACEAE)

Averrhoa carambola L.	CARAMBOLA	ed. fruit

F. BALSAMINACEAE

Impatiens balsamina L.	GARDEN BALSAMINE	ornamental medicinal

APPENDIX III

F. BIGNONIACEAE

Jacaranda filicifolia D.Don	SEE TRANG (LOCAL)	ornamental medicinal
Oroxylum indicum Vent.	INDIAN TRUMPET FLOWER	vegetable medicinal
Pachyptera hymenaea A. Gentry	GARLIC VINE	ornamental medicinal
Spathodea campanulata Beauv.	AFRICAN TULIP TREE	ornamental
Tecoma stans HBK	YELLOW ELDER	ornamental

F. BOMBACACEAE

Ceiba pentandra Gaertn.	KAPOK	fibre
Durio zibethinus L.	DURIAN	ed. fruit

F. BURSERACEAE

Garuga pinnata Roxb.	TAA KHRAAM (LOCAL)	medicine

F. CACTACEAE

Cereus hexagonus Mill.	TORCH THISTLE	ornamental
Gereus peruvianus Haw.	HEDGE CACTUS	fencing

F. CAESALPINIACEAE

Caesalpinia pulcherrima Sw.	PEACOCK'S CREST	ornamental
Cassia alata L.	RINGWORM BUSH	medicinal
Cassia occidentalis L.	COFFEE SENNA	medicinal
Tamarindus indica L.	TAMARIND	ed. fruit condiment medicinal

F. CANNABINACEAE

Cannabis sativa L.	MARIJUANA	medicinal condiment

F. CANNACEAE

Canna indica L.	INDIAN SHOT	ornamental

Non Swidden Plants

F. CAPPARIDACEAE (CAPPARACEAE)
Capparis sp. ——— vegetable
medicinal

F. CHLORANTHACEAE
Chloranthus officinalis Bl. HOM KLAI (LOCAL) ornamental

F. CLEOMACEAE (CAPPARIDACEAE)
Cleome gynandra L. WILD SPIDER FLOWER vegetable

F. COMBRETACEAE
Quisaqualis indica L. RANGOON CREEPER ornamental

F. COMMELINACEAE
Zebrina pendula Schnizl. KAAMPOO LOOT ornamental
(LOCAL)

F. COMPOSITAE (ASTERACEAE)
Artemisia dubia Wall. ex Bess. PAAK HIA (LOCAL) medicinal
Aster cordifolius L. SILVER LEAF ornamental
Bidens bipinnata L. MEXICAN DAISY ornamental
Chrysanthemum morifolium CHRYSANTHEMUM ornamental
Ramat.
Chrysanthemum sp. ——— medicinal
Dahlia pinnata Cav. GARDEN DAHLIA ornamental
Gerbera jamesonii Bolus ex. TRANSVAL DAISY ornamental
Hook.
Helichrysum bracteatum And. STRAW FLOWER ornamental
Tithonia diversifolia A. Gray MEXICAN SUNFLOWER ornamental
WEED medicinal
Zinnia elegans Jacq. ZINNIA ornamental

F. CONVOLVULACEAE
Ipomoea aquatica Forsk. WATER vegetable
CONVOLVULUS

F. CRASSULACEAE
Kalanchoe pinnata Pers. AIR PLANT ornamental
medicinal
Kalanchoe sp. ——— ornamental

441

APPENDIX III

F. CUCURBITACEAE

Coccinia grandis Voigt	IVY GOURD	vegetable

F. ELAEAGNACEAE

Elaeagnus latifolia L.	BAA LOD (LOCAL)	ed. fruit ceremonial

F. ELAEOCARPACEAE

Muntingia calabura L.	MANILA CHERRY	ed. fruit, shade

F. EUPHORBIACEAE

Acalypha hispida Burm.f.	RED HOT CAT'S TAIL	ornamental medicinal
Baccaurea ramiflora Lour. (*B. sapida* Muell. Arg.)	RAMBEH	ed. fruit
Codiaeum variegatum Bl.	CROTON	ornamental
Euphorbia milii des Moulins	CROWN OF THORNS	ornamental
Euphorbia pulcherrima Willd.	POINSETTIA	ornamental
Jatropha curcas L.	PHYSIC NUT	fencing medicinal
Pedilanthus smallii Millsp.	SAAYAEK BAI YIK (LOCAL)	ornamental
Pedilanthus tithymaloides Poit.	SLIPPER PLANT	ornamental
Phyllanthus acidus Skeels	STAR GOOSEBERRY	ed. fruit
Sauropus androgynus Merr.	PAAK WAAN BAAN (LOCAL)	vegetable

F. GRAMINEAE (POACEAE)

Bambusa arundinacea Willd.	BAMBOO	many
Bambusa blumeana Schult.	BAMBOO	many
Bambusa natans Wall.	BAMBOO	many
Bambusa tulda Roxb.	BAMBOO	many
Cephalostachyum pergracile Munro	BAMBOO	many
Cephalostachyum virgatum Kurz	BAMBOO	many

Non Swidden Plants

Cymbopogon nardus Rendle	CITRONELLA GRASS	condiment
Dendrocalamus asper Back.	BAMBOO	many
Dendrocalamus brandisii Kurz	BAMBOO	many
Dendrocalamus hamiltonii Nees	BAMBOO	many
Dendrocalamus membranaceus Munro	BAMBOO	many
Dendrocalamus strictus Nees	BAMBOO	many
Thyrsostachys oliveri Gamble	BAMBOO	many
Thyrsostachys siamensis Gamble	BAMBOO	many
Zizania latifolia Turcz.	MANCHURIA WATERRICE	vegetable

F. HYDRANGEACEAE (CAPRIFOLIACEAE)

Hydrangea macrophylla Ser.	HYDRANGIA	ornamental

F. LABIATAE (LAMIACEAE)

Coleus amboinicus Lour.	INDIAN BORAGE	vegetable
Coleus atropurpureus Benth.	COLEUS	ornamental
Orthosiphon grandiflorus Bolding	PAAYAAP MEK (LOCAL)	medicinal ornamental

F. LILIACEAE

Aloe barbadensis Mill.	STAR CACTUS	medicinal
Chlorophytum elatum R. Br.	WAAN SETHEE RUEN NOK (LOCAL)	ornamental
Chlorophytum elatum R. Br. var. vittatum	SPIDER PLANT	ornamental
Yucca gloriosa L.	SPANISH DAGGER	ornamental medicinal

F. LYTHRACEAE

Lagerstroemia indica L.	CRAPE MYRTLE	ornamental

F. MAGNOLIACEAE

Talauma candollei Bl.	YEE HOOP (LOCAL)	ornamental

APPENDIX III

F. MALVACEAE

Hibiscus cannabinus L.	KENAF	fibre
Hibiscus mutabilis L.	CHANGEABLE ROSE	ornamental
Hibiscus rosa - sinensis L.	SHOE FLOWER	ornamental
Hibiscus sabdariffa L.	ROSELLE	vegetable condiment
Hibiscus schizopetalus Hook. f.	FRINGED HIBISCUS	ornamental
Hibiscus syriacus L.	ROSE OF SHARON	ornamental
Sida acuta Burm.	YAA KHAAD MON (LOCAL)	utensil medicinal

F. MARANTACEAE

Calathea ornata Koehne	WAAN NOKE YOONG TUA MEER (LOCAL)	ornamental
Calathea veitchiana Hook. f.	WAAN NOKE YOONG (LOCAL)	ornamental
Maranta arundinacea L. var. variegata Hort.	SAAKOO DAANG (LOCAL)	ornamental

F. MELIACEAE

Sandoricum koetjape Merr.	SANTOL	ed. fruit

F. MENISPERMACEAE

Tinospora crispa Miers ex. Hook f. & Thoms.	CHUNG CHAA LING (LOCAL)	medicinal
Tinospora glabra Merr.	CHUNG CHAA LING (LOCAL)	medicinal

F. MIMOSACEAE

Acacia farnesiana Willd.	SPONGE TREE	ornamental
Acacia pennata Willd. subsp. insauvis Nielsen.	CHA-OM (LOCAL)	vegetable
Acacia rugata Merr.	SOM POI (LOCAL)	vegetable ceremonial
Leucaena leucocephala de Wit	LEUCAENA	vegetable
Neptunia oleracea Lour.	EDIBLE WATER MIMOSA	vegetable medicinal
Pithecellobium dulce Benth.	MANILA TAMARIND	ed. fruit

Non Swidden Plants

F. MORACEAE
Artocarpus heterophyllus Lam.	JACK FRUIT	ed. fruit
Morus indica L.	MULBERRY	ed. fruit

F. MORINGACEAE
Moringa oleifera Lam.	HORSE RADISH TREE	vegetable

F. MYRISTICACEAE
Myristica fragrans Houtt.	NUTMEG TREE	medicinal

F. MYRTACEAE
Eugenia caryophyllus Bullock & Harrison.	CLOVE	medicinal
Eugenia malaccensis L.	MALAY APPLE	ed. fruit
Psidium guajava L.	GUAVA	ed. fruit medicinal

F. NYCTAGINACEAE
Bougainvillea spectabilis Willd.	PAPER FLOWER	ornamental
Mirabilis jalapa L.	4 O'CLOCK FLOWER	ornamental
Pisonia grandis R.Br.	LETTUCE TREE	ornamental

F. OLEACEAE
Jasminum sambac Ait.	JASMINE	ornamental

F. ORCHIDACEAE
Ascocentrum curvifolium Schltr.	UEANG KHEM DAENG (LOCAL)	ornamental
Dendrobium chrysotoxum Lindl.	UEANG KHAAM (LOCAL)	ornamental
Dendrobium lindleyi Steud.	UEANG PHUENG (LOCAL)	ornamental
Dendrobium spp.	———	ornamental ceremonial
Rhynchostylis gigantea Ridl.	CHAANG KRAA (LOCAL)	ornamental
Vanda coerulea Griff.	FAA MUI (LOCAL)	ornamental

APPENDIX III

F. PALMAE (ARECACEAE)

Areca catechu L.	BETELNUT PALM	masticatory medicinal
Calamus rudentum Roxb.	RATTAN	vegetable construction
Calamus spp.	RATTAN	vegetable construction
Cocos nucifera L.	COCONUT	ed. fruit utensil

F. PANDANACEAE

Pandanus amaryllifolius Roxb.	TOEI HOM (LOCAL)	condiment beverage

F. PAPILIONACEAE

Canavalia ensiformis (L.) DC.	JACK BEAN HORSE BEAN	vegetable
Canavalia gladiata (Jacq.) DC.	SWORD BEAN	vegetable
Clitoria ternatea L.	BLUE PEA, BUTTERFLY PEA	ornamental
Crotalaria pallida Ait.	HING MEN (LOCAL)	medicinal
Gliricidia sepium (Jacq.) Steud.	NICARAGUAN COCOA SHADE	ornamental
Indigofera tinctoria L.	INDIGO	dye
Sesbania grandiflora (L.) Poir.	SESBAN	vegetable

F. PASSIFLORACEAE

Passiflora quadrangularis L.	GIANT GRANADILIA	vegetable ed. fruit

F. PIPERACEAE

Piper betle L.	BETEL PEPPER	masticatory ceremonial cash crop medicinal
Piper chaba Hunt	DEE PLEE (LOCAL)	medicinal
Piper sarmentosum Roxb.	WILDBETAL-LEAF BUSH	vegetable

Non Swidden Plants

F. PLUMBAGINACEAE
    Plumbago indica L.   ROSY LEADWORT   medicinal
    Plumbago zeylanica L.   WHITE LEADWORT   medicinal

F. POLYGONACEAE
    Fagopyrum esculentum Moench   BUCKWHEAT   cereal
    Rumex crispus L.   YELLOW DOCK   vegetable

F. POLYPODIACEAE
    Platycerium wallichii Hook. f.   STAGHORN FERN   ornamental
    medicinal

F. PORTULACACEAE
    Portulaca grandiflora Hook. f.   PORTULACA ROSE, MOSS ROSE   ornamental
    Talinum paniculatum Gaertn.   WAAN PAAK PLANG (LOCAL), FAME FLOWER   vegetable medicinal

F. PUNICACEAE
    Punica granatum L.   POMEGRANATE   ed. fruit medicinal

F. RHAMNACEAE
    Zizyphus mauritiana Lam.   INDIAN JUJUBE   ed. fruit

F. ROSACEAE
    Rosa chinensis Jacq.
    var. minima Voss   FAIRY ROSE   ornamental
    Rosa damascena Mill.   DAMASK-ROSE   ornamental vegetable

F. RUBIACEAE
    Gardenia jasminoides Ellis   GARDENIA   ornamental
    Ixora sp.   KHEM (LOCAL)   ornamental
    Morinda citrifolia L.   INDIAN MULBERRY   vegetable
    Morinda coreia Ham.   YOR PAA (LOCAL)   weaving
    Mussaenda erythrophylla Schum. & Thonn.   RED MUSSAENDA   ornamental

APPENDIX III

Mussaenda philippica A.Rich.
var. donya-aurora Sulit   WHITE MUSSAENDA   ornamental

F. RUTACEAE
Aegle marmelos Corr.   INDIAN BAEL   ed. fruit
                                            medicinal

Citrus aurantifolia Swing.   LIME   condiment
                                             medicinal

Citrus hystrix DC.   LEECH LIME,   condiment
                          KAFFER LIME
Citrus maxima Merr.   PUMMELO   ed. fruit
Citrus medica L.   CITRON   vegetable
Citrus reticulata Blanco   ORANGE   ed. fruit
Citrus sinensis Osb.   SWEET ORANGE   ed. fruit
Murraya paniculata Jack   ORANGE JASMINE ornamental

F. SAMBUCACEAE (CAPRIFOLIACEAE)
Sambucus simpsonii Rehd.   AMERICAN ELDER   ornamental
                                              medicinal

F. SAPINDACEAE
Dimocarpus longan Lour.   LONGAN   ed. fruit
Sapindus rarak A. DC.   SOAP NUT TREE   soap
                                            shampoo

F. SAPOTACEAE
Manilkara kauki Dubard   THAI SAPODILLA   ed. fruit
                           PLUM

F. SAURURACEAE
Houttuynia cordata Thunb.   PAAK COW TONG   vegetable
                              (LOCAL)

F. SOLANACEAE
Cestrum nocturnum L.   QUEEN OF THE   ornamental
                          NIGHT
Nicotiana tabacum L.   TOBACCO   medicinal
Solanum indicum L.   SPARROW'S BRINJAL vegetable
                                            medicinal

Non Swidden Plants

Solanum stramonifolium Jacq.	MAA EUK (LOCAL)	condiment

F. STERCULIACEAE

Sterculia guttata Roxb.	GOLDAR	fibre

F. STRELITZIACEAE

Strelitzia reginae Banks	BIRD OF PARADISE	ornamental

F. THEACEAE (TERNSTROEMIACEAE)

Camellia sinensis Ktze.	TEA	beverage
		vegetable
		masticatory
		cash crop
		medicinal

F. TRAPACEAE

Trapa bicornis Osb.	WATER CHESTNUT	medicinal
		ed. fruit

F. UMBELLIFERAE (APIACEAE)

Centella asiatica Urban	ASIATIC PENNYWORT	vegetable
		medicinal

F. VERBENACEAE

Lantana camara L.	CLOTH OF GOLD	ornamental
Verbena erinoides Lamk.	MOSS VERBENA	ornamental
Verbena sp.	VERBENA	ornamental

F. ZINGIBERACEAE

Alpinia spp.	———	vegetable
		medicinal
Amomum krervanh Pierre	SIAM CARDAMOM	cash crop
Boesenbergia pandurata Holtt.	KAEMPFER	condiment
		medicinal
Curcuma sp.	TRUMERIC	dye
		medicinal
		condiment
		ceremonial
Languas galanga (L.) Stuntz	GARANGAL	condiment

APPENDIX III

Zingiber cassumunar Roxb.	CASSUMUNAR GINGER	ceremonial medicinal
Zingiber ottensii Valeton	PLAI DAAM (LOCAL)	medicinal ceremonial

Appendix IV
List of Some Exotic Plants Introduced into the Highlands.

FAMILY & SCIENTIFIC NAME	COMMON NAME	USE
F. ACANTHACEAE		
Thunbergia spp.	———	ornamental
F. ACTINIDIACEAE		
Actinidia chinensis Planch.	KIWI FRUIT, CHINESE GOOSEBERRY	ed. fruit
F. ALLIACEAE (LILIACEAE)		
Allium aflatunense B. Fedtsch.	———	ornamental
Allium cepa L.	ONION	vegetable
Allium fistulosum L. cv. *Japanese*	JAPANESE ONION	vegetable
F. ALSTROEMERIACEAE		
Alstroemeria aurantiaca D. Don	PERUVIAN LILY	ornamental
F. AMARANTHACEAE		
Amaranthus caudatus L. cv. hybrid	AMARANTHUS	ornamental
Amaranthus tricolor L.	JOSEPH'S COAT	vegetable
Celosia cristata Ktze.	CRESTED CELOSIA, COCKSCOMB	ornamental
Celosia plumosa (syn. *C. pyramidalis* Burm. f.)	PLUMED CELOSIA, WOOL FLOWER	ornamental
F. AMARYLLIDACEAE (LILIACEAE)		
Haemanthus spp.	———	ornamental
Hippeastrum spp.	AMARYLLIS	ornamental

APPENDIX IV

F. ANACARDIACEAE
Anacardium occidentale L. CASHEW NUT nut, vegetable

Mangifera indica L.
cv. *heo maan* (local) MANGO ed. fruit
cv. *hongsa* (local) MANGO ed. fruit
cv. *keo luem raang* (local) MANGO ed. fruit
cv. *khiao saawoei* (local) MANGO ed. fruit
cv. *naam dok mai* (local) MANGO ed. fruit
cv. *ngaa* (local) MANGO ed. fruit
cv. *nong saeng* (local) MANGO ed. fruit
cv. *oakrong khiao* (local) MANGO ed. fruit
cv. *oakrong thong* (local) MANGO ed. fruit
cv. *pimsen maan* (local) MANGO ed. fruit
cv. *praayaa saawoei* (local) MANGO ed. fruit
cv. *rad maan* (local) MANGO ed. fruit
cv. *saam pee* (local) MANGO ed. fruit
cv. *suan thip* (local) MANGO ed. fruit
cv. *taalaap naag* (local) MANGO ed. fruit
cv. *thong daam* (local) MANGO ed. fruit
Pistacia vera L. PISTACHIO NUT nut
Spondias cytherea Sonn. OTAHEITE APPLE ed. fruit

F. ANNOACEAE
Annona cherimolia Mill. CHERIMOYA ed. fruit

F. APOCYNACEAE
Rauvolfia serpentina Benth. ex Kurz SERPENT WOOD medicinal

F. ARACEAE
Zantedeschia aethiopica Spreng. CALLA LILY, ARUM LILY ornamental

Zantedeschia albo- maculata (Hook.) Baill. ornamental

Zantedeschia elliotiana YELLOW ARUM LILY ornamental

Exotic Plants

Zantedeschia hybrida cv. *dwarf pink*	———	ornamental
F. *ARALIACEAE*		
Panax ginseng C.A. Meyer	GINSENG	herb.
Panax quinquefolia L.	AMERICAN GINSENG	herb.
F. AZOLLACEAE		
Azolla bicol	AZOLLA	green manure
Azolla caroliniana Willd.	AZOLLA	green manure
Azolla filiculoides Lam.	AZOLLA	green manure
Azolla mexicana Presl	AZOLLA	green manure
Azolla microphylla Kaulf.	AZOLLA	green manure
Azolla pinnata R.Br.	AZOLLA	green manure
Azolla pinnata R.Br. var. pinnata R.Br.	AZOLLA	green manure
var. imblica (Roxb.) Bonap.	AZOLLA	green manure
F. BEGONIACEAE		
Begonia spp. cv. *hybrid*	BEGONIA	ornamental
F. BORAGINACEAE		
Borago officinalis L.	BORAGE	herb
Cynoglossum amibile Stapf. & Drumm.	CHINESE FORGET ME NOT	ornamental
F. CAESALPINIACEAE		
Cassia angustifolia Vahl.	INDIAN SENNA	medicinal
Tamarindus indica L.		
cv. *muen jonk* (local)	TAMARIND	ed. fruit
cv. *see chompoo* (local)	TAMARIND	ed. fruit
F. CANNABINACEAE		
Humulus lupulus L.	HOP	herb
F. CANNACEAE		
Canna lucifer	———	ornamental

APPENDIX IV

F. CARYOPHYLLACEAE

Dianthus caryophyllus L.	CARNATION	ornamental
Dianthus chinensis L.	CHINESE PINK	ornamental
Gypsophila elegans Bieb.	ANNUAL BABY'S BREATH	ornamental
Gypsophila paniculata L.	GYPSOPHILA	ornamental

F. CHENOPODIACEAE

Beta vulgaris L.	BEET, BEET ROOT	vegetable
Spinacia oleracea L.	SPINACH	vegetable

F. CLEOMACEAE (CAPPARIDACEAE)

Cleome spinosa Raffn.	SPIDER FLOWER	ornamental

F. COMPOSITAE (ASTERACEAE)

Ageratum houstonianum Mill.	TASSEL FLOWER, FAIRY PINK	ornamental
Anthemis nobilis L.	COMMON CHAMOMILE, NOBLE CHAMOMILE	herb
Artemisia dracunculus L.	TARRAGON	herb
Calendula officinalis L.	ENGLISH MARIGOLD	ornamental
Callistephus chinensis Nees	ASTER	ornamental
Centaurea cyanus L.	CORN FLOWER	ornamental
Chrysanthemum cinerariaefolium (Trev.) Brocc.	PYRETHUM	insecticide
Chrysanthemum coronarium L.	VEGETABLE CHRYSANTHEMUM	vegetable
Chrysanthemum indicum L.	CHRYSANTHEMUM TEA	beverage
Chrysanthemum morifolium Ramat. cv. Japanese	JAPANESE CHRYSANTHEMUM	ornamental
Cichorium endivia L.	ENDIVE	condiment
Cichorium intybus L. var. *sativum* Lam. & DC.	CHICORY	condiment

Cosmos bipinnatus Cav.   COSMOS   ornamental
Cynara scolymus L.   ARTICHOKE, GLOBE ARTICHOKE   vegetable
Dahlia pinnata Cav.
cv. *improved varieties*   DAHLIA   ornamental
Gaillardia pulchella Foug.   ANNUAL GAILLARDIA   ornamental
Gazania splendens Hort.   TREASURE FLOWER   ornamental
Gerbera jamesonii Bolus (European strain)   TRANSVAAL DAISY   ornamental
Helichrysum bracteatum And.   STRAW FLOWER   ornamental
Inula helenium L.   ELECAMPANE   herb
Lactuca sativa L.
var. *capitata* L.   HEAD LETTUCE   vegetable
Liatris spp.   BLAZING STAR   ornamental
Matricaria chamomilla L.   CHAMOMILE   herb
Stevia rebaudiana Bertoni   STEVIA   sugar
Tagetes erecta L.
cv. *improved varieties*   AFRICAN MARIGOLD   ornamental
Tagetes patula L.
cv. *improved varieties*   FRENCH MARIGOLD   ornamental
Taraxacum officinalis Weber   DANDELION   herb
Tithonia rotundifolia (Mill.) Blake   MEXICAN SUNFLOWER   ornamental
Tragopogon porrifolius L.   SALSIFY   vegetable
Zinnia elegans Jacq.
cv. *improved varieties*   ZINNIA   ornamental

F. CONVOLVULACEAE
Impomoea reptans Poir.   CHINESE CONVOLVULUS   vegetable

F. CRUCIFERAE (BRASSICACEAE)
Alyssum serphyllifolium Desf.   ALYSSUM   ornamental
Brassica chinensis Jusl.

APPENDIX IV

var. *parachinensis* Tsen & Lee	FLOWERING WHITE CABBAGE	vegetable
Brassica juncea Czern & Coss.		
var. *rugosa* Tsen & Lee	BROAD LEAFED MUSTARD	vegetable, preserved
Brassica napobrassica (L.) Mill.	SWEDE	animal feed.
Brassica napus L.	RAPE	animal feed
Brassica oleracea L.		
var. *botytris* L.	CAULIFLOWER	vegetable
var. *capitata* L.	CABBAGE	vegetable
var. *gemmifera* Zenk.	BRUSSELS SPROUTS	vegetable
var. *gongylodes* L.	KOHLRABI	vegetable
var. *italica* Plenc.	BROCCOLI	vegetable
Brassica pekinensis Rupr.		
var. *cylindrica* Trsen & Lee	PE-TSAI	vegetable
var. *laxa* Tsen & Lee	CELERY CABBAGE	vegetable
Brassica rapa L.	COMMON TURNIP	vegetable
Eutrema wasabi Max.	WASABI	vegetable
Iberis amara L.	ROCKY CANDYTUFT	ornamental
Iberis umbellata L.	GLOBE CANDYTUFT	ornamental
Lobularia maritima L. Desv.	ALYSSUM	ornamental
Nasturnium officinale R.Br.	WATER CRESS	vegetable
Raphanus sativus L.		
cv. *improved variety*	RADISH	vegetable

F. CUCURBITACEAE

Cucumis melo L.	MUSKMELON	ed. fruit
Cucumis sativus L.		
cv. *Japanese*	JAPANESE CUCUMBER	vegetable
Cucurbita pepo L cv. *zucchini*	ZUCCHINI	vegetable
Cucurbita pepo L. var. *ovifera* Alef.	ORNAMENTAL GOURDS	ornamental

Exotic Plants

F. EBENACEAE
   Diospyros kaki L.   PERSIMMON   ed. fruit
   (astringent and
   non-astringent varieties)

F. ERICACEAE
   Arbutus unedo L   STRAWBERRY TREE   ed. fruit
   Rhododendron spp.   ———   ornamental
   Vaccinium ashei Reade.   RABBITEYE   ed. fruit
                                     BLUEBERRY

F. EUPHORBIACEAE
   Hevea brasiliensis   PARA RUBBER   rubber
   (Willd.ex - Adr. de Juss.)
   Muell-Arg.
   Phyllanthus emblica L.   EMBLIC MYROBOLAN   ed. fruit

F. FAGACEAE
   Castanea crenata Sieb & Zucc.   JAPANESE CHESTNUT   nut
   Castanea mollissima Blume   CHINESE CHESTNUT   nut

F. GERANIACEAE
   Geranium spp.   CRANE'S BILL   ornamental

F. GESNERIACEAE
   Siningia speciosa Benth. & Hook   GLOXINIA   ornamental

F. GRAMINEAE (POACEAE)
   Avena sativa L.   OAT   cereal
   Brachiaria brizantha   PALISADE GRASS   pasture
   (Hochst.) Stapf
   Brachiaria decumbens Stapf   SIGNAL GRASS   pasture
   Brachiaria mutica (Forsk.)   PARA GRASS   pasture
                     Stapf
   Cenchrus ciliaris L.
   cv. *American*   AMERICAN BUFFEL   pasture
                               GRASS
   cv. *malopo*   MALOPO BUFFEL   pasture
                               GRASS

APPENDIX IV

Chloris gayana Kunth	RHODES GRASS	pasture
Cymbopogon winterianus Jowett	CITRONELLA GRASS	oil
Cynodon dactylon (L.) Pers.	STAR GRASS	pasture
Dactylis glomerata L.	COCKSFOOT GRASS	pasture
Hordeum vulgare L.	BARLEY	cereal
Oryza sativa L.		
cv. IR No 1,2,7,9	RICE	cereal
cv. Koshihikora (Japonica type)	RICE	cereal
cv. reimei (Japonica type)	RICE	cereal
cv. sasashikuri (Japonica type)	RICE	cereal
Panicum antidotale Retz.	BLUE PANIC	pasture
Panicum coloratum L. var. *makarikariensis* Goossens	MAKARIKARI GRASS	pasture
Panicum maximum Jacq.	GUINEA GRASS	pasture
cv. *hamil*	HAMIL GRASS	pasture
Panicum maximum Jacq. var. *trichoglume* Eyles (syn. pubiglume K.Schum.)	GREEN PANIC	pasture
Paspalum dilatatum Poir	DALLIS GRASS	pasture
Paspalum plicatulum Michaux.	PLICATULUM	pasture
Paspalum spp.	PASPALUM GRASS	pasture
Pennisetum clandestimum Hochst. ex Chiov.	KIKUYU GRASS	pasture
Pennisetum purpureum. Schum.	NAPIER GRASS	pasture
Phleum pratense L.	TIMOTHY GRASS	pasture
Setaria anceps Stapf. ex Massey		
cv. *Kazungula*	KAZUNGULA SETARIA	pasture
cv. *nandi*	NANDI SETARIA	pasture
Setaria sphacelata (Schum.) Stapf & Hubbard	GOLDEN TIMOTHY GRASS	pasture
Tripsacum laxum Nash	GUATEMALA GRASS	pasture

Exotic Plants

Triticum aestivum L.	COMMON WHEAT	cereal
Triticum durum Desf.	DURUM WHEAT	cereal
Urochloa mosambicensis (Hack.) Dandy	SABI GRASS	pasture
Vetiveria zizanioides (L.) Nash.	VETIVER	oil, medicinal
Zea mays L.	BABY CORN	canning
cv. pacific (local)	MAIZE	cereal, animal feed
cv. *suwaan* No. 1-3 (local)	MAIZE	cereal, animal feed
cv. *Thai opaque* No. 1-3	MAIZE	ed. cob, cereal
Zea mays L. var. saccharata Bailey	SWEET CORN	ed. cob

F. IRIDACEAE

Crocus sativus L.	SAFFRON	herb
Freesia spp.	FREESIA	ornamental
Gladiolus sp.	GLADIOLUS	ornamental
cv. *acidanthera*	GLADIOLUS	ornamental
Iris hybrida Hort.	IRIS	ornamental

F. JUGLANDACEAE

Carya pecan. Engler & Graebn.	PECAN	nut
Juglans regia L.	WALNUT	nut

F. LABIATAE (LAMIACEAE)

Coleus blumei Benth.	COLEUS	ornamental
Lavandula hybrida	LAVENDER	ornamental
Lavandula officinalis Chaix. (L. angustifolia DC.)	HYSSOP	herb
Lavandula vera DC.	DUTCH LAVENDER	ornamental
Majorana hortensis Moench	MAJORAM	herb
Melissa officinalis L.	COMMON BALM	herb

Mentha arvensis L.
var. piperacens Mal. | JAPANESE MINT | oil
Mentha cardiaca Gerard ex Baker | SCOTCH MINT | oil
Mentha piperita L. | PEPPERMINT | oil
Mentha spicata (L.) Hudson | SPEAR MINT | oil
Mesona chinensis Benth. | CHAO-KUAI (CHINESE) | desert
Ocimum basilicum L. | BASIL | herb
Origanum vulgare L. | WILD MAJORAM, OREGANO | herb
Pogostemon cablin (Blanco) Benth. | PATCHOULI | oil
Rosmarinus officinalis L. | ROSEMARY | herb
Salvia officinalis L. | SAGE | herb
Salvia sclarea L. | CLARY SAGE | herb
Salvia splendens Ker-Gawl | SALVIA | ornamental
Satureja hortensis L. | SUMMER SAVORY | herb
Satureja montana L. | WINTER SAVORY | herb
Thymus vulgaris L. | THYME | herb

F. LAURACEAE
Persea americana Mill. | AVOCADO | ed. fruit

F. LILIACEAE
Agapanthus spp. | AFRICAN LILY | ornamental
Asparagus officinalis L. | ASPARAGUS | vegetable
Hemerocallis flava L. | LEMON DAYLILY | vegetable
Lilium candidum L. | MADONNA LILY | ornamental
Lilium elegans Thunb. | LILY | ornamental
Lilium longiflorum Thunb. | EASTER LILY | ornamental
Sansevieria hahnii Hort. | ——— | ornamental
Tulipa hybrida Hort. | TULIP | ornamental

F. LINACEAE
Linum usitatissimum L. | FLAX, LINSEED | fibre, oil

Exotic Plants

F. MALVACEAE
Althaea rosea Cav.   HOLLYHOCK   ornamental
Hibiscus sabdariffa L.   ROSELLE   beverage

F. MIMOSACEAE
Acacia auriculaeformis A. Cunn. WATTLE   shade
Mimosa invisa Mart. ex Colla
 var. *inermis* Adelb.   THORNLESS GIANT   cover crop
                                  SENSITIVE PLANT

F. MORACEAE
Ficus carica L.   COMMON FIG   ed. fruit

F. MUSACEAE
Musa sapientum L.
 cv. *Kluai haak mook* (local)   banana   ed. fruit
 cv. *Kluai hom khiao* (local)   banana   ed. fruit
 cv. *Kluai hom thong* (local)   banana   ed. fruit
 cv. *Kluai khai* (local)   banana   ed. fruit

F. MYRICACEAE
Myrica rubra Sieb. & Zucc.   CHINESE   ed. fruit
                                  STRAWBERRY TREE

F. MYRTACEAE
Eucalyptus camaldulensis Dehn. LONGBEAK   forest
                                  EUCALYPTUS
Eucalyptus citriodora Hook.   LEMON SCENTED GUM   forest, oil
Eucalyptus globulus Labill.   BLUE GUM   forest
Eucalyptus grandis Hill.   FLOODED GUM   forest
         ex Maiden.
Eucalyptus macarthuri Dean &   EUCALYPTUS   forest, oil
         Maiden.
Eucalyptus piperita J.E. Smith EUCALYPTUS   forest, oil
Eucalyptus smithii R.T.Baker   EUCALYPTUS   forest, oil
Eucalyptus staigeriana   EUCALYPTUS   forest, oil
 F.Muell.ex F.M.Bail.
Eugenia javanica Lamk.   JAWA APPLE   ed. fruit

APPENDIX IV

F. ONAGRACEAE
Fuchsia hybrida Hort.
  cv. Mrs Popple   FUCHSIA   ornamental

F. ORCHIDACEAE

Cymbidium lowianum Reichb.f.	CYMBIDIUM ORCHID	ornamental
Cymbidium traceyanum Hort.	CYMBIDIUM ORCHID	ornamental
Paphiopedilum appletonianum Rolfe	LADY'S SLIPPER ORCHID	ornamental
Paphiopedilum bellatulum Pfitz.	LADY'S SLIPPER ORCHID	ornamental
Paphiopedilum villosum Pfitz.	LADY'S SLIPPER ORCHID	ornamental
Paphiopedilum sp.	LADY'S SLIPPER ORCHID	ornamental
Paphiopedilum hybrida Hort.	LADY'S SLIPPER ORCHID	ornamental
Vanilla fragans (Salisb.) Ames.	VANILLA	flavoring
Vanilla pompona Schiede.	WEST INDIAN VANILLA	flavoring
Vanilla tahitensis J.W. Moore	TAHITIAN VANILLA	flavoring

F. PAPAVERACEAE

Papaver bracteatum Lind.	POPPY	medicinal

F. PAPILIONACEAE

Alysicarpus vaginalis DC.	ALICE CLOVER	cover crop
Arachis hypogaea L.	PEANUT	ed. seed
cv. *tainan* (local)	PEANUT	ed. seed
cv. *U - thong* (local)	PEANUT	ed. seed
Calopogonium mucunoides Desv.	CALOPOGONIUM	cover crop
Centrosema pubescens Benth.	BUTTERFLY PEA	cover crop
cv. *belato*	BELATO	cover crop
Cicer arietinum L.	CHICK PEA	ed. seed
Crotalaria juncea L.	SUNN HEMP	cover crop
Desmodium codariocalyx (Roxb. ex Link) DC.	CODARIOCALYX	cover crop

Exotic Plants

Desmodium intortum (Mill.)Urb.
cv. greenleaf   GREENLEAF   cover crop
         DESMODIUM

Desmodium uncinatum (Jacq.)DC.
cv. silverleaf   SILVERLEAF   cover crop
         DESMODIUM

Glycine max Merr.
cv. *orba*   SOYABEAN   ed. seed
cv. *S.J.* No. 1-5   SOYABEAN   ed. seed

Glycine wightii Verdc.   TINAROO, PHODESIAN cover crop
         KUDZU VINE
cv. *clarence*   CLARENCE   cover crop
cv. *cooper*   COOPER   cover crop

Lens esculenta Moench   LENTIL   ed. seed
Lotonosis bainesii Baker.   LOTONOSIS   cover crop
Lupinus angustifolius L.   BLUE LUPINE   cover crop
Lupinus cosentini Guss.   SAND PLAIN LUPINE cover crop

Macroptilium atropurpureum SIRATO   cover crop
(DC.) Urḃ.

Macroptilium lathyroides   PHASEY BEAN   cover crop
(L.) Urb.

Macroptilium sativa
cv. *hunter river*   HUNTER RIVER   cover crop
         LUCERNE

Macrotyloma axillare   AXILLARE   cover crop
(E. Mey.) Verdc.

Macrotyloma uniflorum   UNIFLORUM   cover crop
(Lam.) Verdc.

Medicago sativa L.   LUCERNE,   cover crop
         BLUE ALFALEA

Medicago truncatula Gaertn. BARREL MEDIC   cover crop
Medicago spp.   LUCERNES   cover crop
Mucuna utilis Wall.ex Wight VELVET BEAN   vegetable
Mucuna sp.   VELVET BEAN   vegetable,
                   cover crop

APPENDIX IV

Phaseolus angularis (Willd.) Wight	SNAP BEAN, ADZUKI BEAN	vegetable
cv. bush type		
cv. pole type		
Phaseolus lunatus L.	LIMA BEAN	vegetable, edible seed
Phaseolus vulgaris L.	RED KIDNEY BEAN	ed. seed
Pisum sativum L.	GARDEN PEA	vegetable
Pueraria phaseoloides (Roxb.) Benth.	TROPICAL KUDZU	cover crop
Samanea saman Merr.	RAIN TREE	Lac insect's host plant
Stylosanthes hamata (L.) Taub.	HAMATA STYLO	cover crop
Stylosanthes humilis H.B. et K.	PATERSON TOWNSVILLE STYLO	cover crop
cv. *gordon*	GORDON TOWNSVILLE STYLO	cover crop
cv. *lawson*	LAWSON TOWNSVILLE STYLO	cover crop
Stylosanthes fruticosa (Retz.) Alston	WILD LUCERNE	cover crop
Stylosanthes guyanensis Sw.		
cv. *cook*	COOK STYLO	cover crop
cv. *endeavor*	ENDEAVOR STYLO	cover crop
cv. *oxley*	OXLEY FINESTEMMED STYLO	cover crop
cv. *schofield*	SCHOFIFLD STYLO	cover crop
Stylosanthes scabra Vog.	STYLO	cover crop
Stylosanthes viscosa Sw.	STYLO	cover crop
Trifolium repens L.		
cv. *Louisiana*	LOUISIANA WHITE CLOVER	cover crop

cv. *ladino*	WHITE CLOVER	cover crop
Trifolium semipilosum Fresen. cv. *safari*	KENYA CLOVER	cover crop
Trifolium spp.	CLOVERS	cover crop
Trigonella foenum - graecum L.	FENUGREEK	herb
Vigna unguiculata (L.) Walp.	COW PEA	cover crop, vegetable

F. PASSIFLORACEAE

Passiflora edulis Sims.	PASSION FRUIT	ed. fruit, beverage

F. PIPERACEAE

Piper nigrum L.	BLACK PEPPER	medicinal, condiment, ceremonial

F. PLANTAGINACEAE

Plantago ovata Forsk.	PLANTAGO	medicinal

F. PLUMBAGINACEAE

Limonium latifolium Moench	SEA LAVENDER, STATICE	ornamental
Limonium perezii	SEA LAVENDER, STATICE	ornamental
Limonium sinuatum Mill.	SEA LAVENDER, STATICE	ornamental
Limonium suworowii (Regel) O.Ktze	SEA LAVENDER, STATICE	ornamental
Limonium tatarica Mill.	SEA LAVENDER, STATICE	ornamental
(Limonium = Statice)		

F. POLEMONIACEAE

Phlox drumondii Hook.	PHLOX	ornamental

F. POLYGONACEAE

Fagopyrum esculentum Moench	BUCKWHEAT	cereal
Rheum rhaponticum L.	RHUBARB	vegetable

APPENDIX IV

F. PORTULACACEAE

Portulaca grandiflora Hook.f.	SUN PLANT, PORTULACA, MOSS ROSE	ornamental

F. PRIMULACEAE

Primula acaulis (L.) Hill.	PRIMROSE	ornamental

F. PROTEACEAE

Macadamia integrifolia L.S. Smith	SMOOTH-SHELLED MACADAMIA	nut
Macadamia tetraphylla L. Johnson	ROUGH-SHELLED MACADAMIA	nut

F. PUNICACEAE

Punica granatum L. cv. middle east type	POMEGRANATE	ed. fruit

F. RANUNCULACEAE

Delphinium hybrida Hort.	DELPHINIUM	ornamental
cv. *pacific*	DELPHINIUM	ornamental
Rananculus asiaticus L.	BUTTER CUP	ornamental

F. RHAMNACEAE

Zizyphus jujuba Mill.	CHINESE JUJUBE, CHINESE DATE PLUM	ed. fruit

F. ROSACEAE

Cydonia oblonga Mill.	QUINCE	ed. fruit
Eriobotrya japonica (Thunb.) Lindl.	LOQUAT	ed. fruit
Fragaria ananassa Duch.	STRAWBERRY	ed. fruit
cv. *cambridge favorite*	STRAWBERRY	ed. fruit
cv. *sequoia*	STRAWBERRY	ed. fruit
cv. *tioga*	STRAWBERRY	ed. fruit
Malus pumila Mill.	APPLE	ed. fruit
cv. *anna*	APPLE	ed. fruit
cv. *ein shemer*	APPLE	ed. fruit

Exotic Plants

Prunus amygdalus Batsch	ALMOND	nut
Prunus armeniaca L.	APPRICOT	ed. fruit
Prunus avium L.	SWEET CHERRY	ed. fruit
Prunus domestica L.	PLUM	ed. fruit
Prunus mume Sieb. & Zucc.	JAPANESE APPRICOT	ed. fruit
Prunus persica Batsch cv. improved varieties	PEACH	ed. fruit
Pyrus communis L.	EUROPEAN PEAR	ed. fruit
Pyrus pyrifolia (Burm.) Nakai	ASIAN PEAR	ed. fruit
Rosa indica L.	ROSE	ornamental
Rosa multiflora Thunb.	ROSE	rootstock
Rosa spp. (improved varieties)	ROSE	ornamental
Rubus sp.	RASPBERRY	ed. fruit

F. RUBIACEAE

Coffea arabica L.		
cv. *catimor*	ARABICA COFFEE	beverage
cv. *bourbon*	ARABICA COFFEE	beverage
cv. *arusha*	ARABICA COFFEE	beverage
cv. *blue mountain*	ARABICA COFFEE	beverage
cv. *catuai*	ARABICA COFFEE	beverage
cv. *cattura*	ARABICA COFFEE	beverage
cv. *typica*	ARABICA COFFEE	beverage
cv. *villalobos*	ARABICA COFFEE	beverage
Coffea canephora Pierre ex Froehner	ROBUSTA COFFEE	beverage
Coffea liberica Bull ex Hiern.	LIBERICA COFFEE	beverage
Ruta graveolens L.	RUE	herb

F. RUTACEAE

Citrus limon Burm.	LEMON	condiment
Citrus maxima Merr.		
cv. *khao paen* (local)	PUMMELO	ed. fruit
ed. *khao puang* (local)	PUMMELO	ed. fruit

APPENDIX IV

cv. thong dee (local)	PUMMELO	ed. fruit
Citrus paradisi Macf.	GRAPE FRUIT	ed. fruit
Citrus reticulata Blanco		
cv. *baang mod* (local)	SWEET ORANGE	ed. fruit
cv. *som jook* (local)	SWEET ORANGE	ed. fruit
Citrus sinensis Osb.		
cv. *cheng* (Chinese)	SWEET ORANGE	ed. fruit
Clausena lansium Skeels	WAMPEE	ed. fruit
Xanthoxylum limonella Alston	MAA KHAEN (LOCAL)	condiment, medicinal

F. SAPINDACEAE

Dimocarpus longan Lour.		
cv. *biao khiao* (local)	LONGAN	ed. fruit
cv. *chompoo* (local)	LONGAN	ed. fruit
cv. *dor* (local)	LONGAN	ed. fruit
cv. *haew* (local)	LONGAN	ed. fruit
Litchi chinensis Sonn.		
cv. *chaakraapaat* (local)	LITCHI	ed. fruit
cv. *hong huay* (local)	LITCHI	ed. fruit
cv. *kim jeng* (local)	LITCHI	ed. fruit
cv. *O - hia* (local)	LITCHI	ed. fruit
Nephelium lappaceum L.		
cv. *ngor rong rian* (local)	RAMBUTAN	ed. fruit
cv. ngor si chompoo (local)	RAMBUTAN	ed. fruit

F. SAPOTACEAE

Chrysophyllum cainito L.	STAR APPLE	ed. fruit
Madhuca grandiflora Fletch.	LAAMOOD SIDAA (LOCAL)	ed. fruit

F. SCROPHULARIACEAE

Antirrhinum majus L.	SNAP DRAGON	ornamental
Digitalis purpurea L.	FOXGLOVE	ornamental medicinal
Digitalis spp.	DIGITALIS	medicinal

F. SOLANACEAE

Capsicum anuum L.	RED PEPPER	vegetable
var. grossum Sendt.	BELL PEPPER	vegetable
Capsicum frutescens L.		
cv. *Dubai*	HOT PEPPER	condiment
cv. *shotai*	HOT PEPPER	condiment
cv. *Spanish*	HOT PEPPER	condiment
cv. *suntaka*	HOT PEPPER	condiment
cv. *tabasco*	HOT PEPPER	condiment
Hyoscyamus niger L.	HENBANE	herb
Lycopersicon esculentum Mill.		
cv. VHF 134	TOMATO	vegetable
Nicoticana alata Link & Otto	TOBACCO FLOWER	ornamental
Nicotiana tabacum L.		
cv. Turkish (oriental)	TOBACCO	narcotic
cv. *virginia*	TOBACCO	narcotic
cv. *burley*	TOBACCO	narcotic
Petunia hybrida Hort.	PETUNIA	ornamental
Solanum melongena L.		
cv. aubergine	AUBERGINE	vegetable
Solanum muricatum Ait.	PEPINO	ed. fruit
Solanum tuberosum L.		
cv. binje	POTATO	ed. root
cv. *burbank*	CHIP POTATO	snag
cv. *spunta*	POTATO	ed. root

F. VALERIANACEAE

Valeriana officinalis L.	VALERIAN	vegetable

F. VERBENACEAE

Verbena hybrida Hort.	GARDEN VERBENA	ornamental

F. VIOLACEAE

Viola cornuta L.	VIOLA	ornamental
Viola tricolor L.	PANSY	ornamental

APPENDIX IV

F. VITACEAE (AMPELIDACEAE)
Vitis vinifera L.	SEED GRAPE	ed. fruit
cv. *seedless varieties*	SEEDLESS GRAPES	ed. fruit

F. UMBELLIFERAE (APIACEAE)
Anethum graveolens L.	DILL	herb
Angelica acutiloba Kitakawa	DANGGUI	cul. herb, condiment
Apium graveolens L.	CELERY	vegetable
Carum carvi L.	CARAWAY	herb
Coriandrum sativum L.	CORIANDER	cul. herb
Cuminum cyminum L.	CUMIN	condiment
Daucus carota L.	CARROT	vegetable
cv. *baby carrot*	BABY CARROT	vegetable
Foeniculum azoricum Mill.	ITALIAN FENNEL	vegetable
Foeniculum dulce Mill.	SWEET FENNEL	vegetable
Foeniculum vulgare Mill.	FENNEL	vegetable
Pastinaca sativa L.	PARSNIP	vegetable
Petroselinum crispum (Mill.) Nym.ex A.W. Hill	PARSLEY	vegetable
Pimpinella anisum L.	ANISE PLANT	vegetable, condiment

Appendix V (See note)
Target Areas for Prevention of Forest Destruction by Hilltribes

Briefly speaking, prevention and suppression of forest destruction by the hilltribes has not yet succeeded due to several problems and obstacles, despite the use of cautions policy measures. Obstacles found are:

(1) Large number of hilltribe people are scattered all over the northern territories, in at least 22 provinces. These people move around here and there, making their living from shifting cultivation, wood cutting, forest destruction, opium growing and even burning forests for cropping maize etc. Some of them are being financed by certain businessmen to further the interests of these sponsors. It is therefore, hard to make an exact estimate of the hilltribes population.

(2) For the reasons stated in (1), the responsible authorities unable to allocate suitable territories for hilltribe use with proper facilities to control, to prevent and to suppress their misdemeanour or crimes.

(3) Apart from the reasons and facts mentioned in (1) and (2), it also found that the government official units agencies in charge and the assistance and development project had never sought permission for local use of the areas, either of the national forests, the national parks or the national wildlife conservations offices, which created problems to maintenance and supervision work of the authorities concerned.

NB: This document is reproduced from the original. Neither misspellings nor grammatical vagarities have been changed. The paper was not written for publication.

(4) It now appears that prevention and suppression work of the responsible authorities and of the project operation has not proceeded as smoothly and effectively as it should. Hence there is some confusion among the hilltribes, both positively and negatively. For the negative side suppression has detered the hilltribe for making any violations and at the same time from a more positive side, the suppression also encouraged the people to take hold of spaces for permanent living. In the people became confused and undecided. They do not know whether to remain in permanent location or otherwise. Such a situation led hilltribes from other areas, or from neighbouring territories, to come in and take over the unoccupied areas for their own use.

(5) There are still plenty of problems arising from gaps in the work of the project and of the authorities responsible, in areas apart from the coordination gap. Field workers who follow the laid down policy and measures are found to be operating without sufficient support and promotion from the official units. With the facts referred to, it is now appropriate to fix target areas of operation, with a view to synchronizing the work of both the prevention and suppression units and of the project. Work can then proceed according to the policy and measures laid down as well as to the committee's resolutions, which are:

(a) Absolutely Restricted Zones the first target zone selected. This will include the forest areas around the water resources, still assuming its natural condition of being as natural forests, or the partly destructed less than 60% as well as, those on the hilly or mountain terrains with certain portion had been destroyed. Ecologically speaking such area should be absolutely reserved and restricted, such as, the high hilly terrain or the hilly slopes. Suitable for being kept as natural reservation that can also help to prevent future trouble to our natural environments. There should be strict prevention measure to stop its further destruction and not to allow neither Thai nor hilltribe to reside or make use of the area in question. Any violating in this respect should be seriously dealth with either by means of evacuation

Clearance Strategy

or otherwise reasonable period of duration. On the other hand, there seemed to be no other working unit on project provide support or asistance to these people anymore.

(b) Intermediate Zones or the second target zone which are to include areas with almost similar characteristics to the previous zone area. Its only difference is that these areas are mostly destroyed more than 60% which certainly required reforestation and unable to push the people who previously occupied or were allowed to further their temporary stay waiting for suitable terrain either plain or slopes for their new dwelling and living. The work is to be carried out by the sole authority in charge without help or support or intention in concern from outside units, project or individuals. If such are to be permitted it could promote delay and misconception to our officially laid down policy. Only the official units or project directly responsible to the supervision policy will be allowed.

(c) Zones for General Relaxation or the third target zone, consisting the area of the same nature as of target zone No. 1. Only difference is that all forests had been cut down or destroyed, reforestation condition appeared to be very low or the hilltribe violation are not able to be pushed out or evacuated, unable to obtain suitable area for their new dwelling and living. They might be permitted to continue residing as long as the solution could be found.

For the third target zone, other official units or project should be allowed to support and assist in the development of their dwelling and living, promoting their earning, state of living and organize proper administration with the purpose to changing. The hilltribe's habit of destroying forests, as well as, promoting the love of land the live in the feeling of being their citizens. (emphasis added).

Appendix VI
Notes on Plates.

Front cover. "Lahu Sheleh women". This section of a photograph of Lahu Sheleh women at a food demonstration workshop was taken at Pha Peuak, Mae Hong Son, 1988. The photo was taken by John Connell an associate scientist with CIMMYT (International Maize and Wheat Improvement Center) South-East Asian Wheat Programme based at Chiang Mai University. The full photograph is reproduced as Plate 99.

Back cover "Akha Swing" taken in Pa Ka Suk Chai, Mae Chan during the Akha "women's New Year" which falls in late August when the rice is well established. Bernard Vienne took this photograph in the course of the celebration in 1987. The image is reproduced on a full page, Plate 31.

The information provided in brackets is as follows (photographer, village, district, province, date). Where this full set of information was not available the same order is followed but no indication given of missing names.

Plate 1 "Akha Dzoema" (Vienne, Mae Salaep, Mae Chan Chiang Rai, 1987). "Dzoema" in Akha literally means ruler or leader. He is more than a village headman. He is an exemplary elder who has earned a reputation for his honesty and his knowledge of, and adherence to, Akha ways. According to Alting von Geusau he "is generally also the founder of the village (or the founder's son), and leader of the many calendric communal village ceremonies...has final word in judicial affairs and is considered to be father and coordinator of the village" (Leo Alting von Geusau, in McKinnon & Wanat (eds) ***High-Landers of Thailand,*** Oxford University Press, 1986; 268).

APPENDIX VI

Plate 2 "Hmong" (Hobday, Doi Pui, Muang Chiang Mai, Chiang Mai, 1979). From an early age young Hmong girls wear the distinctive, pleated skirt worn by adults. The skirts are made from hemp and the batik design is applied before the material is immersed in an indigo dye. The skirt as well as the jacket is typically hemmed or bordered with a margin of needlework and applicate. Clothing and ornaments of the Hmong are more fully described in Paul and Elaine Lewis's book **Peoples of the Golden Triangle** Thames and Hudson, 1984: 100-133 and **Clothings and Ornaments of China's Miao People** Chinese National Press, Beijing, 1985.

Plate 3 "Mlabri" (McKinnon, Huai Bo Hoi, Nan, 1986). The Mlabri ["(*mal,* 'human beings', *bri* 'forest')" Trier citation below, page 3] or *phii tong luang* (Spirits of the Yellow Leaves) as they are known in Thai are described in the literature as migratory hunters and gatherers. In a personal conversation about their Thai name a Mlabri complained about this less than substantial appellation. "Look at me. See, I am made of flesh and bone. I am a real man". It is as Tier notes, "an interesting fact—and one worth contemplating—that their general name for all non-Mlabri, *guarl,* means "monkey" (citation below, page 9). Collectors of the quaint and exotic prefer to photograph them in their traditional loin cloth but such an image misrepresents the conditions under which most currently live. The few Mlabri in Thailand mostly work as agricultural labourers for Hmong farmers. Mlabri women (see Plate 63) also prefer to dress in a manner dictated by lowland culture. A recent publication on the Mlabri worth reading, Jesper Trier, "The Mlabri of Northern Thailand: Social Organization and Supernatural Beliefs" **Contributions to Southeast Asian Ethnography: Studies of Religions and Worldviews** Anthony R. Walker (ed.) No. 5, August 1986: 3-41.

Plate 4 "Lua" (Kampe, Hoa, Mae Chaem, Chiang Mai, 1988). Lua woman with grandson. In the distant past the Lua were the dominant occupants of the district. Today only six out

Plates

of a total of 220 villages are formally identified as Lua.

The term "Lua" is used to identify Austro-Asiatic speaking people who settled in the North before the arrival of the Tai whose culture and language gradually became dominant. The Lua in fact make up many different groups and have for a long time been subject to deculturation and assimilation. As the linguist David Bradley notes, "change and acculturation are a continuous process. On the one hand, these minorities have been living in a symbiotic relationship with Tai peoples for a very long time; on the other hand, many Thais are descendants of other people who have become Thai" (Bradley in McKinnon & Wanat [eds] **Highlanders of Thailand** Oxford University Press, 1986: 54-55). A recent book on the Lua (in Thai) written by Chonthira Sattaya - Wattana is entitled **Lua Muang Nan** Bangkok, 1987.

Plate 5 "Akha grandmother" (Hobday, Pa Ya Pai, Mae Chan, Chiang Rai, 1978). Life expectancy has always been low in the highlands and older people are somewhat revered. As elders, Akha women exercise a strong authority. Those who have earned the right to wear a white skirt by holding a special ceremony *(yayeum)* are particularly honoured as *yayeama.*

Plate 6 "Mien mother" (Connell, Nam Yao, Pua, Nan, 1982). Mien mythology has it that one of their two original ancestors was a Chinese princess. A Chinese document known as the Yao Charter passed to French officials in 1900 and now held in the Societe Asiatique de Paris appears to be, "a Ch'ing dynasty copy of a document originally dated the fifth year of the medieval Sui dynasty (A.D. 595)" (Lemoine in McKinnon & Wanat ibid. 1986 : 197). This Charter gave the Mien the right, amongst other things "the freedom to cultivate swidden rice in all the mountains of the empire" (ibid. : 197). The myth attests to the strong customary role women occupy in Mien society.

This photograph was taken outside the hospital of the Nam Yao refugee camp. Nobody wants to live in a refugee camp

APPENDIX VI

but the conditions and atmosphere here are considerably better than the highly publicised Khmer camps along the southern sector of the North-East. The authorities provided bamboo, thatch and binding and the people were able to build their houses in the traditional way.

One positive aspect of such camps is that it brought together specialists such as craft people, musicians and religious leaders from previously widely separated villages which resulted in something of a cultural rennaissance. This also served to heightened self awareness of ethnic identity.

Plate 7 "Lua boy" (Hobday, Jung Nong, Mae La Noi, Mae Hong Son, 1985). According to the anthropologist Peter Kunstadter the Lua "value children highly" and through delayed marriage in consultation with village leaders deliberately attempt to keep family size in proportion to village resources (ibid.: 37). From an early age children undertake a wide range of domestic tasks such as collecting firewood and water, feeding animals and minding other children (see Plate 52).

Plate 8 "Lisu grandfather" (Kampe, Pang Sa, Mae Chan, Chiang Rai, February 1988). This senior citizen has seen a lot of changes in his village, particularly over the past 10 years. A string of Royal Thai Government, NGO and donor assisted projects have followed each other in an attempt to ease the community's transition to modernity. Many tourists visit. The village is still strongly Lisu.

Plate 9 "Akha village" (Hobday, Mae Nam Khun, Wiang Pa Pao, Chiang Rai, 1987).

Plate 10 "Akha village" (Hobday, Pa Yai Pai, Mae Chan, Chiang Rai, 1978). The morning mix of mist and haze as fires are stoked for cooking and comfort.

Akha villages are built on carefully chosen sites. The prefered location is on a ridge close to a good supply of clean water for drinking, bathing and washing clothes, preferably under the cover of a grove of trees. There should be space for a public gathering place used as a playground by children, a courting area by the young and a dancing ground for all. A good site for the swing is taken into consideration and if possible should afford a view out to the rice fields. All this should lie inside the main gate into the village.

Plate 11 "Akha pounding cooked rice" (Vienne, Mae Salaep, Mae Chan, Chiang Rai, 1987). Stored swidden rice is first steamed, pounded and stretched, cut and formed into flat cakes which are covered with crushed sesame seed. Rice cakes are an important part of ceremonial meals.

Plate 12 "Lahu butchering a barking deer" (Connell, Huai Hia, Mae Hong Son, 1988). The best time to hunt is after a shower of rain when game come out from under the wet canopy of the forest into the open. If the hunt is successful, wherever possible, the kill is carried back to the village for butchering. An offering is made before the meat is divided up and distributed amongst neighbours and kin.

Game is becoming increasingly scarce. It is for good reasons that the Wildlife Division of the Royal Forestry Department has pressed for both the declaration of more areas in which hunting is prohibited and the formation of additional wildlife sanctuaries. The preservation of the natural flora and fauna as a national heritage is reason in itself. The survival of many endangered species is seriously threatened by collectors, hunters and traders of rare species and the felling of Thailand's forests. As yet the extent to which the cooperation of highlanders should be secured to assist in this task has not been seriously considered. Some people in positions of authority want those who are already there removed altogether. Other conservationists like Dr Ardith A. Eudey, regional coordinator for Asia of the IUCN/Species Survival Commission's Primate Specialist Group believes that their presence is desirable and their cooperation is necessary to ensure protection (Chapter 10 this volume).

APPENDIX VI

Plate 13 "Lahu Sheleh cooking" (Connell, Luk Khao Lum, Mae Hong Son, 1986). In Lahu houses meals are generally cooked inside the house on a clay hearth resting on top of a split bamboo floor. Unlike the Thai, Chinese and Akha who blend herbs and spices to enhance the flavour of their food the Lahu make do by adding salt and chillies. In many villages MSG is becoming and essential ingredient. In its absence people complain about tasteless food.

The hearth serves many purposes. Light for evening gatherings. Hot water is kept on the boil, considerable quantities of tea are taken, and in the middle of the cool season when temperatures can drop as low as five degrees celsius the fire provides a welcome warmth. The smoke from the fire keeps insect life to a minimum and prolongs the life of the bamboo and thatching. Food is hung to dry and seeds, tobacco and tea are also stored above the fire.

This village has built modern houses with several rooms. These dwellings are kept scrupulously clean. The hearth has been relegated to detached bamboo structures and these have become the prefered place for members of the household and neighbours to meet.

Plate 14 "Akha bride" (Ralana, Mae Salaep village, Mae Chan, 1987). Mii Yuu La-che wears her best clothes prepared over a long period before the event. She must sit with her face modestly covered.

The household is the cornerstone of community life. A proper household must have both a man and woman. Tasks are divided between men and women following strict cultural guidelines.

Plate 15 "Pigs, Hmong village" (Connell, Pha Kluai, Chom Thong, Chiang Mai, 1987). This photograph was taken in the course of a visit by a team of nutritionists well trained in their science by modern academic institutions. They were of the opinion that although the presence of many pigs in a village indicated a certain type of wealth the nutritional status of the children was particularly poor. This situation was credited to the fact that in this village, as in many others, wet season cash cropping had displaced upland rice production and the people had come to rely on the purchase of polished rice from the lowlands.

As is noted in the text, "The identification of problems through formal categories preserve and reinforce a hierarchical distance between *chao khao* and the dominant culture which further validates a mixture of stereotyped judgements and naive evidence as a sort of meta-objectivity the main purpose of which is obviously to construct a good self image for those who devote themselves to the *chao khao* (Vienne, Chapter 2 this volume).

Plate 16 "Pigs, Akha village" (Vienne, Mae Salaep, Mae Chan, Chiang Rai, 1987). A piglet had been taken for an offering. The sow was responding to the squeals.

Pork is an important food and an offering is an important feature of many ceremonies. Last year (1987) at Pha Kluai when the mother of several elders died, 23 pigs were killed over a period of seven days. Pigs are also raised for sale to other householders and neighbouring villagers who need to make prestations. The annual cycle provides many opportunities for people to eat meat.

Plate 17 "Mae Tho village, 1964" (Geddes, Mae Tho, Chom Tong, Chiang Mai, 1964) This photograph was taken by Bill Geddes whose book **Migrants of the Mountains** provides an account of the Hmong of Mae Tho before the Royal Thai Government and foreign projects undertook large scale development work in the highlands.

This book is the poorer for the absence of any detailed discussion of specific cultures and readers interested in the Hmong could well refer to both the Geddes and Robert Cooper

APPENDIX VI

books *(Resource Scarcity and the Hmong Response).*

Plate 18 "Mae Tho village 1986" (McKinnon Mae Tho, Chom Tong, Chiang Mai, June 1986) These two photographs of Mae Tho graphically illustrate the changes which have taken place over the past two decades. The site of the village has been moved a few kilometers but a completely new idea of what a developed village should look like can be seen. Concrete block houses, a sealed road and traffic signs. What is a typical highland village?

Plate 19 "Food demonstration" (Connell, Khun Wang, San Pa Tong, 1986) As part of a programme to promote the growing and use of selected traditional, and new, higher yielding varieties of rice, suitable for growing at higher elevations, the Department of Agricultural Research holds demonstrations which provide villagers with an opportunity to taste grain before it is promoted in extension work.

On the day this photograph was taken, wheat boiled as whole grain, cracked and boiled again as a gruel with chicken bone soup was offered for tasting. Although none of those present had ever eaten wheat prepared in this way before the dish was readily consumed.

This "acceptance" needs to be qualified. Wheat, black bean and etc are common components of demonstrations. Although the offering is usually eaten this does not mean that after returning to their homes people will cook such foods even if they are growing them as cash crops. Food preferences are such a deeply structured aspect of culture that it takes more than a demonstration or two to inspire them to change their eating habits.

Plate 20 "Buddhist monks" (Kampe, unidentified highland village, Chiang Mai, 1988). The Royal Thai Government has set up its own missionary programme, the Dhammacarik Bikkhu. Monks are trained to establish centres of Buddhist

Plates

teaching in highland villages and many youngsters are brought to Chiang Mai where they undergo secular and religious training at Wat Sri Soda sited in the foothills of Doi Suthep. Generally speaking, monks are well received in the highlands and shown a respect consistent with their status on the lowlands. Many participate positively in community activities and demonstrate a good understanding of village life. For a recent evaluation of the programme see Sanit Wongsprasert "Impact of the Dhammacarik Bhikkhus' Programme on the Hill Tribes of Thailand" in de Silva, K.M. et. al. (eds) ***Ethnic Conflict in Bhuddhist Societies: Sri Lanka, Thailand and Burma***, Pinter, London 1988: 126-137.

Buddhist proselytization is no match for the pervasive efforts of Christian missionaries, especially fundamentalists committed to a strong ideological position. They ethnocentrically promote their own cultural mythology with little thought for the detrimental impact their activities may have on communities fighting for their cultural survival. Such missionaries are fortunately in a minority and many of a more gentle persuasion have made valuable practical, humanitarian and scholarly contributions to the welfare, education and the task of maintaining the dignity as well as strengthening the political position of highlanders.

Plate 21 "Lisu students" (Kampe, Bang Sa, Mae Chan, Chiang Rai, February 1988). Initially girls were less likely to take advantage of schooling opportunities offered by the government or other agencies. Ralana Maneeprasert has observed that "The status of girls or daughters is generally beneath that of male offspring; consequently fewer resources are invested in them including food, health care and education, because it is expected that on marriage they will leave the family" (Ralana, Chapter 5 this volume). Others point out that this is not always the case today. Where good schools are provided by the government most young girls attend until they marry which can be quite young (14 years).

APPENDIX VI

A tremendous effort has been made over the past two decades to provide highlanders with access to a Thai education. Started by the Border Patrol Police, the Hill Tribe Welfare Division of the Department of Public Welfare and Christian missionaries, responsibility for providing educational services has long been dominated by the Ministry of Education. The Ministry provides schooling through both the Department of Non-Formal Education and the Office of the National Primary Education Commission.

Education in Bang Sa began as a private voluntary effort, evolved into Non-Formal Education and eventually formal schooling was provided. Highlanders regard schools run under the Office of the National Primary Education Commission as "real education" and as such it carries much greater prestige.

Plate 22 "Joys of school" (Kampe, Mae Satop, Mae Chaem, Chiang Mai, February 1988). This Karen village has a two roomed, bamboo and leaf school with one teacher provided by the Royal Forestry Department and another (on the far left of the Plate) provided by the social development component of a foreign assisted project. Mae Satop is considered to be a problem village by project people. It has a high rate of addiction to opium and its inhabitants refuse to take all the advice they are given. As Vienne points out in Chapter 2 of this volume, "community development can be successful only if the 'target people' really feel as though they are full participants in the challenges presented".

Plate 23 "Lisu tomato harvest" (Hobday, Doi Lan, Mae Suai, Chiang Rai, 1986). Commercial cropping of tomatoes on Doi Lan was first promoted by the Thai-German Development Programme in 1983. Over the past five years both tomato and cabbage have deeply affected both social and economic relationships within the village. Accumulation of capital and access to credit increasingly determines household welfare. The old semi-subsistence economy is everywhere giving way to cash cropping. Although not responsible for the commercial revolution which is a part of the process under which the highlanders are becoming integrated into the lowland economy, projects help by giving their seal of approval and providing material support for the transformation.

Plate 24 "Karen mat maker" (Kampe, Pa Kluai, Mae Chaem, Chiang Mai, May 1988). Some traditional crafts survive especially in more remote and traditional villages but it is difficult for crafts people to compete with the low cost and high functional utility of plastic. Mat making is one area in which readily available materials and the comfort provided by leaf and rattan has enabled it to hold its own. Tourism has provided a boost for the revival of handicrafts especially weaving and other textiles decorated with embroidered and applique designs.

A community development worker assigned to this village a year ago is just beginning to understand how the community works and how it is changing. Government and donor agencies seldom make proper provision for consultation with villagers. Consultation takes time. It is much easier to manage and to produce results by building roads, schools and clinics.

Plate 25 "Shan dentist: Akha patient" (McKinnon, A Bae village, Mae Chan, Chiang Rai, November 1986). Itinerant dentists and injection doctors bring their skills and pecuniary interests to isolated villages. This dentist is fitting a fashionable gold cap or covering to the front teeth of a young man. In this case display is the objective rather than functional repair. This dentist is known for his special effects, he has been known to fit coloured covers on the front teeth of his clients.

Plate 26 "Mien house with TV" (Connell, Mae San, Mae Chai, Payao, 11 October 1988). Mae San village has a well developed cash crop nexus. The household income ranges from 10,000-100,000 baht and is likely to increase as coffee trees mature. Many houses run television sets off car batteries. Whether we call it the seduction of modernity or a measure of the power of the market makes no difference to the reality of a prefered choice which makes people members of a national TV culture.

These Mien are watching the World Junior Bantamweight title holder, Khaosai Galaxy (Thai boxers choose their own fighting names) defend his title against the South Korean Choi Chang-ho in Seoul. Galaxy won with a knockout in the eighth. All those watching this telecast were from the very outset, cheering in Yao for a Thai victory.

Plate 27 "School" (Kampe, Huai Bong, Mae Chaem, Chiang Mae 1988). This Karen boy is a student in a Non-Formal Education school. Community development workers employed by a large development project also play the role of teachers. The village is too small to warrant the building of a normal primary school. When the project closes so will the school. Government allocations to education are not enough to support the establishment and maintenance of a multitude of schools in small scattered villages. Even where such schools are set up the quality of education is indifferent. The lack of supervision and the absence of incentives makes such an assignment difficult for teachers accustomed to living in towns. Because of the hardships teachers do not stay long. While on a highland assignment many spend little time at their posts.

Plate 28 "School" (Kampe, Huay Bong, Mae Chaem, Chiang Mai, May 1988). An instructor from the Chiang Mai Teachers College helps to supervise a Non-Formal Education primary school. The curriculum designed to better serve the practical educational needs and likely life chances of those living in isolated villages is seen to provide a second rate chance, a substitute for the real thing. As soon as their children secure a basic literacy in Thai language those families who can afford it, send their children to schools using the formal, national syllabus. Note the ABC's on the blackboard.

Plate 29 "Army consultants" (McKinnon, Khlong Lan, Kamphaeng Phet, June 1987). Rangers or *thahaan pran*, a special task force are responsible for the surveilance and maintenance of a few resettled communities. This photograph was taken in the course of a meeting between a Mien spokesman and a local commanding officer. The spokesman reminded the officer that the community did not have enough rice. The officer could offer little promise of further supplies beyond the coming month when provisions made available for relocation would run out.

Plate 30 "Villagers repairing road" (Kampe, Hoa, Mae Chaem, Chiang Mai, May 1988). These Lua villagers are carrying out road maintenance under a community development effort initiated by a donor project fieldworkers. From an outsiders point of view shortcomings within the village such as opium addiction and weak village leadership are often cited as being the cause of the lack of development. In such a context "development" becomes a measure of the willingness of the target population to do what the developers think is good for them. The authoritarian and paternalistic attitude exercised by most government officers and the confusing mutiplicity of government agencies carrying out work effectively rules out the possibility of a better understanding and the development of a more coordinated and cooperative approach.

Plate 31 "Akha swing" (Vienne, Pa Ka Suk Chai, Mae Chan, Chiang Rai, 26 August, 1986). The Swinging Ceremony "literally means 'drawing and eating rain' or 'drawing rain to eat'. One year as I watched men rebuild the four-posted community swing in Mountain Village, I flet glum because a steady misty drizzle made the taking of photographs a hassle. I was, however, obviously the only person present bothered by the rain; the smiling Blacksmith assured me that the drizzle I disliked was a sign of a blessing during this rite held to ensure plentiful rain and with it the promise of abundant rice.

"The structure of this four-day ceremony parallels that of the New Year Festival to which it is often compared. I have heard Akha refer to it as 'women's New Year...'" (Cornelia Ann

APPENDIX VI

Kammerer *Gateway to the Akha World: Kinship, and Community Among Highlanders of Thailand*. Unpublished PhD dissertation, University of Chicago, 1986: 264. This will be published under the same title in the Illinois Studies in Anthropoly Series of the University of Illinois Press).

Plate 32 "Akha consulting liver" (Vienne, Mae Salaep, Mae Chan, Chiang Rai, May 1987). The Akha follow their own calendar which is close to that of the Chinese and a long way from that of the west. The change from the dry to the rainy season is celebrated in a pre-dawn ceremony *(mii sa law-eu)* conducted after the new gate is constructed and before the ceremony of Planting the New Rice by the *yayeama*. Two or three exemplary males, in this case the blacksmith *(baji)* and reciter *(boemo)* offer on behalf of the whole community, a pig to the Spirit of the Land and the Water to purify the water source (see notes for plate 33). After the pig is killed the liver is removed, washed rubbed and placed back in the body cavity. The liver is then taken out once more and as an oracle examined for omens.

Plate 33 "Akha *mii sa law-eu* ceremony, offerings for the 'landlord'" (Vienne, Mae Salaep, Mae Chan, Chiang Rai, May 1988). This ceremony is held in a special forested grove beyond the village gate. The elders meet in this fenced off area to make their offerings. All the food must be consumed on the spot. Women do not participate and are expected to remain in the house. A small altar can be seen in the background and replicates that used by the Shan *(tai yai)* attesting to a long period of contact. The ceremony is a blessing of all the spirits associated with the water and the land. The ceremony is also celebrated to ensure good fortune for the people. This is shown by making offerings in a symbolic way.

Plate 34 "Lahu Sheleh ceremony" (Supachai). Here a Lahu farmer is making an offering to the Spirit of the Land and asking permission to grow rice. In his prayer he promises not to kill any wild animals he may come across in the immediate vicinity of the field.

Plate 35 "Preparing Akha rice cakes" (Vienne, Mae Salaep, Mae Chan, Chiang Rai, 1988). See the notes for Plate 11.

Plate 36 "Akha sacrifice" (Vienne, Mae Salaep, Mae Chan, 1987). A chicken has been killed as part of a ceremony honoring household ancestors. These ceremonies are held quite frequently often in association with bigger community occassions. This chicken has been killed with a blow to the neck. No blood must be spilt. It is plucked, boiled with rice, ginger and salt. When cooked it is dismembered and five pieces placed in a bowl. Four other bowls are prepared. One containing tea, another a substitute for alcohol, another cooked rice and another rice cake. These five bowls are then placed on the altar of the ancestors. On this occassion the head of the family presents each member of the household, guests and any others present at the time with a piece of chicken.

Plate 37 "Burning forest" (McKinnon, Doi Sam Sow, Mae Chan, April 1988). Close to the Chiang Rai border with Burma little forest remains. Here a forest fire is running through an area in which the trees have not been felled and which is unlikely to be used in the year in which it was burnt. It is distressing to see such wanton destruction of the habitat but when this emotional response is structured into a sociology of knowledge that can be used against the hill tribes it becomes dangerously misleading.

Talk of dessertification is exaggerated. "The natural coincidence of forest cover and higher precipitation has undoubtedly caused, or at least reinforced, the popular notion that forests increase or 'attract' rain and other precipitation forms...Objectively, however, the arguments in favor of positive forest influence are severely weakened when the alleged mechanisms for the influence are critically examined" (Lee **Forest Hydrology** Columbia University, New York: 101).

Plate 38 "Burnt-over garden" (Hobday, Doi Lan, Mae Suai, Chiang Rai, 1986).

Plate 39 "Cut swidden ready to burn" (Connell, Mae Sarieng, 1987). The nutrients and minerals released from the burn assist the growth of the crop. The lighter the biomass the lower the release of nutrients.

Although highland farmers continue to burn the weeds, grass and shrubby growth that becomes established in their fallowed fields and everybody still refers to these fields as "swiddens", the descriptive category, "shifting cultivation" or "slash and burn" becomes increasingly misleading. With the evolution of permanent fields cropped in rotation and associated with sedentary settlements "shifting" comes to mean very little.

Shifting cultivation as a form of semi-subsistence agriculture is something which has traditionally been practised on forested land only marginally suited to annual cropping. This "marginal" classification is an empirical category which means something "natural" defined in structural opposition to fertile lowland plains. Taken in isolation such a category tends to take on an authority that can justifiably be called into question in a broader cultural context. The significance of "marginal" in a "natural" category changes in relationship to how farmers are equipped to get what they need from available land resources. It is a static definition which precludes consideration of changes in agricultural practises and technological advances. With increased investment of labour, fertilizers, pesticides and herbicides as well as the use of sophisticated cropping systems, commercial arable farming is clearly possible. If this was not so commercial cropping systems would not be seen everywhere. The fact that the new system remains highly vulnerable to erosion and adverse changes in the market makes it marginal in both an ecological and economic sense but we still talking about shifting cultivation? The reality appears to have outgrown the category but the classification persists because it is part of an accepted way of talking about agriculture in the highlands.

Plate 40 "Wheat field" (Connell, Pha Daeng, Mae Chi, Phayao, February 1987). Wheat requires cool temperatures and is drought resistant. It is well adapted to be grown as a rain fed crop in the highlands following the harvest of maize, sesame, soya beans and some early maturing varieties of rice. Partly because it is grown at the same time of year as opium and because it augments food production it is being promoted as a replacement crop.

There is a certain irony in this. It is still possible to meet highlanders who grew wheat in Thailand using seed they brought with them from China. Apparently, between 10 and 20 years ago production stopped. At that time opium production and marketing faced so few obstacles and provided such good returns wheat could not compete.

In Yunnan wheat is still grown by Lisu, Lahu, Hmong, Mien and Akha as a fall-back crop in case the rice harvest is poor. It is hoped that wheat can once again fill this role in Thailand. In the near future intensification of the cropping system by reintroducing wheat to follow the maize harvest could pose soil fertility problems. Highland farmers are recommended, following the example of minority groups in Yunnan to plant small areas (0.1 ha per family should provide 100 kg of grain). However, farmers who are chronically short of cash may well choose to grow wheat on a larger commercial scale.

Plate 41 "Fields of Red Kidney bean" (Connell, Pha Daeng, Mae, Chai, Phayao, November 1987). Over the past decade Red Kidney bean was promoted as a crop substitute for opium. It requires chemical fertilizer and the application of fungicides. Despite these constraints the crop has established a market. Merchants are now promoting the crop and farmers are responding by growing as much as they can.

The pressure on land resources is clearly shown by the intensive use made of these steep slopes. The usual explanation given for this is population pressure. Such a general observation does not come close enough to the heart of the matter. Generally speaking the availability of better land to which access is also limited by government intervention, reafforestation schemes and the formation of national parks are other factors which should be taken into account.

In the area depicted here the commercial incentive is paramount. In the year in which this photograph was taken these slopes were double-cropped. Although farmers were aware that this greatly accelerated erosion and that this was already manifest in declining soil fertility they were unwilling to invest the greater labour costs and accept lower returns which the introduction of soil and water conservation measures would have entailed. Until farmers are granted secure and legal forms of land tenure they are unlikely to adopt measures that will ensure sustained production.

Plate 42 "Irrigated rice terraces" (Connell, Pai district, Mae Hong Son, November 1987). These terraces were constructed by Shan *(tai yai)*. The plate reminds us that the highlands are not only occupied by those officially indentified as *chao khao* (hill tribes).

Indicated by the range of different colours various varieties of rice can be seen. Early maturing varieties are planted in contiguous plots.

Plate 43 "Akha ploughing, Doi Chang" (McKinnon, Doi Chang, Mae Suai, Chiang Rai, August 1988). An Akha farmer ploughing his irrigated rice fields with a buffalo. There is nothing in this photograph that cannot be found on the lowlands. To promote the image of "exotic hill tribes" and to ignore evidence of daily activities is a risky business. The received knowledge of a consensus view can take on such authority that it becomes a real impediment to perception let alone understanding.

Plates

Plate 44 "Highland town, Doi Chang" (McKinnon, Doi Chang village, Mae Suai, Chiang Rai, July 1988). Doi Chang is a community of over one thousand people. Half the population are Lisu who have lived there for over 60 years. Before they arrived Hmong settlers had cleared the land and for reasons that are no longer known, moved away. A few years ago Akha, seeking a refuge from the turmoil of modern Burma moved in, worked in Lisu fields and began to buy Land. Doi Chang, like neighbouring Wawi is a frontier town. It has a history. Its inhabitants are heavily engaged in commercial cropping. Most men speak Thai as well as several other languages. They use banks, both lend and borrow money, buy and rent land, own pick-up trucks, speculate on crop futures, send their children to Thai schools, make contributions to official representatives of national public institutions and for entertainment watch television and go to local video theatres.

Plate 45 "Doi Chang fields" (McKinnon, Doi Chang, Mae Suai, Chiang Rai, June 1988). The range of different types of cultivation, various crops and small fields attests to a sophisticated and careful management of resources.

Plate 46 "Akha land use, Mae Salaep" (Vienne, Mae Salaep, Mae Chan, Chiang Rai, 1988). In the foreground can be seen irrigated rice terraces which were built and are managed by Akha farmers. On the steeper slopes and along the ridges trees remain as part of a community conservation measure. In the middle distance can be seen small fields planted in a wide variety of crops. In this area there is considerable pressure on farmers to keep as much land as possible under cultivation. There is little evidence of serious erosion. This is intelligent use of mountain land in an area of high population densities.

Plate 47 "Grass strips, Doi Chang" (McKinnon, Doi Chang, mae Suai, Chiang Rai, June 1988). Grass strips are being promoted by several of the larger, partly foreign funded projects. The most sensible argument used to extend this form of land use runs as follows, that it is a relatively easy and low cost strategy under which to promote both stabilised agriculture and conservation farming in the highlands. In so far as it fails to take into account the fact that most farmers already practise a system of extensive stable farming and advances the idea that a more intensive system of farming is a longterm possibility on fragile soils and consolidated holdings in the absence of project support, it could produce its own problem for development. Intensive commercial cropping constitutes the single biggest danger to the highland environment.

Farmers are sceptical and in Doi Chang where this photo was taken only those interested in both being seen to cooperated with an official development effort and in securing the material incentives offered by the project are willing to take part. As has been observed "People respond to development policies according to their own understanding rather than to the objective suitability of what is being implemented" (Vienne, Chapter 2, this volume).

Plate 48 "Tomato field, Doi Chang" (McKinnon, Doi Chang, Mae Suai, Chiang Mai, July 1988). Contour planting of tomatoes is largely determined by the need to conserve ground moisture. The method is also environmentally sound.

The use made of chemical sprays is less well managed. Several deaths have been reported following prolonged use of herbicides and pesticides. In the absence of autopsies it is not possible, with any certainty, to determine the cause of death.

Plate 49 "Akha child" (Ralana, Mae Salaep, Mae Chan, Chiang Rai, 1987). "Highland women and children are regarded as second class citizens in their own communities. As a consequence they are sometimes ignored, perhaps, inadvertently, when assistance is offered by outside agencies. In a very real structural sense they belong to a disadvantaged group within a disadvantaged population" (Ralana, Chapter 5 this volume).

This observation provides an outsiders, objective point

of view. Ralana also reports that in the Akha community in which this photograph was taken considerable care is taken of children and a strong spirit of family affection is clearly manifest.

Plate 50 "Food demonstration" (Connell)

Plate 51 "Akha mother" (Hobday, Mae Tam Mui, Mae Suai, Chiang Rai, 1986). Much is expected of Akha mothers. They work long days in the fields, carry heavy loads back to their homes; they are expected to be dutiful, obedient and honest.

Plate 52 "Akha boy and baby" (Vienne, Khiew Satai, Mae Chan, Chiang Rai, 1986). Explanations for high infant mortality rates which focus on poor nutrition such as the substitution of breast milk for powdered milk miss the point. A bottle that frequently falls to the ground and is rarely, if ever sterilized, presents a considerable hazard to continuing good health. "The highest death rates are among infants and young children, and the leading causes of death include primary infective and parasitic diseases, especially those of the gasto-intestinal and respiratory systems" (Kunstadter in McKinnon & Wanat [eds] **Highlanders of Thailand** 1983: 30).

Plate 53 "Poppy field" (Vienne, Chiang Rai, 1986). Crop substitution projects produce mixed results. In this case cabbage and poppy.

Plate 54 "Opium smoker" (Supachai). "Over 70 percent of the addicts interviewed have undertaken cures. Most treatments currently in use do not work. Some 23 percent of those interviewed were not interested in considering treatment. As far as they were concerned opium gave them the strength to work and they felt that their indulgence was not a problem" Sanit, Chapter 6 this volume).

Plate 55 "Harvesting opium" (Connell, Pua district, Nan, 1986). Opium fields are not as easy to find as they were just five years ago. Highlanders are actively discouraged from growing the crop and fewer are doing so. Those who continue to do so either grow small plots to provide opium for household addicts or scatter their plots in more remote areas where they are unlikely to be found. With the help of financial support from the USA the army mobilises men to cut down the crop during the growing season. Although not as much is destroyed in this way as could be by aerial spraying, Thailand has wisely resisted pressure from the USA Drug Enforcement Agency (DEA) to adopt this draconian alternative. Aerial spraying of 2,4-D presents a considerable risk to communities in close proximity to targeted fields. For a report of its use in Burma see the *New York Times* 30 November, 1986.

Plate 56 "Lisu farmers" (McKinnon, Doi Lan, Mae Suai, July 1988). Mature women cultivate the land alongside the men; plant, weed and harvest as well as take primary responsibility for cooking, child raising and feeding domesticated livestock. The Lisu bride price is high and women occupy a strong customary and moral role in Lisu society.

Plate 57 "Lisu tomato harvest" (Hobday, Doi Lan, Mae Suai, 1986). Tomatoes were introduced into this area by a foreign funded project. In 1987 many Doi Lan farmers made a lot of money from the sale of tomatoes and in 1988 decided to step up production. Given the high investment cost in fertiliser, herbicides, pesticides, transport and labour the risks are considerable. The very wet season of 1988 resulted in the rapid deterioration of the road and rising transport costs. Production in areas closer to the roadhead brought prices down. From July through to October many farmers paid one baht per kilogramme for transport to the market and received only one to two baht per kilogramme for their tomatoes. The net loss has resulted in serious indebtedness.

A purely technocratic approach to development which does not take into account the likely impact on diet (with cash crops being grown in place of food) and long run marketing and economic considerations can be detrimental.

Plates

Plate 58 "Lisu women" (Connell, Thathon, Fang, Chiang Mai, 1984).

Plate 59 "Lisu children" (Hobday, Doi Lan, Mae Suai, Chiang Rai, 1985). This photo was taken at the New Year festival. This is an occassion on which most people wear their best clothes.

Plate 60 "Hydraulic rice pounder" McKinnon, Pang Mai Daeng, Mae Taeng, October 1986). This rice pounder is something of an oddity.Although it appeals as a form of appropriate technology it is sited at some distance from the village and householders are more likely to either mill their own rice with a foot pounder or pay the charge to use a mechanical mill. The time spent in standing guard over their rice and the effort required to carry the grain and polishings, the mix of husk, germ and bran removed during pounding and used to feed animals back to the house, diminishes its utility. It is viewed more favourably by younger people who have other, good social reasons for using it.

Plate 61 "Lisu girl" (Vienne, Pang Mai Daeng, Mae Taeng, Chiang Mai, 1986). Lisu girl returning from the hydraulic rice pounder.

Plate 62 "Mlabri victim of malaria" (Vienne, Huai Bo Hoi, Nan, September 1986). One of the heavy costs of being a marginal group within a marginal population is that they not only lack access to services but often the knowledge of where to go for help.

Plate 63 "Mlabri women" (McKinnon, Huai Bo Hoi, Nan, 1987). The Mlabri are a very gentle and witty people. The Lahu describe them as "the people who can laugh you to death". It is a pity that so many popular reports play up their supposedly primitive nature. Not all those who have something to say about the Mlabri are as honest as the Thai who was overheard to remark at an exhibition in Bangkok "featuring real Mlabri....

APPENDIX VI

'After all they look like us, and if they were dressed like us they could be mistaken for Thai''' (Baffie, Chapter 15 this volume). Not a lone voice. Pathom Puapansakul, the Thai artist, now a lecturer in the Faculty of Fine Arts, Chiang Mai University who sculptured the Mlabri figure which stands just inside the entrance to the Tribal Research Institute used himself as a model.

Plate 64 "Karen woman cutting melon" (Kampe, Mae Sa, Mae Chaem, Chiang Mai, November 1987). This woman is a member of a relatively prosperous and thoroughly Christian village which prohibits the use of opium and alcohol. By making these religious and moral changes people place themselves in a more dignified social and political category. Many officials classify villagers who hold to traditional belief systems as "having no religion".

Plate 65 "Lahu Sheleh farmers" (Supachai).

Plate 66 "Lahu Sheleh farmers" (Supachai). Both of these Plates show Lahu Sheleh weeding their rice. The large group are involved in reciprocal labour exchange. Each participant agrees to help the other. Sanit, the senior Lahu researcher at the Tribal Research Institute remarks that among the many Lahu sub-groups the Sheleh are most concerned to follow tradition. What he calls a greater Chinese influence is evident in the way they continue to wear their distinctive clothes, follow the twelve day week and take careful note of the day before deciding what can be done. Chicken day is a good day on which to mount a weeding gang. Hens are industrious and look after their chickens by scratching the ground. Rice weeded on a Chicken day will grow well.

Plate 67 "Lahu Sheleh field gang" (Supachai). A crowd of people mobilised for work in the fields must be fed properly.

Plate 68 "Karen wedding" (Connell, Mae Tho, Chiang Mai, 1984). While waiting for the bride to appear these guests are drinking rice whiskey specially distilled for the occassion.

Plates

Each household is obliged to provide alcohol to drink in reciprocal toasts. Connell remarks "Some brews are good, others quite bad." The bridegroom has travelled from a distant village and will take up residence in his wife's household.

Plate 69 "Hmong mother, Huai Yew Yee" (Eudey, Huai Yew Yee, Uthai Thani, April 1986. Acknowledgement, *National Geographic).* This 40 year old woman is the mother of 10 children of whom nine survive. She is pictured here with her youngest child, a three month old daughter. The villagers of Huai Yew Yee and their relatives had gathered to commemorate the 14th anniversary of the death of a "Mother".

Plate 70 "Mock assault" (Eudey, Huai Yew Yee, Uthai Thani, April 1986. Acknowledgement, *National Geographic).* A mock assault on one of the Huai Yew Yee men by a ranger *thahaan pran).*

Plate 71 "Village officials, 1982" (Eudey, Huai Yew Yee, Uthai Thani, 1982. Acknowledgement, New York Zoological Society). The headman of Huai Yew Yee with staff and members of his family including his mother (far left) and other villagers. The man in uniform (second from left) is a forest ranger from Khai Nang Rum Research Station in Huai Kha Khaeng Wildlife Sanctuary.

Plate 72 "Phop Phra relocation area" (Eudey, Mae Sot, Tak, 26 March 1986. Acknowledgement, *National Geographic).* Sector between 48 to 45 kilometers along the Mae Sot-Umphang road. "An area devoid of water and denuded of vegetation" (Eudey, Chapter 10 this volume).

Plate 73 "Soldiers, Huai Yew Yee" (Eudey, Huai Yew Yee, Uthai Thani, 14 April 1986. Acknowledgement, *National Geographic).* the arrival of the Third Army Lt. General at Huai Yew Yee.

Plate 74 "Soldiers & Hmong confer" (Eudey, Huai Yew

APPENDIX IV

Yee, Uthai Thani, 14 pril 1986. Acknowledgement, *National Geographic).* Reported fragments of the discussion are reproduced in the text. "When the Lt.- General stated that to be a good citizen one must comply with the decisions of the Government, each Hmong man raised an identity card indicating that he was a Thai citizen" (Eudey, Chapter 10 this volume).

Plate 75 "Raising the flag" All over Thailand the school day begins with the singing of the national anthem and the raising of the flag.

Plate 76 "Akha bride" (Ralana, Mae Salaep, Mae Chan, Chiang Rai, 19 March 1988). This woman's name is Aa Mii Voi-zoe. She is 24 years old and could have been married much younger. She is the daughter of the headman. Her parents are kind and she dutiful and affectionate.

Aa Mii Voi-zoe delayed her marriage as a mark of respect towards her parents but by doing so, as the oldest daughter, she was also blocking her younger sister's and brother's matrimonial ambitions. They could not marry until she did. With marriage the lineage links with her parents have been broken and she has joined her husband's clan. Such celebrations are not conducted without regret.

Plate 77 "Akha ceremony" (Vienne, Mae Salaep, Mae Chan, 1988). Akha culture in behaviour with formal meaning. Accompanying recitations provide an occassion to repeat accumulated wisdom on how to maintain harmony between people living and dead as well as between the community and the environment.

Plate 78 "Akha thatching roof" (Ralana, Pra Ya Prai, Mae Chan, Chiang Rai, 20 March 1988). Thatching is a man's job and women have no place climbing around on a roof. Ralana took this photograph by proxy. It was taken by Bob Newell who declared himself a "window cleaner from Brisbane, California".

Plates

Plate 79 "Lahu felling a tree" (Supachai). "Trees are felled in sets rather than individually. To avoid accidents cutting commences with axemen working uphill and abreast of each other on the same contour. The trees are cut so that they remain standing. When the axemen reach the top of the ridge they wait until their group is entirely accounted for and out from under the canopy before the trees at the top of the ridge are felled. As these trees fall their weight triggers a domino effect and with a loud series of cracks the forest comes crashing down" (Chantaboon, Chapter 4 this volume).

Plate 80 "Lisu studying liver" (Conrad, Pai district, Mae Hong Son 1988). "Whether the occassion is a celebration or a ceremony performed to avert adversity the killing of a chicken or a pig is always a ritual sacrifice to spirits. The configuration of the holes in the upper leg bones of a chicken or the lobes in a pigs liver provide an indication of the future, the outcome of a specific issue for which the ceremony is held. Old respected men are routinely asked to study the liver and offer an interpretation" (Yves Conrad, personal communication).

Plate 81 "Lahu field ceremony" (Supachai). Before the fields are cleared a proper ceremony must be held to ensure that nobody is injured with a knife, axe or falling tree.

Plate 82 "Htin mother and child" (Connell, Sob Tuang refugee camp, Mae Charim, Nan, 1981). The Htin occupy the borderlands of Nan and Laos. Many in the camp were born in Thailand and lived there until hostilities between guerrillas and government armed forces became too violent. They then fled into Laos in search of a sanctuary. At the end of the war events brought them back into Thailand with a flood of refugees. Their citizenship by birthright was eventually recognised by the Royal Thai Government and they are now settled in Pua district.

Plate 83 "Akha children skipping" (Hobday, Saen Chareon, Mae Suai, Chiang Rai, 1986). This event was staged by a visiting Japanese television crew. The production team paid for everybody to put on their best clothes and a good time was had by all.

Many such stories can be told. One recounted by a very lively and attractive American girl recalls an experience worth recording.

"The Night I Mastered an Akha Dance"

"It was the night of a celebration to mark the opening of an Akha cultural and educational centre in Pha Kluai Gow, Mae Chan, Chiang Rai. The adults were all engaged in a vigorous round of drinking and enjoying a dance which hovered ambiguously between something Akha and something Thai. A few young girls felt left out and retired to the back of the building to do their own thing and it was there that I learned my lesson.

"They asked me to stand in line and do what they did. They instructed me to put my left foot forward and wiggle it, then my right foot forward and wiggle that too. Then it was hands, bottom and so on (I can't remember the order). I began to realise there was something familiar about all this. Then it dawned on me: They were doing the Ball'n the Jack!

Plate 84 "Mien women" (Connell, Mae Chaem, Chiang Rai, 1983). After the photographer had spent the night in their house the family asked if they could have their picture taken. It took sometime before they felt they looked their best. The women adjusting her earring was not well enough to walk and had to be carried out of the house.

Plate 85 "Lahu mother" (Connell, Nong Keo, Chiang Dao, Chiang Mai, 1987). This community is a cluster of hamlets made up of Lua, Karen, Kachin, Akha, and Lahu, all of whom are Christian. The King's Project is active in this area and assists the villagers in growing various cash crops. These people apparently do not experience a compulsion to live in a culturally homogeneous settlement. There is nothing ingrained, fixed or sacred about ethnic identity. Historically, linguistically and culturally Thailand is a nation with a multitude of ethnic groups. How did highlanders come to be singled out?

Plate 86 "Opium replacement crop" (Kampe, Khun Klang Agricultural Research Station, Chom Thong, Chiang Mai, 1988). As can be seen from the 20 pages presented in Appendix IV a considerable number of temporate and sub-tropical crops have been introduced into the highlands under opium crop substitution projects. These range from the simple to the complex. Flowers are amongst the more demanding plant materials and are marketed under preferential arrangements set up and maintained by the projects.

To speed maturation these flowers are being grown under incandescent lighting. They are picked and in some cases placed in coolers for delivery to the market. Under urban based management, with free electricity and a marketing infrastructure already in place, the system works. However, it is an extremely difficult (if not impossible) model for highlanders to replicate in the absence of a benevolent donor. "In order to demonstrate the viability of the on-going process of development, management is more and more taking over by superimposing external structures in which action is more directed by their own interests than by proper consideration of the interests of the so called 'target population'" (Vienne, Chapter 2 this volume).

Plate 87 "Highland land use" (Connell, Pha Kluai, Chom Thong, Chiang Mai, 1987). Springs are tapped and light weight plastic pipes used to activate sprinklers. Vegetable cash crops are grown throughout the year. Although this was initiated by highland development projects it has taken on a life of its own. Local merchants provide inputs, often on credit and encourage farmers in suitable areas to enter into production. The penetration into the highlands of the market economy is the most powerful engine of change.

APPENDIX VI

Plate 88 "Karen burnt swidden" (McKinnon, Mae San, Lampang, March 1986). The Karen are often presented as the environmentally aware, cyclical swiddeners of the highlands. Here the forest has been reduced to a scattered cover of trees and the bulk of the burn provided by bamboo. Under increased population pressure the fallow period must be shortened and there is not enough time for the forest to recover.

Plate 89 "Reafforested farmland" (McKinnon, A'Bae, Mae Chan, Chiang Rai, November 1986). Most of the land throughout the Mae Chan district has been cleared of forest by highland farmers. Exercising their legal rights and formal responsibilities, the Royal Forestry Department has planted pine trees in close proximity to many villages. In any but the most general terms the rationale for doing so is difficult to establish. Pine trees do not appear to promise very much as an economic crop and their protective, watershed characteristics leave much to be desired. Villagers complain about the acidic affect of pine needles spread over their fields from neighbouring plantations. By decreasing the amount of arable land available to farmers reafforestation increases pressure on what remains. An uncoordinated, purely technical approach to development can create as many, if not make more problems than it resolves.

Plate 90 "Road erosion, Doi Thung" (McKinnon, Huai Khrai Mai, Doi Thung, Chiang Rai, July 1988). As Sheng points out in his study of the Mae Sa watershed, "Government road building activities alone accounted for 30 percent of erosion" (Sheng, *Management and Conservation Farming in North Thailand* UNDP/FAO, Chiang Mai, 1979: 52). Erosion is a problem but it cannot be evaluated in isolation from the natural dynamics of watershed hydrology and the impact of human intervention. A lot of basic research remains to be done.

Plate 91 "Field (rill) erosion" (McKinnon, Doi Chang, Mae Suai, Chiang Rai, July 1988). Swiddens cleared under shifting cultivation and planted in food crops are usually dibbled. Interference with the surface is kept to a minimum. Erosion rates are low. When land is brought under sedentary agriculture weeds become a problem and cultivation becomes necessary. This results in considerable localised loss of soil. Although this material rarely enters streams to add to either turbdity or the sedimentary load carried to the lowlands, it still has an adverse impact: loss of fertility in farmers fields. It is in the farmers interest to keep this down. On fragile highland soils the answer is not to consolidate farms and risk the deterioration which follows intensification but maintain an extensive form of cyclical clearing of small plots under which periods of fallow follow cultivation. Projects need to introduce conservation methods into the current system rather than attempt an ambitious programme of landscape architecture.

Plate 92 "Road construction" (McKinnon, Doi Thung, Mae Chan, July 1988). Development means roads, highways are a more developed form of roads. The bigger the road the greater the displacement of earth.

Plate 93 "Two generations, Karen" (McKinnon, Mae San, Lampang, March 1986). The older man was born into a relatively isolated, largely self-sufficient village. The six year old boy was born into a community that was already transformed beyond that which could have been imagined by his grandfather at the same age. The planning horizon for most projects varies between three and five years. Given a normal life this boy will be 16 in the year 2000, 66 in the year 2050. It is helpful to remember, "If economic change and even social welfare can be planned and implemented in such a way as to produce additional income, better education, efficient health services and so forth, the subsequent ineluctable process of social transformation is, generally speaking, unpredictable" (Vienne, Chapter 2 this volume).

Plate 94 Mlabri *"talap manut"* (Baffie, Bangkok, 1986)

Plate 95 Lisu *pla ra wok* (Baffie, Bangkok, 1986)

Plate 96 Hmong *tao phu khao* (Baffie, Bangkok, 1986)

APPENDIX VI

Plate 97 Akha *pu chong ai phi ba* (Baffie Bangkok 1986)

Plate 98 "Tourist exotica" (McKinnon, Tha Phae road, Chiang Mai, 1987). There are more than 60 trekking agencies registered in Chiang Mai with the Tourist Authority of Thailand. There are many more that are not registered. They each attempt to outdo their competitors by offering tours that go to "places off the beaten track" or "hardly visited". They promise adventure and more. As Duangta notes in Chapter 16, "One of the most important obligations faced by guides is to provide answers to questions. They do not know the phrase 'I don't know". This business needs to be better managed or it may become a problem. Why not leave it in the hands of the highlanders themselves?

Plate 99 "Lahu Sheleh women" (Connell, Pha Peuak, Mae Hong Son, 1988). The girls good humour has nothing to do with the *farang* in the background. They are at play in their own way for their own reasons. Food habits are extremely difficult to change. In the presence of such ambience manifest in genuine, lively participation it is possible to communicate.

This was a particularly successful food demonstration. While waiting the one and a half hours it takes to boil wheat grains and produce serious "traditional food", whole meal flour was ground to make rotis. The flour was mixed with water and salt and kneaded into dough. Once it was thoroughly mixed, pieces of dough were broken off and patted into flat cakes which were cooked on a hot pan. This can all be done quite quickly and before the first batch of dough was ready some of the participants were already grinding more flour. A few hours later as the demonstrator was leaving the village dough was still being kneaded and the cooking and eating of rotis was proceeding with gusto. The demonstration had jumped that experiential barrier which lies between a formal demonstration and a real event.

Plate 100 "Hmong seller: *farang* buyer" (Connell, Nam Yao refugee camp, Pua, Nan, 1981). The sale of handicrafts has become an important economic activity in many villages. A recent report on a Mien village visited daily by tourists states that "32 households combined make between 250,000-300,000 baht per year" ($US 10,000-12,000) from this trade (Somkiat Chumlong, *Home Sweet Home* [mimeo. in English] Tribal Research Institute, Chiang Mai, 1987: 26). Special projects have promoted the sale of products overseas and hill people in refugee camps have come to rely on these sales as their only significant source of income. In many villages throughout the North this has both added to the work load and strengthened the position of women.

This photograph shows a French nurse working for the Medecins sans Frontieres (who spoke Hmong) bargaining with one of the residents of the camp.

Plate 101 "Night Bazaar, Chiang Mai" (Hobday, Night Bazaar, Muang Chiang Mai, Chiang Mai, 1980). The Night Bazaar has become an important tourist destination. The local market accommodates big sellers and small. It provides an entry to commercial trading. Many Hmong and Akha have taken the risk to open stalls and shops. Whether as small traders they can compete in the long run with industrial "handicrafts" and meet rising costs has yet to be seen.

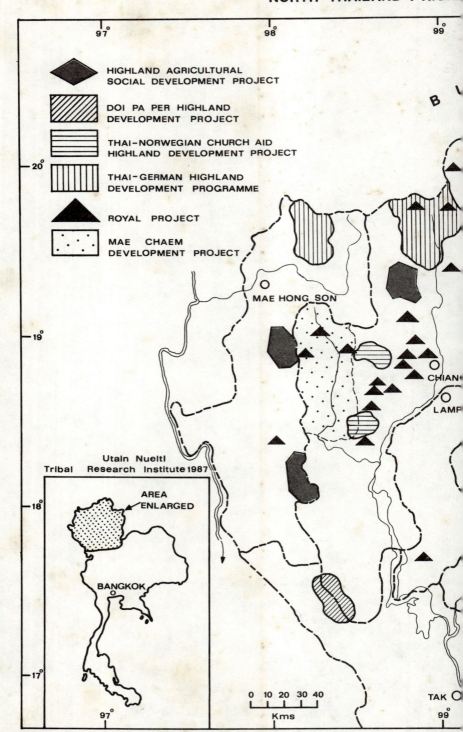